GENERAL EQUILIBRIUM THEORY
AND
INTERNATIONAL TRADE

STUDIES
IN MATHEMATICAL AND
MANAGERIAL ECONOMICS

Editor

HENRI THEIL

VOLUME 13

1972

NORTH-HOLLAND PUBLISHING COMPANY, AMSTERDAM·LONDON
AMERICAN ELSEVIER PUBLISHING CO., NEW YORK

GENERAL EQUILIBRIUM THEORY
AND
INTERNATIONAL TRADE

TAKASHI NEGISHI

University of Tokyo

1972

NORTH-HOLLAND PUBLISHING COMPANY, AMSTERDAM·LONDON
AMERICAN ELSEVIER PUBLISHING CO., NEW YORK

Library of Congress Catalog Card Number: 79-183281
ISBN North-Holland: 0 7204 3399 1
ISBN American Elsevier: 0 444 10340 6

25 Graphs

PUBLISHERS:

NORTH-HOLLAND PUBLISHING COMPANY – AMSTERDAM
NORTH-HOLLAND PUBLISHING COMPANY, LTD. – LONDON

SOLE DISTRIBUTORS FOR THE U.S.A. AND CANADA:

AMERICAN ELSEVIER PUBLISHING CO., INC.
52 VANDERBILT AVENUE, NEW YORK, N.Y. 10017
FH

PRINTED IN BELGIUM

Introduction to the series

This is a series of books concerned with the quantitative approach to problems in the behavioral science field. The studies are in particular in the overlapping areas of mathematical economics, econometrics, operational research, and management science. Also, the mathematical and statistical techniques which belong to the apparatus of modern behavioral science have their place in this series. A well-balanced mixture of pure theory and practical applications is envisaged, which ought to be useful for universities and for research workers in business and government.

The Editor hopes that the volumes of this series all of which relate to such a young and vigorous field of research activity, will contribute to the exchange of scientific information at a truly international level.

THE EDITOR

To Aiko

Preface

This is a book of general equilibrium theory *and* of international trade. It is not merely a book of general equilibrium theory in international trade. In economic science general equilibrium theory plays a role similar to that played in university curricula by mathematics and language studies. It must certainly have its own discipline (i.e., the demonstration of the consistency of its theoretical structure), but at the same time it should also offer services to other branches of study. To tell the story of general equilibrium theory, therefore, one must talk of its applications as well as of its pure theory. Thus, in this book, some chapters are devoted to applications in international economics of the ideas developed in other chapters. Although we start with the problem of the optimality and existence of a competitive equilibrium and then devote a considerable number of pages to the stability problem, both of which are well studied areas of general equilibrium theory, the rest of the book is concerned with such unexplored or unsolved problems as increasing returns, externality, monopolistic competition, second best theory and the dichotomy of price and monetary theories.

Chapters 6, 12 and 15 appeared in essentially their present form, respectively, in *Economic Record*, 34 (1968), *International Economic Review*, 10 (1969) and 9 (1968). I thank the editors of these journals for their permission to make use of these papers. Some of the other chapters are completely revised versions of papers published in such learned journals as *Econometrica*, *Metroeconomica*, *Review of Economic Studies*, etc., and of mimeographed papers privately circulated. I am extremely grateful to Professors K.J. Arrow, J.S. Chipman, F.H. Hahn, M.C. Kemp, R. Komiya, M. Morishima, T. Murakami and H. Uzawa for valuable comments received when I prepared these papers originally. I also received, with many thanks, very helpful comments on these papers from Professors A. Amano, P.K. Bardhan, A.D. Brownlie, L. Hurwicz, K. Inada, R.W. Jones, H. Kanemitsu, K. Kuga, F. Nikaido and A. Takayama. Professors M. Aoki, K. Hamada and K. Suzumura were kind enough to read and improve some parts of the manuscript of this book.

As a Japanese, I am particularly happy since my first book in a non-Japanese language is published by a Dutch company. The Dutch were the only western people who kept contact with Japan in her long period of isolation from foreign countries, 1639–1858. All the modern sciences, including political economy, were first imported from The Netherlands and called Dutch studies in Japan. Therefore, let me express my gratitude to North-Holland Publishing Company and Mr. F. Snater for their kind effort to make this publication possible. It is my pleasant duty to state that my study has been supported by Stanford University (Office of Naval Research, U.S.A.), University of New South Wales, Asia Foundation, Hill Foundation, University of Minnesota, Tokyo Center for Economic Research and the Faculty Research Fund of University of Tokyo (Department of Economics). Finally, but not the least, my thanks go to Mrs. H. Bliss for the linguistic check of the manuscript and to Miss S. Enosawa and Miss M. Takahata for their kind help in the preparation of the manuscript and in the proofreading.

Tokyo   TAKASHI NEGISHI

Contents

Introduction

1. How useful general equilibrium analysis is can best be seen in the controversy between Keynes and neo-classical economists like Pigou and Patinkin. What distinguishes Keynes from neo-classical economists is his view on the partial equilibrium between investment and saving.[1]) According to Keynes, neo-classical economists considered the rate of interest essential to the adjustment between investment and saving. Keynes, on the other hand, emphasized the importance of the level of output which determines, and is determined by, investment and saving. Since the difference between investment and saving is nothing but the excess demand for aggregate output, the role of the level of output is most important in the adjustment of the market for the aggregate output, if prices are rigid. However, it is one thing to emphasize the role of the level of output in the so-called Keynesian situation, but quite another to insist on the possibility or even the necessity of the equilibrium level of output with unemployment even when the full flexibility of prices is assumed.

Figure 1 is the famous one drawn by Klein, which aims to show the impossibility of full employment equilibrium.[2]) Saving S and investment I in real terms are measured horizontally and the rate of interest r, vertically.

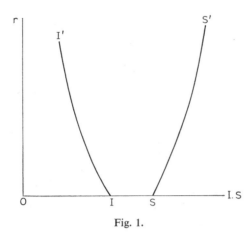

Fig. 1.

[1]) Keynes, J. M., *The general theory of employment, interest and money*, Macmillan, 1936, pp. 175–185.
[2]) Klein, L. R., *The Keynesian revolution*, Macmillan, 1947, p. 85.

Curves II' and SS' indicate respectively investment and saving as functions of the rate of interest, when the level of output is that of full employment. Both investment and saving are assumed inelastic with respect to the rate of interest and there exists no positive rate of interest which equates investment and saving at the full employment level of output. In other words, irrespective of the level of the interest rate, supply exceeds demand for aggregate output when laborers are fully employed. This may imply the necessity of under-employment equilibrium when prices are rigid. However, it by no means implies the impossibility of full employment equilibrium when prices are flexible. The partial equilibrium demand and supply curves, i.e., II' and SS', are drawn under the assumption that other things are equal. The level of prices, which is included in 'other things', must be changed if supply exceeds demand in the aggregate output market. The reduction of the price level will firstly shift the SS' curve to the left, as was emphasized by Pigou and Patinkin,[3]) through the favorable effect of the increased real cash balance on consumption, and secondly shift the II' curve to the right since the increased real balance induces an increase in the demand for real assets in the portfolio of the firms. Then, there is no reason to deny the eventual crossing of II' and SS', i.e., the existence of full employment equilibrium from the point of view of general equilibrium analysis.[4])

Partial equilibrium analysis gets a first approximation by strategically concentrating on a certain aspect of the economy and by assuming that other things are equal. It is certainly most convenient to grasp what one considers as the essence of the matter, without being troubled by the complexities caused by less important factors. No one can deny its significance as a heuristic method. But there is the danger of a sweeping generalization if one forgets its basic assumption that other things are equal. The role of general equilibrium analysis is, on the other hand, to construct a bird's eye view of the entire economy, to transplant the partial equilibrium analysis properly to the general setting and to check the general applicability and relevance of the results obtained under the assumption that other things are equal.

[3]) Pigou, A.C., 'The classical stationary state,' *Economic Journal*, 53 (1943), pp. 343–51, Patinkin, D., 'Price flexibility and full employment,' *American Economic Review*, 38 (1948), pp. 543–64.

[4]) We cannot agree with the interpretation of Keynesian arguments in chapter 19 of *General theory* that there exists no full employment equilibrium. Our interpretation is that the full employment equilibrium is unstable. See chapter 13.

2. In several chapters of this book (i.e., chapters 1, 2, 5, 7, 8), we shall often be concerned with the question of the existence of an equilibrium. Why is it necessary, however, to demonstrate the existence of an equilibrium? Is it not enough simply to observe an economy to see if there exists a general equilibrium, i.e., the system of prices such that demand and supply of all commodities are equalized? To answer these questions, we have to reflect on a more fundamental question, i.e., what is an economic theory? If a theory is a mere description of the facts of economic life, it is certainly not necessary to prove the existence of what actually exists. In such a description theory, however, there is no place for the general equilibrium, since there always exist some disequilibria in a real economy. Our theory is something quite different. It is a *model* of the reality, i.e., a system which is independent of facts, though expected to work in parallel with facts. To be operational, i.e., to be useful to us, it cannot be a completely detailed description of facts. It is not the reality itself, but a measure which we can apply to the reality. The concept of the general equilibrium is a part of such an operational theory, a convenient device by which we hope we can analyze an economy. Since it is not a fact of an economy but a statement of a theoretical model of an economy, we have to observe the logical structure of the model rather than the real economy to see if it really exists.

To prove the existence of a general equilibrium is, therefore, to check the logical consistency of the concept of an equilibrium in the given structure of a theoretical model. To show the importance of this proof, let us first give an example of the case in which a general equilibrium does not exist. Consider an economy of two commodities, i.e., the service of labor and a product which can be produced by the input of labor service. Suppose there exists a firm with a given production function and m consumers with identical utility functions and identical initial stocks of labor services. Let us further assume that the profit of each firm is equally distributed among consumers. If there ever exists a competitive equilibrium in such an economy, then the same equilibrium must also exist for an economy of one firm and one aggregated consumer, since consumers are completely identical. Such an economy is shown in figure 2. The amount of the product is measured horizontally and that of the labor service (time), vertically. Curves I_1 and I_2 are consumer's indifference curves. OA represents the initial amount of labor service held by the consumer. It is assumed that an overhead cost is incurred to produce the product. It is represented by the input AB of labor service, the only one factor of production in the model. On the other hand, the variable cost of production is shown by the curve BC, expressing the relation between the input of labor service measured downward from *B* and the output of the product measured to the right from *O*. Since the variable cost is increasing, the average cost is expressed by a typical U-shaped curve.

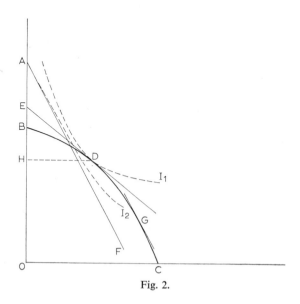

Fig. 2.

If a positive amount of the product is produced in a competitive equilibrium, the marginal rates of substitution of consumer and firm must be equal, as they are at *D*, to the price ratio. The price ratio of the product and labor service at *D* is equal to the slope of the common tangent *DE* of curves *BC* and I_1. Then, the profit of the firm is negative, since the value, in terms of labor service, of product *DH* produced from the input *AH* of labor service is merely *EH*. The profit at *D* is, under the price ratio *DE*, the maximum on *BC*, but smaller than that at *A* where no input and output are made at all. Therefore, *D* cannot be a competitive equilibrium. In terms of cost curves, equilibrium conditions for a competitive firm are not satisfied at *D*, since the average cost curve is diminishing even though the marginal cost curve is increasing. How about, then, the point of no production *A* as an equilibrium? If *A* is an equilibrium, the price ratio is equal to the slope of the tangent *AF* to the indifference curve I_2 at *A*. However, it is profitable for the firm to produce, under the price ratio *AF*. The maximum profit is realized at *G*. Therefore, *A* cannot be an equilibrium. Neither the equilibrium with production nor the one without production is possible. Since points between A and B are inefficient, we must conclude that there exists no competitive equilibrium in the economy of figure 2. We may note that the feasible production set $AEBDGCOHB$ is not convex. Since the set $BDGCOHB$ is convex and D is the competitive equilibrium if A and B coincide, we may infer that the difficulty is due to the existence of the overhead cost AB.[5])

The assumptions of perfect competition, laissez faire, internal economies due to overhead costs and the existence of a general equilibrium are mutually inconsistent. To get rid of this difficulty, we have to forsake some of these assumptions. Thus, we assumed away economies of scale in chapters 1 and 2. On the other hand, laissez faire is given up and government interference with subsidy is called for in chapters 3 and 6 to deal with internal economies. Perfect competition is replaced by monopolistic or imperfect competition in chapter 7 and it is shown that the general equilibrium is then reconciled with internal economies in chapter 8. However, as will be shown in chapter 5, economies of scale themselves can dispense with internal economies and depend on external economies which are consistent with perfect competition.

3. Perhaps, one of the most neglected problems in this book will be the problem of income distribution. The reason for this neglect is two-fold. In the normative analysis (as in chapters 1, 4, 6, 12, etc.) we can evade the issue by postulating the social welfare function or by confining ourselves to the study of Pareto optimal resource allocation. On the other hand, positive economics can make use of assumptions under which the problem disappears.

Firstly, although competitive prices allocate resources efficiently, this system does not succeed in distributing income among different individuals efficiently. Since the market fails in this respect, the resultant distribution of income should be, and nowadays is, easily subject to the changes caused by income redistribution policies. However, the problem of the optimal distribution of income, as well as the problem of the optimal supply of public goods,[6]) cannot be solved by the market mechanism and is therefore beyond the scope of the present book. Individuals have different views on the optimal

---

[5]) See Chipman, J.S., 'A survey of the theory of international trade, 2,' *Econometrica*, 33 (1965), pp. 685–760, for another counter-example to the existence of an equilibrium.
[6]) Income distribution and public goods are jointly considered as public concern in Kolm, S. Ch., 'The optimum production of social justice,' *Public Economics* (Margolis and Guitton ed.), Macmillan, 1969, pp. 145–200.

income distribution, i.e., their own social welfare functions. Perhaps, the problem of forming the social welfare function must be solved by a properly designed system of majority voting. This is why we sometimes confine ourselves to the Pareto optimality of resource allocation, a distribution free concept, which is a necessary condition for the maximum of any social welfare function, provided it is individualistic and Paretian.[7])

Secondly, under certain assumptions on the individual indifference maps, the competitive equilibrium prices and therefore the resultant allocation of resources is independent of income redistribution. The social amount of demand can be obtained from the well behaved social indifference map and therefore is independent of income distribution, if individual indifference maps are identical and the marginal rates of substitution are unchanged for any proportional changes in the amount of goods, as we will assume some-where in several chapters (chapters 2, 3, 5, 6, 8, 14, 16, etc.). The latter assumption on the marginal rates of substitution can also be stated as that individual Engel curves are straight lines through the origin or that the individual utility functions are homogeneous with respect to the amount of goods. Because of this assumption, the individual demand for goods is proportional to the level of income, if prices are given. Since individual indifference maps are identical, the coefficients of the proportionality are the same for all individuals. Therefore, the social demand, i.e., the sum of individual demands, is proportional to the level of the total income, independent of its distribution. Identical individual indifference maps can also serve as the social indifference map. There is no possibility of the crossing Scitovsky social indifference curves.[8])

4. A brief summary of the following chapters is in order. Seventeen chapters are grouped into six parts, i.e., Optimality and existence, Increasing returns and externality, Monopolistic competition, Second best, Stability, and Dichotomy. In each part, the first one or two chapters discuss the pure theory of the general equilibrium, while the remaining chapters are devoted to the applications in the theory of international trade.

Part 1 is a story of an economic utopia. The existence of a competitive equilibrium is demonstrated by making use of its Pareto optimality in chapter 1. A graphical exposition of a simple case as well as the mathe-matical demonstration of the general case will be given. Chapter 2 is an

---

[7]) See chapter 1.
[8]) See chapter 3.

international trade version of chapter 1, with the cost of transportation properly introduced.

The first two chapters in part 2 deal with cases of market failure, i.e., internal and external economies and diseconomies. Chapter 3 considers how far profit can be used as an indicator of increases in social welfare, when the average cost is diminishing due to the existence of the overhead cost. This is related to the problems of cost–benefit analysis of an investment project and of the optimal number of firms in an industry. Externality, which is an important aspect of the problem of environmental disruption,[9]) is considered and various policies towards externality are compared in chapter 4. We will insist that the classical Pigouvian policy is as efficient as other policies despite some recent criticism against it. Other two chapters in part 2 are essays on international trade, critical of traditional theory of free trade. Chapter 5 tries to develop a theory of international trade without assuming the international difference in factor endowments, which is the essence of the traditional Heckscher–Ohlin theory. Gains from trade due to increasing returns are demonstrated under the assumption of Marshallian external economies. Classical infant industry dogma will be defended from recent criticism in chapter 6 on the ground that it can be based on the dynamic internal economy even if there exists no externality. This is an application of chapter 3.

The assumption of perfect competition is given up in part 3. The existence of a general equilibrium with monopolistic competitions is demonstrated in chapter 7, with proper consideration of the differentiation of commodities by monopolistically competitive firms. Chapter 8 follows chapter 5 to develop another theory of trade without assuming international difference in factor endowments. Gains from trade due to internal economies are demonstrated under imperfect competition. Chapter 9 is a Fisherian (two-period) analysis of optimal trade and optimal foreign investment for a single country which has monopolistic powers in international markets of commodities and investments.

Part 4 deals with the theory of the second best, which is surveyed in chapter 10. Two kinds of domestic distortions, i.e., the wage differentials between industries and non-optimal domestic saving are considered in chapter 11. The possibility of the second best policies for international trade and/or foreign investment are discussed in the presence of these domestic distortions. Chapter 12 is an analytical counterpart of Vanek's geometry of

---

[9]) Another important aspect is the fact that the environment is a public good.

customs union which is a second best situation in comparison with free trade.

The stability problem of competitive markets is discussed in part 5. After the consideration of the difference between Walrasian and Marshallian stability, chapter 13 is wholly devoted to the study of Walrasian tâtonnement under gross substitutability. The Keynesian problem of why the flexible wage does not lead to full employment is discussed as an application of the stability analysis. The so-called non-tâtonnement stability is considered in chapter 14. Our view is that stability is more easily established if the highly special tâtonnement assumption is relaxed. Chapter 15 applies Hicksian stability condition in the study of the stability of the foreign exchange market.

Finally, part 6 deals with the question why non-monetary theory can be useful in a monetary world. Dichotomy controversies are critically surveyed in chapter 16 from this point of view. Chapter 17 applies the dichotomy in international economics to consider the relation between economic growth, terms of trade and the balance of payments.

PART 1

Optimality and existence

CHAPTER 1

Optimality and existence of a competitive equilibrium

1. Walras, the father of general equilibrium theory, developed two arguments to show the consistency of his theory. The first one, i.e., the theoretical or mathematical demonstration of the existence of a solution to his model of general equilibrium was, however, based on the mere counting of the number of unknowns and of equations and therefore quite unsatisfactory.[1]) The rigorous proof of this existence problem of a perfectly competitive equilibrium is given much later by Arrow and Debreu and many others.[2]) The demand and supply of each commodity are considered as functions of all the prices and the crux of the proof is to show the existence of an equilibrium price vector which equalizes demand and supply of all the commodities.

On the other hand, the recent development of the theory of mathematical programming sheds a new light on the basic theorem of welfare economics, i.e., the Pareto optimality of a competitive equilibrium. Equilibrium prices are derived as Lagrangean multipliers in the constrained maximization. An equilibrium point of an economic system under perfect competition is an efficient state in Pareto's sense in which we cannot make any one better off without making someone worse off. Conversely, a Pareto optimal allocation of resources in which individual budget constraints are satisfied is a competitive equilibrium if a positive income is imputed to each individual.[3]) In other words, it can be said that a competitive equilibrium

---

[1]) See Walras–Jaffé [25], pp. 237–42. The second argument, i.e., the empirical demonstration of how markets can solve the problem of general equilibrium (Walras–Jaffé [25], pp. 243–54) will be discussed below in chapter 13.

[2]) For early predecessors, see Wald [24]. In addition to Arrow–Debreu [2], we must mention, among others, Gale [9], Kuhn [12], [13], McKenzie [15], [16], [17] and Nikaido [21].

[3]) See Arrow [1], Debreu [6] and Hurwicz [10].

is a maximum point of some properly defined social welfare function subject to the resource and technological constraints.

The purpose of this chapter is, following Negishi [19],[4]) to relate these two problems, i.e., existence and optimality of equilibrium, to each other, and to give an alternative proof of the existence of an equilibrium putting emphasis on the welfare aspect of competitive equilibrium. We shall first show that a competitive equilibrium is a maximum point of a social welfare function which is a linear combination of utility functions of individual consumers, with the weights in the combination in inverse proportion to the marginal utilities of income. Then, the existence of an equilibrium is equivalent to the existence of a maximum of this special welfare function and we can prove the former by showing the latter.[5])

2.   Before presenting the proof of the general case, it might be better to consider the simple case graphically so that the gist of the proof can be easily understood. Let us consider the case of pure exchange of two commodities between two persons by using the familiar Edgeworth box diagram. The Edgeworth box is a model of pure trade or exchange, that is, a model in which economic activity consists entirely of trading and consuming, with the exclusion of production.

We assume that the first person has an endowment of $\overline{X}_{11}$ units of commodity 1 and $\overline{X}_{12}$ units of commodity 2. Similarly, we assume that the second person has an endowment of $\overline{X}_{21}$ units of commodity 1 and $\overline{X}_{22}$ units of commodity 2. Since this is a model with no production, the total amount of commodity 1 in the economy before and after trade is given by $\overline{X}_1 = \overline{X}_{11} + \overline{X}_{21}$, and the total amount of commodity 2 is given by $\overline{X}_2 = \overline{X}_{12} + \overline{X}_{22}$.

It follows that the only possible states of the economy are those represented by a set of points contained in a rectangle having dimensions $\overline{X}_1$ by $\overline{X}_2$ (figure 1.1). Any point in the box represents a particular distribution of the

---

[4]) This is developed from Negishi, T., 'Welfare economics and existence of an equilibrium for a competitive economy, I and II,' Technical Report No. 62 and No. 65, Office of Naval Research, Contract N6onr–25133, NR–047–004, Department of Economics, Stanford University (1958, December), and

Negishi, T., 'Existence and stability of an economic equilibrium' (in Japanese), presented to University of Tokyo as a partial requirement for M.A. in 1957. For further developments, see Takayama–El Hodiri [22] and Takayama–Judge [23].

[5]) It may be interesting to note that in this approach we can dispense with the concept of demand and supply functions altogether. See also a recent existence proof given in chapters III–V of Arrow–Hahn [3].

commodities between the two persons. For example, if the distribution of commodities is given by point M, the quantities of commodity 1 and commodity 2 consumed by the first person, X_{11} and X_{12} respectively, are measured by the coordinates of M, using the south-west corner O as the origin; the quantities consumed by the second person, X_{21} and X_{22} respectively, are measured by the coordinates of point M, using the north east corner O' as the origin. The indifference map of the first person is drawn, using O as the origin, and the indifference map of the second person, using O' as the origin. The marginal rates of substitution of two persons are equal where an indifference curve of the first person is tangent to an indifference curve of the second person. The locus of all such points is the contract curve CC'.

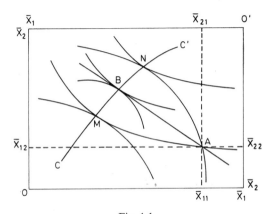

Fig. 1.1.

The marginal rates of substitution are unequal at points not on the contract curve, say point A of the initial endowments, and it is possible to increase the utility level of both persons by altering the existing distribution of commodities. For example, if the final position after a redistribution of commodities is between M and N, both persons would have gained, since both would be on higher indifference curves than at A. If a point on the contract curve is reached, it is not possible to improve further the position of either person without a deterioration in the position of the other. In other words, points on the contract curve are Pareto optimal.

Although it is a bit strange to assume perfect competition in the case of the bilateral exchange, let us suppose for heuristic purposes that two persons are acting as quantity adjusters to the given market prices. Denoting the price ratio, i.e., the price of commodity 1 in terms of commodity 2 by p, the first person will choose the best combination of two commodities (X_{11}, X_{12}) being subject to his budget constraint, $pX_{11}+X_{12}=p\overline{X}_{11}+\overline{X}_{12}$. Similarly the second person will choose (X_{21}, X_{22}) being subject to $pX_{21}+X_{22}=p\overline{X}_{21}+\overline{X}_{22}$. Equilibrium conditions for each person are (1) the equality of the marginal rate of substitution and the price ratio (i.e., the tangency of indifference curve and price line) and (2) the budget constraint. The market equilibrium is attained when demand and supply of two commodities are equal, i.e., $X_{11}+X_{21}=\overline{X}_1$, $X_{12}+X_{22}=\overline{X}_2$. It should be noted that among two budget constraints and two market clearing conditions any one condition is implied by the remaining three conditions.

At any point in the box diagram market equilibrium conditions are satisfied. If the common tangent of two indifference curves is considered as the price line, the condition (1) of the equilibrium of each person is realized at any point on the contract curve CC'. Therefore, all the conditions for the competitive equilibrium are satisfied at such a point as point B on the contract curve, where the price line BA passes the initial endowment point A, i.e., the budget constraint is satisfied for each person.

Is the existence of such a point generally guaranteed? If an instructor of *Introduction to economics* is smart enough and always produces point B on the blackboard very easily, happy students might not have such a question. However, being a bit clumsy, the instructor may draw a price line from B which does not pass through point A or the one from point A which is not tangent to indifference curves at point B and may not produce point B properly without twisting indifference curves favorably. The existence of a competitive equilibrium, i.e., the point B, in general must be demonstrated so as to save the face of such a clumsy instructor.

Since markets are always cleared in the box we have only to find a point on the contract curve CC' at which a budget constraint is satisfied. Let us first consider the point M, i.e., the point of intersection of the contract curve and the indifference curve of the first person passing through point A. If difference curves are strictly convex to the origin, we have

$$F(X_{11}, X_{12})=p(X_{11}, X_{12})X_{11}+X_{12}-p(X_{11}, X_{12})\overline{X}_{11}-\overline{X}_{12}<0$$

at point M, where p is the marginal rate of substitution of the first person. Budget constraint is not satisfied and M is not a competitive equilibrium. Similarly we have at point N, i.e., the point of intersection of the contract curve and the indifference curve of the second person passing point A,

$$F(X_{11}, X_{12})=p(X_{11}, X_{12})X_{11}+X_{12}-p(X_{11}, X_{12})\overline{X}_{11}-\overline{X}_{12}>0.$$

If the marginal rate of substitution of the first person p is assumed to be a continuous function of the amount of two commodities consumed by the same person, $F(X_{11}, X_{12})$ is also a continuous function. The movement on the contract curve from M to N can be expressed as $X_{11} = X_{11}(t)$, $X_{12} = X_{12}(t)$, $0 \leq t \leq 1$, where $\{X_{11}(0), X_{12}(0)\}$ is the coordinates of M, $\{X_{11}(1), X_{12}(1)\}$ is the coordinates of N and X_{11} and X_{12} are continuous function of t. Then, $F\{X_{11}(t), X_{12}(t)\}$ is a continuous function of t such that $F < 0$ at $t = 0$ and $F > 0$ at $t = 1$. By the theorem of intermediate values on a continuous function, we are sure that $F = 0$ at some $\bar{t}$ such that $0 < \bar{t} < 1$. The point whose coordinates from the origin O is $\{X_{11}(\bar{t}), X_{12}(\bar{t})\}$ is a competitive equilibrium, i.e., point B in the box diagram.

We may summarize as

Theorem 1. If indifference curves are strictly convex to the origin and the marginal rate of substitution is a continuous function of the amount of commodities consumed, then there exists a competitive equilibrium for the bilateral exchange of two commodities.

The gist of the proof of the above is to find a point with budget constraints satisfied (point B) among Pareto optimal points (curve CC') by changing the social importance of individuals in the society (the movement from M to N). It may be interesting to note that the case of figure 1.2 given below violates the assumption in theorem 1.

3.   Let us now construct an economic model of the general m commodity, n consumer, r firm case.

Let $X_i \, (\geq 0)$ be a consumption vector (whose element $X_{ij} \geq 0$ is the amount of the jth commodity consumed, $j = 1, ..., m)$, $\bar{X}_i \, (\geq 0)^6)$ be an initial holding vector (whose element $\bar{X}_{ij} \geq 0$ is the amount of the jth commodity initially endowed) and $U_i(X_i)$ be the utility function of the ith consumer, $i = 1, ..., n$.

Next let y_k be a production vector of the kth firm, $k = 1, ..., r$, whose element $y_{kj} \geq 0 \, (\leq 0)$ is the output (input) of the jth commodity, and Y_k be the possible set of y_k, or the set of y_k which satisfies the restriction on production $F_k(y_k) \geq 0$. Conventional production function is defined in terms of equality as $F_k(y_k) = 0$. By permitting the free disposal of commodities,

---

6) For a vector x, $x \geq 0$ denotes that all the elements of x are non-negative and at least some of them are positive.

we can extend it into inequality. For example, in the case of Cobb–Douglas production function, we can convert $Y - AK^\alpha L^{1-\alpha} = 0$ into $Y - AK^\alpha L^{1-\alpha} \leq 0$, where Y, K and L are respectively the amount of output, of input of the service of capital and of input of the service of labor, and A (> 0) and α ($0 \leq \alpha \leq 1$) are constants.

Let P (≥ 0) be a price vector whose element $P_j \geq 0$ is the price of the jth commodity. Let finally λ_{ik} be the proportion of the profit of the kth commodity distributed to the ith consumer such that $\lambda_{ik} \geq 0$, $\Sigma_i \lambda_{ik} = 1$.

We define a general equilibrium under perfect competition:

Definition 1. The following are conditions of a competitive equilibrium $(X_i, y_k, P)_{i=1,\ldots,n,\, k=1,\ldots,r}$.

(a) Equalities of demand and supply of non-free commodities,

$$\Sigma_i X_{ij} - \Sigma_k y_{kj} - \Sigma_i \overline{X}_{ij} \leq 0, \quad P_j(\Sigma_i X_{ij} - \Sigma_k y_{kj} - \Sigma_i \overline{X}_{ij}) = 0 ,$$

for $j = 1, \ldots, m$.

(b) The equilibrium of consumers, i.e., X_i is a maximum point of $U_i(X_i)$ subject to the budget constraint $\Sigma_j P_j X_{ij} = M_i$, with P and

$$M_i = \Sigma_j P_j \overline{X}_{ij} + \max(0, \Sigma_k \lambda_{ik} \Sigma_j P_j y_{kj})$$

given, for $i = 1, \ldots, n$.

(c) The equilibrium of firms, i.e., y_k is a maximum point of $\Sigma_j P_j y_{kj}$ subject to $F_k(y_k) \geq 0$ ($y_k \in Y_k$), with P given, $k = 1, \ldots, r$.

Next let us define two highly related but slightly different concepts, i.e., a welfare maximum and a Pareto optimal allocation as follows:

Definition 2. Consider a weighted sum of utility functions $\Sigma_i \alpha_i U_i(X_i)$, with weights $\alpha_i \geq 0$, $\Sigma_i \alpha_i = 1$, $i = 1, \ldots, n$, as a social welfare function. An allocation $(X_i, y_k)_{i=1,\ldots,n,\, k=1,\ldots,r}$ which maximizes this welfare function, subject to the conditions of no excess of demand over supply, $\Sigma_i X_i \leq \Sigma_i \overline{X}_i + \Sigma_k y_k$ and those of production $F_k(y_k) \geq 0$, $k = 1, \ldots, r$, is called a welfare maximum.

Definition 3. An allocation $(X_i, y_k)_{i=1,\ldots,n,\, k=1,\ldots,r}$ which satisfies the condition of no excess of demand over supply and those of production, is said to be Pareto optimal if there exists no allocation $(X'_i, y_k)_{i=1,\ldots,n,\, k=1,\ldots,r}$ which satisfies the same conditions and $U_i(X'_i) \geq U_i(X_i)$, for all i, the strict inequality holding for at least one i ($i = 1, \ldots, n$).

The assumptions on utility functions and production restrictions are as follows:

Assumption 1. $U_i(X_i)$ is continuous, increasing and concave; more precisely we can make it concave by a strictly positive monotone transformation.

A function is increasing if $f(X) > f(X')$ for $X > X'$. The concavity of a function implies that $f(\beta X + (1-\beta)X') \geq \beta f(X) + (1-\beta)f(X')$ for any $0 \leq \beta \leq 1$. Roughly speaking, this assumption implies that there is a utility function with non-increasing marginal utility among utility functions which correspond to the same indifference map. Usually, a utility function is assumed to be quasi-concave, i.e., indifference curves are convex to the origin. Concavity implies the quasi-concavity, but not vice versa. However, note that under certain regularity conditions a quasi-concave function can be transformed to a concave function by a strictly positive monotone transformation, while utility ordering is usually supposed to be invariant under such a transformation.[7])

Assumption 2. $F_k(y_k)$ is continuous and concave, and $F_k(y_k^*) > 0$ for some y_k^* such that $-\Sigma_k y_k^* < \Sigma_i \overline{X}_i$. Furthermore, the sets Y_k and their vector sum (i.e., the possible set of $\Sigma_k y_k$) $Y = \Sigma_k Y_k$ satisfy the following conditions: $0 \in Y_k$, $Y \cap B = 0$ (B is the closed positive orthant), $Y \cap (-Y) = 0$.

The concavity of F_k implies non-increasing returns and the convexity of Y_k. The condition on y_k^* is needed for the application of the Kuhn–Tucker theorem given below as is seen in lemma 2. The implications of the three conditions on Y_k and Y are respectively the possibility of no production, the negation of the land of Cockaigne and the irreversibility of the production process.[8])

Although it is a rather strict assumption, we make it for the sake of the simplicity:[9])

---

[7]) See de Finetti [7] and Fenchel [8], pp. 115–137. We may also note that the concavity defined in an open convex set implies the continuity and the existence of the left hand and right hand derivatives. But we are defining utility functions on a closed set, i.e., $X_i \geq 0$. See Berge [5], p. 201 (Berge–Patterson [5], p. 193).

[8]) See Arrow–Debreu [2], p. 276.

[9]) For weaker but more complicated assumptions, see, for example, Arrow–Debreu [2], Arrow–Hahn [3] and McKenzie [17].

Assumption 3. $U_i(X_i)$ is strictly increasing (i.e., $U_i(X') > U_i(X_i)$ for $X' \geq X_i$), or $\overline{X}_i > 0$, for all i.

From assumptions 1, 2 and the conditions of no excess of demand over supply in definitions 2 and 3 or of equalities of demand and supply for non-free commodities in definition 1, the following lemma is obtained.

Lemma 1.   The domain of X_i and y_k is convex and compact and can be restricted as $X_i \in \Gamma_i$, $y_k \in \Gamma_k$, Γ_i, Γ_k being suitably large convex, compact sets, without causing any change in the definitions of a welfare maximum, Pareto optimal allocation and a competitive equilibrium.[10])

Other lemmas we shall use in this chapter are,

Lemma 2.   (Kuhn–Tucker theorem). Let $f(x)$ and $g(x) = \langle g_1(x), ..., g_n(x) \rangle$ be concave in $x \geq 0$ and $g(x)$ satisfy Slater's condition that there is a vector x^0 such that $x^0 \geq 0$ and $g(x^0) > 0$. Then $\bar{x}$ maximizes $f(x)$ subject to the restrictions that $x \geq 0$ and $g(x) \geq 0$, if and only if there is a vector $\bar{u}$ such that $(\bar{x}, \bar{u})$ is a non-negative saddle point of the Lagrangean $\psi(x, u) = f(x) + ug(x)$, i.e., $\psi(x, \bar{u}) \leq \psi(\bar{x}, \bar{u}) \leq \psi(\bar{x}, u)$ for all $x \geq 0$ and $u \geq 0$.[11])

Lemma 3.   (Kakutani's Fixed Point theorem). Let K be a compact convex set in n dimensional Euclidian space R^n and $f(x)$ be a point-to-set, upper-semicontinuous mapping from K into K, whose image is non-void and convex. Then, there is a fixed point $\hat{x}$ such that $\hat{x} = f(\hat{x})$.[12])

4.   Now we are in the position to state the following theorems on a welfare maximum and a Pareto optimal allocation.

Theorem 2.   For any set of weights α_i, there is a welfare maximum under assumptions 1 and 2. Furthermore, if all weights are strictly positive, an allocation is a welfare maximum if and only if it is Pareto optimal.

Proof.   From assumption 1 and definition 2, the social welfare function is continuous. From lemma 1, the domain is compact. Therefore, from

---

[10]) See Arrow–Debreu [2], pp. 276–279.
[11]) See Kuhn–Tucker [14] and Arrow–Hurwicz–Uzawa [4], pp. 32–37.
[12]) See Kakutani [11] and Debreu [6], p. 26.

Weierstrass theorem, the social welfare function has a maximum, as a continuous function on the compact domain. Suppose next a welfare maximum (X_i, y_k) is not Pareto optimal. From definition 3 there exists an allocation (X_i', y_k) such that $U_i(X_i') \geq U(X_i)$ for all i and $U_i(X_i') > U_i(X_i)$ for some i. Then we have $\Sigma_i \alpha_i U_i(X_i') > \Sigma_i \alpha_i U_i(X_i)$, a contradiction. Therefore, a welfare maximum is Pareto optimal. Finally consider the feasible set of utility combinations under conditions of no excess of demand over supply and those of production, i.e., the set of $U = (U_1, ..., U_n)$ such that $U_i = U_i(X_i)$, $\Sigma_i X_i - \Sigma_k y_k - \Sigma_i \bar{X}_i \leq 0$, $F_k(y_k) \geq 0$, $i = 1, ..., n$, $k = 1,..., r$. Let us denote this set by A. The boundary of this set, or more precisely, a set of U such that $U \in A$ and there is no $U' \geq U$, $U' \in A$, is sometimes called the utility frontier or, in the case of $n = 2$, the utility possibility curve. From assumptions 1 and 2, the set A is convex. This is seen as follows. Let allocations (X_i, y_k) and $(X_i' y_k')$ respectively correspond to U and U' such that $U \in A$ and $U' \in A$. Any positive combination of these two allocations, i.e., $\beta(X_i, y_k) + (1-\beta)(X_i', y_k')$, $0 \leq \beta \leq 1$, satisfies the conditions of no excess of demand over supply and those of production, and we have $\{U_i(\beta X_i + (1-\beta)X_i')\}_{i=1,...,n} \in A$. Since U_i's are concave, $U_i(\beta X_i + (1-\beta)X_i') \geq \beta U_i(X_i) + (1-\beta)U_i(X_i')$. It follows, from the fact that U_i's are increasing, that $U^2 \in A$ if $U^1 \in A$ and $U^1 \geq U^2$. Therefore, $\beta U + (1-\beta)U' \in A$, i.e., A is convex. Suppose now that $U^0 \in A$ is Pareto optimal. Since U^0 is on the boundary of a convex set, there is a supporting hyperplane containing U^0, $\Sigma_i \alpha_i U_i^0 = c$, α_i and c being constants, such that for any $U \in A$, $\Sigma_i \alpha_i U_i \leq c$. From the definition of A we can make $\alpha_i \geq 0$ for all i. Therefore, a Pareto optimal allocation corresponding to U^0 is a welfare maximum for such α_i's.

Theorem 3. A welfare maximum is a saddle point of Lagrangean

$$\psi(X_i, y_k, P_j, \mu_k) = \Sigma_i \alpha_i U_i(X_i) - \Sigma_j P_j(\Sigma_i X_{ij} - \Sigma_k y_{kj} - \Sigma_i \bar{X}_{ij})$$
$$+ \Sigma_k \mu_k F_k(y_k) ,$$

where $X_i \geq 0$ and y_k are maximizing variables and $P_j \geq 0$, $\mu_k \geq 0$ are minimizing variables. The necessary and sufficient condition for it is as follows:

$$\alpha_i U_{ij}^{-0} - P_j \geq 0, \quad \alpha_i U_{ij}^{+0} - P_j \leq 0, \quad \text{for} \quad i = 1, ..., n, j = 1, ..., m,$$

$$P_j + \mu_k F_{kj}^{-0} \geq 0, \quad P_j + \mu_k F_{kj}^{+0} \leq 0, \quad \text{for} \quad k = 1, ..., r, j = 1, ..., m,$$

$$\Sigma_i X_{ij} - \Sigma_k y_{kj} - \Sigma_i \bar{X}_{ij} \leq 0, \quad P_j(\Sigma_i X_{ij} - \Sigma_k y_{kj} - \Sigma_i \bar{X}_{ij}) = 0,$$

$$\text{for} \quad j = 1, ..., m,$$

$$\mu_k F_k(y_k) = 0, \quad F_k(y_k) \geq 0, \quad \text{for} \quad k = 1, ..., r,$$

where U^{-0}_{ij} (U^{+0}_{ij}) stands for the left (right)-hand derivative of U_i with respect to X_{ij} and the like.

Proof. A social welfare function is called individualistic if it is expressed as a function of individual utilities only, like $W(X_1, \ldots, X_n) = V\{U_1(X_1) \ldots, U_n(X_n)\}$ and V is said to be Paretian if marginal social importance of each individual is positive, $\partial V/\partial U_i > 0$, for all i. Since U_i's are concave with respect to X_i, W is concave with respect to X_i, $i = 1, \ldots, n$, if V is concave with respect to U_i, $i = 1, \ldots, n$. This is seen as follows. Consider $X^1 = (X^1_1, \ldots, X^1_n)$, $X^2 = (X^2_1, \ldots, X^2_n)$ and $X^3 = \beta X^1 + (1 - \beta) X^2$ for any $0 \leq \beta \leq 1$. Since U_i is concave, $U_i(X^3_i) \geq \beta U_i(X^1_i) + (1 - \beta) U_i(X^2_i)$, where $X^3_i = \beta X^1_i + (1 - \beta) X^2_i$, $i = 1, \ldots, n$. From the fact that W is individualistic and V is Paretian and concave, we have

$$W(X^3) = V(U^3) \geq V\{\beta U^1 + (1 - \beta) U^2\} \geq \beta V(U^1) + (1 - \beta) V(U)^2$$

$$= \beta W(X^1) + (1 - \beta) W(X^2),$$

where $U^s = (U^s_1, \ldots, U^s_n)$ and $U^s_i = U_i(X^s_i)$ for $s = 1, 2, 3$. Therefore, W is concave with respect to X_i, $i = 1, \ldots, n$.[13] Since our social welfare function $V = (U_1, \ldots, U_n) = \Sigma_i \alpha_i U_i$ is linear and therefore concave, $W(X_1, \ldots, X_n) = \Sigma_i \alpha_i U_i(X_i)$ is also concave. On the other hand, by putting $X_i = 0$, the assumption $F(y^*_k) > 0$, $-\Sigma_k y^*_k < \Sigma_i \overline{X}_i$ guarantees the satisfaction of the Slater condition in lemma 2. Then, we can apply the Kuhn–Tucker theorem. The second half of the theorem follow from the definition of a saddle point.

The Lagrangean multiplier P_j in theorem 3 is sometimes called a shadow or an efficiency price of the jth commodity since it signifies the scarcity of the jth commodity. It may be noted that from assumption 1 (U_i's are increasing) at least some of P_j's are positive, while the first half of assumption 3 (U'_i's are strictly increasing) implies that all P_j's are positive.

5. Next we shall prove the following theorem on the relation between a welfare maximum and a competitive equilibrium.

Theorem 4. Suppose the Lagrangean multiplier P_j attached to the condition of no excess of demand over supply of the jth commodity in a welfare maximum is interpreted to be equal to the price P_j of the same jth commodity

[13] See Negishi [20].

in an equilibrium. Then, at any welfare maximum, the conditions (a) and (c) of an equilibrium in definition 1 are always satisfied while the condition (b) of an equilibrium is satisfied at a welfare maximum if and only if the weight α_i of consumers in the latter state are all positive and happen to be identical to the inverse of the marginal utility of income of consumers in the former state, or, in other words, if and only if the budget constraints in a competitive equilibrium happen to be satisfied in a welfare maximum, when weights α_i's are all positive.

Proof. Conditions (b) and (c) of an equilibrium in definition 1 can be written in the following form:
(b') x_i is a saddle point of Lagrangean

$$\phi_i(X_i, \delta_i) = U_i(X_i) - \delta_i(\Sigma_j P_j X_{ij} - M_i) ,$$

where $X_i \geq 0$ are maximizing variables and $\delta_i \geq 0$ is a minimizing variable. It is well known that δ_i is the marginal utility of income. The necessary and sufficient condition for a saddle point is,

$$U_{ij}^{-0} - \delta_i P_j \geq 0, \quad U_{ij}^{+0} - \delta_i P_j \leq 0, \quad \text{for} \quad j = 1, ..., m,$$

and

$$\sum_j P_j X_{ij} - M_i = 0,$$

(c') y_k is a saddle point of Lagrangean

$$\phi_k(y_k, \mu_k) = \Sigma_j P_j y_{kj} + \mu_k F_k(y_k) ,$$

where y_k are maximizing variables and $\mu_k \geq 0$ is a minimizing variable. The necessary and sufficient condition for it is

$$P_j + \mu_k F_{kj}^{-0} \geq 0, \quad P_j + \mu_k F_{kj}^{+0} \leq 0, \quad \text{for} \quad j = 1, ..., m,$$

and

$$F_k(y_k) \geq 0.$$

The equivalence of (b) and (b') is seen as follows. Since $M_i > 0$ from assumption 3, Slater's condition in lemma 2 can be satisfied by putting $X_i = 0$ and the Kuhn–Tucker theorem can be applied. The conditions (c) and (c') are equivalent since the assumption $F_k(y_k^*) > 0$ implies Slater's condition and Kuhn–Tucker theorem can be applied. Then, comparing definitions 1 and 2 and using theorem 3 and the equivalence of (b) and (b'), and of (c) and (c'), the theorem is easily obtained.

We may note that both in theorem 2 (the relation of a welfare maximum and a Pareto optimal allocation) and theorem 4 (the relation between a welfare maximum and a competitive equilibrium) the case of $\alpha_i = 0$ is excluded. This is an anomalous case in which a Pareto optimal allocation may not be achieved by competitive mechanism. Consider the case of the bilateral exchange of two commodities. Figure 1.2 is a box diagram similar to the figure 1.1. I_1 and I_2 are indifference curves of the first person with the

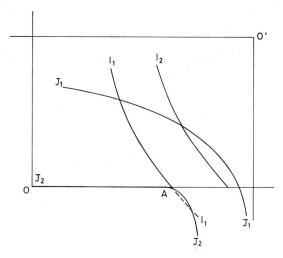

Fig. 1.2.

origin at O and J_1 and J_2 are those of the second person with the origin at O'. Note that the utility of the commodity 1 is satiated for the second person at points between O and A (including O and A) while it is not so for the first person. Therefore, OA in figure 1.2 corresponds to BA in figure 1.3 which is the utility frontier or the utility possibility curve, i.e., the curve of the maximum combination of U_1 and U_2. If $\alpha_1 = 0$, then points between OA (including O) in figure 1.2 or points between BA (including B) in figure 1.3 are welfare maximum but certainly not Pareto optimal. Point A which is also a welfare maximum when $\alpha_1 = 0$ is Pareto optimal, but not a competitive equilibrium as is pointed out by Arrow [1], since there can be no price line which is tangent to both I_1 and J_2 at A. If A is a welfare maximum the shadow price of commodity 1 is zero and the value of the consumption of the first person which is to be equal to M_1 at equilibrium is also zero in terms of shadow prices. In theorem 5 below the exclusion of this anomalous case is guaranteed by the fact that $M_i > 0$ from assumption 3.[14])

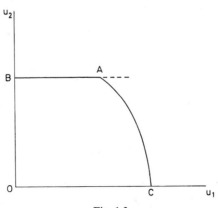

Fig. 1.3.

6. From theorem 4 we know that if condition (b) of an equilibrium is satisfied at a welfare maximum for some set of positive weights α_i, then it is an equilibrium. We have to seek such a set of weights to prove the existence of an equilibrium. For this purpose, we construct the following mapping:

(a) For any point $\alpha = (\alpha_1, \ldots, \alpha_n)$ on the $n-1$ dimensional simplex S^{n-1} we obtain a welfare maximum $(X_i', y_k', P', \mu_k')_{i=1,\ldots,n,\, k=1,\ldots,r}$ and by the normalization $P_j'' = P_j'/\Sigma_j P_j'$, we have (X_i', y_k', P''), where $X_i' \in \Gamma_i$, $y_k' \in \Gamma_k$, $P' = (P_1', \ldots, P_m')$, $P'' = (P_1'', \ldots, P_m'')$ and $P'' \in S^{m-1}$.

(b) For any point (X_i, y_k, P) contained in a convex, compact set $K = \Pi_i \Gamma_i \times \Pi_k \Gamma_k \times S^{m-1}$, we can have $\Sigma_i |M_i - \Sigma_j P_j X_{ij}| < B$, where B is a positive constant. Then, for any $\alpha \in S^{n-1}$ and $(X_i, y_k, P) \in K$, we obtain $\alpha'' = (\alpha_1'', \ldots, \alpha_n'') \in S^{n-1}$ by

$$\alpha_i' = \max(0, \alpha_i + (M_i - \Sigma_j P_j X_{ij})/B)$$

and the normalization $\alpha_i'' = \alpha_i'/\Sigma_i \alpha_i'$.

(c) Combining (a) and (c) we have a mapping from a convex compact set into itself $S^{n-1} \times K \ni (\alpha, X_i, y_k, P) \to (\alpha'', X_i', Y_k', P'') \in S^{n-1} \times K$.

---

[14]) It is also known that the demand function may not be continuous when $M_i = 0$. In figure 1.2, the demand for the first commodity (measured horizontally) of the first individual is less than OA if its price is positive while it is infinite when its price is zero.

Some remarks may be in order. In (a), the range of $P' = (P'_i, ..., P'_m)$ can be considered compact from assumption 2 and theorem 3 since U_i's and F_k's are continuous and have compact domains.[15] It may be noted that $P' \neq 0$, since U_i's are increasing. In (b), $\Sigma_i \alpha'_i > 0$, since $\Sigma_i \alpha_i = 1$ and $\Sigma_i \{|M_i - \Sigma_j P_j X_{ij}|/B\} < 1$. The idea of the mapping (b) is to change the social importance of individual consumers in the social welfare so as to make budget constraints satisfied.

Finally we can prove that the above mapping has a fixed point and the corresponding welfare maximum is a competitive equilibrium, and so establish the following existence theorem for a competitive equilibrium.

Theorem 5. Under assumptions 1, 2 and 3, there exists a competitive equilibrium.

Proof. (A) The mapping has a fixed point.
(1) The point to set mapping $\alpha \in S^{n-1} \to (X'_i, y'_k, P')$ is the mapping from α to saddle points of $\psi(X_i, y_k, P, \mu_k)$ in theorem 3. From theorem 2 its image is non-void. It is convex because ψ is concave with respect to X_i and y_k and linear with respect to P. This mapping is upper-semi-continuous because its graphical representation is closed and its range is compact. The normalization mapping $P' \to P''$ preserves the upper-semi-continuity and the convexity of the image, since it is a continuous point to point mapping when $P' \neq 0$. Therefore, mapping (a) is upper-semi-continuous, having non-void and convex image.[16]
(2) The point to point mapping $(\alpha, X_i, y_k, P) \to \alpha''$ is continuous when $\Sigma_i \alpha'_i > 0$.
(3) From 1 and 2, the mapping $(\alpha, X_i, y_k, P) \to (\alpha'', X'_i, y'_k, P'')$ is an upper-semi-continuous mapping from a convex compact set $S^{n-1} \times K$ into itself whose image is non-void and convex. Therefore, there is a fixed point $(\bar{\alpha}, \bar{X}_i, \bar{y}_k, \bar{P})$ from Kakutani's Fixed Point theorem in lemma 3.
  (B) A fixed point $(\bar{\alpha}, \bar{X}_i, \bar{y}_k, \bar{P})$ is an equilibrium.
The point $(\bar{X}_i, \bar{y}_k, \bar{P})$ is the welfare maximum corresponding to $\bar{\alpha}$. Therefore, to demonstrate that it is also an equilibrium, it is sufficient to show that condition (b) is satisfied. In order to see this, we first note that $\Sigma_j \bar{P}_j \bar{y}_{kj} \geq 0$ since $0 \in Y_k$ and therefore

$$\Sigma_j \bar{P}_j \bar{X}_{ij} = \bar{M}_i (\equiv \Sigma_j \bar{P}_j \bar{X}_{ij} + \Sigma_k \lambda_{ik} \Sigma_j \bar{P}_j \bar{y}_{kj}) .$$

---

[15] See Moore [18].
[16] See Berge [5], pp. 114–12**2** (Berge–Patterson, 109–117).

This is because all $\bar{M}_i - \Sigma_j \bar{P}_j \bar{X}_{ij}$ cannot be of unequal sign by the construction of the mapping and because from theorem 3,

$$\Sigma_i (\Sigma_j \bar{P}_j \bar{X}_{ij} - \bar{M}_i) = \Sigma_j \bar{P}_j (\Sigma_i \bar{X}_{ij} - \Sigma_k \bar{y}_{kj} - \Sigma_i \bar{X}_{ij}) = 0 .$$

Also from theorem 3, $(\bar{X}_i, \bar{y}_k, \bar{P})$ satisfies the following conditions,

$$\bar{\bar{\alpha}}_i U_{ij}^{+0} - \bar{P}_j \leqq 0, \quad \bar{\bar{\alpha}}_i U_{ij}^{-0} - \bar{P}_j \geqq 0, \quad \text{for} \quad j = 1, ..., m, \; i = 1, ..., n.$$

Because of the assumption of the strictly increasing U_i (i.e., the positive P_j for all j) or that of $\bar{X}_i > 0$ for all i (assumption 3) we have $\bar{M}_i > 0$. Then, we are sure that $\bar{\bar{\alpha}}_i > 0$, since otherwise $\Sigma_j \bar{P}_j \bar{X}_{ij} = 0$. Therefore, we obtain

$$U_{ij}^{+0} - \frac{1}{\bar{\bar{\alpha}}_i} \bar{P}_j \leqq 0, \quad U_{ij}^{-0} - \frac{1}{\bar{\bar{\alpha}}_i} \bar{P}_j \geqq 0, \quad \text{for} \quad j = 1, ..., m, \; i = 1, ..., n.$$

Replacing $1/\bar{\bar{\alpha}}_i$ by $\bar{\bar{\delta}}_i$, we get

$$U_{ij}^{+0} - \bar{\bar{\delta}}_i \bar{P}_j \leqq 0, \quad U_{ij}^{-0} - \bar{\bar{\delta}}_i \bar{P}_j \geqq 0, \quad \text{for} \quad j = 1, ..., m, \; i = 1, ..., n.$$

These, together with $\bar{M}_i = \Sigma_j \bar{P}_j \bar{X}_{ij}$, $i = 1, ..., n$, are the necessary and sufficient condition of (b) as is seen in theorem 4.

Thus, we proved the existence of an equilibrium for a competitive economy as a welfare maximum, with the weight of a consumer being in inverse relation to the equilibrium marginal utility of income, since δ_i is the so-called marginal utility of income of the ith consumer.

References

[1] Arrow, K.J., 'An extension of the basic theorems of classical welfare economics,' J. Neyman (ed.), *Proceedings of the Second Berkeley Symposium on Mathematical Statistics and Probability*, University of California Press, 1951, pp. 507–532 (P. Newman (ed.), *Readings in Mathematical Economics, I*, Johns Hopkins University Press, 1968, pp. 365–390).

[2] Arrow, K.J. and G. Debreu, 'Existence of an equilibrium for a competitive economy,' *Econometrica*, 22 (1954), pp. 256–291.

[3] Arrow, K.J. and F.H. Hahn, *Competitive equilibrium analysis*, Holden–Day, forthcoming.

[4] Arrow, K.J., L. Hurwicz and H. Uzawa, *Studies in linear and non-linear programming*, Stanford University Press, 1958.

[5] Berge, C., *Espaces topologiques et fonctions multivoques*, Dunod, 1959 (Patterson tr., *Topological Spaces*, Macmillan, 1963).

[6] Debreu, G., *Theory of value*, John Wiley, 1959.

[7] De Finetti, B., 'Sulle stratificazioni convesse,' *Annali di Matematica Pura e Applicata*, 30 (1949), pp. 173–183.

[8] Fenchel, W., *Convex cones, sets and functions*, Princeton University (mimeographed), 1953.

[9] Gale, D., 'The law of supply and demand,' *Mathematica Scandinavica*, 3 (1955), pp. 155–169 (P. Newman (ed.), *Readings in Mathematical Economics*, *I*, Johns Hopkins University Press, 1968, pp. 87–101).

[10] Hurwicz, L., 'Optimality and informational efficiency in resource allocation processes,' K.J. Arrow and others (ed.), *Mathematical Methods in the Social Sciences, 1959*, Stanford University Press, 1960, pp. 27–46 (K.J. Arrow and T. Scitovsky (ed.), *Readings in Welfare Economics*, Irwin, 1969, pp. 61–80).

[11] Kakutani, S., 'A generalization of Brouwer's fixed point theorem,' *Duke Mathematical Journal*, 8 (1948), pp. 457–459 (P. Newman (ed.), *Readings in Mathematical Economics*, *I*, Johns Hopkins University Press, 1968, pp. 33–35).

[12] Kuhn, H.W., 'On a theorem of Wald,' H.W. Kuhn and A.W. Tucker (ed.), *Linear Inequalities and Related Systems*, Annals of Mathematics Studies, 38 (1956), pp. 265–273 (P. Newman (ed.), *Readings in Mathematical Economics*, *I*, Johns Hopkins University Press, 1968, pp. 106–115).

[13] Kuhn, H.W., 'A note on 'The law of supply and demand," *Mathematica Scandinavica*, 4 (1956), pp. 143–146 (P. Newman (ed.), *Readings in Mathematical Economics*, *I*, Johns Hopkins University Press, 1968, pp. 102–105).

[14] Kuhn, H.W. and A.W. Tucker, 'Nonlinear programming', J. Neyman (ed.), *Proceedings of the Second Berkeley Symposium on Mathematical Statistics and Probability*, University of California Press, 1951, pp. 481–92 (P. Newman (ed.), *Readings in Mathematical Economics*, *I*, Johns Hopkins University Press, 1968, pp. 3–14).

[15] McKenzie, L.W., 'On equilibrium in Graham's model of world trade and other competitive systems,' *Econometrica*, 22 (1954), pp. 147–161.

[16] McKenzie, L.W., 'Competitive equilibrium with dependent consumer preferences,' H.A. Antosiewicz (ed.), *Proceedings of the Second Symposium on Linear Programming*, *I*, USAF, 1955, pp. 277–294 (P. Newman (ed.), *Readings in Mathematical Economics*, *I*, Johns Hopkins University Press, 1968, pp. 129–146).

[17] McKenzie, L.W., 'On the existence of general equilibrium for a competitive market,' *Econometrica*, 27 (1959), pp. 54–71 (29 (1961), pp. 247–248).

[18] Moore, J.C., 'A note on point-set mapping,' J.P. Quirk and A.M. Zarley (ed.), *Papers in Quantitative Economics*, University of Kansas Press, 1968, pp. 129–140.

[19] Negishi, T., 'Welfare economics and existence of an equilibrium for a competitive economy,' *Metroeconomica*, 12 (1960), pp. 92–7.

[20] Negishi, T., 'On social welfare function,' *Quarterly Journal of Economics*, 77 (1963), pp. 156–8.

[21] Nikaido, H., 'On the classical multilateral exchange problem,' *Metroeconomica*, 8 (1956), pp. 135–145, 9 (1957), pp. 209–210 (P. Newman (ed.), *Readings in Mathematical Economics*, *I*, Johns Hopkins University Press, 1968, pp. 116–128).

[22] Takayama, A. and M. El Hodiri, 'Programming, Pareto optimum and the existence of competitive equilibria,' *Metroeconomica*, 20 (1968), pp. 1–10.

[23] Takayama, T. and G. Judge, *Spatial and temporal price and allocation Models*, forthcoming.

[24] Wald, A., 'Über einige Gleichungssysteme der mathematischen Ökonomie,' *Zeitschrift für Nationalökonomie*, 8 (1936), pp. 637–670 ('On some systems of equations of mathematical economics,' *Econometrica*, 19 (1951), pp. 368–403).

[25] Walras, L., *Éléments d'économie politique pure*, Corbaz (Lausanne), 1874–77 (1st ed.), 1926 (definitive ed.) (W. Jaffé tr., *Elements of pure economics*, Irwin, 1954).

CHAPTER 2

Equilibrium and efficiency of free trade

1. The theory of international trade is the old home of general equilibrium theory. The theory of reciprocal demand developed by J.S. Mill is one of the earliest examples of general equilibrium analysis. After Mill, most of the theories of international trade, including those of Edgeworth, Heckscher, Graham, Yntema and even of Marshall, are constructed essentially in terms of general equilibrium, to say nothing of more recent works of e.g., Mosak, Samuelson and Meade.[1])

In this chapter, three applications in international trade theory of the theorems considered in the preceding chapter will be discussed.

As is pointed out by Chipman, the model of international trade considered in chapter 18, book 3 of the *Principles* of Mill, the chapter called the 'great chapter' by Edgeworth, can be analyzed by the method of non-linear programming. Therefore, the optimality and existence of an equilibrium in this highly simplified case under stringent conditions can be easily proved as corollaries to our theorems.[2])

Mill's theory of reciprocal demand is further developed by Meade [11] in terms of the trade indifference map. This is a typical case of the bilateral exchange of two commodities, for which our theorem 1 will find a twin theorem of existence and optimality of an equilibrium. As a matter of fact, the plausibility of the competitive assumption is much greater in this case.

Finally, the most extensive application of our theorems can be found in the theory of international trade with the cost of transportation considered by Hadley and Kemp [5]. Since an identical commodity located at different places should be regarded as different commodities commanding different prices, the counterpart of assumption 3 which guarantees a positive weight of welfare or a positive income for each country is somewhat different from the original one.

[1]) See Mill [12], book 3, chapter 18, Edgeworth [3], Heckscher [6], Graham [4], Yntema [18], Marshall [9], Mosak [13], Samuelson [16] and Meade [10]. For further references, see Chipman [1] and Kemp [8].
[2]) Chipman [1], I, pp. 483–91, Mill [12], 1915, pp. 597–601.

2. It is one thing to prove, as is done in the preceding chapter, the existence of an equilibrium in a general model under rather weaker conditions, which had not been done until quite recently. However, it is quite another to show essentially the existence of an equilibrium in a particular simplified model by explicitly solving equations in the model either numerically or graphically.

What Mill did in his *Principles* (book 3, chapter 18) is certainly a classical example of such an attempt. In addition to the classical assumption of production that returns to scale are constant and essentially there exists only a single factor of production, Mill made the following assumption on demand. 'In both countries any given increase of cheapness produces an exactly proportional increase of consumption; or, in other words, that the value expended in the commodity, the cost incurred for the sake of obtaining it, is always the same, whether that cost affords a greater or smaller quantity of the commodity.' For example, let us suppose that in Germany 100 yards of cloth was exchanged for 200 yards of linen and that England wants to sell 1,000,000 yards of cloth to Germany. If German demand for cloth is 800,000 yards, this is equivalent to 1,600,000 yards of linen at German exchange ratio. Since German expended value in cloth is constant, England will receive 1,600,000 yards of linen in exchange of 1,000,000 yards of cloth, replacing German supply of cloth entirely. Under this assumption, Mill explicitly solved for the international exchange ratio of two commodities in terms of coefficients of production in two countries and by so doing showed the existence of an equilibrium.[3]

As is pointed out by Chipman, the case analyzed by Mill can be considered as a problem of non-linear programming and therefore the existence of an equilibrium can be proved, even without solving equations explicitly, by the existence theorem of a solution of non-linear programming. We shall show below that this is a simple degenerate case of the problem we discussed in the preceding chapter, where the choice of welfare weights α_i is irrelevant because of the stringent assumption on demand.

Let us construct a formal model of Mill's case. It is a two-country (Germany and England), two-commodity (cloth and linen), single factor model of an international economy.

Let $y_{11} \, (\geqq 0)$, $y_{21} \, (\geqq 0)$, $y_{12} \, (\geqq 0)$ and $y_{22} \, (\geqq 0)$ be respectively the amount of cloth produced in Germany and in England, and the amount of linen produced in Germany and in England. If we denote the total amount of cloth produced in Germany when she is completely specialized in it by

---

[3] See footnote 2 above.

a_{11} (>0) and the corresponding amount of linen by a_{12} (>0), the possible set of y_{11} and y_{12} has to satisfy

$$y_{11}/a_{11}+y_{12}/a_{12} \leqq 1 . \tag{1}$$

Similarly, for England, we have

$$y_{21}/a_{21}+y_{22}/a_{22} \leqq 1 , \tag{2}$$

where a_{21} (>0) and a_{22} (>0) are respectively the maximum amounts of cloth and linen produced. (1) and (2) signify, in other words, that the demand for the factor of production does not exceed the supply in each country, the total amount of the supply in each country, which is a given constant, being the unit of measurement. The equilibrium of production (y_{11}, y_{12}) and (y_{21}, y_{22}) maximize ($p/q)y_{11}+y_{12}$ and ($p/q)y_{21}+y_{22}$ subject to (1) and (2), respectively, where p and q are prices of cloth and linen.

Suppose that Germany has the comparative advantage in linen, i.e., $a_{11}/a_{12}<a_{21}/a_{22}$. Between total amounts of cloth and linen, i.e., $y_1 = y_{11}+y_{21}$ and $y_2 = y_{12}+y_{22}$, we obtain

$$y_1/a_{11}+y_2/a_{12} \leqq a_1/a_{11} \tag{3},$$

by multiplying a_{11} and a_{21} respectively to (1) and (2) and then summing them up and considering $a_{11}/a_{12} < a_{21}/a_{22}$, where $a_1 = a_{11}+a_{21}$. Similarly,

$$y_1/a_{21}+y_2/a_{22} \leqq a_2/a_{22} \tag{4}$$

is derived by multiplying a_{12} and a_{22} respectively to (1) and (2) and summing them up, where $a_2 = a_{12}+a_{22}$.[4]) We may note that both (3) and (4) can be satisfied with strict inequalities for some (y_1^*, y_2^*). Let us denote, for later use, as $U^* = y_1^* y_2^*$.

As for the demand, let x ($\geqq 0$), y ($\geqq 0$), p ($\geqq 0$), q ($\geqq 0$) and R (>0) respectively denote the demand for cloth, demand for linen, the price of cloth, price of linen and income (p, q and R all in terms of the factor of production) in an economy. By choosing appropriate units of commodities, we can without loss of generality derive demand functions satisfying Mill's assumption, i.e., $x = R/2p$ and $y = R/2q$ from the maximization of utility $U = xy$ subject to the budget constraint $px+qy = R$. There is a unit own-elasticity of demand with respect to price, zero cross-elasticities and unit income elasticity. The value expended in cloth is $R/2$ and that in linen is

---

[4]) Chipman [1], I, p. 485.

also $R/2$, being constant in terms of the factor. If Germany is producing linen as in Mill's example above, q is constant from the assumption of constant returns to scale and a single factor of production and the value expended in cloth is constant in terms of linen, since $px/q = R/2q$ and R is constant. For example, the value expended in 800,000 yards of cloth is equivalent to 1,600,000 yards of linen when 100 yards of the former exchanged for 200 yards of the latter ($p/q = 2$). Since this value is constant, England will receive 1,600,000 yards of linen when she wants to sell 1,000,000 yards of cloth ($p/q = 1.6$), replacing German supply of cloth entirely.

With linen as numeraire, $x = qR'/2p$, $y = R'/2$, where $R' = R/q$. Let us suppose that the taste of consumers is identical both in Germany and in England. If R' represents German income, x and y give German demands for cloth and linen. If R' represents English income, x and y are English demands. Finally, if R' is the joint income of two countries, x and y represent total demands of two countries for cloth and linen. Therefore, German demands for cloth and linen, respectively denoted by X_{11} ($\geqq 0$) and X_{12} ($\geqq 0$) are derived by the maximization of $U = X_{11} X_{12}$ subject to $(p/q) X_{11} + X_{12} = R'$, R' being German income, English demands for two commodities, X_{21} ($\geqq 0$) and X_{22} ($\geqq 0$), are obtained from the maximization of $U = X_{21} X_{22}$ subject to $(p/q) X_{21} + X_{22} = R'$, R' being English income, and total demands for two commodities, X_1 ($= X_{11} + X_{21}$) and X_2 ($= X_{12} + X_{22}$) respectively, can be derived from the maximization of $U = X_1 X_2$ subject to $(p/q) X_1 + X_2 = R'$, R' being joint income, independently from the distribution of income between two countries.

Finally, markets for cloth and linen must be cleared, i.e., demands for commodities cannot exceed supplies at an equilibrium of free international trade,

$$X_1 \leqq y_{11} + y_{21} \tag{5}$$

$$X_2 \leqq y_{12} + y_{22} . \tag{6}$$

Consider now the maximization of $U = X_1 X_2$ subject to (1), (2), (5) and (6). Since it is apparent that the maximum U is strictly larger than U^*, we can restrict the domain of X_1 and X_2 to the set $(X_1, X_2; X_1 X_2 \geqq U^*)$ without changing the problem. Nor does the logarithmic transformation of U change the problem and $\log U = \log X_1 + \log X_2$ is concave for X_1, X_2 such that $X_1 X_2 \geqq U^*$. Therefore, as in the preceding chapter (theorems 2 and 3), there exists $(X_1, X_2, y_{11}, y_{12}, y_{21}, y_{22})$ which maximizes U subject to (1), (2), (5) and (6) and we may consider it as a non-negative saddle point $(X_i, y_{ij}, p, q, r, s)_{i,j=1,2}$ of the Lagrangean,

$$\log X_1 + \log X_2 + p(y_{11} + y_{21} - X_1) + q(y_{12} + y_{22} - X_2)$$

$$+ r(1 - y_{11}/a_{11} - y_{12}/a_{12}) + s(1 - y_{21}/a_{21} - y_{22}/a_{22}). \tag{7}$$

It is easily seen that X_1, X_2, p, q, r and s are all positive, with the result that (1), (2), (5) and (6) are satisfied with equality at a saddle point.

By theorem 4 of the preceding chapter, we can see a saddle point of (7) is an equilibrium of a free international trade, with p/q, r/q and s/q respectively signifying the price of cloth, the price of the factor of production in Germany and that in England, all in terms of linen, since $(p/q)X_1 + X_2 = (r/q) + (s/q) = R'$ (joint income of two countries). With p, q, r and s given, equilibrium demands of each country are easily obtained from $X_{11} = (q/2p) \times (r/q)$, $X_{12} = (1/2)(r/q)$, $X_{21} = (q/2p)(s/q)$ and $X_{22} = (1/2)(s/q)$, since German R' is r/q and English R' is s/q.

3.   Without making Mill's stringent assumption on demand, a more general two-country two-commodity two-factor model of an international economy can be analyzed by the use of the trade indifference map invented by Meade. The situation is exactly identical to that of the bilateral exchange considered in the preceding chapter and an equilibrium can be proved to exist in a similar way as in the case of theorem 1.

Consider the geometric representation given in figure 2.1. Measure up the axis Oy the amount of commodity y consumed in the home country and along the axis Ox' (i.e., to the left of O) the amount of commodity x consumed in the home country. Then in the quadrant $x'Oy$ we can draw a map of consumption indifference curves of which I_c is a representative. Let the block $QPSR$ represent the production possibility curve of the home country, with the origin at Q. RQ is the maximum amount of commodity y produced and PQ is the maximum amount of commodity x produced. Now let the block $QPSR$ slide up the indifference curve I_c in such a way that the curve PSR remains tangential to I_c and the line PQ remains in a horizontal position. The corner of the block, Q, will trace out the curve I_t which is called the trade indifference curve of the home country corresponding to the consumption indifference curve I_c. When we measure up the axis Oy the amount of import of commodity y, down the axis Oy' (i.e., below O) the amount of the export of commodity y, along the axis Ox' the amount of import of commodity x and along the axis Ox the amount of export of commodity x, I_t represents indifferent combinations of export and import which can give the satisfaction corresponding to I_c to consumers in the home country. For example, coordinates of point Q represent the amount of export (excess of production over consumption) of commodity x and the amount of import (excess of consumption over production) of commodity y, since the coordinates of point S with the origin at O represent amounts of consumption of two commodities and those with the origin at Q represent amounts of production of two commodities.

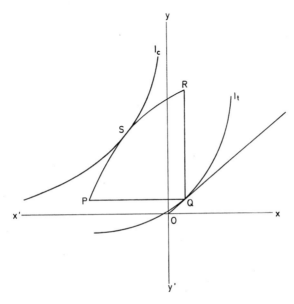

Fig. 2.1.

By construction, the slope of a trade indifference curve at any point (say, Q) is equal to the slope of the corresponding consumption indifference curve at the corresponding point (S).[5]

At an equilibrium under free international trade, the slope of a consumption indifference curve is equal to the price ratio of two commodities as a result of the competitive behavior of domestic consumers[6] and the slope of the production possibility curve is equal to the price ratio as a result of

[5] Meade [11], pp. 13–4.
[6] For the possibility of a social or community indifference map, see Chipman [1], II, pp. 689–698.

the competitive behavior of domestic producers. Therefore, the production possibility curve is tangential to a consumption indifference curve and the slope of the corresponding trade indifference curve at the corresponding point is equal to the price ratio. Furthermore, the balance of trade condition requires that the value of imports must be equal to the value of exports, and therefore the tangent to the trade indifference curve at this point must pass through the origin. In other words, if the price ratio is given, we can draw a price line whose slope is equal to the price ratio, and find a point of tangency to a trade indifference curve, whose coordinates give the amount of import and of export.

Since imports of one country are the exports of the other, we can draw trade indifference maps of two countries in the same figure. In figure 2, I_1, I_2, I_3 are trade indifference curves of the home country and J_1, J_2, J_3 are those of the foreign country. The origin O represents the autarky situation. The curve AD is the contract curve on which indifference curves of two countries are tangential to each other. If an equilibrium under free international trade does exist, it must be represented by a point on the curve AD such that the tangent to two indifference curves passes through the origin. As in the case of theorem 1 in the preceding chapter, we can show

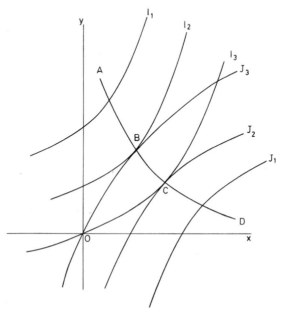

Fig. 2.2.

the existence of such a point between the points of intersection (*B* and *C*) of two indifference curves (I_3 and J_3) passing the origin and the curve *AD*. The existence of an equilibrium under free international trade is proved as a corollary to theorem 1; if trade indifference curves of the home country are strictly concave from above and those of the foreign country are strictly concave from below and the slopes of indifference curves are continuous then exists an equilibrium under free international trade.

4. Costs of transportation between countries had never been satisfactorily integrated with the competitive general equilibrium theory of international trade, until Kemp tried to do it, adopting an explicit programming approach to subdue the general analytical difficulties posed by elements of jointness, both in the supply of and in the demand for carriage.[7]) The cost of transportation is derived as one of the efficiency prices in a non-linear programming model, in which the objective function is a positive linear combination of national utilities.

However, the weights in the combination are simply given and the balance of payments condition, which corresponds to budget constraints in the case of interpersonal trade, is not successfully taken account of. Therefore, efficiency prices there derived are not necessarily competitive equilibrium prices. Following our suggestions, Hadley–Kemp [5] takes up this point by changing weights in the combination parametrically in accordance with the condition of the balance of payments. Hadley–Kemp [5] is in this sense an international version of Negishi [14] which we discussed in the preceding chapter. However, in the case of international trade with transportation costs, a physically identical commodity must be regarded as different commodities according to its location, since the prices are different by the addition of transportation costs. Therefore, it is impossible by definition to assume that every country is not satiated with respect to every commodity or that every country has a positive stock of every commodity. The analogy to the case of interpersonal trade in a closed economy considered in the preceding chapter is not perfect in regard to assumption 3 and the positivity of national income of each country should be checked carefully.[8])

---

[7]) Kemp [8], pp. 143–155. For an earlier use of nonlinear programming in the theory of international trade, see Uzawa [17].

[8]) Although the element of jointness in the provision of transport services is ignored, this point is ingeniously taken care of in Isard–Ostroff's [7] interregional study. See also Debreu [2].

Let us consider a two-country world, each country being assumed to produce a different commodity and offer a round trip transportation service.[9])

Let $W_1(c_{11}, c_{12})$ and $W_2(c_{21}, c_{22})$ be social utility functions of two countries, where c_{ij} signifies the amount of the commodity produced by the jth country and consumed by the ith country. W's are assumed to be concave and strictly increasing, i.e., increasing with respect to each variable. Technological constraint of production for the ith country is,

$$f_i(X_i) - C_i \geq 0 \qquad i = 1, 2, \tag{8}$$

where X_i is the amount of the commodity produced and C_i is the amount of round trip transportation service offered. It is assumed that $f_i' > 0$ and $f_i'' < 0$. It is further assumed that both C_i and X_i can be positive. Finally, let p_i, w_j and q_i be respectively the price of the commodity produced by and located at the ith country, one way transportation cost from the jth country to the other and the price of the round trip transportation service offered by the ith country ($i = 1, 2$). The unit of commodities is chosen according to the unit transportation service.

Producers and consumers behave as follows. Producers in the ith country maximize the revenue, $q_i C_i + p_i X_i$, being subject to (8). This revenue of producers then is distributed to consumers in the same country in the form of wage, rent, dividend, etc., and the national income of the ith country is,

$$Y_i = q_i C_i + p_i X_i, \qquad i = 1, 2. \tag{9}$$

Consumers in the ith country maximize W_i being subject to

$$Y_i = p_i c_{ii} + (p_j + w_j) c_{ij} \qquad i \neq j, i, j = 1, 2. \tag{10}$$

It is clear that an equilibrium demand and supply of commodities and of transportation service must satisfy

$$X_i - c_{ii} - c_{ji} \geq 0, \qquad p_j(X_i - c_{ii} - c_{ji}) = 0, \qquad i \neq j, i, j = 1, 2, \tag{11}$$

$$C_i + C_j - c_{ij} \geq 0, \qquad w_j(C_i + C_j - c_{ij}) = 0, \qquad i \neq j, i, j = 1, 2. \tag{12}$$

If we construct a positive linear combination of W's, i.e.,

$$\alpha_1 W_1(c_{11}, c_{12}) + \alpha_2 W_2(c_{21}, c_{22}) \tag{13}$$

---

[9]) See Negishi [15]. It suffices to discuss the simple model of Kemp [8], pp. 143–155 and the arguments below can easily be extended for the model of Hadley–Kemp [5].

and maximize it being subject to (8) and the first conditions of (11) and (12), and interpret Lagrangean multipliers corresponding to (8) and the first half of (11) and of (12) as q_i, p_i and w_j, then from theorems 3 and 4 in the preceding chapter the solution is a competitive equilibrium under free international trade, provided that it satisfies (9) and (10) with positive Y_i's. This is possible if weights α_i's are properly chosen. The existence of such proper weights in the case of interpersonal trade in a closed economy is proved as theorem 5 in the preceding chapter, where we note that the role of assumption 3 is important, which guarantees that incomes of all individual consumers are positive even if some α_i's are zero.

Since the exact counterpart of assumption 3 is impossible in the case of international trade with transportation costs included, we are interested in the problem of how the positivity of national income of each country is assured in our present model. From the assumption of non-satiation, prices of two commodities are positive at least in one country at a maximum of (13). Furthermore, this is true even if one of α_i is zero. Suppose prices are positive in the second country, i.e., $p_1 + w_1 > 0, p_2 > 0$. Then the revenue of producers in this country is positive, i.e., $p_2 X_2 + q_2 C_2 > 0$ and therefore the national income Y_2 is positive. Now since $p_1 + w_1 > 0$, either $p_1 > 0$, $w_1 \geqq 0$ or $p_1 \geqq 0, w_1 > 0$. If $p_1 > 0$, the revenue of producers in country 1, $p_1 X_1 + q_1 C_1$ is positive. If, on the other hand, $w_1 > 0$, again $p_1 X_1 + q_1 C_1$ is positive, since we have $q_1 = q_2 \geqq w_1 + w_2 > 0$, from conditions for a maximum in terms of Lagrangean multipliers. Therefore, in any case, Y_1, the national income of the first country is positive.

To sum up, we can prove the existence and efficiency of a competitive equilibrium under free international trade with transportation cost by applying theorems in the preceding chapter, if each country can produce a positive amount of transportation service and if the social utility of each country is not satiated with respect to every commodity it can consume.

References

[1] Chipman, J. S., 'A survey of the theory of international trade, I, II, III,' *Econometrica*, 33 (1965), pp. 477–519, 33 (1965), pp. 685–760, 34 (1966), pp. 18–76.
[2] Debreu, G., 'New concepts and techniques for equilibrium analysis,' *International Economic Review*, 3 (1962), pp. 257–273.
[3] Edgeworth, F. Y., *Papers relating to political economy*, II, Macmillan, 1925.
[4] Graham, F. D., *The theory of international values*, Princeton University Press, 1948.
[5] Hadley, G. and M. C. Kemp, 'Equilibrium and efficiency in international trade,' *Metroeconomica*, 18 (1966), pp. 125–141.

[6] Heckscher, E., 'The effect of foreign trade on the distribution of income,' *Economisk Tidskrift*, 21 (1919), pp. 497–512 (in Swedish), reprinted in translation by S. and N. Laursen, in S. Ellis and L.A. Metzler (ed.), *Readings in the theory of international trade*, Blakiston, 1949, pp. 272–300.

[7] Isard, W. and D.J. Ostroff, 'Existence of competitive interregional equilibrium,' *Papers and Proceedings of the Regional Science Association*, 4 (1958), pp. 49–76.

[8] Kemp, M.C., *The pure theory of international Trade*, Prentice Hall, 1964.

[9] Marshall, A., *The pure theory of foreign trade*, London School of Economics, 1930.

[10] Meade, J.E., *The theory of international economic policy*, I, II, Oxford University Press, 1951, 1955.

[11] Meade, J.E., *A geometry of international trade*, George Allen and Unwin, 1952.

[12] Mill, J.S., *Principles of political economy*, 1st ed., Parker, 1849, Longmans–Green, 1915.

[13] Mosak, J., *General equilibrium theory in international trade*, Principia Press, 1944.

[14] Negishi, T., 'Welfare economics and general existence of an equilibrium for a competitive economy,' *Metroeconomica*, 12 (1960), pp. 92–97.

[15] Negishi, T., 'Equilibrium and efficiency in international trade with costs of transportation,' *Economic Studies Quarterly*, 16–1 (1965, Nov.), pp. 74–77.

[16] Samuelson, P.A., *The collected scientific papers of P.A. Samuelson*, II, M.I.T. Press, 1966.

[17] Uzawa, H., 'Prices of the factors of production in international trade,' *Econometrica*, 27 (1959), 448–68.

[18] Yntema, T.O., *A mathematical reformulation of the general theory of international trade*, University of Chicago Press, 1932.

PART 2

Increasing returns and externality

CHAPTER 3

The role of profit in the total conditions for optimality

1. Under the assumption of non-diminishing cost, the existence and the Pareto optimality of perfect competition is demonstrated in chapter 1. The implication of optimality here is two-fold. First, the marginal conditions for optimality are satisfied and the level of outputs and inputs are optimal when the number of firms is fixed. Secondly, the number of firms itself is optimal, i.e., a total condition for optimality[1]) is also achieved. Since the set of firms is regarded as fixed, we suppose that all conceivable firms are included in the model. Then, some firms might find it most preferable to produce (and to consume) nothing. Hence, what is ordinarily called entry here appears as a change from zero to positive output levels. The necessary and sufficient condition for the entry of a firm from a welfare viewpoint is simply its non-negative profit when prices are equalized to marginal costs. More generally, no pecuniary spillovers or secondary benefits should be taken into account in the cost–benefit analysis of investment projects.[2])

In the case of a U-shaped cost curve due to the existence of some fixed, overhead inputs, things are not so simple since no output does not imply no input and therefore non-existence of a firm. Marginal cost pricing should still be applied as the marginal condition for optimality. What is then the condition for entry, a total condition for optimality? With significantly large fixed, overhead cost, perfect competition or the application of the marginal cost pricing rule may imply running at a loss for some firms. There may be, however, a situation in which it pays to introduce some such firms and cover their losses by subsidies. But of course not all firms running at a loss should be subsidized. Since the profit of a firm is no longer the perfect

---

[1]) For marginal and total conditions for optimality, see Hicks [7].
[2]) McKean [16], pp. 134–167. Since the entry of a firm is a special case of investment projects, the condition for entry to be discussed below can also be applied in the cost–benefit analysis of investment projects.

indicator of the desirability of its existence, some rules for entry might be proposed by taking into consideration the pecuniary external economies and diseconomies, i.e., the changes of profit of other firms caused by entry.[3])

In classical welfare economics, this problem is discussed in terms of consumers' surplus.[4]) It is, therefore, subject to the ceteris paribus assumption of partial equilibrium analysis[5]) and the non-operationality of the consumers' surplus concept. The main purpose of this chapter is, on the contrary, to give some sufficient conditions for the entry of firms with fixed costs, in terms of general equilibrium analysis of a closed economy. Conditions are operational in the sense that only price and input–output data before and after entry are needed to see when conditions are satisfied.

Without subsidies, a firm running at a loss cannot remain in the economy. Therefore, it is possible that the number of firms in perfect competition is less than optimal under laissez-faire. On the other hand, discussions of monopolistically competitive economy by Kahn [12] and Meade [19] in terms of marginal productivity of an entrepreneur suggest the possibility of the redundancy of firms even in a Pareto optimum. As McKenzie [17] points out, this is due to the special properties of their model, in which proportionality, not necessarily equality, of price and marginal cost is the marginal condition for optimality. However, the marginal productivity of an entrepreneur analysis exaggerates the possibility of redundancy, since indivisibility of the entry of firms is assumed away in the marginal analysis. In the final part of this chapter, the redundancy proposition is reformulated in terms of our indivisible entry.[6])

2.   In this section, let us construct a model of a competitive economy. Let there be m commodities. Vectors are defined in m dimensional Euclidean space.

---

[3]) For the pecuniary and technological external effects, see Scitovsky [26]. Technological external effect, which is not discussed here, is analyzed in chapter 4.
[4]) See Dupuit [5], Hicks [8], Hotelling [11], Kahn [12], Meade [19]. Related to these are Marshall–Pigou proposals of tax upon industries with diminishing returns and bounty for those with increasing returns. See, Marshall [15], pp. 467–9, Pigou [22], pp. 803–8 and Ellis–Fellner [6]. Below we shall support the proposal for bounty on increasing return industries, but not that for tax on diminishing return industries. See also Knight [13] and Samuelson [24], pp. 207–8.
[5]) The attempt in Hotelling [11] of the extension to the multi-commodity case is not successful.
[6]) This chapter is based on a revised version of Negishi [20].

Let there be n consumers denoted by $i = 1, ..., n$. The consumption vector and utility function of the ith consumer are respectively denoted by $X_i \geq 0$ and $U_i(X_i)$.

Assumption 1. $U_i(X_i)$ is strictly quasi-concave and strictly increasing, i.e., the set of X_i' such that $U_i(X_i') \geq U_i(X_i)$ is strictly convex for any X_i and there exists X_i' such that $U_i(X_i') > U_i(X_i)$ for any X_i, $i = 1, ..., n$.

Total consumption vector is defined as $X = \Sigma_i X_i$.

Let there be r firms denoted by $k = 1, ..., r$. The production (input–output) vector of a firm consists of a variable production vector and a fixed, overhead input vector. The variable production vector and its possible domain of the kth firm are denoted by y_k and Y_k. Positive (negative) element of production vector $y_{kj} > 0$ (< 0) denotes output (input) of the jth commodity.

Assumption 2. (1) $0 \in Y_k$, (2) Y_k is strictly convex and compact, (3) there is no y_k such that $y_k \geq 0$, $y_k \in Y_k$.[7])

In addition to the variable inputs denoted by the negative y_{kj}'s, which correspond to the variable cost of production to produce outputs denoted by the positive y_{kj}'s, fixed, overhead inputs $-a_k = -(a_{kl}, ..., a_{km}) \leq 0$, which correspond to the fixed, overhead cost of production, are required irrespective of the levels of outputs. Therefore, the combined production vector of the kth firm is $y_k - a_k$. The existence of the fixed inputs $-a_k$ upsets the law of diminishing returns to scale, since it is impossible to make $y_k - a_k = 0$, i.e., $0 \notin Y_k - a_k$. The total variable production vector, its possible domain and the total fixed input vector are defined respectively as $y = \Sigma_k y_k$, $Y = \Sigma_k Y_k$, $a = \Sigma_k a_k$, $k = 1, ..., r$.

The initial distribution to consumers of, and the total amount of resources are denoted by $Z_i > 0$ and $Z = \Sigma_i Z_i$. The ratio of the profit of the kth firm distributed to the ith consumer is denoted as $\lambda_{ki} > 0$, $\Sigma_i \lambda_{ki} = 1$. Finally, price vector is denoted by $P > 0$.

Definition 1. A competitive equilibrium is defined as a set of vectors $(X_i^0, y_k^0, P^0)_{i=1,...,n, k=1,...,r}$ which satisfies the following conditions.
(1) Utility maximization subject to budget constraint, $U_i(X_i^0) = \max U_i(X_i)$, s.t., $P^0 X_i = P^0 Z_i + \Sigma_k \lambda_{ki} P^0 (y_k^0 - a_k)$, for $i = 1, ..., n$.

---

[7]) See assumption 2 in chapter 1.

(2) Profit maximization, $P^0 y_k^0 = \max P^0 y_k$, s.t., $y_k \in Y_k$, for $k = 1, ..., r$.
(3) Equality of demand and supply, $X^0 - y^0 - a = Z$, where $X^0 = \Sigma_i X_i^0$, $y^0 = \Sigma_k y_k^0$.

The existence of an equilibrium can be discussed in the same way as in chapter 1. The difference, however, is that there is no assurance of non-negative profit $P^0(y_k^0 - a_k) \geq 0$ and therefore we have to assume fairly large initial resources (i.e., $Z_i > \Sigma_k \lambda_{ki} a_k$, unless some redistribution of income is considered) so that the income of individual consumers can be positive.

Let us now define sets of vectors which are preferred or indifferent to equilibrium vectors as $\overline{U}_i^0 = (X_i : U_i(X_i) \geq U_i(X_i^0))$, $\overline{U}^0 = \Sigma_i \overline{U}_i^0$, and $3^0 = \overline{U}^0 - Y$. The set $\overline{U}_i^0$ is the set of consumption vectors of the ith consumer which is preferred or indifferent to X_i^0. The set $\overline{U}^0$ is the set of total consumption vectors which can be decomposed into X_i such that $X_i \in \overline{U}_i^0$. Finally, the set 3^0 is the set of commodity vectors which can be transformed by production into a vector X such that $X \in \overline{U}^0$.

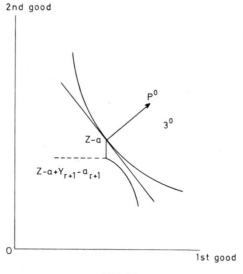

Fig. 3.1.

A minimal element $A^{\min}$ of a set A is an element of A such that there is no other element of A which is smaller than it. Then, under assumptions 1 and 2, the following results on the optimality of a competitive equilibrium are obtained.

Lemma 1. (1) $Z - a \in 3^{0\min}(X^0 \in \bar{U}^{0\min})$.

(2) $P^0 Z' \geqq P^0(Z-a)$ for any $Z' \in 3^0$.

$(P^0 X' \geqq P^0 X^0$ for any $X' \in \bar{U}^0)$.

(3) $P^0 Z' > P^0(Z-a)$ if $Z' \in 3, {}^0 Z' \neq Z - a$

$(P^0 X' > P^0 X^0$ if $X' \in \bar{U}^0, X' \neq X^0)$.

In words, among sets of resources which can also produce the welfare attained at an equilibrium, Z has the minimum value evaluated by equilibrium prices P^0.[8])

3. Suppose there is a new firm with variable production vector y_{r+1} and its possible set Y_{r+1} which satisfies conditions (1), (2) and (3) in assumption 2. It is also supposed that for the entry of this firm to the economy a fixed input $-a_{r+1} = -(a_{r+1,1}, \ldots, a_{r+1,m}) \leqq 0$ is needed. Therefore, the combined production vector is denoted by $y_{r+1} - a_{r+1}$. After the entry of this firm the resources which are still left available to the economy other than the new firm are $Z - a + y_{r+1} - a_{r+1}$. If this vector does not belong to the set 3^0 the entry should not be encouraged. What is, then, the implication of the profit of the new firm in this respect?

Theorem 1. If it is known that positive profit is impossible for the new firm under prices ruling before entry, entry should not be made.

Proof. If max $P^0(y_{r+1} - a_{r+1}) \leqq 0$, $y_{r+1} \in Y_{r+1}$, then $P^0(Z - a + y_{r+1} - a_{r+1}) \leqq P^0(Z-a)$ for any $y_{r+1} \in Y_{r+1}$. From lemma 1, then, $Z - a + y_{r+1} - a_{r+1} \notin 3^0$. For the case of $m = 2$, figure 1 explains theorem 1, indicating the fact that for the new firm consuming the second good and producing the first good there is no positive profit under P^0 and no intersection of the set 3^0 and the set $Z - a + Y_{r+1} - a_{r+1}$ (i.e., the set of $Z - a + y_{r+1} - a_{r+1}$).

A corollary to theorem 1 is that if there is some firm k ($k = 1, \ldots, r$) such that $P^0(y_k^0 - a_k) \leqq 0$ and $Y_k = Y_{r+1}$, $a_k = a_{r+1}$, then the new $r+1$th firm should not enter. In other words, duplicate facilities should not be constructed unless the existing one is making positive profit.[9]) Another corollary

---

[8]) For the proof of lemma 1, as well as lemma 2 and 3 below, see Debreu [4]. For the case of $m = 2$, figures 3.1–3.5 are self-explanatory.

[9]) However, we may note the so-called common-sense position in cost–benefit analysis that the building of duplicate facilities is uneconomical (McKean [16], pp. 145–6) is not always true. If the existing one is making a profit, it may be economical.

is that if what can be done by the entering firm can also be done by the changes of activities of the existing firms, i.e., if $y^0 + Y_{r+1} - a_{r+1} \subset Y$, then the entry should not be made, since $\max P^0(y^0 + y_{r+1} - a_{r+1}) < P^0 y^0$, i.e., $\max P^0(y_{r+1} - a_{r+1}) < 0$, from the fact that $P^0 y^0 = \max P^0 y$, $y \in Y$.

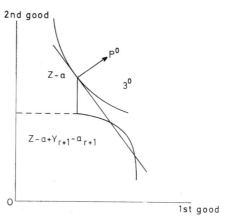

Fig. 3.2.

As is seen from figure 3.2, which indicates that the newly entering firm can make positive profit under P^0 but there is still no intersection of 3^0 and $Z - a + Y_{r+1} - a_{r+1}$, the converse of theorem 1 that the new firm with positive profit under prices ruling before entry should enter into the economy is not necessarily true.

After entry, a new competitive equilibrium $(X_i^1, y_i^1, P^1)_{i=1,\ldots,n, k=1,\ldots,r+1}$ is established. Conditions for this new equilibrium are similar to those given in definition 1. Sets of vectors which are preferred or indifferent to equilibrium vectors are defined as $\bar{U}_i^1 = (X_i : U_i(X_i) \geq U_i(X_i^1))$, $\bar{U}^1 = \Sigma_i \bar{U}_i^1$, and $3^1 = \bar{U}^1 - Y$, where $Y = \Sigma_{k=1}^{k=r} Y_k$. Then, as in the case of lemma 1, the following is established.

Lemma 2.   (1) $Z - a + y_{r+1}^1 - a_{r+1} \in 3^{1 \min}(X^1 = \Sigma_i X_i^1 \in \bar{U}^{1 \min})$.

(2) $P^1 Z' \geq P^1(Z - a + y_{r+1}^1 - a_{r+1})$ for any $Z' \in 3^1$.

   $(P^1 X' \geq P^1 X^1$ for any $X' \in \bar{U}^1)$.

(3) $P^1 Z' > P^1(Z - a + y_{r+1}^1 - a_{r+1})$ for any $Z' \in 3^1$ if $Z' \neq Z - a$
   $+ y_{r+1}^1 - a_{r+1}$.

   $(P^1 X' > P^1 X^1$ for any $X' \in \bar{U}^1$ if $X' \neq X^1)$.

If $Z-a$, the resource which is available to the economy other than the $r+1$th firm does not belong to the set 3^1, then the $r+1$th firm should not be withdrawn.

Theorem 2. If the new firm is running without a loss after entry, the firm should have entered after all.

Proof. If $P^1 y^1_{r+1} - P^1 a_{r+1} \geq 0$, then $P^1(Z-a) \leqq P^1(Z-a+y^1_{r+1}-a_{r+1})$ and $Z-a \notin 3^1$.

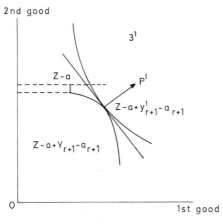

Fig. 3.3

For the case of $m = 2$, figure 3.3 explains theorem 3, indicating that the $r+1$th firm which consumes the first good and produces the second has a positive profit and $Z-a \notin 3^1$.

As is seen in figure 3.4, which shows the case of negative profit for the $r+1$th firm and $Z-a \notin 3^1$, however, the converse of theorem 2 that the firm with a loss after entry should not have entered and should be shut down, does not hold generally.

Similar results are conjectured in terms of partial equilibrium analysis in classical welfare economics, since positive profit, i.e., positive producers' surplus implies, with positive consumers' surplus, a positive total surplus, i.e., an increase of welfare, while sufficiently large consumers' surplus still implies a positive total surplus even if profit is negative.[10]

---

[10]) Hicks [8], Hotelling [11], Kahn [12] and Meade [19], part 2.

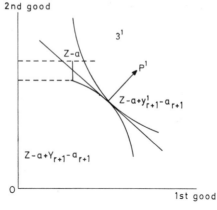

Fig. 3.4

If prices are not changed by the entry of the firm $(P^0 = P^1)$, theorem 1 and theorem 2 give a complete rule for the entry in terms of the profit of the entering firm. However, the indivisibility of the entry with fixed inputs changes prices before and after the entry, i.e., $P^0 \neq P^1$.[11]) Therefore, there may be a situation such that profit before the entry and loss after the entry and simple profit rules of the above theorems cannot tell whether to introduce the firm into the economy. In the long run, a firm remains in the economy if and only if profit after the entry is non-negative. Under laissez faire, therefore, the number of firms in perfect competition can be less (can not be more) than optimal, in view of the fact that the converse of theorem 2 does not hold.

4.   In cost–benefit analysis of the partial equilibrium type, it is sometimes suggested that profit should be calculated from average prices before and after entry, i.e., the average of profits before and after entry.[12]) Since profit before entry (theorem 1) is a necessary and profit after entry (theorem 2) is a sufficient condition for entry, however, there is no reason why such a rule of average can be used, even as an approximation, from a general equilibrium point of view. The original intention in considering such an

[11]) See Lerner [14], p. 189. This does not necessarily contradict the assumption of perfect competition. In perfect competition, individual consumers and firms behave *assuming* that market prices are constant. But market prices themselves are affected by the joint action of individual participants. If the number of individuals is finite, therefore, market prices are affected, however slightly it may be, by the action of a single individual.

[12]) McKean [16], pp. 168–70, Prest–Turvey [23], p. 163.

average, on the other hand, lies in measuring the changes in the surplus of consumers and other firms caused by the entry, i.e., the pecuniary spillovers and secondary benefits. What we need now is to consider the pecuniary external effects of entry from a general equilibrium point of view. Pecuniary external effects, being changes of profits of other firms, can be net changes of social welfare and by no means exhausted by mere transfer of rent, though it is often so regarded in cost–benefit analysis.[13]) Though it is not a change in physical efficiency of the economy as in the case of technological external effects, it is a change in the value or welfare productivity of the economy, i.e., a change in the surplus imputed to other firms. When some of the consumers of a product of a firm are other firms, the so-called consumers' surplus certainly does include such pecuniary external effects.[14])

Consider two sets $\overline{U}^0$ and $\overline{U}^1$ defined in the above, i.e., sets of commodity vectors which can be distributed to consumers so that they are not worse off than at equilibria $(X_i^0, y_k^0, P^0)_{i=1,...,n, k=1,...,r}$ and $(X_i^1, y_k^1, P^1)_{i=1,...,n, k=1,...,r+1}$, respectively. X^0 is on the boundary of $\overline{U}^0$ and X^1 is on the boundary of $\overline{U}^1$. However, it must be noted that generally $X^0 \notin \overline{U}^1$ does not mean $X^1 \in \overline{U}^0$ (i.e., $\overline{U}^0 \supset \overline{U}^1$) and vice versa. The reason is the different distribution of income at two equilibria among consumers with different taste. In other words, $\overline{U}^{0\min}$ and $\overline{U}^{1\min}$ (the boundary of $\overline{U}^0$ and that of $\overline{U}^1$) are two different Scitovsky community indifference curves which may intersect with each other.[15]) In this section, to strengthen results we exclude this possibility by the following assumption.

Assumption 3. All the consumers have the same utility function which is positive homogeneous, i.e., $U_i(X_i) = U(X_i)$, for $i = 1, ..., n$, and $U(\lambda X_i) = \lambda^k U(X_i)$, where k is some positive constant, for any $\lambda > 0$.

The homogeneity of utility function implies that the income consumption (Engel) curves are straight lines through the origin. Assumption 3 is a

---

[13]) Prest–Turvey state that it is double counting if they are included (Prest–Turvey [23], p. 160) and Margolis insists that gains to one group are offset by the losses of another (Margolis [18]). It seems that McKean ([16], pp. 134–167) really insists that only the marginal conditions (i.e., the marginal changes of surplus) are necessary to find a maximum surplus in the case of divisibility and non-increasing returns. Otherwise, total conditions (i.e., the total changes of surplus) must be directly considered. This point is not properly understood by Prest–Turvey [23] and Margolis [18].

[14]) See Hotelling [10].

[15]) Scitovsky [25].

sufficient condition for the existence of a consistent system of community indifference curves.[16])

Theorem 3. Under assumption 3, if the loss of the new firm after entry is within a certain limit, i.e., $P^1(a_{r+1} - y_{r+1}^1) \leq P^1(y^1 - y^0)$, it is possible to make every consumer better off than before the entry by some proper redistribution of income among consumers.

Proof. If $P^1(a_{r+1} - y_{r+1}^1) \leq P^1(y^1 - y^0)$, we have $P^1(Z - a + y^0) \leq P^1(Z - a + y^1 + y_{r+1}^1 - a_{r+1})$, which implies by the equality of demand and supply at two equilibria $P^1 X^1 \geq P^1 X^0$. Then, by lemma 2, we have $X^0 \notin \bar{U}^1$. Under assumption 3, this implies $X^1 \in \bar{U}^0$ and $X^1 \notin \bar{U}^{0\min}$, X^1 is an inner point of $\bar{U}^0$. Then, some proper changes in distribution of income make an equilibrium $(X_i, y_k^1, P^1)_{i=1, \ldots, n, k=1, \ldots, r+1}$, with $U(X_i) > U(X_i^0)$ for all i, possible since under assumption 3 consumers' total demand for commodities X remain undisturbed by the changes of income distribution. It may be noted that $X^0 \notin \bar{U}^1$ does not necessarily imply $Z - a \notin 3^1$ in the absence of assumption 3 and that $P^1(y^1 - y^0) > 0$, provided that $P^0 \neq P^1$.

The idea of theorem 3 is essentially that of the weak axiom of revealed preference and can be interpreted in terms of index number theorems.[17]) The implication of the theorem is that entry should be made if the loss is covered by the increase of profit of other firms when prices after entry are deflated by a Laspeyres price index with weights y^0 (i.e., $P^0 y^0 / P^1 y^0$) so that we have $P^0 y^0 = P^1 y^0$, since $P^1(y^1 - y^0) = P^1 y^1 - P^0 y^0 + (P^0 y^0 - P^1 y^0)$.

This is a sufficient condition for the case in which the entry of a new firm should be subsidized so as to cover its loss under marginal cost pricing. If there is a conglomerate merger of the firm to be subsidized and other firms, the loss of the former is easily compensated by the increased profit of the latter, in so far as the increase of profit is larger than the loss.[18]) Clearly any entry subsidized by conglomerate power is desirable from the point of view of social welfare, but not vice versa. On the other hand, if public subsidies are needed, there is a problem of how to finance them. If they are to be financed by taxation, it must be done without upsetting marginal conditions of optimality.

---

[16]) Chipman [3], pp. 690–8. Or alternatively we may assume the social welfare function with Bergsonian indifference curves convex to the origin. See Negishi [21].
[17]) Hicks [9], Bergson [1], p. 428.

In view of theorems 1, 2 and 3, the role of prices which prevail after entry is important. Although perfect information concerning such prices cannot be obtained before the entry, at least a part of it can be conjectured from prices formed by speculators in anticipation of the entry. Therefore, for example, it seems objectionable from the point of view of allocative efficiency, though understandable from the distribution point of view, to prevent the realization of speculative profit by forcing landowners to sell necessary land for public investment projects with prices which prevailed, say, two years before.

5. In sections 3 and 4, it is assumed that all the contracts made before the entry of a new firm – $(X_i^0, y_k^0, P^0)_{i=1,\ldots,n, k=1,\ldots,r}$ – are cancelled and overall recontracts – $(X_i^1, y_k^1, P^1)_{i=1,\ldots,n, k=1,\ldots,r+1}$ – are made after the entry. This corresponds to the assumption of tâtonnement in the analysis of the stability of a competitive economy. In this section, on the contrary, it is assumed that all contracts made before the entry are still effective and some new contracts – $(X_i^*, y_k^*, P^*)_{i=1,\ldots,n, k=1,\ldots,r+1}$ – are added, partly offsetting the former contracts, when a new firm enters into the economy. This corresponds to the assumption of non-tâtonnement or barter process in the theory of stability.[19]

With previous contracts effective, the domain of possible y_k for new contracts is now $Y_k - y_k^0$ for $k = 1, \ldots, r$, and, instead of resources Z_i, a stock of commodities X_i^0 or a right of claim to them are available to the ith consumer. An equilibrium $(X_i^*, y_k^*, P^*)_{i=1,\ldots,n, k=1,\ldots,r+1}$ for newly added contracts is defined as follows.

Definition 2. (1) $U_i(X_i^*) = \max U_i(X_i)$, s.t., $P^* X_i^* = P^* X_i^0$

$$+ \sum_{k=1}^{k=r} \lambda_{ik} P^* y_k^* + \lambda_{i,r+1} P^* (y_{r+1}^* - a_{r+1}).$$

(2) $P^* y_k^* = \max P^* y_k$, $y_k \in Y_k - y_k^0$, for $k = 1, \ldots, r$.

(3) $P^* y_{r+1}^* = \max P^* y_{r+1}$, $y_{r+1} \in Y_{r+1}$.

(4) $X^* - y^* + a_{r+1} = X^0$, where $X^* = \sum_i X_i^*$, $y^* = \sum_k y_k^*$.

We must note here that prices in the old and new contracts are generally different $P^0 \neq P^*$, and that fixed inputs are not required for newly added contracts except for the new $r+1$th firm which enters only in the new contract.

Theorem 4. Under assumption 3, if the loss of a new firm can be covered by the profit of other firms obtained from new contracts, every consumer can be better off than before the entry.

Proof. If $P^*(a_{r+1} - y^*_{r+1}) \leq P^* y^*_k$, then from 4 of definition 2 we have $P^* X^* \geq P^* X^0$. The rest of the proof is similar as in the case of theorem 3.

As a matter of fact, since equilibrium prices are unchanged by redistribution of income under assumption 3, it is easily seen that $P^* = P^1$ and the allocation of resources is identical in theorems 3 and 4.

6. So far we have explored the conditions for entry under the assumption that perfect competition (or the marginal cost pricing rule) is prevailing everywhere in the economy, i.e., the whole economy is efficiently organized as far as marginal conditions are satisfied. In this section we drop this assumption and assume that the new $r+1$th firm can enjoy monopolistic profit while other firms and all consumers are still perfectly competitive, i.e., the economy consisting of units other than the new firm is efficiently organized. It does not make any sense to go further and drop this latter assumption, since the condition for entry should be an increase in welfare in comparison with the efficiently organized state.

In partial equilibrium analysis where perfect knowledge of the demand and marginal cost functions are assumed, the increase of welfare by the entry of a firm can be expressed by the difference between the values of the area surrounded by the price axis and the demand and marginal cost curves, and of the overhead cost. It is certainly positive when the monopolistic profit of the firm is positive. In general equilibrium analysis, however, the difficulty is two-fold. Because of the possibility of shifts of demand and cost curves, firstly such a simple measure of welfare change is inapplicable, and, secondly, perfect knowledge of the demand function of the firm cannot be expected.[20]

Our problem is to consider whether the monopolistic profit of a firm can justify entry even if it is based on imperfect knowledge of the demand function. Let $((X^m_i, y^m_k, P^m)_{i=1,...,n, k=1,...,r+1}$ be an equilibrium for an

[20] See chapter 7 below.

economy where only the $r+1$th firm is monopolistic. Let us define $\bar{U}_i^m = (X_i : U_i(X_i) \geq U_i(X_i^m))$, $\bar{U}^m = \Sigma_i \bar{U}_i^m$, $3^m = \bar{U}^m - Y$, where $Y = \Sigma_{k=1}^{k=r} Y_k$. Then as before we have the following since resources $Z + y_{r+1}^m - a_{r+1}$ are efficiently allocated among consumers and r firms other than the $r+1$th firm.

Lemma 3.   (1) $Z - a + y_{r+1}^m - a_{r+1} \in 3^{m\,\min}(X^m \in \bar{U}^{m\,\min}$, where $X^m = \Sigma_i X_i^m)$.

          (2) $P^m Z' \geq P^m(Z - a + y_{r+1}^m - a_{r+1})$ for any $Z' \in 3^m$.

          $(P^m X' \geq P^m X^m$ for any $X' \in \bar{U}^m)$.

          (3) $P^m Z' > P^m(Z - a + y_{r+1}^m - a_{r+1})$ for any $Z' \in 3^m$ such that

          $Z' \neq Z - a + y_{r+1}^m - a_{r+1}$.

          $(P^m X' > P^m X^m$ for any $X' \in \bar{U}^m$ such that $X' \neq X^m)$.

Theorem 5.   If the monopolistic profit is non-negative, the new firm should remain in the economy.

Proof.   If $P^m(y_{r+1}^m - a_{r+1}) \geq 0$, then $P^m(Z - a + y_{r+1}^m - a_{r+1}) \geq P^m(Z - a)$, and $Z - a \notin 3^m$. It must be noted that $P^m y_{r+1}^m \geq P^m y_{r+1}$ for any $y_{r+1} \in Y_{r+1}$ does not hold and that the theorem holds for any conceivable pricing behavior of the monopolist. Figure 3.5 shows a plausible way for the monopolist to behave in the case of $m = 2$. Finally, it goes without saying that marginal cost pricing should be applied to the new firm after the entry is admitted by theorem 5.

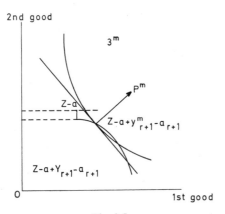

2nd good

3^m

P^m

$Z-a$

$Z-a+y^m_{r+1}-a_{r+1}$

$Z-a+Y_{r+1}-a_{r+1}$

O

1st good

Fig. 3.5.

7. We have shown that the possibility of the number of firms' being less than optimal under perfect competition. Under monopolistic competition, on the other hand, there is a possibility of the redundancy of firms. Our final task in this chapter is to examine the so-called Kahn–Meade proposition on the redundancy of firms.[21]

The following assumption is implicitly made in the Kahn–Meade model of the economy.

Assumption 4. Commodities are divided into two categories, i.e., factors of production which are not desired by consumers and the desirables (consumers' goods). Firms are integrated in the sense that the desirables are produced directly from inputs of factors and there is no transaction of commodities among firms.

Let us denote the ith consumer's initial holding vector of the desirables and factors respectively by $\bar{X}_i$ and $\bar{\bar{X}}_i$ so that $Z_i = (\bar{X}_i, \bar{\bar{X}}_i)$, the kth firm's output vector of the desirables and combined input vector of factors be respectively v_k and u_k so that $y_k - a_k = (v_k, u_k)$, $k = 1, \dots, r+1$, and price vectors of the desirables and factors respectively q and r so that $P = (q, r)$.

Suppose all $r+1$ firms are monopolistically competitive while consumers are assumed to be perfectly competitive. Then we have,

Theorem 6. Under assumption 4, if $(X_i'', v_k'', u_k'', q'', r'')_{i=1\dots,n, k=1,\dots,r+1}$ is an equilibrium of monopolistic competitions, and $(v_k'', u_k'', \lambda q'', \mu r'')$, where λ is some positive scalar and μ is some positive diagonal matrix, is such that $\lambda q'' v_k'' - \mu r'' u_k''$ is the maximum for $(v_k, u_k) = y_k - a_k \in Y_k - a_k$, then $(X_i'', v_k'', u_k'', \lambda q'', \mu r'')_{i=1,\dots,n, k=1,\dots,r+1}$ is a competitive equilibrium under some proper redistribution of income, and therefore $(X_i'', v_k'', u_k'')_{i=1,\dots,n, k=1,\dots,r+1}$ satisfies marginal conditions for optimality.

Proof. Consumers' total income is $\Sigma_i (q'' \bar{X}_i + r'' \bar{\bar{X}}_i) + \Sigma_k q'' v_k'' - \Sigma_k r'' u_k'' = \Sigma_i q'' \bar{X}_i + \Sigma_k q'' v_k''$, since we have from assumption 4, $\Sigma_i \bar{\bar{X}}_i = \Sigma_k u_k''$. The real total income, then, is invariant for any price change in which the prices of the desirables move proportionally, with v_k constant. If income is redistributed among consumers so as to keep the individual real income constant, i.e., in proportion to $(q'', r'') X_i''$, then $(X_i'', v_k'', u_k'', \lambda q'', \mu r'')_{i=1,\dots,n, k=1,\dots,r+1}$

---

[21]) Kahn [12], Meade [19], part 2, McKenzie [17].

is a competitive equilibrium, since consumers are competitive and $\lambda q'' v_k''$ $- \mu r'' u_k''$ is maximum for $y_k \in Y_k$.

In the Kahn–Meade case of no joint output and perfect competition in factor markets (μ is an identity matrix), the condition that $\lambda q'' v_k'' - \mu r'' u_k''$ is maximum for $y_k \in Y_k$ implies that the degree of monopoly is equal for all firms (i.e., $((1/\lambda)-1)$) and the price is proportional to marginal cost. Proportionality, not necessarily equality, of price and marginal cost is required for optimality. Marginal conditions for optimality are achieved not only in perfect competition but also in monopolistic competition with equal degree of monopoly.[22])

Now we are concerned with the total conditions for optimality. Even if $(X_i'', v_k'', u_k'')_{i=1,...n, k=1,...,r+1}$ satisfies the marginal condition there is a possibility of redundancy of firms. Suppose the $r+1$th firm is redundant and $Z - a \in 3''$, where $a = \Sigma_{k=1}^{k=r} a_k$ and $3''$ is similarly defined as in the preceding sections. Then, we have from theorem 2 that $\lambda q'' v_{r+1}'' - \mu r'' u_{r+1}'' \leq 0$, i.e., the loss of the $r+1$th firm under competition. Under laissez faire, however, the firm remains in the economy so far as its monopolistic profit, $q'' v_{r+1}''$ $- r'' u_{r+1}''$ is positive. In the Kahn–Meade case, the loss under competition implies falling average cost and possibility of redundancy arises from the sufficiently high degree of monopoly to make the profit under monopolistic competition positive. The loss under competition, however, does not necessarily imply redundancy, if prices are affected by the entry of a firm with large overhead cost, as is seen from figure 3.4 in section 3 and theorem 3 in section 4.

In the Kahn–Meade analysis of the marginal productivity of an entrepreneur (or management),[23]) it is argued that marginal productivity is negative (redundancy), if average cost is falling, each monopolistic competition having an equal degree of monopoly (i.e., marginal productivity is same in every industry). This is true only in such marginal analysis, where prices are assumed not to be affected by entry.[24]) Since the coexistence of

---

[22]) See Kahn [12], pp. 22, 29, Meade [19], p. 177. It may be noted that consumers' total real income is invariant for any price change in which the prices of the desirables move proportionally even if commodities are divided into three categories, i.e., the desirables, intermediates and factors. It is easily seen that an equal degree of monopoly in the desirables' markets and perfect competition in intermediates' markets as well as factor markets are sufficient for marginal conditions. See McKenzie [17], p. 792.

[23]) Kahn [12], p. 32, Meade [19], p. 157.

[24]) McKenzie [17], p. 786.

falling average cost and no overhead cost (i.e., no price change by the entry) is rather unlikely, the Kahn–Meade proposition exaggerates the possibility of the redundancy of firms in monopolistic competitions. It may be said that the proposition of excess capacity under falling average cost due to Chamberlin [2] is also subject to the same qualification.[25])

References

[1] Bergson, A., 'Socialist economics,' Ellis, ed., *A survey of contemporary economics, 1,* Irwin, 1948.

[2] Chamberlin, E.H., *The theory of monopolistic competition,* Harvard University Press, 6th ed., 1948.

[3] Chipman, J.S., 'A survey of the theory of international trade, 2,' *Econometrica,* 33 (1965), 685–760.

[4] Debreu, G., 'The coefficient of resource utilization,' *Econometrica,* 19 (1951), 273–282.

[5] Dupuit, J., 'De la mesure de l'utilité des travaux publics,' *Annales des Ponts et Chaussées,* 2d series, vol. 8, 1844 (Barback, tr., 'On the measurement of the utility of public works,' *International Economic Papers,* 2 (1952), 83–110, Arrow and Scitovsky, ed., *Readings in Welfare Economics,* Irwin, 1969, 255–283).

[6] Ellis, H.S. and W. Fellner, 'External economies and diseconomies,' *American Economic Review,* 38 (1943), 493–511 (Stigler and Boulding, ed., *Readings in price theory,* Irwin, 1952, 242–263).

[7] Hicks, J.R., 'The foundation of welfare economics,' *Economic Journal,* 49 (1939), 696–711.

[8] Hicks, J.R., 'The rehabilitation of consumers' surplus,' *Review of Economic Studies,* 9 (1941), 108–16. (Arrow and Scitovsky, ed., *Readings in welfare economics,* Irwin, 1969, 325–35).

[9] Hicks, J.R., 'Consumers' surplus and index numbers,' *Review of Economic Studies.*

[10] Hotelling, H., 'Demand function with limited budgets,' *Econometrica,* 3 (1935), 66–78.

[11] Hotelling, H., 'The general welfare in relations to problems of taxation and of railway and utility rates,' *Econometrica,* 3 (1938), 242–70 (Musgrave and Shoup, ed., *Readings in economics of taxation,* Irwin, 1959, 139–167, Arrow and Scitovsky, ed., *Readings in welfare economics,* Irwin, 1969, 284–308).

[12] Kahn, R.F., 'Some notes on ideal output,' *Economic Journal,* 45 (1935), 1–35.

[13] Knight, F.H., 'Some fallacies in the interpretation of social cost,' *Quarterly Journal of Economics,* 38 (1924), 586–606. (Arrow and Scitovsky, ed., *Readings in welfare economics,* Irwin, 1969, 213–227, Stigler and Boulding, ed., *Readings in price theory,* Irwin, 1952, 160–179, Knight, *The ethics of competition,* Harper, 1935, 215–236).

[14] Lerner, A.P., *The economics of control,* Macmillan, 1946.

[15] Marshall, A., *Principles of economics,* Macmillan, 8th ed., 1920.

---

[25]) Chamberlin [2], pp. 104 ff.

[16] McKean, R. N., *Efficiency in government through systems analysis*, John Wiley, 1958

[17] McKenzie, L W., 'Ideal output and the interdependence of firms,' *Economic Journal*, 61 (1951), 785–803.

[18] Margolis, J., 'Secondary benefits, external economies, and the justification of public investment,' *Review of Economics and Statistics*, 39 (1957), 284–91 (Arrow and Scitovsky, ed., *Readings in welfare economics*, Irwin, 1969, 372–83).

[19] Meade, J. E., *An introduction to economic analysis and policy*, 2nd ed., Oxford University Press, 1937.

[20] Negishi, T., 'Entry and optimal number of firms,' *Metroeconomica*, 14 (1962), 86–96.

[21] Negishi, T., 'On social welfare function,' *Quarterly Journal of Economics*, 77 (1963), 156–8.

[22] Pigou, A. C., *Economics of welfare*, Macmillan, 4th ed , 1932.

[23] Prest, A. R. and R. Turvey, 'Cost–benefit analysis : A survey,' *Surveys of Economic Theory, III*, Macmillan and St, Martin's, 1966, 155–207.

[24] Samuelson, P. A., *Foundations of economic analysis*, Harvard University Press, 1947.

[25] Scitovsky, T., 'A reconsideration of the theory of tariffs,' *Review of Economic Studies*, 9 (1941), 89–110 (Ellis and Metzler, ed., *Readings in the theory of international trade*, Blakiston, 1949, 358–89).

[26] Scitovsky, T., 'Two concepts of external economies,' *Journal of Political Economy*, 62 (1954), 143–51 (Agawala and Singh, ed., *The economics of under-development*, Oxford University Press, 1958, 295–308, Arrow and Scitovsky, *Readings in welfare economics*, Irwin, 1969, 242–52).

[27] Singer, E. M., *Antitrust economics*, Prentice-Hall, 1968.

CHAPTER 4

Optimal policies with externality

1. So far we have been concerned with interactions through markets among individual participants of an economy (i.e., consumers and firms). However, there also exist non-market interactions among individuals which are known by the name of technological external economies and diseconomies.[1]) Technological external economies (diseconomies) are defined as the favorable (unfavorable) non-market, i.e., free (uncompensated) effects of actions of a firm (input nd/or output of commodities) or those of a consumer (consumption of commodities) on production function of other firms or utility function of other consumers.[2]) It is well known that competitive markets fail to produce Pareto optimal allocation of resources if technological external economies and diseconomies are present. Some interference with the market mechanism is necessary so that the modified market system can bring forth Pareto optimal allocation.

As policy measures for such a purpose, Pigou proposed taxes on (bounties to) the party which effects external diseconomies (economies) on others, i.e., the party which has discrepancies between the social and private marginal productivities (costs) in Pigouvian terminology.[3]) Of course, such a Pigouvian policy of taxes and bounties is not the only conceivable remedy to external economies and diseconomies. Bargaining or trade among parties

---

[1]) See Scitovsky [11].

[2]) Pecuniary external economies (diseconomies) are, on the other hand, defined as the favorable (unfavorable) effect through markets of actions of a firm or those of a consumer on profits of other firms or on the budget of other consumers. See chapter 3.

[3]) Pigou [9], (1932), p. 192. Meade refined Pigouvian discussion. See Meade [6], particularly his case of the creation of the atmosphere. It must be noted, however, that the reward to capital (hiring factor) is assumed here to be determined not by its marginal productivity but as the residual after the wage (equal to marginal productivity of labor) is paid and that the party which receives the external effect must also be taxed in his example of the case of the unpaid factors since there exists the divergence between the social and private productivities (costs) with such an externally affected rather than affecting party.

concerned[4]) is certainly another solution, which amounts to creating additional markets for artificially created commodities, i.e., the services due to the external economy effects and the disservices or negative services (the negative amount of services) due to the external diseconomy effects. A classical example is the creation of the patent system, a new market for technological knowledge and information, the free use of which is a typical case of external economies. The internalization of external effects made possible by the merger of parties concerned is also conceivable as a remedy for distortions due to external effects.[5])

The purpose of this chapter is to demonstrate that these various policies on external economies and diseconomies are equivalent, if the costs of the policy measures themselves[6]) are ignored, in the sense that Pareto optimal allocation is achieved by the modified market system under any of these policies. The only difference between various policies is the difference in the resulting income distribution, which is beyond the scope of Pareto optimal allocation and can be modified by redistribution policies. In other words, the identical resources allocation can be produced by any of these policies combined with suitable redistributions of income. Some readers may consider, and we wish to agree with them, that this is too obvious and need not be demonstrated. But unfortunately we must admit that such is not the case with the current doctrines of external effects, in view of the criticism by Coase [4] and Buchanan and Stubblebine [2] of the Pigouvian proposals. Coase states that the fairly well defined oral tradition (Pigouvian tradition) which emerged though the original doctrine of Pigou was not clear and that both the analysis and the policy conclusions of Pigouvian tradition are incorrect. Buchanan and Stubblebine argued that the Pigouvian terminology (i.e., marginal social and private products (costs)) through its concentration on the decision making of the externally acting party (rather than externally affected party) alone tends to obscure the two-sidedness of a single externality relationship and that full Pareto equilibrium (i.e., optimality) can never be attained via the imposition of unilaterally imposed taxes and subsidies. The sources of these authors' confusion will be discussed below.

---

[4]) Buchanan–Stubblebine [2] and Coase [4] emphasized this solution.
[5]) Coase [4] suggested this solution. See also Coase [3] and Davis and Whinston [5]. As for the internalization in general, see Bohm [1], pp. 13–16.
[6]) For example, the cost of gathering information needed to determine the rates of taxes and bounties, administration cost of additionally created markets, etc.

Murakiam and Negishi [7] demonstrated that in certain cases of externality, i.e., when outputs of a firm effect external diseconomies and inputs effect external economies, the technological efficiency of individual firms and the optimal allocation of resources may be mutually inconsistent. The balance of this chapter will be devoted to examining such cases with regard to various optimal policies with externality. It will be argued that the combination of output external diseconomy and input external economy is more prevalent than is expected in Murakami and Negishi [7].

2. Our model is an extension of the one considered in chapter 1. Let there be m commodities (denoted by $j = 1, ..., m$), n consumers (denoted by $i = 1, ..., n$) and r firms (denoted by $k = 1, ..., r$). Because of the external economies and diseconomies, utility and production functions U_i and F_k are generally functions of activities of all the participants of the economy, i.e., of all X_{ij}, y_{kj} and Z_{kj}'s, where U_i, F_k, X_{ij} (≥ 0), y_{kj} (≥ 0) and Z_{kj} (≥ 0) are, respectively, the utility function of the ith consumer, the production function of the kth firm, the amount of consumption of the jth commodity by the ith consumer and the output and input of the jth commodity in the kth firm.[7]

The constraints in our optimal allocation problems are

$$F_k(X, Y) \leq 0, \qquad k = 1, ..., r , \tag{1}$$

where X is a matrix of X_{ij} for all i, j and Y is a matrix of y_{kj} and Z_{kj} for all k, j, and

$$\Sigma_i X_{ij} \leq \Sigma_k y_{kj} - \Sigma_k Z_{kj} + \Sigma_i \overline{X}_{ij}, \qquad j = 1, ..., m , \tag{2}$$

where $\overline{X}_{ij}$ denotes the initial holding of the jth commodity by the ith consumer. We are interested in Pareto optimal allocations, i.e., the combinations of utilities $U_i(X, Y)$, $i = 1, ..., n$, which satisfy (1) and (2) and are such that it is impossible to increase U_i without decreasing U_s, $s \neq i$, and without violating (1) and (2). Conditions for such allocations are obtained, for example, by assigning arbitrary (but feasible, i.e., possible under (1) and (2)) values $\overline{U}_2, ..., \overline{U}_n$ to $U_2, ..., U_n$, and maximizing U_1 being subject to $U_i(X, Y) \geq \overline{U}_i$, $i \neq 1$, (1) and (2).[8]

Throughout this chapter we assume,

---

[7] Either y_{kj} or Z_{kj}, but not both of them are defined for any k, j.

[8] For an alternative way to derive conditions for Pareto optimality as well as definitions, assumptions and lemmata which are not explicitly given in this chapter, see chapter 1.

Assumption 1. U_i and F_k are concave with respect to X and Y. Then, from the theory of non-linear programming, we have,

Theorem 1. Conditions for Pareto optimality are derived from Lagrangean,

$$U_1(X, Y) + \Sigma_{i \neq 1} \alpha_i (U_i(X, Y) - \overline{U}_i) - \Sigma_k \gamma_k F_k(X, Y)$$
$$- \Sigma_j P_j (\Sigma_i X_{ij} + \Sigma_k Z_{kj} - \Sigma_k y_{kj} - \Sigma_i \overline{X}_{ij}),$$

and, in addition to the utility assignments, as follows.

$$F_k(X, Y) = 0 \qquad (\leqq 0, \text{ if } \gamma_k = 0), \qquad k = 1, ..., r, \qquad (1')$$

$$\Sigma_i X_{ij} + \Sigma_k Z_{kj} - \Sigma_k y_{kj} - \Sigma_i \overline{X}_{ij} = 0 \quad (\leqq 0, \text{ if } P_j = 0), \quad j = 1, ..., m, \quad (2')$$

$$\alpha_i U_{i/ij} - P_j + \Sigma_{s \neq i} \alpha_s U_{s/ij} - \Sigma_k \gamma_k F_{k/ij} = 0 \qquad (\leqq 0, \text{ if } X_{ij} = 0),$$
$$i = 1, ..., n, \quad j = 1, ..., m, \qquad (3)$$

$$- \gamma_k F_{k/kj} + P_j \operatorname{sign}(F_{k/kj}) - \Sigma_{s \neq k} \gamma_s F_{s/kj} + \Sigma_i \alpha_i U_{i/kj} = 0$$
$$(\leqq 0, \text{ if } y_{kj} \text{ or } Z_{kj} = 0), \qquad k = 1, ..., r, \quad j = 1, ..., m, \qquad (4)$$

where $\alpha_1 = 1$ and $U_{s/ij}$ and $F_{s/kj}$ signify the partial derivatives of U_s and F_s with respect to X_{ij} and y_{kj} or Z_{kj}, and the like.

Since marginal rates of substitution are not equal for different consumers and firms in (3) and (4), i.e., the ratios of $U_{i/ij}$ for various j and those of $F_{k/kj}$ for various j are not equal for different i and k, perfect competition does not achieve Pareto optimal allocation.

However, if the market price of the jth commodity is P_j while the price to be faced by the ith consumer (the kth firm) is equalized, by the combination of taxes and bounties, to $P_j - \Sigma_{s \neq i} \alpha_s U_{s/ij} + \Sigma_k \gamma_k F_{k/ij} (P_j + \Sigma_i \alpha_i U_{i/kj} - \Sigma_{s \neq k} \gamma_s F_{s/kj})$, then perfect competition modified with taxes and bounties satisfies optimal conditions.[9] It is clear that the positive (negative) $U_{s/ij}$ or $U_{s/kj}$ implies the external economy (diseconomy) to the sth consumer from the ith consumer or the kth firm. On the other hand, since the implicit form of the production function can be viewed, e.g., as

$$F_k(X, Y) = y_{k1} - f_k(X, Y') \leqq 0,$$

[9] The balance of taxes and bounties is assumed to be imposed on or returned to consumers in a lump sum.

where Y' is equal to Y except that y_{k1} is deleted, the positive (negative) $F_{s/ij}$ or $F_{s/kj}$, i.e., the positive (negative) $-f_{s/ij}$ or $-f_{s/kj}$, implies the external diseconomy (economy) to the sth firm from the ith consumer or the kth firm. Lagrangean multipliers α_i and γ_k are non-negative.

Therefore, we have, as proposed by Pigou [9] and Meade [6],

Theorem 2. To satisfy marginal conditions for optimality, a tax must be imposed on (a bounty must be given to) an activity (consumption, input or output of a commodity) of a party, which produces external diseconomy (economy) to other parties. Since only marginal conditions are relevant, here a tax on (bounty to) an increase of the level of an activity is to be understood equivalent to a bounty to (tax on) a reduction of the level of the same activity, the only difference resulting in income distribution.

Suppose a group of firms form a closed circle of externality in the sense that external effects of actions of a member firm extend only to other member firms of the same group, i.e.,

Assumption 2. $U_{i/kj} = 0$, $k \in K$, $F_{s/kj} = 0$, $s \notin K$, $k \in K$, where K is a group of firms.

If all the firms in the group merged into a single firm, the merged firm will maximize, under competitive condition, the profit,

$$\Sigma_j P_j \Sigma_{k \in K}(y_{kj} - Z_{kj}),$$

being subject to $F_k(X, Y) \leqq 0$, $k \in K$, where prices P_j's are given constant. Then, it is easily checked that the optimal conditions (4) are satisfied for $k \in K$.

Theorem 3. If a group of firms forming a closed circle of externality (assumption 2) merge into a single firm, the competitive allocation is Pareto optimal.[10])

3. Suppose markets for artificial commodities are created corresponding to the effects of external economy and diseconomy. In general, there can exist $nm(n+r-1) + rm(n+r-1)$ new artificially created commodities in all corresponding to external effects on each party caused by actions X_{ij}, y_{kj}, Z_{kj} of other parties. Let us denote the amount of effect received by the sth

---

[10]) See Coase [4] and Davis and Whinston [5].

consumer from the activities X_{ij} and y_{kj} (or Z_{kj}) respectively by $X_{s/ij}$ and $X_{s/kj}$. Similarly, the amount of effect received by the sth firm from X_{ij} and y_{kj} (or Z_{kj}) is respectively denoted by $y_{s/ij}$ and $y_{s/kj}$.

Now condition (1) must be replaced by

$$F_k(X_k, Y_k) \leqq 0, \qquad k = 1, ..., r, \tag{5}$$

where X_k is the matrix of $y_{k/ij}$ for all i, j, and Y_k is the matrix of $y_{k/sj}$ for $s = 1, ..., r$, $j = 1, ..., m$, $y_{k/kj}$ being identical with y_{kj} or Z_{kj}, while, in addition to (2), we have

$$X_{ij} \geqq (\leqq) X_{s/ij}, \qquad s = 1, ..., n, \ s \neq i, \ \text{if} \ U_{s/ij} > 0 \ (< 0), \tag{6a}$$

$$X_{ij} \leqq (\geqq) y_{k/ij}, \ \text{if} \ F_{k/ij} > 0 \ (< 0), \tag{6b}$$

$$y_{kj} + Z_{kj} \geqq (\leqq) X_{i/kj}, \ \text{if} \ U_{i/kj} > 0 \ (< 0), \tag{6c}$$

$$y_{kj} + Z_{kj} \leqq (\geqq) y_{s/kj}, \qquad s = 1, ..., r, \ s \neq k, \ \text{if} \ F_{s/kj} > 0 \ (< 0),$$
$$i = 1, ..., n, \quad j = 1, ..., m, \quad k = 1, ..., r.^{11}) \tag{6d}$$

Utility functions are similarly modified, i.e., $U_i = U_i(X_i, Y_i)$, where X_i is the matrix of $X_{i/sj}$ for $s = 1, ..., n$, $j = 1, ..., m$, $X_{i/ij}$ being equal to X_{ij}, and Y_i is the matrix of $x_{i/kj}$ for all k, j.

Conditions for optimality are derived by maximizing $U_1(X_1, Y_1)$ being subject to $U_i(X_i, Y_i) \geqq \overline{U}_i$, $i \neq 1$, (2), (5) and (6).

Theorem 4. Conditions for optimality are derived from Lagrangean

$$U_1(X_1, Y_1) + \Sigma_{i \neq 1} \alpha_i (U_i(X_i, Y_i) - \overline{U}_i) - \Sigma_k \gamma_k F_k(X_k, Y_k)$$
$$- \Sigma_j P_j (\Sigma_i X_{ij} + \Sigma_k Z_{kj} - \Sigma_k y_{kj} - \Sigma_i \overline{X}_{ij})$$
$$- \Sigma_{ij} \Sigma_{s \neq i} q_{sij} (X_{s/ij} - X_{ij}) - \Sigma_{kij} q_{kij} (y_{k/ij} - X_{ij})$$
$$- \Sigma_{ikj} q_{ikj} (X_{i/kj} - y_{kj} - Z_{kj}) - \Sigma_{kj} \Sigma_{s \neq k} q_{skj} (y_{s/kj} - y_{kj} - Z_{kj})$$

and, in addition to utility assignments and (2'), as follows.

$$F_k(X_k, Y_k) = 0, \quad (\leqq 0, \text{if} \ \gamma_k = 0), \quad k = 1, ..., r, \tag{5'}$$

$$X_{ij} = X_{s/ij}, \quad s = 1, ..., n, \quad s \neq i, \tag{6a'}$$

$$X_{ij} = y_{k/ij}, \tag{6b'}$$

$$y_{kj} + Z_{kj} = X_{i/kj}, \tag{6c'}$$

$$y_{kj} + Z_{kj} = y_{s/kj}, \quad s = 1, ..., r, \quad s \neq k, \tag{6d'}$$

$^{11})$ Since either y_{kj} or Z_{kj} is not defined, $y_{kj} + Z_{kj}$ should read as y_{kj} or Z_{kj} as the case may be.

(a', b', c', d' are replaced respectively by a, b, c, d in (6) if q_{sij}, $s \neq i$, q_{kij}, q_{ikj}, q_{skj}, $s \neq k$, are respectively zero, i.e., there exist no external effects at the margin),

$$\alpha_i U_{i/ij} - P_j + \Sigma_{s \neq i} q_{sij} + \Sigma_k q_{kij} = 0, \quad (\leq 0, \text{ if } X_{ij} = 0), \tag{7}$$

$$\alpha_s U_{s/ij} - q_{sij} = 0, \quad (\leq 0, \text{ if } X_{s/ij} = 0), \quad k = 1, ..., r, \quad s = 1, ..., n,$$
$$s \neq i, \tag{8}$$

$$-\gamma_k F_{k/ij} - q_{kij} = 0, \quad (\leq 0, \text{ if } y_{k/ij} = 0), \quad i = 1, ..., n, \quad j = 1, ..., m, \tag{9}$$

$$-\gamma_k F_{k/kj} + P_j \text{ sign}(F_{k/kj}) + \Sigma_i q_{ikj} + \Sigma_{s \neq k} q_{skj} = 0, \quad (\leq 0, \text{ if } y_{kj} \text{ or}$$
$$Z_{kj} = 0), \tag{10}$$

$$\alpha_i U_{i/kj} - q_{ikj} = 0, \quad (\leq 0, \text{ if } X_{i/kj} = 0), \tag{11}$$

$$-\gamma_s F_{s/kj} - q_{skj} = 0, \quad (\leq 0, \text{ if } y_{s/kj} = 0), \quad s = 1, ..., r, \quad s \neq k,$$
$$k = 1, ..., r, \quad j = 1, ..., m, \tag{12}$$

where $\alpha_1 = 1$ and $F_{s/kj}$ signifies the partial derivative of F_s with respect to $y_{s/kj}$ and the like.[12])

In view of (6'), we can easily see that conditions (7), (8) and (9) are identical with condition (3) and that conditions (10), (11) and (12) are identical with condition (4). Since (1) and (5') are also identical, conditions in theorem 1 are identical with conditions in theorem 4.

Since the situations in the newly created markets for external effects are those of bilateral monopoly, the optimal conditions, i.e., equalities of marginal rates of substitution are likely to be satisfied.[13]) Positive (negative) Lagrangean multipliers q_{sij}, $(s = 1, ..., n, s \neq i)$, q_{kij}, q_{ikj}, q_{skj}, $(s = 1, ..., r, s \neq k)$, are prices to be paid by externally affected parties (by externally affecting parties) for the effect of external economy (diseconomy). Then, we have

Theorem 5. The solution of externality proposed by Coase [4] and Buchanan and Stubblebine [2], i.e., trade or bargaining among parties

---

[12]) It must be noted that $F_{k/kj} > (<)0$ in (10) if the jth commodity is an output (input) of the kth firm and $y_{kj}(Z_{kj})$ is relevant.

[13]) Davis and Whinston's [5] argument to the contrary may be partly due to their assumption of the non-cooperative case. Generally, the existence of a core solution is likely since consumers are expected to trade between themselves at a point on the contract curve and firms to divide between themselves the jointly maximized profit.

concerned (both externally affecting and affected) is identical to the one proposed by Pigou [9], i.e., taxes and bounties on the externally affecting party alone.

Of course, the resulted distribution of income is different in the two solutions, since, e.g., the party which enjoyed external economy free in the Pigouvian solution must pay for such an economy in the trade or bargaining solution. As a matter of fact, the distribution of income is not uniquely determined even in the latter solution. For example, consider a case of external diseconomy. The affecting party must pay for it if it is legally decided as guilty. On the other hand, if it is not guilty, the affected party must pay so as to induce the affecting party to reduce the effect. Clearly, as is emphasized by Coase, the difference in legal decisions implies different distributions of income, though the marginal conditions for allocation are unchanged, since the affecting party still has to pay for the increase of the effect in the opportunity cost sense. Theorem 5 is, however, free from this fact, since the income distribution can be modified by redistribution policies and is beyond the scope of Pareto optimal allocations.

If the external effect of activities of a party extend to many other parties and the public goods aspect of externality (i.e., non-excludability) is prevalent, the solution of externality by trade and bargaining is very difficult. It is also difficult, however, to find proper taxes and bounties in the case of public goods. Anyway, the problem of public goods, like that of income distribution, is outside the scope of the present study since it cannot be solved by the price system.[14]

4. After careful studies of many legal examples, Coase insists quite correctly on the equivalence of various solutions for externality, particularly of different solutions through bargaining.[15] However, his criticism on Pigouvian policies is wrong and seems to be based on his misunderstanding. He states that a Pigouvian 'tax should be equal to the damage done and should therefore vary with the amount of the harmful effect', and that it 'is undoubtedly the result of not comparing the total product obtainable with alternative social arrangements'. This is clearly not the case with Pigouvian policies. Since they are remedies for the divergence between the

---

[14] For public goods, see Musgrave [7], pp. 61–89.
[15] Coase [4], pp. 39–42.

social and private marginal product (costs), i.e., $\Sigma_{s \neq i}\alpha_s U_{s/ij} - \Sigma_k \gamma_k F_{k/ij}$ in (3) ($\Sigma_i \alpha_i U_{i/kj} - \Sigma_{s \neq k}\gamma_s F_{s/kj}$ in (4)), they are undoubtedly derived from the comparison of total product obtainable with alternative social arrangements and need not be equal to the total damage done.

A Pigouvian tax is based, 'not on the damage caused, but on the fall in the value of production (in its widest sense) resulting from e.g., the emission of smoke'. As such, it is subject to his criticism that he is 'unable to imagine how the data needed for such a taxation system could be assembled', but not to the criticism that it 'would not necessarily bring about optimal conditions'. Since the externally affected parties are also assumed to behave, given external diseconomy, so as to increase the value of production, i.e., to do their best to get rid of the effect of diseconomy, it is not correct to say that the Pigouvian tax fails to consider the total value of production and 'tends to lead to unduly high costs being incurred for the prevention of damage'. Pigouvian proposals, as well as solutions by trade or bargaining among parties concerned, amount to maximizing the total value of production, not by eliminating 'smoke pollution' but by securing the optimal amount of 'smoke pollution'.

It is strange that Coase who clearly states that the only difference between various bargaining solutions is that of distribution of income fails to see that the difference between bargaining solutions and Pigouvian solutions is also limited to that of income distribution. Incidentally, Coase's arguments based on numerical examples where the value of production is calculated by non-optimal prices are dangerous. Unless prices are optimal prices, the value of production cannot be a proper measure of the social welfare.[16])

Following Coase, Buchanan–Stubblebine [2], which is the most rigorous and complete analysis of the subject to date, also criticised Pigouvian policies. They state that Pareto optimality cannot be attained via the imposition of unilaterally imposed taxes and subsidies, i.e., until and unless those benefitting from changes are required to pay some price for securing the benefits and that if a tax-subsidy method, rather than trade, is to be introduced, it should involve bilateral taxes and subsidies. However, their arguments, based on an example of external effects between two individuals, in leading to this conclusion seem to be confused.

Suppose two individuals are buying two commodities and the consumption of the first commodity by the second individual has an external effect on the

---

[16]) Coase [4], p. 33. For the so-called second best theory, see chapter 10.

first individual. The optimal condition given by Buchanan and Stubblebine [2] is[17])

$$-\frac{U_{1/21}}{U_{1/12}} = \frac{U_{2/21}}{U_{2/22}} - \frac{P_1}{P_2}. \tag{13}$$

This is exactly identical to the condition derived from (3). If a Pigouvian tax or bounty is imposed on the second individual, (13) is satisfied. By using marginal valuation curves, Buchanan and Stubblebine confirmed that a Pigouvian solution of the amount of consumption of the first commodity by the second individual is equal to the level in a Pareto optimal situation at which there is no divergence between private and social marginal costs. However, according to Buchanan and Stubblebine, this is not Pareto optimal, since the condition for the latter is now

$$-\frac{U_{1/21}}{U_{1/12}} = \frac{U_{2/21}}{U_{2/22}} - \left(\frac{P_1}{P_2} - \frac{U_{1/21}}{U_{1/12}}\right) \tag{14}$$

and trade between two individuals is possible in the Pigouvian situation so as to satisfy (14).[18, 19])

Sources of confusion un Buchanan and Stubblebine [2] seem to be as follows. In our view, (14) is not the condition of Pareto optimality, though it is an equilibrium condition for trade between two individuals concerning external effects. If between two parties trade of external effects is possible, a competitive economy without any taxes and bounties is optimal. However if any tax or bounty does exists, a competitive economy with trade concerning external effects is by no means optimal. This is the point of the second best theory. In a Pigouvian situation, the optimal condition is still (13). Once a Pigouvian tax or bounty is introduced, no voluntary trade between externally related individuals is optimal. We must remember that there exists no need for Pigouvian policies if such a trade is possible.[20]) On the

---

[17]) (13) corresponds to (11) and (13) in Buchanan–Stubblebine [2].

[18]) Turvey [12] rightly states that the situation with (14) is sub-optimal. It is curious that Turvey, with his intention to support Buchanan and Stubblebine [2] by the graphical consideration of a simple case, actually arrived at the right conclusion which is given below, by misunderstanding the point made by Buchanan and Stubblebine.

[19]) (14) corresponds to (11 A) in Buchanan–Stubblebine [2]. This is obtained from (13) by substituting Pigouvian corrected price.

[20]) In the terminology of Buchanan–Stubblebine [2], if there is no Pareto relevant externality (as a result of such trade), the situation is Pareto optimal and no policies are needed, even if there remain marginal externalities (i.e., $U_{s/1J}$, $F_{s/kJ}$, etc., are not zero).

other hand, if Pigouvian policies are introduced, no further trade of external effects is needed. They are alternative, mutually exclusive solutions of externality.

If a Pigouvian policy is applied, the question is who pays the subsidy or to whom the revenue of tax is returned. If there is a third party involved in this regard, it must be considered in the definition of Pareto optimality, even though it has nothing to do with the further trade of externalities between the relevant two parties. Such a trade (i.e., (14)) assures the optimality of two parties, but not that of three parties. On the other hand, if tax (subsidy) marginally applied is returned to (collected from) the same party in a lump sum, there is no possibility of trade when (13) is established, i.e., (13) rather than (14) is the condition for the equilibrium.

Davis and Whinston's [5] argument that a Pigouvian policy may be impossible if the externality is mutual and non-separable in terms of cost function should be equally addressed to the solution attained by trading externality. The possible game theoretic indeterminancy may be more serious in the latter solution where both parties must explicitly recognize the variability of externalities while the concept of Nash type non-cooperative equilibrium has less difficulty in the case of the former policy of the omnipotent government which does not require the knowledge of the private parties on the variability of externalities received.

5. If there exist no external effects at all, social optimality (Pareto optimality) implies the individual efficiency (in the technological sense) of each firm which produces and/or consumes non-free commodities, i.e., $F_k(y_{k1}, \ldots, y_{km}, Z_{k1}, \ldots, Z_{km}) = 0$. But, in the case of external economies and diseconomies, such is not always the case as is pointed out by Murakami and Negishi [6]. One of the counter examples to the coexistence of social optimality and individual efficiency will be given below. Before the example, however, let us first consider a formal condition necessary for the occurrence of such abnormal cases.

Suppose that the production of the kth producer at a social optimal point is inefficient from his own individual point of view, that is $F_k(X, Y) < 0$, $\gamma_k = 0$ in (1'). From (4) we can see that $\gamma_k = 0$ implies the existence of some $\gamma_s F_{s/kj} > 0$ or some $\alpha_i U_{i/kj} < 0$ if all the prices are positive, i.e., $P_j > 0$. Following Murakami and Negishi [6], we have

Theorem 6. If, at a social optimal point, some producer is inefficient from his own point of view, then his activity must exert some external diseconomy effect (on some other producers who operate efficiently or consumers whose social significance is not negligible)[21]) via all of his actually produced outputs and must exert some external economy effect via all of his actually needed inputs.

In Murakami and Negishi [7], the combination of output external diseconomy and input external economy is considered rather a strong condition and it is argued that in the normal or standard cases discussed by, e.g., Meade [6] where external effect works only via output the abnormality in question will never occur. However, upon further reflection, we now think that external diseconomies caused by outputs most likely imply the possibility of external economy through inputs and that the case of external effects via outputs only cannot be considered so normal. A classical example which is most instructive in this respect is Pigou in the case of smoke pollution. As is pointed out by Coase,[22]) it is rather astonishing to find that the problem of the smoky chimney is used by Pigou as an example of external economy and is never mentioned explicitly in connection with the external diseconomy. Pigou's point is that factory owners who devote resources to prevent their chimneys from smoking render services for which they receive no payment and that they should be given a bounty to induce them to install smoke preventing devices. Of course it is also true that the owner of the factory with the smoky chimney should be taxed as most modern economists would suggest. Smoke producing, external diseconomy producing outputs must be taxed and smoke preventing, external economy producing inputs must be subsidized.[23]) Since most external diseconomy produced by outputs can be prevented or reduced by increasing inputs, the case for theorem 6 seems to be fairly prevalent.

The technological inefficiency of individual firms at social optimum does not imply the pecuniary inefficiency of those firms when proper measures for externality are taken. Suppose Pigouvian taxes and bounties are introduced. From (4), prices relevant to firms for which the technological inefficiency is required for the social optimality, i.e., $\gamma_k = 0$, are all zero, i.e., $P_j - \Sigma_i \alpha_i U_{i/kj} + \Sigma_{s \neq k} \gamma_k F_{s/kj} = 0$. The social value of outputs as well as that of inputs is zero. For such firms all the feasible combinations of inputs and

---

[21]) I.e., those i for whom $\alpha_i > 0$.

[22]) Coase [4], p. 35. Pigou [9], p. 184.

[23]) See Plott [10]. In the case of smoke, of course, the amount of tax should be greater than the amount of subsidy.

outputs are indifferent from the point of view of profit maximization under competition and the socially optimal allocation is not inconsistent with the individual pecuniary efficiency. On the other hand, if markets for external effects are created, the kth firm will maximize

$$\Sigma_j P_j(y_{kj}-Z_{kj})+\Sigma_{ij}q_{i/kj}(y_{kj}+Z_{kj})+\Sigma_s\neq_k\Sigma_j q_{s/kj}(y_{kj}-Z_{kj})$$

with respect to $(y_{k1}, ..., y_{km}, Z_{k1}, ..., Z_{km})$, being subject to $F_k(X, Y)\leq 0$. From (10, 11) and (12), again any feasible inputs and outputs are indifferent to the firm and there is no pecuniary inefficiency when $\gamma_k = 0$ and $F_k(X, Y) < 0$. In this case production may be considered not inefficient even in the technological sense, since any increase of output is accompanied by an increase of external diseconomy effects which, causing the cost of production to increase, are considered as a sort of input, and any decrease of inputs is accompanied by a decrease of external economy effects which, reducing the revenue of the firm, are considered as a sort of output. In other words, when fictitious outputs and inputs corresponding to external effects are introduced, the rule that each firm should be operated at a technologically efficient level is no longer violated in the enlarged space of commodities. For example, the amount of smoke should be minimized for the given level of other inputs and outputs.

Finally, we reproduce from Murakami and Negishi [7] an example of an economy where some inefficient individual production is required for an optimal social production pattern. Let us assume four kinds of commodities, two of consumers' goods (commodities 1 and 2) and two of labor services (commodities 3 and 4). The social welfare function is

$$W = 100X_1+100X_2+50X_3-5X_1^2-5X_2^2, \tag{15}$$

where X_i denotes the amount of commodity i consumed. The production function of commodity 1 (the first firm) is

$$Y_{11} \leq 10Z_{13}, \tag{16}$$

i.e., commodity $1(Y_{11})$ is produced solely from commodity 3 (labor) (Z_{13}); the production function of commodity 2 (the second firm) is

$$Y_{22} = Z_{24}-Y_{11}+Z_{13}, \tag{17}$$

i.e., commodity $2(Y_{22})$ is produced from commodity 4 (labor) (Z_{24}) but the external effects of production of commodity 1 (the output of commodity 1 and the input of commodity 3) on that of commodity 2 are present. Initial stock of commodities are given as $\overline{X}_1 = 0$, $\overline{X}_2 = 0$, $\overline{X}^3 = 2$, $\overline{X}_4 = 9$. The socially optimal production pattern is determined by maximizing W under the following conditions: all the variables are non-negative; technological restrictions on production (16) and (17) are met; and demands are constrained not to exceed supplies, $X_1 - Y_{11} \leqq 0$, $X_2 - Y_{22} \leqq 0$, $X_3 + Z_{13} - \overline{X}_3 \leqq 0$, and $Z_{24} - \overline{X}_4 \leqq 0$. The Lagrangean expression, in this case, is

$$100X_1 + 100X_2 + 50X_3 - 5X_1^2 - 5X_2^2 - P_1(X_1 - Y_{11}) - P_2(X_2 - Y_{22})$$

$$- P_3(X_3 + Z_{13} - \overline{X}_3) - P_4(Z_{24} - \overline{X}_4) - \gamma_1(Y_{11} - Z_{13})$$

$$- \gamma_2(Y_{22} + Y_{11} - Z_{24} - Z_{13}).$$

The solution of the problem is, according to the theory of non-linear programming, a saddle point of the Lagrangean expression such that $X_1 = Y_{11} = 5$, $X_2 = Y_{22} = 5$, $X_3 = Z_{13} = 1$, $Z_{24} = 9$, $P_1 = P_2 = P_3 = P_4 = 50$, $\gamma_1 = 0$, $\gamma_2 = 50$, and the following conditions corresponding to (1'), (2'), (3), (4) or (2'), (5'), (6'), (7), (8), (9), (10), (11), (12), are satisfied.

$$100 - 10X_1 - P_1 = 0,$$
$$100 - 10X_2 - P_2 = 0,$$
$$5_30 - P = 0,$$
$$P_1 - \gamma_1 - \gamma_2 = 0,$$
$$P_2 - \gamma_2 = 0,$$
$$- P_3 + 10\gamma_1 + \gamma_2 = 0,$$
$$- P_4 + \gamma_2 = 0,$$
$$X_1 - Y_{11} = 0,$$
$$X_2 - Y_{22} = 0,$$
$$X_3 + Z_{13} - 2 = 0,$$
$$Z_{24} - 9 = 0,$$
$$Y_{11} - 10Z_{13} < 0,$$
$$Y_{11} + Y_{22} - Z_{13} - Z_{24} = 0.$$

The technological inefficiency in the production of commodity 1 is required for the sake of a socially optimal production pattern. The output of commodity 1 has an external diseconomy, and the input of commodity 3 for the production of commodity 1 has an external economy for the production of commodity 2.

References

[1] Bohm, P., *External economies in production*, Stockholm Economic Studies, Almqvist and Wiksell, 1964.

[2] Buchanan, J. M. and Wm. Craig Stubblebine, 'Externality,' *Economica*, N.S. 29 (1962), 371–84 (Arrow and Scitovsky, ed., *Readings in welfare economics*, Irwin, 1969, 199–212).

[3] Coase, R. H., 'The nature of the firm,' *Economica*, N.S. 4 (1937), 386–405 (Stigler and Boulding, ed., *Readings in price theory*, Irwin, 1952, 331–351).

[4] Coase, R. H., 'The problem of social cost,' *The Journal of Law and Economics*, 3 (1960), 1–44.

[5] Davis, O. A. and A. Whinston, 'Externalities, welfare and the theory of games,' *Journal of Political Economy*, 70 (1962), 241–62.

[6] Meade, J., 'External economies and diseconomies in a competitive situation,' *Economic Journal*, 62 (1952), 54–67 (Arrow and Scitovsky, ed., *Readings in welfare economics*, Irwin, 1969, 185–198).

[7] Murakami, Y. and T. Negishi, 'A note on a formulation of external economy,' *International Economic Review*, 5 (1964), 328–334.

[8] Musgrave, R. A., *The theory of public finance*, McGraw-Hill, 1959.

[9] Pigou, A. C., *The economics of welfare*, Macmillan, 1920 (first ed.), 1932 (fourth ed.).

[10] Plott, C., 'Externalities and corrective taxes,' *Economica*, N.S. 33 (1966), 84–87.

[11] Scitovsky, T., 'Two concepts of external economies,' *Journal of Political Economy*, 17 (1954), 143–51 (Arrow and Scitovsky, ed., *Readings in welfare economics*, Irwin, 1969, 242–252, Argawala and Singh, ed., *The economics of underdevelopment*, Oxford University Press, 1958, 295–308).

[12] Turvey, R., 'On divergences between social cost and private cost,' *Economica*, N.S. 30 (1963), 309–313.

[13] Wellisz, S., 'On external diseconomies and the government-assisted invisible hand,' *Economica*, N.S. 31 (1964), 345–362.

CHAPTER 5

External economies and
trade between similar countries

1. Trade or autarky, i.e., whether a country should be opened to inter-national dealings or not, is typically a question of a total condition for optimality. The elegance of the traditional theory of the gains from inter-national trade may induce a response of breathless admiration or a mood of deep despair, or both. It all depends on one's point of view: the subject is difficult and one cannot fail to admire the glitter of the theorems which have been established; on the other hand, the theorems rest on very special assumptions. Specifically, it has been shown that in the absence of external economies and diseconomies and internal economies of scale, free trade is better than no trade.[1]) When these assumptions are relaxed, we must confess that the subject is in a mess. Of course, we are now occupied with comparisons of non-optimal situations, and for some this observation will serve both as an explanation and expiation, since in such a case many strange things are believed to be possible. Nevertheless one need not jump overboard in the belief that literally anything can happen and generalization is impossible; that is what we hope to show in this chapter.

The purpose of relaxing traditional assumptions is not mere generalization for the sake of generalization. It is badly needed for the development of a new theory of international trade which can explain the gains from trade between similar countries. To explain the gains from trade, traditional doctrines emphasize the difference between countries, i.e., the difference in autarky prices is the condition for the gains from trade. For example, the so-called Heckscher–Ohlin theory assumes international difference in factor endowments as the crucial and sole factor determining comparative advantage.[2]) Therefore, it cannot explain trade heavily carried on between

---

[1]) See Leontief [11], Samuelson [16].
[2]) For example, see Bhagwati [2], pp. 159–181. However, as for Ohlin himself, see foot-note 3 below.

industrial areas that are very similar. Furthermore, such a theory is an exogeneous explanation of trade in the sense that only the one way effect on trade of the comparative advantage which exists before trade is emphasized. It is, however, preferable to develop an endogeneous theory of trade since there is a possibility that international trade and specialization as such creates the comparative advantage which did not exist in autarky.

Ohlin himself has already suggested economies of scale as an endogeneous factor explaining international trade.[3]) To be consistent with competition, economies of scale must be coupled with the so-called Marshallian external economies which are external to the firm but internal to the industry.[4]) Recently, Chipman emphasized the importance of this line of approach to international trade.[5]) As pioneering studies in this approach, we have, of course, Matthews and Kemp.[6]) As far as the gains from trade are concerned, however, their result is rather disappointing. Assuming continuously decreasing reversible cost curves in both industries with such equal intensity of cost decreasing that the transformation curve is convex to the origin and the price line is still tangent to it, it is shown that both countries may not be better off with international trade than in autarky.

On the other hand, such a use of Marshallian external economies may be subject to some criticisms. Firstly, as is argued by Sraffa quite persuasively, such economies are not likely to be called forth by small increases in production.[7]) Supply curves showing continuously decreasing costs are not to be found. There must be certain threshold levels of changes in production for economies to be effective. Secondly, as is pointed out by Anderson, Marshallian external economies should be regarded as irreversible, i.e., the economies once attained will not be lost even if industrial output is contracted.[8]) Certainly this would have been the view of some of the original neo-classical writers. However, the existence of such a threshold and/or irreversibility is rather favorable to demonstrate the gains from trade. The

---

[3]) See Ohlin [14], pp. 50–58 and 106–111.
[4]) Ohlin himself, however, does not seem to emphasize this point. Of course, the economies of scale can be consistently coupled with monopolistic competition. See chapter 8.
[5]) Chipman [5], pp. 736–749.
[6]) Matthews [12], Kemp [8], pp. 110–127 and 173–175.
[7]) Sraffa [17], p. 540. This does not necessarily contradict with the relative *smallness* of the contribution of an individual firm to industrial output, which is essential to such economies, i.e., the effect of the industrial output on the individual production functions, *external* to the firm. However, see Chipman [5], p. 742.
[8]) Anderson [2], Caves [4], pp. 172–3.

first aim of this chapter is to show, following Negishi [13], two cases of gains from trade for both countries. In the first case it is assumed that there is a threshold for the effect of economies of scale and that each country can enjoy economies of scale when specialized in one industry but cannot enjoy them in autarky. Alternatively, in the second case, irreversibility of economies of scale is assumed with the result that the contraction of the import competing industry would not cause it to lose its economies attained under autarky.

It is rather apparent that the joint gains from trade of similar countries are positive if all the industries are similar and subject to sufficiently strong economies of scale. Since two industries in a simple two country two commodity model of an international economy are actually aggregated or composite industries, we can change the demand and/or supply conditions of these industries by changing the composition of the two industries, i.e., by changing the grouping of the original industries into two. If demand and supply conditions of two aggregated industries can be made similar in this way, the positive joint gains from trade can be equally distributed and each of the similar countries can enjoy the trade gains. This is the point suggested by Kojima, i.e., the theory of agreed specialization in the similar industries or *intra*-industry specialization in the discussion of gains from customs union.[9] However, Kojima's condition is too stringent since generally industrial difference in demand conditions and those in supply conditions are independent. Furthermore, it is not certain whether by *intra*-industrial specialization industries can enjoy Marshallian external economy. Our second aim in this chapter is to demonstrate that the similarity of only the demand conditions (relative to the biased supply conditions) for two aggregated industries, particularly the marginal propensity to consume of the output, is sufficient to guarantee the gains from trade and *inter*-industry specialization for each of the similar countries, provided the degree of increasing returns to scale is fairly strong.

Of course, the demonstration of the gains from trade is subject to the existence of a trade equilibrium. If there exists no equilibrium other than the autarky equilibrium, the gain from trade, even if it is formally proved, does not exist. The final part of this chapter is devoted to keeping the theorems on trade gains from being vacuous, i.e., to the demonstration of the existence of an equilibrium in which each country specializes in a different industry and therefore international trade exists. Under some simplifying assump-

---

[9]) Kojima [10], p. 70.

tions, the existence of sufficiently strong effects of economies of scale in two industries is sufficient for such a demonstration.

2. Let us begin with the demonstration of the trade gains under traditional assumptions. Consider a two-country two-commodity factor model of an international economy. Let $X_i = (X_{i1}, X_{i2})$ denote the consumption of the ith country, where X_{ij} signifies the amount of the jth commodity consumed by the ith country $(i, j = 1, 2)$. Well behaved indifference curves are assumed on X_i, with an index $U_i = U_i(X_{i1}, X_{i2})$.[10] Technology is assumed to be identical between countries. Assuming away the joint output, the production function of the individual firm

$$y_j = f_j(v_{j1}, v_{j2}) \tag{1}$$

is linear homogeneous, with isoquants strictly convex to the origin, where y_j and v_{jk} are, respectively, the individual output of the jth commodity and the input of the kth factor for the production of the jth commodity $(k = 1, 2)$. Let us signify by Y_{ij} and V_{ijk}, respectively, the total output of the jth commodity in the ith country and the total input of the kth factor for the production of the jth commodity in the ith country. Since they are linear homogeneous, f_j's are also production functions of the industries, i.e.,

$$Y_{ij} = f_j(V_{ij1}, V_{ij2}) . \tag{2}$$

Consider a free trade equilibrium $(X_i^0, Y_{ij}^0, V_{ijk}^0, p_j^0, w_{ik}^0)$ such that:

Definition 1. (a) $U_i(X_i)$ is maximized with respect to X_i, being subject to

$$\sum_j p_j^0 X_{ij} = \sum_j p_j^0 Y_{ij}^0 \text{ (the condition of the trade balance),} \tag{3}$$

(b) $p_j^0 Y_{ij} - \sum_k w_{ik}^0 V_{ijk}$ is maximized with respect to Y_{ij} and V_{ijk}, being subject to (2),

(c) $\sum_i Y_{ij} = \sum_i X_{ij}, \sum_j V_{ijk} = \bar{V}_{ik}$,

where p_j, w_{ik} and $\bar{V}_{ik}$ are, respectively, the price of the jth commodity, the price of the service of the kth factor in the ith country and the given amount of the total supply of the kth factor in the ith country.[11] This is to be compared with the autarky equilibrium $(X_i^1, Y_{ij}^1, V_{ijk}^1, p_{ij}^1, w_{ik}^1)$ defined by:

---

[10] This simplifies, but is not necessary for, the discussion. See Samuelson [16], Kemp [8], pp. 159–183.

[11] Conditions (a), (b), (c) represent respectively the aggregation of consumer's behavior, the aggregation of profit maximization of individual firms, and the clearance of commodity and factor markets.

Definition 2. (a′) $U_i(X_i)$ is maximized with respect to X_i, being subject to

$$\sum_j p_{ij}^1 X_{ij} = \sum_j p_{ij}^1 Y_{ij}^1, \tag{3′}$$

(b′) $p_{ij}^1 Y_{ij} - \sum_k w_{ik}^1 V_{ijk}$ is maximized with respect to Y_{ij} and V_{ijk}, being subject to (2),

(c′) $X_{ij} = Y_{ij}$, $\sum_j V_{ijk} = \bar{V}_{ik}$, where p_{ij} is the price of the jth commodity in the ith country.

If there are international differences in taste U_i and/or in factor endowments $\bar{V}_{ik}$ and therefore in the autarky prices p_{ij}^1, there exists international trade, i.e., $X_{ij}^0 - Y_{ij}^0 \neq 0$, and we can show that each country is better off in a trade equilibrium than in the autarky.

Theorem 1. Each country is better off in $(X_{ij}^0, Y_{ij}^0, V_{ijk}^0, p_j^0, w_{ik}^0)$ than in $(X_{ij}^1, Y_{ij}^1, V_{ijk}^1, p_{ij}^1, w_{ik}^1)$, if $X_{ij}^0 - Y_{ij}^0 \neq 0$.

Proof. Suppose not. Then, from (a) in definition 1, we must have

$$\sum_j p_j^0 X_{ij}^0 < \sum_j p_j^0 X_{ij}^1. \tag{4}$$

By (3) and the second half of (c) in definition 1 and (c′) in definition 2, this leads to

$$\sum_j (p_j^0 Y_{ij}^0 - \sum_k w_{ik}^0 V_{ijk}^0) < \sum_j (p_j^0 Y_{ij}^1 - \sum_k w_{ik}^0 V_{ijk}^1). \tag{5}$$

However, this contradicts with the result of the profit maximization, (b) in definition 1,

$$(p_j^0 Y_{ij}^0 - \sum_k w_{ik}^0 V_{ikj}^0) \geq (p_j^0 Y_{ij}^1 - \sum_k w_{ik}^0 V_{ijk}^1). \tag{6}$$

So far, so good, but there can be no international trade and therefore no gains from trade, unless there are differences in taste and/or in factor endowments between countries. To explain trade between similar countries, one must introduce economies of scale so that an industry with no comparative advantage at autarky can create it by itself by expanding production and exporting outputs. To be consistent with competition, economies of scale must be based on Marshallian external economies which are external to the firm but internal to the industry. The production function of the individual firm is assumed to be shifted by the change of total output of the industry, i.e., (1) is replaced by

$$y_j = f_j(v_{j1}, v_{j2}, Y_j), \qquad \partial f_j / \partial Y_j > 0, \tag{7}$$

where f_j is linear homogeneous with respect to v_{j1} and v_{j2} and Y_j is the total output of the jth industry. Industrial production function (2) is similarly replaced by

$$Y_{ij} = f_j(V_{ij1}, V_{ij2}, Y_{ij}), \qquad \partial f_j/\partial Y_{ij} > 0, \qquad (8)$$

and (b) and (b') in definitions 1 and 2 should now read as
(b") $p_j^0 Y_{ij} - \Sigma_k w_{ik}^0 V_{ijk} (p_{ij}^1 Y_{ij} - \Sigma_k w_{ik}^1 V_{ijk})$ is maximized being subject to

$$Y_{ij} = f_j(V_{ij1}, V_{ij2}, Y_{ij}^0) \ (Y_{ij} = f_j(V_{ij1}, V_{ij2}, Y_{ij}^1)). \qquad (8')$$

The implication of (b") is that competitive firms pay no attention to the changes of industrial output caused by a change in their own individual output. This externality to the firm is rather easy to swallow. In our opinion, the difficulty lies in the fact that the economy is internal to the industry, though it is not so to the firm. Marshallian external economies are often explained by the improved organization of the industry, for example, the increased specialization of firms made possible by an enlargement in an industry as a whole.[12] However, there is no reason why such specialization is impossible from the beginning, i.e., when the scale of the industry is small, unless there is internal economy in the firm.[13] Therefore, the burden of the proof seems to be still placed on those who believe that competitive conditions could be reconciled with increasing returns. Fortunately, for our present purpose, it is not necessary to make the economy, which is external to the firm, internal to the industry. Since two industries are competing for the given amount of factors and the expansion of one industry implies the contraction of the other, the effect on the individual firm is the same if we consider the external diseconomy caused by the change of the output of the other industry instead of the internal economy of scale of the industry to which the firm belongs. Such external diseconomy between industries can be explained by the fact that two industries are competing for the free public resources, e.g., highways and other transportation services, training and education of labor, research and development activities, etc.

3.   If industries are under increasing returns to scale, there may exist a trade equilibrium defined by definition 1 (with (b) replaced by (b")), i.e., $X_{ij}^0 \neq Y_{ij}^0$, even if two countries are exactly alike.[14] However, gain from

[12] For example, Chipman [5], p. 744.
[13] Robinson [15], pp. 337–343.
[14] See section 5 below.

trade is not assured for each country, as is shown by Matthews and Kemp under rather stringent assumptions. This is seen, in terms of the proof of theorem 1, as follows.

If an industry is expanded in a trade equilibrium in comparison with its autarky state (the case of export industry), (6) is established since at trade equilibrium, given prices and industrial output, the profit of individual firms are being maximized subject to the production function $f_j(V_{ij1}, V_{ij2}, Y_{ij}^0)$ which is superior to the production function prevailing under autarky, i.e., $f_j(V_{ij1}, V_{ij2}, Y_{ij}^1)$. On the other hand, if an industry is contracted in a trade equilibrium in comparison with its autarky state (the case of import competing industry), (6) may not be obtained since the production function in a trade equilibrium is inferior to the one in autarky. If gains from trade do not exist, the lost economy of scale in the import competing industry is responsible. An easy consequence from this argument is:

Theorem 2. If as a result of trade industries subject to increasing returns to scale are expanding and industries under non-increasing returns are contracted, there exist gains from trade.[15])

It must be noted that no assumption is made about the shape of the transformation curve to demonstrate theorem 2.

Theorem 2 is concerned with a historically celebrated case of Graham and Tinbergen.[16]) Assuming the watch industry is under increasing returns and the wheat industry is under diminishing returns, Graham suggested that the expansion of the former and the constraction of the latter by trade restriction is favorable. Using figure 5.1, Tinbergen demonstrated that the expansion of the increasing return industry and contraction of the diminishing return industry by trade is favorable. The output of watches is measured horizontally and that of wheat, vertically. The transformation curve is *ab*. A trade equilibrium under incomplete specialization is such that the production is carried out at *g* and consumption, at *f* on the price line *gf* which is tangent to the curve *ab* at the point *g*. The point *f* is inferior to the point of autarky, *e*. On the other hand, a trade equilibrium under complete specialization in watches, the production point and consumption point being *b* and *d*, respectively, on the price line *bc*, is superior to the autarky point *e*.

---

[15]) See Kemp–Negishi [9], which is partly based on Negishi, T., 'Increasing returns, factor market distortions and trade,' mimeographed, University of New South Wales, 1967.
[16]) Graham [6], Tinbergen [18], appendix 1 and [19], appendix 2.

However, this argument of Tinbergen based on his much reproduced diagram[17]) is wrong in essentials. (1) It is constructed on the assumption that the price ratio (the slope of the price line) is equal to the ratio of marginal social costs (the slope of the transformation curve *ab*), which it clearly cannot be, since the marginal social cost is lower than the marginal private cost and therefore than the price in the increasing return industry. (2) The locus of the competitive outputs in the diagram, i.e., transformation curve *ab*, has a shape which is inconsistent with the assumption made about scale returns in the two industries.[18]) (3) The world prices of two commodities are assumed to be constant, since two price lines *gf* and *cb* are drawn parallel.

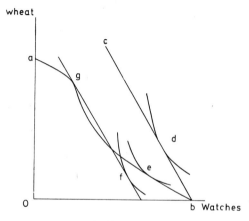

Fig. 5.1.

If the price is constant, however, the equilibrium of the increasing return industry is unstable.[19]) (4) While a country which specializes in the watch industry obtains trade gains, the rest of the world which specializes in wheat may not enjoy the gains from trade, to say nothing of the possibility that such a trade equilibrium does not exist. Our theorem 2 is free from (1), (2) and (3), but shares (4) with Tinbergen.

To assure trade gains for each country, we have to return to the case of increasing returns in all industries, and assume either:

---

[17]) Caves [4], p. 172, Bhagwati [3], p. 221.
[18]) Herberg–Kemp [7].
[19]) Adams–Wheeler [1].

Assumption 1.[20]) Suppose the ith country is specialized in the ith industry at trade equilibrium, i.e., $Y_{ij}^0 = V_{ijk}^0 = 0$, $i \neq j$. There exists the threshold level of the total output, $\bar{Y}_j$, for the external economy effect of the industry to individual firms, which is below the specialization level of production Y_{ij}^0 ($i = j$) but above the autarky level of production Y_{ij}^1, and (8) and (8′) are respectively replaced by

$$Y_{ij} = f_j(V_{ij1}, V_{ij2}, s), \quad \partial f_j/\partial s > 0, \quad s = \max(Y_{ij}, \bar{Y}_j), \tag{9}$$

$$Y_{ii} = f_i(V_{ii1}, V_{ii2}, Y_{ii}^0), \quad Y_{ij} = f_j(V_{ij1}, V_{ij2}, \bar{Y}_j), \quad i \neq j,$$

$$(Y_{ij} = f_j(V_{ij1}, V_{ij2}, \bar{Y}_j)). \tag{9′}$$

or, alternatively,

Assumption 2. Suppose the ith country is completely specialized in the ith industry at trade equilibrium. The external economies are irreversible in the sense that the economies already attained under autarky are not to be lost when the level of output is contracted in the trade equilibrium and (8) and (8′) in the above are raplaced by

$$Y_{ij} = f_j(V_{ij1}, V_{ij2}, s), \quad \partial f_j/\partial s > 0, \quad s = \max(Y_{ij}, Y_{ij}^1), \tag{10}$$

and

$$Y_{ii} = f_i(V_{ii1}, V_{ii2}, Y_{ii}^0), \quad Y_{ij} = f_j(V_{ij1}, V_{ij2}, Y_{ij}^1), \quad i \neq j,$$

$$(Y_{ij} = f_j(V_{ij1}, V_{ij2}, Y_{ij}^1)). \tag{10′}$$

In either case, we have

$$f_j(V_{ij1}, V_{ij2}, Y_{ij}^1) < f_j(V_{ij1}, V_{ij2}, Y_{ij}^0), \quad i = j,$$

$$f_j(V_{ij1}, V_{ij2}, Y_{ij}^1) = f_j(V_{ij1}, V_{ij2}^0, Y_{ij}^0), \quad i \neq j. \tag{11}$$

Then, we can easily prove

Theorem 3. Under assumption 1 or 2 (i.e., the assumption of the threshold or of the irreversibility), each country is better off in the trade equilibrium than in autarky.

---

[20]) The implication of this assumption is that the threshold is not insignificant relative to the total resources of the country. In other words, the country should be small, not in relation to the other country, but in relation to the threshold.

Proof.   The proof of theorem 1 can be applied since (6) is obtained from (b″) (with (8′) replaced by (9′) or (10′)) and (11), i.e., at the trade equilibrium, given prices and industrial output, the profits of individual firms are being maximized subject to the production function $f_j(V_{ij1}, V_{ij2}, Y_{ij}^0)$, which is, if $i = j$, superior to the production function prevailing under autarky, $f_j(V_{ij1}, V_{ij2}, Y_{ij}^1)$.

According to theorem 3, even if two countries are exactly alike, there are gains from international specialization and trade to both countries. It must be noted that this is true, irrespective of which country specializes in which industry. Therefore, with the introduction of the concept of the threshold and/or the irreversibility of external economies, the economies of scale due to Marshallian external economies can explain the gains from trade between similar countries. Furthermore, the above arguments apply even if the specialization is incomplete, provided, in the case of threshold, that one industry is above and the other industry is below the threshold level of production at trade equilibrium.

4.   Theorems 2 and 3 demonstrate gains from trade by assuming some restrictions on the production side of the economy. Our next task is, on the other hand, to demonstrate gains from trade between similar countries by imposing restrictions on the taste or consumption side of the economy. Suppose two countries are identical with respect to factor endowments, i.e., $\overline{V}_{ik} = \overline{V}_k$. Let us define the ratio of autarky factor input t_j and the ratio of autarky output s_j $(j = 1, 2)$ as follows.

Definition 3.   The ratio of autarky factor input t_j is defined by

$$Y_{ij}^1 (= Y_{1j}^1 = Y_{2j}^1) = f_j(t_j \overline{V}_1, t_j \overline{V}_2, Y_{ij}^1), \tag{12}$$

i.e., t_j is the ratio of factor inputs needed to produce the autarky level of output in the jth industry Y_{ij}^1 to the total factor endowments when the factor intensity V_{ij1}/V_{ij2} is hypothetically equalized to the factor endowments ratio $\overline{V}_1/\overline{V}_2$.

Definition 4.   Suppose the ith country is completely specialized in the ith industry at trade equilibrium. The ratio of autarky output s_j is defined as

$$s_j = Y_{ij}^1/f_j(\overline{V}_1, \overline{V}_2, Y_{ij}^0) = Y_{ij}^1/Y_{ij}^0, \quad i = j, \tag{13}$$

i.e., s_j is the ratio of the levels of the autarky output and of the output in the completely specialized trade equilibrium.

Given the autarky equilibrium, t_j is constant while s_j is smaller as the degree of increasing returns to scale beyond the autarky level is stronger.

The figure 5.2, which is a box diagram of the factor endowments with isoquants of the jth industry, explains the ratios t_j and s_j. Looking from the origin O, the point A is the point of autarky of the jth industry and t_j is the ratio of Oa and OO' which is larger than $s_j = Y_{ij}^1/Y_{ij}^0$, since the industry is operating under increasing returns to scale. Looking from the

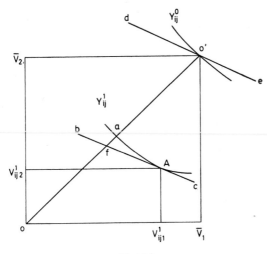

Fig. 5.2.

origin O', A is also the autarky point of the other industry. The slope of the parallel lines bc and de represents the ratio of factor prices in autarky situation. Since individual production functions are linear homogeneous with respect to factor inputs, the value of the output is exhaustively distributed to factors. Therefore the line bc represents the value expended on the jth commodity while the line de represents the value of the total factor income at autarky. The marginal propensity to consume the jth commodity at autarky, m_j, is the ratio of fO to OO', if the social income-consumption curve is a straight line through the origin. In such a case, m_j is generally not larger than t_j. Now we are ready to state

Assumption 3. The social income-consumption curve is a straight line through the origin.[21]

---

[21] This implies that the corresponding utility function is positive homogeneous. See assumption 3 in chapter 3.

Assumption 4.   The marginal propensity to consume the jth commodity at trade equilibrium m_j^* satisfies

$$s_i < m_j^* < 1 - s_j, \quad i, j = 1, 2, \quad i \neq j. \tag{14}$$

and

Assumption 5.   The degree of increasing returns to scale is strong relative to the industrial difference in factor intensities and the elasticity of factor substitution in the sense that $t_j - s_j \ (>0)$ is larger than $t_j - m_j \ (\geq 0)$.

The non-vacuousness of assumption 4 is assured by assumption 5. Since assumption 4 implies that $1 - (1 + m_i^* - s_i)/2 < m_j^* < (1 + m_j^* - s_j)/2, m_1 = m_1^* = 1/2$ satisfies assumption 4 if assumption 5 is made. Assumption 5 is innocent if there is no industrial difference in factor intensities or if two factors are perfectly substitutable, so that $t_j = m_j$.

Then we have

Theorem 4.   Suppose two countries are exactly identical with respect to taste and factor endowments and each country is completely specialized in a different industry. Then, under assumptions 3, 4 and 5 there exist trade gains for each country if each industry is subject to increasing returns to scale, i.e., (b) and (b′) in definitions 1 and 2 are replaced by (b″).

Proof.   Suppose $p_1^1/p_2^1 < p_1^0/p_2^0$ and the first country is better off than the second at a trade quilibrium.[22] Let us first consider the case where a country specialized in a commodity whose relative price is raised by trade can enjoy higher real income, i.e., the first (second) country is specialized in the first (second) commodity. If the second country, the country with the lower real income at a trade equilibrium is worse off than at autarky, we have a situation shown as in figure 5.3. Autarky point is A, trade equilibrium of the ith country is T_i, respectively on higher and lower indifference curves. The movement from A to T_i can be divided into the movement AT_i' on Engel curve OE due to income effect and the movement $T_i' T_i$ on indifference curve due to the substitution effect. Clearly, the substitution effect in both countries is to decrease the demand for the first commodity and so is the income effect in the second country. Therefore, the change in the demand

---

[22] Since autrarky prices of two countries are identical, p_{ij}^1 is denoted by p_j^1.

for the first commodity caused by the trade ΔD_1, which must be equal to that in the supply ΔS_1, is smaller than the change in the first country,

$$\Delta S_1 = Y_{11}^0 - 2Y_{11}^1 = \Delta D_1 < m_1^* Y_{11}^0 - m_1 Y_{11}^1 - m_1 (p_2^1/p_1^1) Y_{12}^1, \qquad (15)$$

where use is made of assumption 3 and the fact that $Y_{11}^1 = Y_{21}^1$. From the definition of m_1,

$$Y_{11}^1 = m_1 (Y_{11}^1 + (p_2^1/p_1^1) Y_{12}^1). \qquad (16)$$

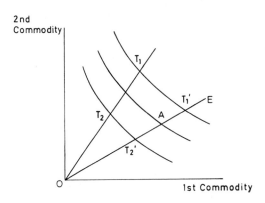

Fig. 5.3.

Therefore, (15) is reduced to $Y_{11}^0 - Y_{11}^1 < m_1^* Y_{11}^0$, and to

$$1 - s_1 < m_1^* \qquad (17)$$

by using definition 4. By changing the role of two commodities, we have similarly

$$1 - s_2 < m_2^* = 1 - m_1^*. \qquad (18)$$

Either (17) or (18) is necessary for the second country, i.e., the country relatively worse off at a trade equilibrium than the other, to be worse off at a trade equilibrium than at autarky. However, both (17) and (18) contradict assumption 4. Therefore, in this case two countries are better off at a trade equilibrium than at autarky. Let us next consider the case where a country with higher real income is specialized in a commodity whose relative price is lowered by trade, i.e., the first (second) country is specialized in the second (first) commodity, still assuming $p_1^1/p_2^1 < p_1^0/p_2^0$. In this case, both countries can enjoy the trade gains. Suppose not. Then the second country must be worse off at a trade equilibrium than at autarky. In figure 3, the value of T_2 evaluated by the relative price p_1^0/p_2^0 is smaller than the value of A. From (c') in definition 2,

$$p_1^0 X_{21}^0 + p_2^0 X_{22}^0 < p_1^0 Y_{21}^1 + p_2^0 Y_{22}^1. \tag{19}$$

This is reduced by using (3) to

$$p_1^0 Y_{21}^0 < p_1^0 Y_{21}^1 + p_2^0 Y_{22}^1. \tag{20}$$

Since $p_1^1/p_2^1 < p_1^0/p_2^0$, we have from (20)

$$p_1^1 Y_{21}^0 < p_1^1 Y_{21}^1 + p_2^1 Y_{21}^1. \tag{21}$$

On the other hand, from definition 4 and (c') in definition 2, we have

$$p_1^1 Y_{21}^0 = p_1^1 Y_{21}^1/s_1 = (p_1^1 Y_{12}^1 + p_2^1 Y_{21}^1) m_1/s_1. \tag{22}$$

Jointly from (21) and (22) it follows

$$m_1 < s_1, \tag{23}$$

which is in contradiction with assumption 5.

5. The above demonstrations of the gains from trade under increasing returns to scale are of course subject to the existence of a trade equilibrium. However, before demonstrating the existence of a trade equilibrium, something must be said on the existence of the autarky equilibrium, since a straightforward application of the existence theorem developed in chapter 1 is impossible when economies of scale exist and the feasible set of total production is not convex. Fortunately the argument is rather simple, since the feasible set of individual production is convex in the case of economies of scale due to external economy.

Theorem 5. There exists an autarky equilibrium as defined in definition 2 (with (b') replaced by (b'')) if the usual assumptions on utility and individual production functions are satisfied except for the assumption concerning external effects between individual productive activities.[23]

---

[23] See assumptions 1 and 2 in chapter 1.

A sketch of Proof. Let us denote by $\bar{Y}_j$ the maximum possible output of the jth commodity under the given amount of factors, $\bar{V}_{i1}, \bar{V}_{i2}$. For any given amount of industrial output Y_j such that $0 \leq Y_j \leq \bar{Y}_j$ $(j = 1, 2)$, consider the individual production function (7) in inequality form $y_j \leq f_j$ (v_{j1}, v_{j2}, Y_j) and its aggregation

$$Y_{ij} \leq f_j(V_{ij1}, V_{ij2}, Y_j), \qquad j = 1, 2. \tag{24}$$

If we consider the maximization of $U_i(X_i)$ subject to (24) and inequality version of (c') in definition 2, i.e., $X_{ij} \leq Y_{ij}$, $\Sigma_j V_{ijk} \leq \bar{V}_{ik}$, $j, k = 1, 2$, we have a degenerate case of the existence theorem in chapter 1 and the constrained maximum is an autarky equilibrium, provided that $Y_{ij} = Y_j$. By considering a fixed point of the mapping from Y_1, Y_2 to Y_{i1}, Y_{i2} which also satisfy $0 \leq Y_{ij} \leq \bar{Y}_j$, we can demonstrate the existence of an autarky equilibrium.

To demonstrate the existence of a trade equilibrium, we need, in addition to assumption 3, the following assumptions.

Assumption 6. The social utility of each commodity is not satiated, i.e., $\partial U_i/\partial X_{ij} > 0$ for all i and j.

Assumption 7. The external economy is neutral for factor inputs,[24] i.e., industrial production function (8) is written in the form of

$$Y_{ij} = g_j(Y_{ij})f_j(V_{ij1}, V_{ij2}) \tag{25}$$

and the severity of the external effect is equal in both industries at the output level of complete specialization in the sense that $\bar{Y}_{i1}/\bar{Y}_{i2} = \bar{\bar{Y}}_{i1}/\bar{\bar{Y}}_{i2}$, where $\bar{Y}_{ij}$ (output at complete specialization without external economy) satisfies $\bar{Y}_{ij} = f_j(\bar{V}_{i1}, \bar{V}_{i2})$ and $\bar{\bar{Y}}_{ij}$ (output at complete specialization with external economy) is obtained from $\bar{\bar{Y}}_{ij} = g_j(\bar{Y}_{ij}) \bar{Y}_{ij}$.

Theorem 6. Under assumptions 3, 6 and 7, there exists a trade equilibrium defined in definition 1 (with (b) replaced by (b″)) where each similar country is completely specialized in a different commodity, provided the effect of the external economy is sufficiently strong.

Proof. Without loss of generality, let us assume that the ith country is specialized in the ith commodity. Consider a competitive pure exchange

[24] Kemp [8], pp. 127–8.

between two countries, each having $\overline{Y}_{ii}$ amount of the commodity defined in assumption 7. Because of assumption 6, the box-diagram analysis gives us a finite positive relative price p_1/p_2. Let us make the second commodity numeraire, i.e., $p_2 = 1$. Then, w_{1k}, w_{2k} corresponding to $\overline{Y}_{11}, \overline{Y}_{22}$ are obtained from

$$w_{1k} = p_1 g_1 (Y_{11}) \partial f_1 (\overline{V}_{11}, \overline{V}_{12}) / \partial V_{11k}$$
$$w_{2k} = g_2 (Y_{22}) \partial f_2 (\overline{V}_{21}, \overline{V}_{22}) / \partial V_{22k} \tag{26}$$

by assuming $g_1 = g_2 = 1$.

The condition of non-profitability (i.e., the unit cost is higher than the price) of the production of the jth commodihy in the ith country $(i \neq j)$ when the level of industrial output is zero is

$$\min_{V_{12k}} \{\textstyle\sum_k w_{1k} V_{12k} / g_2(0) f_2 (V_{121}, V_{122})\} > 1$$
$$\min_{V_{21k}} \{\textstyle\sum_k w_{2k} V_{21k} / g_1(0) f_1 (V_{211}, V_{222})\} > p_1, \tag{27}$$

when $g_1 = g_2 = 1$, i.e., at w_{1k}, w_{2k} corresponding to $\overline{Y}_{11}, \overline{Y}_{22}$, (27) may not be satisfied. Now consider $\overline{Y}_{11}, \overline{Y}_{22}$ defined in assumption 7. Because of assumption 7, p_1 (with $p_2 = 1$) in the pure exchange is unchanged when $\overline{Y}_{11}, \overline{Y}_{22}$ are replaced by $\overline{\overline{Y}}_{11}, \overline{\overline{Y}}_{22}$. Since w_{1k}, w_{2k} corresponding to $\overline{\overline{Y}}_{11}, \overline{\overline{Y}}_{22}$ are in proportion to $g_1(\overline{\overline{Y}}_{11}), g_2(\overline{\overline{Y}}_{22})$ from (26), (27) is satisfied if $g_1(\overline{\overline{Y}}_{11})$ and $g_2(\overline{\overline{Y}}_{22})$ are sufficiently large. Then it is easy to see that the conditions in definition 1 (with (b) replaced by (b")) are satisfied from (26) (with Y_{11} and Y_{22}), (27) and the fact that p_1 (with $p_2 = 1$) is obtained in the pure exchange between two countries, when the ith country is specialized in the ith commodity.

References

[1] Adams, R.W. and J.T. Wheeler, 'External economies and the falling supply curve,' *Review of Economic Studies*, 20 (1951), 24–39.
[2] Anderson, K.L., 'Tariff protection and increasing returns,' *Exploration in Economics* (in honor of Professor Taussig), McGraw-Hill, 1936, 157–168.
[3] Bhagwati, J., 'The pure theory of international trade: a survey,' *Surveys of Economic Theory*, 2, Macmillan and St. Martin's, 1965, 156–239.
[4] Caves, R.E., *Trade and economic structure*, Harvard University Press, 1963.
[5] Chipman, J.S., 'A survey of the theory of international trade, 2, The Neo-Classical Theory,' *Econometrica*, 33 (1965), 685–760.

[6] Graham, F.D., 'Some aspects of protection further considered,' *Quarterly Journal of Economics*, 37 (1923), 199–227.

[7] Herberg, H. and M.C. Kemp, 'Some implications of variable returns to scale,' *Canadian Journal of Economics*, 2 (1969), 403–415.

[8] Kemp, M.C., *The pure theory of international trade*, Prentice-Hall, 1964.

[9] Kemp, M.C. and T. Negishi, 'Variable returns to scale, commodity taxes, and their implications for trade gains,' *Swedish Journal of Economics*, 72 (1970), 1–11.

[10] Kojima, K., *EEC no Keizaigaku* (Economics of EEC), Nihonhyoron, 1962.

[11] Leontief, W.W., 'The use of indifference curves in the analysis of foreign trade,' *Quarterly Journal of Economics*, 47 (1933), 493–503 (Ellis and Metzler, ed., *Readings in the theory of international trade*, Blakiston, 1949, 229–238).

[12] Matthews, R.C.O., 'Reciprocal demand and increasing returns,' *Review of Economic Studies*, 17 (1949–50), 149–158.

[13] Negishi, T., 'Marshallian external economies and gains from trade between similar countries,' *Review of Economic Studies*, 36 (1969), 131–135.

[14] Ohlin, B., *Interregional and international trade*, Harvard University Press, 1933.

[15] Robinson, *The economics of imperfect competition*, Macmillan, 1933.

[16] Samuelson, P.A., 'The gains from international trade,' *Canadian Journal of Economics and Political Science*, 5 (1939), 195–205. (Ellis and Metzler ed., *Readings in the theory of international trade*, Blakiston, 1949, 239–52).

[17] Sraffa, P., 'The laws of returns under competitive conditions,' *Economic Journal*, 36 (1926), 535–550. (Stigler and Boulding ed., *Readings in price theory*, Irwin, 1952, 180–197).

[18] Tinbergen, J., *International economic cooperation*, Elsevier, 1945.

[19] Tinbergen, J., *International economic integration*, Elsevier, 1954.

CHAPTER 6

Dynamic internal economies and protection of the infant industry

1. The so-called infant industry dogma (arguments for a tariff aiming at the protection of an infant industry) has a long history and has been generally accepted by international trade theorists. According to Samuelson, it is the only serious exception among the mostly shallow economic arguments for tariff protection. However, since the critical survey by Kemp [2], [3], of the proposed tests as to whether an industry (or a firm) should be protected in its infancy or not, the argument seems to have lost most of its special *ad hoc* flavor and to have been regarded merely as one kind of external economies phenomenon so common in economics. However, the conclusion from our analysis is different. There are cases in which the classical infant industry dogma is still valid and in which interference with the competitive allocation, i.e., the protection of infant industries is desirable even if no external effects are present.[1])

The first of the tests proposed by Kemp derives from Mill, to the effect that protection should be confined to cases in which there are grounds for believing that the industry will, after a time, be able to dispense with it, i.e., that the industry can be expected to be profitable in the future. Of course, there may be cases in which profitability can never be expected even under an optimal price system (i.e., marginal cost prices if no externality exists), since the static average cost is falling, and yet permanent protection is necessary. However, the essence of the infant industry dogma is the temporary protection of an industry for the period of learning by doing. Mill's test is nothing but the definition of infant protection, which is to be distinguished from the protection of increasing return industries in general. The second test proposed by Kemp is that of Bastable, i.e., the future gain obtained by the matured industry should be sufficiently large to compensate

---

[1]) This chapter is based on Negishi [7]. It is an application of the theory developed by Debreu [1]. See also Negishi [6] and chapter 3.

for costs incurred in the protected learning period when a suitable time discount is applied. It is by no means clear whether 'future gain' includes only the profit accruing in the industry or whether in addition it takes account of consumers' surplus.[2]) However, the difference is very important as will be discussed below. Finally, Kemp criticizes the Mill–Bastable dogma which insists that the industry should be protected if it has passed Mill's and Bastable's tests. Kemp argues that, even if these two tests are passed, protection is not required in the case of dynamic internal economies, i.e., when only the firm that actually carries on production gains in experience so that the accumulating knowledge becomes the exclusive property of that firm. The reason is that the private incentive to undertake investment in the learning period is sufficient, since losses of the unprotected firm in its learning period are more than offset by the profits it enjoys later (i.e., Bastable's test). Therefore the third or Kemp's test is necessary, i.e., the existence of the dynamic external economies, with non-appropriable knowledge and experience which can be tapped by any newcomer.

If Bastable's test is interpreted in terms only of the profitability of the private firm in the long run, its significance from the point of view of welfare economics will be lost. There may be a case which does not pass this interpretation of Bastable's test but is still socially useful and should be protected. On the other hand, if Bastable's test is understood in terms of increases in social welfare in some sense, then it by no means requires private profitability and Kemp's test is not necessary (though sufficient) for protection.

Meade [5] reaches the same conclusion as Kemp as to the unlikelihood of the need for protection, by arguing that the growth of an infant industry as such does not necessarily imply the existence of external effects and/or indivisible factors of production.[3]) However, it will be shown below that the growth of an infant industry implies, by definition, the existence of something like an indivisible factor of production. The traditional infant industry dogma will be defended from the point of view of the intertemporally optimal allocation of resources, i.e., protection may be necessary even if no external effects exist. The reason lies in the existence of the dynamic internal economies, specifically in the indivisibility which is inherent in the learning process of infant industries.

---

[2]) Kemp seems to adopt the former interpretation in [3] and for the case of monopoly in [2]. It is not clear which interpretation is adopted in the case of the competitive firm in [2].

[3]) See Meade [5], 255–6.

2.   As Kindleberger [4] has justly emphasized, the infant industry dogma is primarily concerned with the optimal allocation of world resources.[4])

Our model assumes that the infant industry cannot at present compete with foreign mature industries, since its cost is too high in comparison with the current price of its product in the international market. However, it is possible that in the future the cost curve will be lower and the industry profitable, provided it produces some output (at a loss) at present. This is the learning process of the industry. If the level of activity at present is nil, then there can be no shift in the cost curve and no profit in the future. The higher the level of activity in the present, the larger will be the shift in the cost curve and the greater profitability of the industry in the future. Unless the industry is just at the point of break-even from the beginning, there must be a certain minimum activity level and therefore a minimum loss to be incurred in the present which is necessary for profitability in the future. Therefore, for any industry which passes Mill's test (profitability in the future), this minimum cost in the present is a sort of indivisible factor of production which is the reason for the dynamic internal economy. Particularly from the point of view of production in the future, it is a fixed or overhead cost by which the falling part of the average cost curve is explained.

Consider a two-period model of the world economy, x and x^* being respectively the world consumption vector of commodities in the first period (the present) and in the second period (the future). For example, if there exist m commodities and the amount of consumption of the ith commodity is x_i, then $x = (x_1, \ldots, x_i, \ldots, x_m)$. The world indifference map of two-period consumption vectors (x, x^*) is assumed to exist, with indifference surfaces being convex to the origin. Next consider the world vector of input and output (y, y^*), which does not include the input–output of the infant industry in question, where y refers to the present and y^* to the future, and where the ith component of each vector signifies the output (input) of the ith commodity if it is positive (negative).

The technologically possible set of (y, y^*) is denoted by Y, which is assumed to be closed and convex.

---

[4]) However, the arguments below can be applied to the analysis from the point of view of a single country, provided the foreign offer curve with the optimal tariff imposed is interpreted as a kind of input–output relation.

Suppose the infant industry does not exist and competition prevails in the world (resources are optimally allocated). We have at equilibrium

$$x - y - c = 0$$
$$x^* - y^* - c^* = 0,$$

where c and c^* are vectors of initial resources in the present and future. Let $\bar{p}$ and $\bar{p}^*$ be price vectors in the present and future. The rate of interest is implicitly difined by the price system $(\bar{p}, \bar{p}^*)$. Denote the set of commodity vectors preferred or indifferent to (x, x^*) by U and define Z as $U - Y$. Z is a set of vectors of initial resources which make consumption preferred or indifferent to (x, x^*) possible if production is carried on properly. From the equilibrium conditions of consumption and production, we have $\bar{p}'c + \bar{p}^{*'}c \leq \bar{p}'z + \bar{p}^{*'}z^*$ for any $(z, z^*) \in Z$, the inequality being strong if Z is strongly convex.

The model of the infant industry is as follows. The industry produces the first commodity and q and q^* are input–output vectors of this industry in the present and future. In particular, $q_1 \geq 0$ and $q_1^* \geq 0$. The set of possible q is Q, and that of q^* is $Q^*(q_1)$, which signifies the shift of the production function in the future caused by the existence of production in the present. If $q_1 = 0$, then Q and Q^* coincide, and if $q_1' > q_1$ then $Q^*(q_1') \supset Q^*(q_1)$. To exclude static increasing returns, Q is assumed to be closed, convex and such that $0 \in Q$, and Q^* is also assumed to be closed, convex and that $0 \in Q^*$ for any given q_1.[5] It is also assumed that external effects, static or dynamic, do not exist at all. Therefore there is no need to distinguish the industry and the firm.

Since this industry is in its infancy and cannot compete with foreign industries, the maximum of $\bar{p}'q$ $(q \in Q)$ and that of $\bar{p}^{*'}q^*$ $(q^* \in Q^*(0))$ are zero for the prices $(\bar{p}, \bar{p}^*)$ which are established when this industry does not exist. Moreover, we assume that there exists $\bar{q}_1 > 0$ such that max $\bar{p}^{*'}q^* > 0$ if $q_1 > \bar{q}_1$ and max $\bar{p}^{*'}q^* = 0$ if $q_1 \leq \bar{q}_1$. This means there is a finite cost differential between the infant industry and its foreign competitors. In other words, the marginal cost of the first good is definitely higher than $\bar{p}_1^*$, when $q_1 = q_1^* = 0$.

3. We do not insist that all infant industries should be protected. Then, we have to ask under what circumstances an infant industry should, or should not, be protected. The problem is to devise tests the passing of which is either necessary or sufficient to justify protection. Suppose current prices

---

[5] The set of possible (q, q^*) need not be convex, since dynamic increasing returns are the essence of the infant industry dogma.

and expected prices in the future, including international prices of products as well as domestic prices of factors, remain unchanged in the course of the growth of an infant industry. Actually, the price of the product would fall and factor prices would rise as a result of the growth of the industry. Therefore, such unchanged prices are more favorable for the industry than prices which would actually prevail in the course of its growth. If the expected profit of an industry in the future (properly discounted) falls short of the loss incurred in the present when calculated on the basis of the favorable assumption of unchanged prices, then it can be shown that such an industry should not be protected. Conversely, for the protection to be justified, it is necessary (but not sufficient) that, considered together, the present and future activities of the industry should prove profitable at prices which would prevail in the absence of such activities.

The input–output of the industry in the present and future are q and q^*. Then, the resources available to consumers and other industries change from c and c^* to $z = c + q$ and $z^* = c^* + q^*$. If $(z, z^*) \in Z$, then such a change is not undesirable, and if it belongs to the inner points of Z then the change is preferable. As is mentioned above, if $(z, z^*) \in Z$, then $\bar{p}'z + \bar{p}^{*\prime}z^* \geq \bar{p}'c + \bar{p}^{*\prime}c^*$, and $\bar{p}'q + \bar{p}^{*\prime}q^* \geq 0$. If Z is strongly convex, we have $\bar{p}'q + \bar{p}^{*\prime}q^* > 0$. Therefore, if the growth of the infant industry is desirable, the industry must be profitable in the long run under the assumption that prices p and p^* are not changed by the growth of the industry.

Thus our test 1 is $\max(\bar{p}'q + \bar{p}^{*\prime}q^*) > 0$, being subject to the given prices p and p^* and the technological restriction $q \in Q$, $q^* \in Q^*(q_1)$. Of course, this is a necessary but not a sufficient condition for the desirability of the growth of the infant industry. If the industry fails to pass this test, there is no need to go further.

From the assumptions about the infant industry the maximum of $\bar{p}'q$ under $q \in Q$ is zero. Therefore, $\bar{p}'q + \bar{p}^{*\prime}q^* > 0$, $q \in Q$ and $q^* \in Q^*(q_1)$ implies $\bar{p}^{*\prime}q^* > 0$, which in turn implies $q_1 > \bar{q}_1$, again from the assumptions. If the infant industry is to develop, i.e., if $(c + q, c^* + q^*) \in Z$ then there is a certain minimum scale of production in the period of its infancy.[6])

Suppose that our infant industry has passed test 1. This does not necessarily imply the possibility of private profitability in the industry and of its growth without protection. Since prices are changed by the growth

---

[6]) This implies the necessity of the existence of some indivisible factor of production for the growth of the infant industry. The arguments below are based on the possibility of diminishing cost due to the existence of such a factor.

of the infant industry, test 1 does not assure the realization of positive profit in the industry. Entrepreneurs in the infant industry make their decisions deliberately, taking account of their expectations of price changes. Assuming that their expectation are valid, let us consider the situation prevailing after the industry has grown up.

4. If the loss incurred in the present is weighed against the profit available in the future (taking account of the proper discount factor) and the latter is larger than the former, then, as is emphasized by Meade and Kemp, there is no need for an industry to be protected, since the growth of the industry is profitable as a private investment project. However, even if the former is larger than the latter and the growth of an industry is not profitable as a private investment project, there still remains the possibility of the social desirability, and therefore the need for the protection of such an industry, provided there exists a minimum loss in the present which is necessary for the profitability in the future. This is the essence of the infant industry protection based on the dynamic internal economy. Suppose that the infant industry has actually grown up and that world resources are optimally allocated under the restrictions $(y, y^*) \in Y, q \in Q, q^* \in Q^*(q_1)$ and $q_1 \geq \bar{q}_1$.[7]) That is, a point (x, x^*) is chosen on the indifference surface which is most preferred under the restriction $x - y - q - c = 0, x^* - y^* - q^* - c^* = 0$.

Suppose also that such an optimal situation is achieved by the competitive price system with the protection of the infant industry, if necessary. Then $p'y + p^{*\prime}y^*$ is maximized with respect to $(y, y^*) \in Y$ under the given prices (p, p^*) and $p'q + p^{*\prime}q^*$ is maximized under the restrictions $q \in Q, q^* \in Q^*(q_1)$, $q_1 > \bar{q}_1$ and given prices. If we define the set of consumption vectors preferred or indifferent to (x, x^*) as U and $U - Y$ as Z, then Z is the set of commodity vectors preferred or indifferent to $(c + q, c^* + q^*)$ for consumers and industries other than the infant industry. From the conditions of competitive equilibrium, if $(z, z^*) \in Z$, then $p'z + p^{*\prime}z^* \geq p'(c + q) + p^{*\prime}(c^* + q^*)$, the inequality being strong if Z is strongly convex. In what follows, strong convexity is assumed. Now we can consider whether or not we should have allowed the infant industry to grow. For this purpose, compare (c, c^*), which would have been available to consumers and to the other industries if the infant industry had not been developed, with $(c + q, c^* + q^*)$, which would have been available to them as the result of the growth of the infant industry. If $(c, c^*) \in Z$, then we should not have fostered the infant industry.

---

[7]) Since our industry has passed test 1, there is no possibility of $q_1 \leq \bar{q}_1$.

In such a case, we have $0 > p'q + p^{*'}q^*$. Therefore, the growth of the infant industry is justified if $p'q + p^{*'}q^* \geqq 0$, i.e., if it is profitable in the long run.

We assume that our infant industry has passed Mill's test, i.e., $p^{*'}q^* \geqq 0$. If, in addition to this, $p'q > 0$, then our industry should be developed and, moreover, it could have grown without any protection, since it is profitable as a private undertaking. By definition, however, such an industry is not an infant industry.

Thus the typical cases of the infant industry are such that $p'q < 0$ and $p^{*'}q^* \geqq 0$, the long run profit $p'q + p^{*'}q^*$ being either positive or negative. If it is positive, the industry should be fostered, but it could have grown by itself without any protection. This is the case emphasized by Kemp and Meade, with Bastable's test being interpreted as $p'q + p^{*'}q^* > 0$.

However, the converse is not true; even if the infant industry should be developed (i.e., $(c, c^*) \notin Z$), there is a possibility that $p'q + p^{*'}q^* < 0$. (It should be noted that $q_1 > \bar{q}_1$ even in such a case, since Mill's test is passed.) Then, the industry cannot grow without protection. The loss accruing under the competitive price system must be compensated by the subsidy.

5.   Since our test 1 is merely a necessary condition, we need a further test to know wether or not an industry which passes test 1 needs to be protected. Suppose there is a perfect foresight as regards present and future prices that will prevail when an infant industry grows up. Then it can be shown that the protection of an industry may be justified even if present and future activities of the industry, considered together, fail to be profitable at these prices. A test to detect such cases is as follows. The protection of an infant industry is justified, if the loss involved in the growth of the industry at prices actually prevailing in the course of its growth is no greater than a certain amount which also depends on such prices and on changes in the activities of other industries caused by the growth of the industry. In other words, a maximum amount which can safely be paid for the protection of an industry is calculated on the basis of data that, in principle, can be observed or estimated.

Let the consumption vector available when there was no infant industry be denoted by $(\bar{x}, \bar{x}^*)$, and that available when the infant industry is allowed to grow by (x, x^*). The set of vectors indifferent or preferred to (x, x^*) is denoted by U. A sufficient condition for $(\bar{x}, \bar{x}^*) \notin U$ is $p'x + p^{*'}x^* > p'\bar{x} + p^{*'}\bar{x}^*$, where (p, p^*) is the price system when the infant industry is fostered. By the use of equalities of supply and demand, this can be rewritten as $p'(\bar{y} + c) + p^{*'}(\bar{y}^* + c^*) < p'(q + y + c) + p^{*'}(q^* + y^* + c^*)$, where $(\bar{y}, \bar{y}^*)$ and (y, y^*) are respectively the input–output vector of other industries in the absence of an infant industry and the input–output vector of other industries when an infant industry is involved. Therefore, our second test is $p'(y - \bar{y}) + p^{*\prime}(y^* - \bar{y}^*) > -p'q - p^{*\prime}q^*$. In other words, the infant industry should be promoted by protection if its loss is less than $p'(y - \bar{y}) + p^{*\prime}(y^* - \bar{y}^*)$. This test 2 is, in contrast to test 1, a sufficient condition.

If we cannot apply this test to all the industries in the world, we can still apply it to a part of them, e.g., to industries located in the same country as the infant industry in question. If our infant industry passes such a partial test, surely it must pass the original test 2.

It is desirable to protect an industry which passes test 2. Since (p, p^*) is a system of optimal prices, protection needs to be carried out in such a way that no price is changed by protection.

Suppose the consumers and other industries are competitive while the infant industry enjoys a monopolistic profit. We can then argue in the same way as above that such an economic system is not optimal, but superior to the system without the infant industry. Therefore, such an infant industry should be developed. This is our test 3.

6. Let us consider the protection of an infant industry by means of an import tariff. The optimal allocation of resources is not achieved in such a case. But there still is a possibility of a second best situation in that it is better than the situation which would prevail if the infant industry were not fostered.

If the world economy is competitive in other respects, we can apply our arguments above to the case with an import tariff, by differentiating a protected commodity according to its location, i.e., domestic or foreign to the tariff imposing country. The set of the tariff-imposing country's consumption vectors which are indifferent or preferred to its consumption when its infant industry is protected is denoted by U_1. The corresponding set for other countries, when the infant industry is protected in the first country, is denoted by U_2. U is defined as $U_1 + U_2$. The possible set of the first country's input–output vectors of industries other than the infant one is denoted by Y_1. The corresponding set for other countries is denoted by Y_2 and Y is defined as $Y_1 + Y_2$. The import from other countries by the first country of the commodity which is physically the same as the product of its protected infant industry is considered as a sort of input–output relation and denoted, respectively in the present and future, by m and m^*. If the infant industry produces commodity 1 and the same commodity in other countries is denoted as commodity 0, then $m = (m_0, m_1, 0, ..., 0)$, and $m^* = (m_0^*, m_1^*, 0, ..., 0)$, where $m_0 \leqq 0$, $m_1 \geqq 0$, $-m_0 = m_1$, $-m_0^* = m_1^*$. There is a possibility of export in the future for the infant industry. When the infant industry is nurtured by tariff protection, then $p_0 < p_1$ in the present because of the tariff but $p_0^* = p_1^*$ in the future when the industry will have matured and the tariff will have been abolished. The tariff revenue in the present is $(p_1 - p_0)m_1$. The indifference map of countries is assumed to be the same if the same commodity is properly labeled commodity 0 or commodity 1, according to its location. Moreover, we assume that the Engel curves (income consumption curves) are straight lines through the origin. Then competitive equilibrium prices, and therefore input–output, are independent of the international distribution of income. This is the condition for the existence of a consistent indifference map for the world as a whole.

 The optimal consumption vector of the world is denoted by $(\bar{x}, \bar{x}^*)$ in the situation which prevails if there is no tariff and no infant industry. On our assumptions this remains unchanged if the international distribution of income is changed. If $(\bar{x}, \bar{x}^*)$ does not belong to U, then the protection of the infant industry can be justified. Consumers and other industries being assumed to be competitive, a sufficient condition for $(\bar{x}, \bar{x}^*) \notin U$ is $p'x + p^{*\prime}x^* \geqq p'\bar{x} + p^{*\prime}\bar{x}^*$. This is reduced to $p'q + p^{*\prime}q^* + p(m - \bar{m}) > 0$, by the use of equalities $x - y - q - m - c = 0$, $x^* - y^* - q^* - m^* - c^* = 0$, equilibrium conditions which prevail if there is no protective tariff. i.e., $\bar{x} - \bar{y} - \bar{m} - \bar{c} = 0$, $\bar{x}^* - \bar{y}^* - \bar{m}^* - \bar{c}^* = 0$, $p'(y - \bar{y}) \geqq 0$, $p^{*\prime}(y_1^* - \bar{y}_0^*) \geqq 0$ and $p^{*\prime}m^* = p^{*\prime}m^* = 0$, which is obtained from the assumption $p_1^* = p_0^*$. The profit of the protected industry, adjusted for the change in imports caused by the tariff, should therefore be positive. Since the export activity m is not profit maximizing, we do not have $p'(m - \bar{m}) > 0$.[8] It might instead be negative since the import is likely to be reduced by the tariff. This test 4 is similar to test 3. If the test is passed, the protective tariff, though not optimal, turned out to be better than laissez-faire.[9]

References

[1] Debreu, G., 'The coefficient of resource utilization,' *Econometrica*, 19 (1951), pp. 273–292.

[8] m and m^* are equilibrators which correspond to conditions when a tariff is imposed $(p_0 \neq p_1)$ or abolished $(p_0^* = p_1^*)$.
[9] See Negishi [7] for a heuristic partial equilibrium analysis in terms of consumers' surplus.

[2] Kemp, M.C., 'The Mill–Bastable infant industry dogma,' *Journal of Political Economy*, 63 (1960), pp. 65–67.

[3] Kemp, M.C., *The pure theory of international trade*, Prentice-Hall, 1964.

[4] Kindleberger, C.P., *International economics*, Irwin, 1958.

[5] Meade, J.E., *Trade and welfare*, Oxford University Press, 1955.

[6] Negishi, T., 'Entry and optimal number of firms,' *Metroeconomica*, 14 (1962), pp. 86–89.

[7] Negishi, T., 'Protection of the infant industry and dynamic internal economy,' *Economic Record*, 34 (1968), 56–67.

PART 3

Monopolistic competition

CHAPTER 7

Monopolistic competition and general equilibrium

1. It has long been suggested that partial equilibrium analysis in the theory of monopolistic or imperfect competition developed by Chamberlin [5] and Robinson [17] must be extended to general equilibrium analysis. 'The new wine of monopolistic competition should not be poured into the old goatskins of particular equilibrium methodology.'[1]) On the other hand, from the point of view of realism, a general economic equilibrium model should contain at least some imperfections of competition, even though it 'must have very destructive consequences for economic theory'.[2])

We have already dealt with the foundation of this problem in Negishi [15]. The existence of an equilibrium for an economy with some monopolistic competition present is proved by (1) placing essentially the same restrictions on consumption and production as in chapter 1; (2) assuming that monopolistically competitive firms have subjective or imaginary inverse demand (supply) functions for their outputs (inputs), $p = f(y, \bar{p}, \bar{y})$, in which prices p are linear and decreasing (increasing) functions of their outputs (inputs) y; (3) making these functions consistent with the given information about the present state of the market $(\bar{p}, \bar{y})$, i.e., $\bar{p} = f(\bar{y}, \bar{p}, \bar{y})$; and (4) assuming one monopolistic competitor at most in each market. A similar result can be obtained in the case in which there are some kinks in the demand or supply functions. These results are reproduced below in section 3.[3])

However, Kuenne [12] quite rightly criticised that the problem of product differentiation is not coped with in Negishi [15], since there were assumeed to be a set of distinct commodities, all elements of which are held as positive stocks by every consumer (a condition that is sufficient to eliminate a certain

---

[1]) Triffin [21], p. 89.
[2]) Hicks [9], pp. 83–85.
[3]) The stability of a monopolistically competitive economy is also studied in Negishi [15] under the assumption of gross substitutability.

potential discontinuity in consumer demands.[4]) Although the imperfectness of markets, i.e., the slope of demand (supply) curves can also be attributed to the differentiation of the sellers (buyers) rather than the products,[5]) it is certainly true that the central theme of monopolistic competition is product differentiation. Which specific forms of product to produce is to be decided by firms, i.e., the stock of what commodities to exist should not be the data of the model, what are usually regarded as varieties of the same commodity being distinguished as different ones if they are not perfect substitutes.

We have therefore, to demonstrate the existence of an equilibrium for monopolistic competition due to product differentiation without assuming a positive amount of, not only individual but also social,[6]) stock of each commodity. In sections 4 and 5, we will do it by applying the method developed in chapter 1 (i.e., the one which dispenses with the concept of demand functions) under the assumption that each consumer holds positive stocks of some commodities which are always desirable to all consumers. For the existence proof of a competitive equilibrium which uses the concept of demand functions, of course, there are several devices to dispense with the assumption of positive commodity stock and of always desirable commodities. However, being based on the conditions for the efficient organization of production, these are not applicable in the case of monopolistic competition.[7])

Another extension of Negishi [15] we are going to make in sections 4 and 5 is concerned with te fact that a firm must perceive subjective or imaginary demand (supply) functions in which interdependence among commodities are clearly included. The expected price of a certain commodity must be a function of the amount not only of its own output but also of the output of other commodities, since close substitutability should be expected among varieties of the physically same commodity, which are regarded now as different commodities. This fact will be taken care of under the assumption of gross substitutability.[8])

---

[4]) See chapter 1, footnote 14.
[5]) See Kuenne [12], p. 231, Robinson [17], pp. 88–90, Sraffa [18]. In chapter 8 below, we shall discuss a case of imperfection due to the differentiation of the sellers.
[6]) In Nikaido [16], the positive social stock is assumed.
[7]) See Arrow–Debreu [1], McKenzie [13], Debreu [8].
[8]) We have no restrictions on nonnegative profits and are concerned with an equilibrium in the short run or under limited supply of entrepreneurship. Interproduct non-rivalrous competition has nothing to do with this assumption, though Kuenne [12] insists to the contrary.

Finally, we must mention that non-increasing returns to scale (i.e., the convex production set) is assumed throughout this chapter.[9]) Considering that the equilibrium with which we are concerned is a temporary equilibrium with myopic time horizon, there is some plausibility for this assumption.[10]) However, with the introduction of some imperfection of competition, it may deprive economists of some interest, considering the fact that the imperfection of competition has much to do with the case of increasing returns.[11]) If we assume that feasible production sets are contractible, i.e., do not break up into several parts or have holes in the middle, we can still prove the existence of an equilibrium by imposing some conditions on the forms of the perceived demand and supply functions so as to assure the contractibility of the equilibrium set of inputs and outputs chosen by each firm,[12]) though it may be difficult to find proper economic implications of, and therefore, justifications of such conditions.[13])

2. The model to be considered is as follows. Let there be m comodities, n consumers and r firms (r' firms are perfectly competitive and $r-r'$ firms are monopolistically competitive). A consumption vector, the initial holding vector and the utility function of consumer i are respectively denoted by X_i (whose element $X_{ij} \geq 0$ denotes the amount of commodity j), $\bar{X}_i$ (whose element $\bar{X}_{ij} \geq 0$ denotes the amount of commodity j) and $U_i(X_i)$. Let y_k be a production vector of firm k whose element $y_{kj} > (<)0$ is output (input) of the jth commodity, and Y_k be the possible set of y_k. The price vector is denoted by P (whose element $P_j \geq 0$ denotes the price of commodity j). Let $P^*(P_j^*)$ and $y_k^*(y_{kj}^*)$ be the expected values of $P(P_j)$ and $y_k(y_{kj})$, respectively. $100\lambda_{ik}$ per cent of the profit of the kth firm is to be distributed to the ith consumer, i.e., $\lambda_{ik} \geq 0$, $\Sigma_i \lambda_{ik} = 1$. Without loss of generality, let $R^1 = (1, ..., r')$ be the set of competitive firms and $R^2 = (r'+1, ..., r)$ be the set of monopolistically competitive firms, and let $j \in J^k$ imply that the jth commodity's market is dominated by the kth firm, $k \in R^2$.

Assumptions made throughout this chapter are,

[9]) We shall be concerned, however, with the increasing returns to scale in chapter 8.
[10]) Hicks [9], p. 83.
[11]) Sraffa [18].
[12]) See Debreu [7]. In the case of the perfect competition, it is quite likely that the chosen set of inputs and outputs under given prices is not contractible if the feasible set is not convex.
[13]) However, see Arrow–Hahn [2].

Assumption 1.   Utility functions $U_i(X_i)$ are continuous, increasing and quasi-concave.[14])

Assumption 2.   Possible production sets satisfy (1) $0 \in Y_k$, (2) K_k is convex and (3) Y_k is compact.[15])

These two assumptions are essentially the same ones as those in chapter 1.

New assumptions to be introduced with the introduction of the market imperfections are as follows.

Assumption 3.   Every monopolistically competitive firm is separated from every other such firm; that is $J^k \cap J^{k'} = 0$, for any k, $k' \in R^2$, 0 being the null set.

The purpose of this assumption is to exclude from our model the indeterminate case of conscious rivalry among firms so that every firm is completely isolated from unpredictable external feedbacks of its own decision making. The 'large group case' of Chamberlin and more generally any form of non-rivalrous interfirm competitions are allowed.[16]) The case of the oligopoly with product differentiation is also all right in so far as it is determinate, in other words, if each firm will behave according to the well-behaved demand (supply) functions for its outputs (inputs), i.e., if the other firms' feedback effects from its own decision is (believed to be) predictable.

Assumption 4.   The kth firm ($k \in R^2$) takes the current prices of commodities not under its control as given and perceives inverse demand or supply functions for its outputs or inputs on the basis of the observed P and y_k, i.e.,

$$P_j^* = P_j^*(y_k^*, P, y_k),$$

which may or may not be correct but are single valued, continuous, linear homogeneous with respect to P and satisfy

$$P_j = P_j^*(y_k, P, y_k).[17])$$

---

[14]) See chapter 1, assumption 1.
[15]) See chapter 1, assumption 2 and lemma 1.
[16]) Chamberlin [5] (1956), pp. 81–100.
[17]) If P_j^* is constant with respect to y_k^*, then we have the case of the perfect competition.

It is widely agreed that the only demand (supply) function that is relevant in the theory of monopolistic (monopsonic) competition is the perceived, imagined or subjective demand (supply) functions which express the expectation of the firm as to the relationship between the price it charges (offers) and the quantity of its output (input) the market will buy (sell).[18]) The perception of functions is made on the basis of observed prices and quantities. It is assumed that the functions are correct and coincide of necessity with the objective fact of the market at the observed point at which the firm happens to be actually selling or buying at the moment, though not necessarily elsewhere. In other words, for the quantities actually produced or consumed, the firm correctly perceives the prices which will clear the markets but not necessarily the elasticity of demand or supply. It may be possible to derive a true or real demand or supply function of a firm as a residual in the general equilibrium system, i.e., as a function of all the variables in the system. However. one can hardly conceive of any firm being able to observe and take into account all the variables in the system, i.e., not only prices but also inputs and outputs of other firms, etc., since even the modern econometric studies can take into account only a few variables. It is most natural to assume that firms respond to some partial equilibrium type of perceived functions.

Now we can state the conditions for an equilibrium.

Definition 1. A set of vectors $(X_i^0, y_k^0, P^0)_{i=1,\dots,n, k=1,\dots,r}$ is an equilibrium if (1) X_i^0 is the maximum point of $U_i(X_i)$ under the restriction $\Sigma_j P_j^0 X_{ij} = \Sigma_j P_j^0 \overline{X}_{ij} + \Sigma_k \lambda_{ik} \Sigma_j P_j^0 y_{kj}^0 \equiv M > 0$, (2) y_k^0 $(k \in R^1)$ is the maximum point of $\Sigma_j P_j^0 y_{kj}$ subject to the restriction $y_k \in Y_k$, (3) y_k^0 $(k \in R^2)$ is the maximum point of $\Sigma_{j \notin Jk} P_j^0 y_{kj} + \Sigma_{j \in Jk} P_j^*(y_k, P^0, y_k^0) y_{kj}$ under the restriction $y_k \in Y_k$, (4) $\Sigma_i X_{ij}^0 - \Sigma_k y_{kj}^0 - \Sigma_i \overline{X}_{ij} \leqq 0$, $P_j(\Sigma_i X_{ij}^0 - \Sigma_k y_{kj}^0 - \Sigma_i \overline{X}_{ij}) = 0$.

3. In this section, following Negishi [15], let us consider that the differentiation of product is already carried out and that what remains to be done for each firm is only to determine the quantity of the already chosen varieties of products. Following the traditional supposition that only one variety of the physically same commodity is produced in each firm,[19]) we may

---

[18]) Bushaw–Clower [4], p. 181, Davis–Whinston [6], Kaldor [10] and Triffin [21], pp. 62–67.

[19]) Assumption 3 implies that two different monopolistic firms actually produce (consume) non-overlapping sets of commodities whose price they believe to be able to control.

disregard the demand interdependence among commodities in the perceived functions, i.e.,

Assumption 5.   Functions $P_j^*(y_k^*, P, y_k)$ is simplified to $P_j^*(y_{kj}^*, P, y_k)$ which is linear and decreasing with respect to y_{kj}^*,

$$P_j^* = a_j(P, y_k)\, y_{kj}^* + b_j(P, y_k), \quad a_j(P, y_k) < 0, \quad j \in J^k, \quad k \in R^2.$$

Since the domain of y_k is bounded from assumption 2, we can, in view of assumption 1 and condition (4) in definition 1, restrict the domain of X_i in some convex compact set Γ_i without causing any essential changes in the definition of equilibrium.[20])

If we define consumer demand functions as

Definition 2.   Consumer demand function X_i is the maximum point of $U_i(X_i)$ under the restriction of $X_i \in \Gamma_i$ and $\Sigma_j P_j X_{ij} = M_i(P, y_1, ..., y_r)$, where $M_i(P, y_1, ..., y_r)$ is continuous,

then we have

Lemma 1.   Consumer demand functions $X_i(P, y_1, ..., y_r)$ defined in definition 2 are upper semi-continuous if $M_i(P, y_1, ..., y_r) > 0$.[21])

An easy sufficient condition for lemma 1 is

Assumption 6. $\overline{X}_i > 0$ for all i,

if M_i is defined as in condition (1) in definition 1, since from conditions (2) and (3) in definition 1 and assumption 2, $\Sigma_j P_j^0 y_{kj}^0 \geq 0$ for all k.[22])

Now we are ready to state

Theorem 1.   Under assumptions 1, 2, 3, 4, 5 and 6, there exists an equilibrium defined in definition 1.

Proof.   Since conditions in definition 1 have homogeneity of degree zero with respect to P, i.e., remain satisfied when prices are changed propor-

---

[20]) See Ass chapter 1.
[21]) See Arrow–Debreu [1], McKenzie [13], Berge [3], pp. 122 (Berge–Patterson, p. 117).
[22]) Nikaido [16] weakened assumption 6 to $\Sigma_i \bar{x}_i > 0$.

tionally, we can normalize price vector P such that $P \in S^{m-1}$ ($m-1$ dimensional simplex). With $P \in S^{m-1}$ and $y_k \in Y_k$, $k = 1, ..., r$, given, we can get from condition 1 of definition 1 a consumption vector X_i', setting temporarily as $M_i = \Sigma_j P_j \overline{X}_{ij} + \max(0, \Sigma_k \lambda_{ik} \Sigma_j P_j y_{kj})$. Since $M_i > 0$ from assumption 6, lemma 1 assures us that X_i' is an upper semi-continuous function of P and y_k's, whose image is non-void and convex from assumption 1 and the fact that $X_i \in \Gamma_i$. From condition (2) of definition 1, we can have y_k', $k \in R^1$, when $P \in S^{m-1}$ is given. This is also an upper semi-continuous function of P, whose image is non-void and convex from assumption 2. With $P \in S^{m-1}$, $y_k \in Y_k$, given, we have y_k', $k \in R^2$, from condition (3) of definition 1 and assumptions 4 and 5. This is the maximum of a concave quadratic function $\Sigma_{j \in J^k}(a_j y_{kj} + b_j)y_{kj} + \Sigma_{j \notin J^k} P_j y_{kj}$, on the domain of a compact convex set Y_k, where a_j and b_j are given. Therefore, y_k' is a function of P and y_k which is upper semi-continuous, of non-void and convex image. Finally, if $P \in S^{m-1}$, $X_i \in \Gamma_i$, $y_k \in Y_k$, $i = 1, ..., n$, $j = 1, ..., r$, are given, we have a following mapping to $P' = (P_1', ..., P_m')$.[23]

$$P_j' = \max(0, P_j + \mu(\Sigma_i X_{ij} - \Sigma_k y_{kj} - \Sigma_i \overline{X}_{ij}))/\lambda,$$

where $\lambda = \Sigma_j \max(0, P_j + \mu(\Sigma_i X_{ij} - \Sigma_k y_{kj} - \Sigma_i \overline{X}_{ij})) > 0$, if $\mu > 0$ is sufficiently small. Combining all these, we have a mapping from $S^{m-1} \times \Pi_i \Gamma_i \times \Pi_k Y_k$ into itself: $(P, X_i, y_k)_{i=1...,n, k=1,...,r} \to (P', X_i', y^k)_{i=1,...,n, k=1,...,r}$. Because this is an upper semi-continuous mapping from a compact, convex set into itself and its image is non-void and convex, there is a fixed point $(P^0, X_i^0, y_k^0)_{i=1,...,n, k=1,...,r}$, which maps into itself, from the fixed point theorem of Kakutani, i.e., lemma 3 in chapter 1. Then we can show that this fixed point is an equilibrium defined in definition 1. From condition (1) of assumption 2, we have $\Sigma_j P_j^0 y_{kj}^0 \geq 0$. Therefore, we have Walras' law, $\Sigma_j P_j(\Sigma_i X_{ij} - \Sigma_k y_{kj} - \Sigma_i \overline{X}_{ij}) = 0$, from condition 1 of definition 1 and assumption 1. Using Walras' law, we see from $(\lambda - 1)\Sigma_j(P_j^0)^2 = \mu(\Sigma_j P_j^0 (\Sigma_i X_{ji}^0 - \Sigma_k y_{kj} - \Sigma_i \overline{X}_{ij})) = 0$, that $\lambda = 1$ at the fixed point. Then, condition (4) of definition 1 must be satisfied there. From the construction of X_i' and y_k' and assumption 4, we also see that conditions (1)–(3) in definition 1 are satisfied at the fixed point.

Since the role of assumption 5 is to make the profit $\Sigma_j P_j^*(y_{kj}^*, P, y_k)y_{kj}^*$ a concave function of y_{kj}^*, a possible extension is the introduction of the kinked demand or supply function,[24] i.e.,

[23] This mapping was first suggested by Uzawa [22].
[24] See Stigler [19] and Sweezy [20].

Assumption 7.

$$P_j^*(y_{kj}^*, P, y_k) = a_j(P, y_k)\, y_{kj}^* + b_j(P, y_k), \text{ if } y_{kj}^* > y_{kj}$$
$$= a_j'(P, y_k)\, y_{kj}^* + b_j'(P, y_k), \text{ if } y_{kj}^* < y_{kj}$$

and $a_j(P, y_k) < a_j'(P, y_k) < 0$.

Replacing assumptions 7 for assumption 5, we can similarly prove,

Theorem 2. Under assumptions 1, 2, 3, 4, 6 and 7, there exists an equilibrium defined in definition 1.

4. Now let us introduce product differentiation into our model. This is to be done by converting the problem of product differentiation (the change of the quality of a commodity) into the problem of whether each different variety of the same commodity should be produced (consumed) at all and further into the problem of how much it should be (for some, possibly zero). Since all conceivable varieties of the physically same commodity are to be distinguished as different commodities among which a firm is going to choose some (not necessarily one),[25] the interdependence among commodities produced (consumed) by the same firm cannot be ignored (as in assumption 5) even in the perceived demand (supply) functions. The demand (supply) function of commodity j $(J \in J^k)$ perceived by the kth firm when (P, y_k) is observed is assumed to be

$$y_{kj}^* = f_{kj}(P^*, P, y_k). \tag{1}$$

Let us assume that the firm consider the linear approximation of (1) at the observed point, where $P^* = P$, $y_k^* = y_k$, i.e.,

$$y_{kj}^* = \sum_{s \in J^k} (\partial f_{kj}/\partial P_s^*)^0\, P_s^* + g_j(y_k, P), \tag{2}$$

to estimate the relation between y_{kj}^* and P_j^*'s for $j \in J^k$, where $(\partial f_{kj}/\partial P_s^*)^0$ signifies the partial derivative at the observed point. It is reasonable to suppose that the entrepreneur is rational with respect to demand (supply) forecast and that f_{kj} is homogeneous of degree zero with respect to P^*, i.e.,

$$\sum_{s \in J^k} (\partial f_{kj}/\partial P_s^*)\, P_s^* + \sum_{s \notin J^k} (\partial f_{kj}/\partial P_s^*)\, P_s^* = 0. \tag{3}$$

---

[25] The implication of the assumption 3 is now more stringent than in the preceding section. Different monopolistic firms consider a non-overlapping list of commodities whose price they believe they are able to control.

If we further assume the gross substitutability in the demand (supply) forecast of the entrepreneurs, i.e., $\partial f_{kj}/\partial P_s^* \geqq 0$, for $j \neq s$, $j \in J^k$, $s = 1, \ldots, m$ then the matrix $A = [(\partial f_{kj}/\partial P_s^*)^0]_{j, s \in J^k}$ is Hicksian, i.e., its principal minors alternate in sign as given by $(-1)^h$, where h is the order of the minor, provided that A is indecomposable and $P^* > 0$.[26]) This can be seen by applying the theorem in Negishi [14] to (3).

The matrix A is generally not symmetric. A non-zero off-diagonal element of A can be decomposed into the substitution term and income term,[27]) if customers are competitive. Since substitution terms are symmetric and there are income terms for consumers only, we can make A symmetric by assuming symmetric income terms of consumers. If there is no stock of commodities j and s such that $j, s \in J^k$ in the hands of consumers,[27]) an income term is given by $-y_{ks}^*(\partial y_{kj}^*/\partial Y)$, where Y denotes consumer's income. If two commodities are aiming at consumers in different income ranges, perhaps no demand interdependence between commodities is expected and the corresponding off-diagonal element of A is zero. On the other hand, if two commodities which are varieties of the physically same commodity are competing for consumers in the same income range, it is reasonable to suppose that income effect on consumption is neutral and the income term is symmetric, i.e., $(\partial y_{kj}^*/\partial Y)/y_{kj}^* = (\partial y_{ks}^*/\partial Y)/y_{ks}^*$. These arguments suggest that it is not implausible to assume the symmetry of A and therefore the negative definiteness of A, i.e., $x'Ax < 0$ for any non-vanishing column vector x.

Solving (2) for P_j^* $(j \in J^k)$, we have

$$P_j^* = \sum_{s \in J^k} H_{js}^k(P, y_k)\, y_{ks}^* + L_{js}^k(P, y_k), \tag{4}$$

where the matrix $[H_{js}^k]$ is the inverse of the matrix A. Therefore, we may assume,

Assumption 8. The function $P_j^*(y_k^*, P, y_k)$ is given as (4) and the matrix $[H_{js}^k]$ in (4) is negative definite,

since the inverse of negative definite matrix is also negative definite. This makes the profit of the kth firm $(k \in R^2)$ a concave function in definition 1, (3).

---

[26]) The indecomposability, roughly speaking, means that all the commodities are at least indirectly interdependent.

[27]) This implies exclusion of the case of monopsony.

Considering the fact that many of commodities exist merely in the list and are in fact not produced at all, we replace assumption 6 by

Assumption 6'.   Each consumer has positive stock of at least one commodity, say commodity j, such that $\partial U_i/\partial X_{ij} > 0$ for all i.

Assumptions 1 and 2 are slightly strengthened as,

Assumption 1'. $U_i(X_i)$ is continuous, increasing and concave,[28])

Assumption 2'.   In addition to conditions (1), (2) and (3) in assumption 2, (4) y_k, $k = 1, \ldots, r$, which maximizes $\Sigma_j P_j y_{kj}$ over Y_k is unique when $P \in S^{m-1}$ is given.

Assumption 1' is introduced, as in chapter 1, to utilize the following theorem in non-linear programming in the below.

Lemma 2.   Let $f(x)$ be concave and $g(x) = \langle g_1(x), \ldots, g_n(x) \rangle$ be linear in $x \geq 0$. Then $\bar{x}$ maximizes $f(x)$ subject to the restrictions that $x \geq 0$ and $g(x) \geq 0$, if and only if there is a vector $\bar{u}$ (Lagrangean multipliers) such that $(\bar{x}, \bar{u})$ is a non-negative saddle point of the Lagrangean $\psi(x, u) = f(x) + u.g.(x)$, i.e., $\psi(\bar{x}, u) \geq \psi(\bar{x}, \bar{u}) \geq \psi(x, \bar{u})$ for all $x \geq 0$ and $u \geq 0$.[29])

5.   Now we can prove,

Theorem 3.   There exists an equilibrium defined in definition 1 under assumptions 1', 2', 3, 4, 6' and 8.

Proof.
  For any $P \in S^{m-1}$, condition (2) in definition 1 gives $y'_k \in Y_k$, $k \in R^1$. This is a continuous point to point mapping from assumption 2'. We may note that $\Sigma_j P_j s_{kj}$ is maximized uniquely at y'_k if $s_k = (s_{k1}, \ldots, s_{km})$ is restricted as $s_k \in [0, y'_k]$ since $0 \in Y_k$ and Y_k is convex from assumption 2'. Next consider condition (3) in definition 1 and assumptions 4 and 8. In view of assumptions 2' and 8, we have a continuous point to point mapping from $P \in S^{m-1}$,

---

[28]) See assumption 1, chapter 1.
[29]) Karlin [11], p. 203, theorem 7.12.

$y_k \in Y_k$ to $y_k' \in Y_k$, $k \in R^2$. We may note that $s_k = y_k'$ alone maximizes $\Sigma_j P_j s_{kj}$ over $[0, y_k']$, if y_k' ($\neq 0$) happens to be equal to the given $y_k \in Y_k$ (and therefore P_j^* happens to be equal to the given P_j of $P \in S^{m-1}$ from assumption 4),[30]) since $\Sigma_j P_j y_{kj}' > 0$, $0 \in Y_k$ and Y_k is convex from assumption 2'.

Having obtained $y_k'(P)$, $k \in R^1$ and $y_k'(P, y_k)$, $k \in R^2$, when $P \in S^{m-1}$ and $y_k \in Y_k$, $k \in R^2$ are given, consider the feasible set Z of $(X_i, z_k)_{i=1,...,n, k=1,...,r}$ defined by linear inequalities

$$\Sigma_i X_i - \Sigma_{k \in R^1} z_k y_k'(P) - \Sigma_{k \in R^2} z_k y_k'(P, y_k) - \Sigma_i \bar{X}_i \leq 0, \tag{5}$$

$$0 \leq z_k \leq 1. \tag{6}$$

It is clear that Z is non-void. In view of assumptions 1', 2', condition (4) of definition 1, 5 and 6, we can restrict X_i as $X_i \in \Gamma_i$,[31]) Γ_i being convex and compact. We can apply lemma 2 to the maximization of $\Sigma_i \alpha_i U_i(X_i)$ over Z, where $\alpha = (\alpha_1, ..., \alpha_n) \in S^{n-1}$. As in the case of chapter 1, theorem 5, we have as the solution of this maximization problem $X_i' \in \Gamma_i$, $i = 1, ..., n$ and $P' = (P_1', ..., P_n') \in S^{m-1}$, where P' is obtained by normalizing Lagrangean multipliers attached to conditions (5). At the maximum, $z_k = 1$ if $\Sigma_j P_j' y_{kj}' > 0$. Since y_k', $k \in R^1$ is the unique point which maximizes $\Sigma_j P_j s_{kj}$ over $[0, y_k'(P)]$ under given P, $z_k = 1$ if $y_k' \neq 0$ and P' and P are equal. Similarly, since y_k', $k \in R^2$ is the unique point which maximizes $\Sigma_j P_j s_{kj}$ over $[0, y_k'(P, y_k)]$ under given P and y_k, $z_k = 1$ if $y_k' \neq 0$ and $P = P'$, $y_k = y_k'$. The mapping from $\alpha \in S^{n-1}$, $P \in S^{m-1}$, $y_k \in Y_k$ ($k \in R^2$) to $X_i' \in \Gamma_i$, $i = 1, ..., n$, and $P' \in S^{m-1}$ is upper semi-continuous, of non-void and convex image.[32]) The conditions for (1) in definition 1 are satisfied at X_i', if P' is the price vector, with the exception of the budget constraint $\Sigma_j P_j' X_{ij} = M_i$ (this should hold as an equality from assumption 1').

Therefore, the last step is to introduce the adjustment of α in view of budget constraints. Let us construct a mapping from $(X_i, y_k, P, \alpha)_{i=1,...,n, k=1,...,r} \in \Pi_i \Gamma_i \times \Pi_k Y_k \times S^{m-1} \times S^{n-1}$ to $\alpha' \in S^{n-1}$ by

$$\alpha_i' = \max (0, \alpha_i + (M_i - \Sigma_j P_j X_{ij})/B)/\lambda,$$

$$\lambda = \Sigma_i \max (0, \alpha_i + (M_i - \Sigma_j P_j X_{ij})/B),$$

where M_i is as defined in (1) in definition 1 and B is a large positive constant such that $\Sigma_i |M_i - \Sigma_j P_j X_{ij}| < B$.[33])

---

[30]) In other words, if the subjective profit is maximized at the observed point.
[31]) See section 3 above.
[32]) Berge [3], pp. 114–122 (Berge–Patterson, pp. 109–117).
[33]) See section 5, chapter 1.

Now by putting all of these mappings together, we have an upper semi-continuous mapping of non-void and convex image from a convex compact set into itself:

$$(X_i, y_k, P, \alpha)_{i=1,\dots,n, k=1,\dots,r} \in \Pi_i \Gamma_i \times \Pi_k Y_k \times S^{m-1} \times S^{n-1}$$

$$\to (X'_i, y'_k, P', \alpha')_{i=1,\dots n, k=1,\dots,r} \in \Pi_i \Gamma_i \times \Pi_k Y_k \times S^{m-1} \times S^{n-1}.$$

From Kakutani's fixed point theorem (lemma 3 in chapter 1), there exists a fixed point $(X^0_i, y^0_k, P^0, \alpha^0)_{i=1,\dots,n, k=1,\dots,r}$.

We can show that this fixed point is an equilibrium defined in definition 1. We see at first that conditions (2) and (3) are satisfied at the fixed point from the construction of y'_k. Since $z_k y'_k = y'_k$ in the maximization problem (of $\Sigma_i \alpha_i U_i$ over Z) corresponding to the fixed point where $P = P'$ and $y_k = y'_k$, and each condition in (5) is satisfied with equality if the corresponding P_j is positive, condition (4) of definition 1 is satisfied. Finally, by the construction of α' and condition (4) of definition 1 just established, we can see as in the proof of theorem 5 in chapter 1, that budget constraint are satisfied and (1) in definition 1 is established.

References

[1] Arrow, K.J. and G. Debreu, 'Existence of an equilibrium for a competitive economy,' *Econometrica*, 22 (1954), pp. 256–291.

[2] Arrow, K.J. and F.H. Hahn, *Competitive equilibrium analysis*, Holden-Day, forthcoming.

[3] Berge, C., *Espaces topologiques et fonctions multivoques*, Dunod, 1959 (Patterson tr., *Topological spaces*, Macmillan, 1963).

[4] Bushaw, D.W. and R.W. Clower, *Introduction to mathematical economics*, Irwin, 1957.

[5] Chamberlin, E.H., *The theory of monopolistic competition*, Harvard University Press, 1933 (1st ed.), 1956 (7th ed.).

[6] Davis, O.A and A. Whinston, 'Piecemeal policy in the theory of second best,' *Review of Economic Studies*, 34 (1967), 323–331.

[7] Debreu, G., 'A social equilibrium existence theorem,' *Proceedings of the National Academy of Sciences*, 38 (1952), pp. 886–893.

[8] Debreu, G., 'New concepts and techniques for equilibrium analysis,' *International Economic Review*, 3 (1962), pp. 257–273.

[9] Hicks, J.R., *Value and capital*, Oxford University Press, 2nd ed., 1946.

[10] Kaldor, N., 'Market imperfection and excess capacity,' *Economica*, N.S. 2 (1935), pp. 33–50 (Stigler and Boulding, ed., *Readings in price theory*, Irwin, 1952, 384–403).

[11] Karlin, S., *Mathematical methods and theory in games, programming and economics*, 1, Addison–Wesley, 1959.

[12] Kuenne, R.E., 'Quality space, interproduct competition, and general equilibrium theory,' R.E. Kuenne (ed.), *Monopolistic Competition Theory*, John Wiley, 1967, 219–50.

[13] McKenzie, L.W., 'On the existence of general equilibrium for a competitive market,' *Econometrica*, 27 (1959), 54–71, 29 (1961), 247–248.

[14] Negishi, T., 'A note on the stability of an economy where all goods are gross substitutes,' *Econometrica*, 26 (1958), 445–447.

[15] Negishi, T., 'Monopolistic competition and general equilibrium,' *Review of Economic Studies*, 28 (1961), 196–201 (Abstract, *Econometrica*, 28 (1960), pp. 667–8).

[16] Nikaido, H., 'A supplementary note to 'On the classical multilateral exchange problem,'' *Metroeconomica*, 9, 1957 (209–210) (Newman ed., *Readings in mathematical economics*, I, Johns Hopkins University Press, 1968, 127–128).

[17] Robinson, J., *The economics of imperfect competition*, Macmillan, 1933.

[18] Sraffa, P., 'The laws of returns under competitive conditions,' *Economic Journal*, 36 (1926), 535–550 (Stigler and Boulding, ed., *Readings in price theory*, Irwin, 1952, 180–197).

[19] Stigler, G.J., 'The kinky oligopoly demand curve and rigid prices,' *Journal of Political Economy*, 55 (1947), 432–449 (Stigler and Boulding ed., *Readings in price theory*, Irwin, 1952, 410–439).

[20] Sweezy, P., 'Demand under conditions of oligopoly,' *Journal of Political Economy*, 47 (1939), 568–573 (Stigler and Boulding, ed., *Readings in price theory*, Irwin, 1952, 404–409).

[21] Triffin, R., *Monopolistic competition and general equilibrium theory*, Harvard University Press, 1940.

[22] Uzawa, H., 'Walras' tâtonnement in the theory of exchange,' *Review of Economic Studies*, 27 (1960), 182–194,

CHAPTER 8

Increasing returns, imperfect competition and international trade[1]

1. The Ricardian and the so-called Heckscher–Ohlin approaches have dominated thinking on the existence and optimality of international trade and specialization. While the former attributes to international differences in production functions (or the geographical differences) the explanation of comparative advantage and makes the factor supply irrelevant in determining the trade pattern, the latter assumes international differences in factor endowments as the crucial and sole factor determining comparative advantage, postulating explicitly the international identity of production functions. International trade between dissimilar countries, or trade in primary products, for which factors of production such as natural resources are important, can surely be explained in terms of differences in climate, production functions or factor endowments. Trade between similar countries, or trade in manufactures, however, cannot be so explained. It is well known, of course, that most international trade is carried on between large industrial areas that are very similar.

Suppose that two countries have identical conditions, i.e., equal tastes, production functions, factor endowments. To explain the trade and its optimality, one must rely on the existence of economies of scale in production. Once economies of scale are introduced into the model, however, one must face the old dilemma of the inconsistency of the assumption of perfect competition, on one hand, and the existence of diminishing marginal and/or average costs, on the other.[2] There are two escape-routes from this dilemma, both of which are historically celebrated. One is to introduce Marshallian

---

[1] This is to replace my earlier manuscript entitled 'International trade between similar countries with factor mobility,' Mimeographed, University of New South Wales, 1967, and Negishi, T., 'Increasing returns, imperfect competition and international trade,' *Economic Studies Quarterly*, 20–3 (1969), 15–23.

[2] If marginal cost is diminishing profit can not be maximized. On the other hand, if average cost is diminishing, the maximized profit cannot be positive.

external economies as the main factor causing the falling supply curve of the industry (but not that of an individual firm). By so doing we have already discussed the gains from trade between similar countries.[3]) Another escape-route from the dilemma of competition and economies of scale is simply to discard the assumption of perfect competition and to consider the falling average cost curve of individual firms due to the existence of the overhead costs.[4]) For such economies of scale in individual firms to imply economies of scale in the industry, changes in the output of the industry must always be caused, not by changes in the number of firms, but by changes in the output of individual firms, which may be assured by the entry-preventing behaviour of the established firms.

As H.G. Johnson pointed out in a survey dedicated to Chamberlin, the theory of imperfect or monopolistic competition has had virtually no impact on the theory of international trade.[5]) One reason for this may be the fact that the former embodies a partial-equilibrium approach while the latter is mainly concerned with general equilibrium. However, in the theory of location, which has been developed rather independently from the theory of trade but analyzes a similar problem, i.e., interregional trade from a point of view different from that of the theory of trade, we have Loesch's general equilibrium model of a space economy operating under conditions of monopolistic competition.[6]) It is interesting, therefore, to compare the basic assumptions of Hecksher–Ohlin theory of trade and those of Loesch theory of location. In the former, they are (1) perfect competition, (2) constant returns to scale, (3) no transportation cost, (4) international immobility of factors of production and (5) international difference in factor endowments. On the other hand, the latter assumes (1) imperfect competition, (2) increasing returns, (3) transportation cost for goods, (4) ubiquity, i.e., perfect mobility with no cost of factors and materials.

Since we are concerned with the possibility of international trade between similar countries due to increasing returns to scale, our basic assumptions in this chapter will be (1) imperfect competition, (2) increasing returns, (3) no transportation cost, (4) international immobility of factors and (5) no international difference in factor endowments. Assumptions 3 and 4 are

---

[3]) See chapter 5.
[4]) The so-called L-shaped cost curve is widely supported by empirical studies. See Johnston [5].
[5]) Johnson [4].
[6]) Loesch [7], 70–78, Isard [3], 43–49, 274.

traditional simplifying ones. Assumptions 1 and 2 are identical to those of Loesch. Though highly stimulating in this respect, however, Loesch's analysis is unsatisfactory on two points. Firstly, mere counting of numbers of equations and of unknowns is not enough to show the existence of equilibria in the model. Secondly, no analysis of gains from trade can be made since the model is based not on the basic utility and production functions but on the very simplified demand functions. Below, we will first demonstrate carefully the possibility of an autarky equilibrium and an equilibrium with international trade and specialization in our model. Then gains from trade over autarky will be discussed.

2.   Consider an international economy of two completely identical countries. We assume two goods as usual, but only one factor for simplicity.

Alternatively we may suppose two or more factors, no international difference in factor endowments, and identical factor intensity in two industries. Since we are going to explain trade by reasons other than difference in factor endowments, even this drastic assumption may not be inappropriate. Each country is assumed to have the same constant amount L (>0) of this single factor of production. Furthermore, we assume the identical social indifference map for two countries, with Engel curves being straight lines passing through the origin.[7] The cost of production of each firm is divided into the overhead cost and the variable cost. The former is due to the necessary input of the constant amount (a in the first industry, b in the second) of the factor, irrespective of the level of production. We assume that the latter, the variable cost is proportional to the level of output. Then, by taking the unit of goods properly, we can make the marginal cost unity in terms of the factor. For example, if the total amount of the factor input is x in a firm in the first industry, then the amount of output is $x-a$ and the average total cost is $wx/(x-a)$, where w is the price of the factor.

Since the average cost is diminishing, the behavior of firms cannot be perfectly competitive. Each industry is assumed to consist of the given number of identical firms and the market is assumed to be divided equally among these firms. With current prices and demand for output given, each firm estimates the subjective demand function. Due to the differentiation of

---

[7] In other words, the corresponding utility function is homogeneous and the marginal rate of substitution depends only on the ratio of goods.

firms,[8]) estimated demand curves are assumed to be downward sloping. For example, a firm in the first industry estimates the relation between the price of its output p and demand for it $x-a$ as

$$p = A(p^*, w^*. x^* - a) - B(p^*, w^*, x^* - a)(x - a) \tag{1}$$

with the condition

$$p^* = A(p^*, w^*, x^* - a) - B(p^*, w^*, x^* - a)(x^* - a),$$
$$B(p^*, w^*, x^* - a) > 0, \tag{2}$$

satisfied, where p^*, w^* and $x^* - a$ are respectively the current price of output, that of the factor and current demand for output.[9]) Being based on this demand function, each firm wants to maximize its profit. But, at the same time, considerations for the possibility of the entry of new firms are necessary. In this respect, we assume that the already established firms are pessimistic and expect active entry of new firms based on optimistic expectations.[10]) To prevent the entry, therefore, the rate of profit to the total cost is kept at the level of the so-called normal rate. If normal profit is included in the factor price, the condition for the equilibrium of the firm is equality of price and average cost. On the other hand, newly entering firms are also assumed to be pessimistic and to expect the constant amount of output of the established firms.[11])

Let us first consider the possibility of the autarky equilibrium where each country is separated from the other and there is no trade between them. Let there be n firms in the first industry and m in the second. For any combination of the input of the factor of each firm in the first industry x_1 and that in the second industry x_2 such that $x_1 \geq a$, $x_2 \geq b$, $nx_1 + mx_2 = L$, assuming that $na + mb < L$, consider the maximization of $U(D_1, D_2)$ subject to $0 \leq D_1 \leq n(x_1 - a)$, $0 \leq D_2 \leq m(x_2 - b)$, where U is a differentiable utility indicator corresponding to the social indifference map and D_1 and D_2 are

[8]) Product differentiation is not introduced. This is the reason why we say imperfect competition rather than monopolistic competition in this chapter. See footnote 5 in chapter 7.
[9]) Of course, x is the input of the factor. Each firm assumes that others are behaving in the same way. But if we drop this assumption and introduce the so-called kinked demand curve, the discussion below will not be changed essentially. Negishi [9].
[10]) Bain [1], 97–98.
[11]) This is the assumption of Sylos-Labini. Sylos-Labini [11], 43, Bain [1], 105, and Modigliani [8], 217.

consumers' demands for two goods. Since this is a problem of homogeneous programming,[12] we can form a Lagrangean

$$U(D_1, D_2) - p_1(D_1 - nx_1 + \alpha) - p_2(D_2 - mx_2 + \beta), \tag{3}$$

where $\alpha = na$ and $\beta = mb$, and obtain a solution as a saddle point $D_1 \geq 0$, $D_2 \geq 0$, $p_1 \geq 0$, $p_2 \geq 0$ of this Lagrangean.[13] Interpreting Lagrangean multipliers p_1 and p_2 as prices of two goods, the price of the factor w is calculated from

$$wL = p_1 D_1 + p_2 D_2. \tag{4}$$

Assuming the insatiability of each good, we find p_1, p_2, w are positive and the mapping

$$(x_1, x_2) \in \Omega = \{(x_1, x_2) \mid x_1 \geq a, x_2 \geq b, nx_1 + mx_2 = L\} \to p_1, p_2, w$$

is a continuous point to point mapping. Since the utility of each good is insatiable, we have $D_1 = n(x_1 - a)$ and $D_2 = m(x_2 - b)$. These, together with (4), give us

$$n\{(p_1 - w)x_1 - p_1 a\} + m\{(p_2 - w)x_2 - p_2 b\} = 0.$$

Therefore, $(p_1 - w)x_1 - p_1 a = 0$ implies that $(p_2 - w)x_2 - p_2 b = 0$ and vice versa. Consider a continuous function

$$f(x_1) = n\{(p_1 - w)x_1 - p_1 a\}.$$

If $x_1 = a$, then $f(x_1) < 0$. On the other hand, if $x_1 = (L - mb)/n$, then $f(x_1) > 0$, since $nx_1 + mx_2 = L$ and $f(x_1) = -m\{(p_2 - w)x_2 - p_2 b\}$. From the theorem of intermediate values, therefore, there must be a point $\bar{x}_1$ between a and $(L - mb)/n$ such that $f(\bar{x}_1) = 0$. Now it is easy to see that $(\bar{x}_1, \bar{x}_2)$ such that $n\bar{x}_1 + m\bar{x}_2 = L$ with corresponding p_1, p_2, w is an equilibrium, since we have both $(p_1 - w)\bar{x}_1 - p_1 a = 0$ and $(p_2 - w)\bar{x}_2 - p_2 b = 0$.

    To keep such an equilibrium from being disturbed by the entry of new firms, it is sufficient to assume that the elasticity at $(p^*, x^* - a)$ of the demand curve (1) estimated by firms in the first industry[14] is always smaller than $\alpha(1 - m_1)/2nL$, i.e.,

$$e = p^*/B(x^* - a) < \alpha(1 - m_1)/2nL, \tag{5}$$

---

[12] See Eisenberg [2] for homogeneous programming, which is equivalent to concave programming if the degree of homogeneity is positive.

[13] See Karlin [6], p. 203 and lemma 2 in chapter 7 in the above.

[14] As for the second industry, replace a by b, n by m, m_1 by $1 - m_1$, x_1 by x_2 and p_1 by p_2.

where m_1 is the marginal propensity to consume of the first good.

Then, e is smaller than x_1/an at equilibrium [15]) and we have

$$B = p_1/e(x_1-a) > anw/(x_1-a)^2 > aw/(x_1-a)^2 \qquad (6)$$

by the use of $p_1(x_1-a) = wx_1$. Since the slope of the average cost curve $A.C = wx/(x-a)$ at equilibrium is $-wa/(x_1-a)^2$, the demand curve is steeper than the average cost curve. In figure 8.1, $A.C$ and $M.C$ are

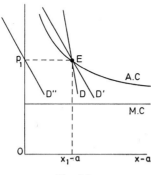

Fig. 8.1.

respectively average and marginal cost curves. Curve D represents the demand function $p = A - B(x-a)$ estimated at equilibrium, E, i.e., p_1 and x_1-a. At E, the profit of established firms is maximized, being subject to the entry preventing condition that it is not more than the normal profit. In a sense the demand curve for these firms can be interpreted as the kinked one of $p_1 ED$. Now, the line D' has the slope of B/n and is still steeper than $A.C$ as is seen from (6). A newly entering firm will behave according to the demand curve D'', i.e., $p = p_1 - B(x-a)/n$, which is obtained by shifting D' horizontally. The reason for this is that the new firm expects to invade markets of all n firms equally. The output of established firms is supposed by an entering firm to be unchanged in spite of the entry. If demand is elastic, a new firm can expect profit greater than normal by producing more than the established firm, even if the latter's profit is not greater than the normal.[16]) In our case, however, this is impossible, since demand is expected to be inelastic. In figure 8.1, D'' remains always below $A.C$. Therefore, there is no entry of new firms and we have,

---

[15]) Since $\alpha = an$, $(1-m_1)<1$, $x_1>a$, $L>an$, we have $\alpha(1-m_1)/2nL < x_1/an$.
[16]) Ruehman [10] , 318

Theorem 1. If the elasticity of the demand curves perceived by firms are sufficiently small and both the established firms and newly entering firms are pessimistic as to the conditions for entry, there exists an autarky equilibrium.

3.   The next thing to do is to consider the possibility of a trade equilibrium where each country is specialized in a different good and there is trade between them. Without loss of generality, we can assume that the ith country is specialized in the ith good and therefore there is no firm and no output in the jth industry $(i \neq j)$ in the ith country. Because of the entry preventing behavior of established firms, we may suppose the number of firms in the first industry of the first country, n, and that of the second industry of te second country, m, are unchanged. The output of the first good is $L-\alpha$, that of the second good is $L-\beta$ and the relative price p_1/p_2 is obtained from the box diagram in figure 8.2. The origin for the first country is O, that of the second, O' and the first good is measured horizontally, the second vertically. The line OO' is the contract curve and marginal rate of substitution on it is p_1/p_2. If p_1 is arbitrary fixed, p_2 is determined. From the equality of price and average cost, the factor price of the ith country w_i is determined as $w_1 = p_1(L-\alpha)/L$, $w_2 = p_2(L-\beta)/L$. Whether this is a trade equilibrium depends on the possibility of entry.

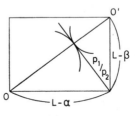

Fig. 8.2.

For the ith industry in the ith country, the situation is similar to the case of autarky. The demand elasticity expected by established firms is smaller than $\alpha(1-m_1)/2nL(\beta m_1/2mL)$ and therefore smaller than $L/ann(L/bmm)$. Since $L = nx_1$ $(L = mx_2)$, the slope of the demand curve B is larger than $aw_1 n(x_1-a)^2 (bw_2 m/(x_2-b)^2)$. Both B and $B/n(B/m)$ are larger than the slope of the average cost curve. Therefore, as in the figure 8.1, there is no entry. Now, without loss of generality we can assume $w_1 > w_2$. Then, there is no possibility of the revival of the second industry in the first country.

This is because new firms in the first country with a higher factor price cannot compete with the established firms in the second country when even the new firms in the latter country cannot. In figure 8.1, this is the situation when $A.C$ is relatively shifted upwards. As for the first industry in the second country, can new firms expect a higher price than average cost, assuming unchanged output in the first country? Price is expected from the demand function obtained from the one estimated in the first country, $p = p_1 - B(x-a)/n$, where $x-a$ is the output of a new firm in the second country, p_1 is the price when only the first country is supplying this good. Putting $B' = B/n$, we must have

$$B'x^2 + (w_2 - p_1 - 2B'a)x + B'a^2 + p_1 a > 0 \qquad (7)$$

so as to have $p_1 - B'(x-a) < w_2 x/(x-a)$, i.e., the average cost is always greater than the price. This requires $B' > (w_2 - p_1)^2/4aw_2$ since $B' > 0$, $p_1 > w_1 > w_2$, and $(w_2 - p_1 - 2B'a) < 0$. From $p_1 > w_2$, we have also $2p_1^2/aw_2 > (p_1 - w_2)^2/4aw_2$. Therefore, it is sufficient if $B > 2p_1^2 n/aw_2$ or $e = p_1/B(x_1 - a) < aw_2 n/2p_1(x_1 - a)$, where e is the demand elasticity in the first industry of the first country. However, since $w_2 = p_2(L-b)/L$ and $p_2/p_1 = (1-m_1)(L-a)/m_1(L-b)$ from $L-a = m_1(L-a+(L-b)p_2/p_1)$, this implies $e < aw_2 n/2p_1(L-a) = an(1-m_1)/2Lm_1 > \alpha(1-m_1)/2L$. Then, this is possible since by assumption $e < \alpha(1-m_1)/2nL$. There is no possibility of revival of the first industry in the second country and a trade equilibrium is possible where the ith country is specialized in the ith industry. We can conclude as,

Theorem 2. If the elasticities of the demand curves perceived by firms are sufficiently small and both the established firms and the newly entering firms are pessimistic about the conditions for entry, there exists a trade equilibrium with complete specialization.

4. We have demonstrated that there are autarky equilibria where each country produces the same amount of goods and a trade equilibrium with complete specialization in our model, provided that the elasticity of the estimated demand curve is sufficiently small, that established firms keep profit at the normal level and that newly entering firms expect unchanged output of established firms. Is there any gain from trade, i.e., can each country be better off in a trade equilibrium? Since each firm is under increasing returns and the number of firms is not increased, it may be possible that the world as a whole is better off in a trade equilibrium.

However, this does not necessarily imply gains from trade for each country. Since we have only one factor, the transformation curve of each country is *ABCD* in figure 8.3. *BC* is the transformation curve when two goods are produced and its slope is -1. Substituting the second good for the first,

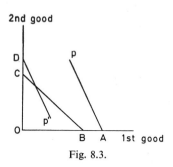

Fig. 8.3.

we approach *C* and when the production of the first good is terminated we jump to *D* since factors corresponding to overhead cost are released from the first industry. Similarly we arrive at *A* when specialized in the first industry. Suppose the first country is at *A* and the second at *D*, and the price ratio of two goods p_1/p_2 is given by the slope of *p* and *p'*. It is evident that the first country is better off in a trade equilibrium since the point on *Ap* at which *Ap* and a social indifference curve are tangents to each other is preferred to any point on *BC*. However, this may not be the case with the second country, since the tangential point of *Dp'* and a social indifference curve may not be preferred to the autarky point on *BC*. In any case, a country with a higher value of output and therefore higher factor price is always better off in a trade equilibrium than in autarky. The remaining question is the case of a country with a lower factor price.

Let the common price ratio at autarky be $\bar{p}_1/\bar{p}_2$, that of a trade equilibrium, p_1/p_2 and the factor price in the *i*th country, w_i. Without loss of generality, we may assume $p_1/p_2 > \bar{p}_1/\bar{p}_2$ and $w_1 > w_2$. First let us suppose that the first country is specialized in the first good, the second country in the second good. This is the case where a country specialised in a good whose relative price is raised can enjoy a higher factor price at the trade equilibrium. If we suppose the second country, the one with the lower factor price is worse off at trade equilibrium, we have a situation shown in figure 8.4. Autarky point is *A*, trade equilibrium of the *i*th country is T_i, respectively on higher and lower indifference curves. The movement from *A* to T_i can be divided into the movement AT'_i on Engel curve OE due to income effect and the movement $T'_i T_i$ on indifference curve due to the substitution effect. Clearly the substitution effect in both countries is to decrease the demand for the first good and so is the income effect in the second country. Therefore,

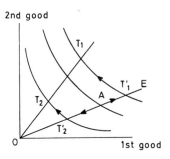

Fig. 8.4.

the change in the demand for the first good caused by the trade is smaller than the income effect in the first country. If the autarky output of two goods in each country is $\bar{L}_1 - \alpha$, $\bar{L}_2 - \beta$, respectively, and the marginal propensity to consume the first good when price ratio is $\bar{p}_1/\bar{p}_2$ is m_1 and the marginal propensity to consume the first good when price ratio is p_1/p_2 is m_1^*, then the change in the demand for the first good is smaller than

$$m_1^*(L-\alpha) - m_1(\bar{L}_1-\alpha) - m_1(\bar{L}_2-\beta)\,\bar{p}_2/\bar{p}_1 \,.$$

On the other hand, the change in the supply which must be equal to that in demand is

$$(L-\alpha) - 2(\bar{L}_1-\alpha) \,.$$

Therefore, we must have

$$(L-\alpha) - 2(\bar{L}_1-\alpha) < m_1^*(L-\alpha) - m_1(\bar{L}_1-\alpha) - m_1(\bar{L}_2-\beta)\,\bar{p}_2/\bar{p}_1 \,. \qquad (8)$$

Since m_1 is the marginal propensity to consume the first good under autarky (price ratio) which is constant for any level of income, we have

$$m_1(\bar{L}_1-\alpha) + m_1(\bar{L}_2-\beta)\,\bar{p}_2/\bar{p}_1 = \bar{L}_1-\alpha \,, \qquad (9)$$

and (8) is reduced to

$$L - \bar{L}_1 < m_1^*(L-\alpha). \qquad (10)$$

If the autarky factor price is $\bar{w}$, then from $\bar{p}_1(\bar{L}_1-\alpha)=\bar{w}L_1$ and $\bar{p}_2(\bar{L}_2-\beta)$ $=\bar{w}L_2$, we have $\bar{p}_2/\bar{p}_1=\bar{L}_2(\bar{L}_1-\alpha)/\bar{L}_1(\bar{L}_2-\beta)$ and $m_1=\bar{L}_1/L$ from (9). Substituting this into (10), we obtain

$$\max\,(m_1,m_1^*)>L/(2L-\alpha)=1/(2-\alpha/L)>1/2. \tag{11}$$

If (11) is not satisfied, i.e., $\max(m_1,m_1^*)<1/(2-\alpha/L)$, the second country cannot be worse off at trade equilibrium. By changing the role of the two goods, we have instead of (11),

$$\max\,(m_2,m_2^*)=1-\min\,(m_1,m_1^*)>1/(2-\beta/L). \tag{12}$$

Therefore, if consumption is not biased very much and m_1 and m_1^* do not differ from $1/2$ very much, even a country specialised in a good whose relative price is diminished and having a lower factor price at trade equilibrium can enjoy gains from trade. A sufficient condition for this is the violation of both (11) and (12), i.e.,

$$1-1/(2-\beta/L)<\min\,(m_1,m_1^*)\leq\max\,(m_1,m_1^*)<1/(2-\alpha/L). \tag{13}$$

Next let us suppose that the first country is specialized in the second good, the second country in the first good, still assuming $p_1/p_2>\bar{p}_1/\bar{p}_2$ and w_1/w_2. This is the case where a country with a higher factor price is specialized in a good whose relative price is diminished by trade. In this case, both countries are better off at the trade equilibrium. Suppose not. Then the second country is worse off. In figure 8.4, the value of T_2 evaluated by the relative price p_1/p_2 is smaller than the value of A. The coordinates of A are $(\bar{L}_1-\alpha)$ and $(\bar{L}_2-\beta)$. If those of T_2 are denoted by D_{21} and D_{22},

$$p_1 D_{21}+p_2 D_{22}<p_1(\bar{L}_1-\alpha)+p_2(\bar{L}_2-\beta)\,. \tag{14}$$

The left-hand side of (14) is equal to $p_1(L-\alpha)$ since the second country is specialized in the first good. Since $p_2/p_1<\bar{p}_2/\bar{p}_1=\bar{L}_2(\bar{L}_1-\alpha)/\bar{L}_1x(\bar{L}_2-\beta)$, (14) is reduced to

$$L-\alpha=\bar{L}_1-\alpha+\bar{L}_2(\bar{L}_1-\alpha)/\bar{L}_1\,. \tag{15}$$

Substituting $m_1=\bar{L}_1/L$, $1-m_1=\bar{L}_2/L$, we have from (15)

$$m_1 L<m_1 L-\alpha\,, \tag{16}$$

which is a contradiction.

In any case, (13) is a sufficient condition for gains from trade of each country. If we regard each of two goods in our model as the aggregate of many goods, then m_1 can be changed by changing the grouping of goods, i.e., changing the trade and specialization pattern. A criterion for the mutually profitable grouping of goods is (13).

Theorem 3. If (13) is satisfied, both countries can enjoy gains from trade and complete specialization.

References

[1] Bain, J.S., *Barriers to new competition*, Harvard University Press, 1956.

[2] Eisenberg, E., 'Duality in homogeneous programming,' *Proceedings of the American Mathematical Society*, 12 (1961), 783–787 (Newman, ed., *Readings in mathematical economics*, I, Johns Hopkins University Press, 1968, 15–19).

[3] Isard, W., *Location and space-economy*, John Wiley, 1956.

[4] Johnson, H., 'International trade and monopolistic competition theory,' *Monopolistic competition theory*, edited by Kuenne, John Wiley, 1967.

[5] Johnston, J., *Statistical cost analysis*, McGraw-Hill, 1960.

[6] Karlin, S., *Mathematical methods and theory in games, programming and economics*, *1*, Addison–Wesley, 1959.

[7] Loesch, A., *Die raeumliche Ordnung der Wirtschaft*, G. Fischer, Jena, second edition, 1944.

[8] Modigliani, F., 'New developments on the oligopoly front,' *Journal of Political Economy*, 66 (1958), 215–232.

[9] Negishi, T., 'Monopolistic competition and general equilibrium,' *Review of Economic Studies*, 28 (1961), 196–201.

[10] Ruehman, P., 'Oligopolistische Preispolitik unter dem Einfluss der latenten Konkurrenz,' *Weltwirtschaftliches Archiv*, 96 (1966), 287–339.

[11] Sylos-Labini, P., *Oligopoly and technical progress*, Harvard University Press, 1962.

CHAPTER 9

Optimal foreign trade and investment for a nation

1. In the preceding two chapters, our basic principle to cope with monopolistic competition was to postulate that firms would behave according to the subjective or perceived demand functions. Although we have demonstrated the consistency of the model and worked out some problems of the comparative statics, we must admit that the subjectivity of demand functions, i.e., of decision rules of firms, is a source of grave difficulty in the analysis of the general equilibrium model of monopolistic competition.[1] Provided that there are many firms which have some price making powers, however, this subjectivity is an essential aspect of the model as was emphasized in chapter 7. Nevertheless there is an exceptional case in this regard, in which we can employ objective demand functions quite safely. This is the case of a country in an international economy with appreciable monopoly power in trade and no possibility of retaliation by other countries, i.e., that of the optimal tariff. The reasons justifying the use of objective demand functions are two-fold. Firstly, true or objective demand functions for a country have less conceptual difficulty and are much easier to estimate than those for a single firm since countries are more separated from each other than firms in an economy. Secondly, the government of a country can mobilize more resources to estimate true demand functions than a single firm can do. Besides, in international trade, a country may also have monopolistic power in international investments. Just as we can conceive of the optimal amount of international trade caused by commercial policies like an optimal tariff or subsidy on trade, so we may estimate for such a country the optimal amount of capital movement controlled by an optimal tax or subsidy on investment. In this chapter, we shall be concerned with

---

[1] For the critical point of view on the use of perceived demand functions, e.g., see Atsumi and Nikaido [1].

such optimal policies on international trade and investment from the nationalistic point of view of one country.

Recent contributions on the theory of optimal capital movements like Kemp [6, 7] and Jones [5], which analyzed an aspect of international trade and capital movements very neatly, interpret capital movements as physical transfer of capital goods between countries. 'It is rare, however, that capital instruments wander about.'[2]) Hence, the essential aspect of capital movements is the transfer of purchasing power over goods and services through trade deficit or surplus. Historically speaking, for example, Japan's prewar foreign capital imports consisted primarily of investment in bonds floated by the Industrial Bank of Japan in London or New York financial markets.[3]) Such capital movements create claims and liabilities between countries, but are not necessarily accompanied by the accumulation of physical capital in the importing country, or the decumulation of physical capital in the investing country. What will happen depends on the change of net investment in countries caused by capital movements. For this reason, it appears that multi-period models should be employed in the analysis of international capital movements.

We reconsider below optimal capital movements policy and its relation to optimal international trade from the above view point. In section 2 we begin with the simplest models of pure international trade with no capital movements and of pure capital movements where international trade is absent. The optimal combination of trade and capital movements is considered in sections 3 and 4. Finally, in section 5, a formal relationship between our analysis of capital movements and those of Kemp and Jones is discussed. In all that follows the formal similarity of the problem of optimal capital movements to the problem of optimal tariff should be noted.[4])

2. Consider first a single period two-commodity two-country model of an international economy. Let q_i and E_i denote respectively the price and excess demand of the ith commodity in the home country and p_i and F_i the price and excess demand of the ith commodity in the foreign country ($i = 1, 2$). The first commodity is taken as numeraire so that $p_1 = q_1 = 1$.

---

[2]) Ohlin [8], p. 404. See also Caves [2], pp. 134–7.
[3]) Okita and Miki [9].
[4]) This chapter is a revision of T. Negishi, 'Optimal capital movements revisited,' mimeographed, University of Minnesota, 1968.

If the second commodity is imported by the home country, $q_2 > p_2$ implies the import tariff and $q_2 < p_2$ implies the import subsidy. Home and foreign countries are subject to balance of trade constraints,

$$E_1 + p_2 E_2 = 0 , \tag{1}$$

$$F_1 + p_2 F_2 = 0 . \tag{2}$$

The reason why p_2 is used is that the foreign country – but not the home country, of course – is assumed to be a laissez faire country. For this reason the foreign price is identical with the price in the international market even though the home country is assumed to make its domestic price deliberately different from the international price. Since the commodity market must be cleared, we have

$$E_1 + F_1 = 0 , \tag{3}$$

$$E_2 + F_2 = 0 . \tag{4}$$

Equations 1–4 are dependent with only 3 degrees of freedom.

The economy of the foreign country is assumed to be competitive and F_1 and F_2 are considered as functions of p_2. Assuming laissez faire in the foreign country, the home country can influence p_2 by changing E_2.

Differentiating (4) with respect to E_2,

$$1 + (\mathrm{d}F_2/\mathrm{d}p_2)(\mathrm{d}p_2/\mathrm{d}E_2) = 0 . \tag{5}$$

Similarly differentiating (2),

$$(\mathrm{d}F_1/\mathrm{d}p_2)(\mathrm{d}p_2/\mathrm{d}E_2) + (\mathrm{d}F_2/\mathrm{d}p_2)(\mathrm{d}p_2/\mathrm{d}E_2)p_2 + F_2(\mathrm{d}p_2/\mathrm{d}E_2) = 0 . \tag{6}$$

But E_1 must be adjusted to the changed E_2 so that markets are cleared. Differentiation of (3) gives

$$(\mathrm{d}E_1/\mathrm{d}E_2) + (\mathrm{d}F_1/\mathrm{d}p_2)(\mathrm{d}p_2/\mathrm{d}E_2) = 0 . \tag{7}$$

From the point of view of the home country, the optimal condition is the equality of the domestic rate of substitution and the foreign rate of substitution $-(\mathrm{d}E_1/\mathrm{d}E_2)$. In a competitive economy, the former is equal to the relative price q_2. Therefore, from (5), (6) and (7) we should have for optimality,

$$q_2 = p_2 - F_2(\mathrm{d}p_2/\mathrm{d}E_2) . \tag{8}$$

As for the sign of dp_2/dE_2, we may consider it as positive. The reason for this is two-fold. Firstly, from the local stability condition of

$$dp_2/dt = F_2(P_2) + E_2, \quad (t = \text{time}), \qquad (9)$$

where E_2 is fixed since it is assumed to be controlled freely by the home country, we have dF_2/dp_2 negative and from (5) dp_2/dE_2 positive. However, one may argue that the stability condition of the market is $(dF_2/dp_2) + (dE_2/dq_2)r < 0$, since the home country is assumed not to control E_2 directly but to fix the ratio r of q_2 and p_2 by imposing the tariffs or subsidies (therefore E_2 is a function of p_2). Then, alternatively we may argue as follows. Suppose $dF_2/dp_2 > 0$. Then from (5), (7) and the optimal condition that $q_2 = -dE_1/dE_2 > 0$, dF_1/dp_2 must be negative. By differentiating (2) with respect to p_2, we have $(dF_1/dp_2) + p_2(dF_2/dp_2) + F_2 = 0$ and therefore $p_2(dF_2/dp_2) + F_2 > 0$. If we may assume the community trade indifference map in the foreign country, we have the Slutsky equation $dF_2/dp_2 = S_{22} - (dF_2/dY)F_2$, where $S_{22} < 0$ is a Hicksian substitution term and Y signifies the national income (in terms of the first commodity) and can see that F_2 must be negative unless the commodity is inferior. However, $p_2(dF_2/dp_2) + F_2 = p_2 S_{22} + (1 - p_2(dF_2/dY))F_2 > 0$ implies that F_2 must be positive, unless there exists an inferior good. Therefore, assuming no inferior goods, we have $dF_2/dp_2 < 0$ at the optimal point.

If the home country is importing the second commodity, $E_2 > 0$ and $F_2 < 0$, then from (8) we have $q_2 > p_2$, i.e., import must be restricted by tariff. On the other hand, if the home country is exporting the second commodity, $E_2 < 0$ and $F_2 > 0$, then from (8), $q_2 < p_2$ and export must be restricted by tariff. In either case, trade must be restricted from the home country's point of view for optimal trade.[5]

Consider now a Fisherian type (present and future) two-period model of two countries. Both countries produce a single identical commodity with the result that there exists no trade between them. However, lending and borrowing are possible. This means that one country can consume more (less) than it produces in the present, and less (more) in the future. Let us call the currently produced commodity the first commodity and that which is produced in the future the second commodity. Since a loan must be paid for, we have again budget constraints of home and foreign countries, (1) and (2). If E_1 is negative and E_2 is positive, the home country is lending

---

[5] If the home country is very small and the foreign elasticity of demand and supply is infinite, free trade is optimal.

since it consumes less at present and more in the future. If E_1 is positive and E_2 is negative, the home country is a borrower. Analogous relationships hold for the foreign country. As in the case of optimal trade, we have (8) as the optimal condition from the home country's point of view.

If the home country is lending, F_2 is negative and $q_2 > p_2$. This implies that the domestic rate of interest is lower than the foreign rate of interest. When the movement of capital is free, this condition can be established only by imposing a tax on interest from investment abroad. Similarly, if the home country is borrowing, F_2 is positive, $q_2 < p_2$, and the domestic rate of interest is higher than the foreign one and a tax should be imposed on interest earned by foreign investers. From the definition of the rate of interest (i.e., $(1-p_2)/p_2$ and $(1-q_2)/q_2$), (5) and (8), the rate of optimal taxation is calculated as $|(F_2/p_2)(\mathrm{d}p_2/\mathrm{d}E_2)|/(1-p_2+F_2(\mathrm{d}p_2/\mathrm{d}E_2))$.[6]

It should be noted that this is formally identical to the case of optimal trade in the two commodity (and single period) trade model. Just as the restriction of trade by tariff is optimal in the trade model, so is the restriction of capital movements by a tax on interest in the pure capital movements model.

3.   Now we extend the model to that of four commodities so as to include international trade as well as international investment. Let the first and second commodities be present commodities while third and fourth are future commodities. Definitions of E_i, F_i, p_i and q_i are the same as in the previous section and either the existence in the present of a market for future commodities or perfect expectation of future prices is assumed. Future prices are discounted present prices of future commodities and the first commodity is chosen as numeraire. Let us assume that the home country is exporting the first and third commodities ($E_1, E_3 < 0$), and importing the second and fourth ones ($E_2, E_4 > 0$).

Instead of (1) and (2), we now have

$$E_1 + p_2 E_2 + p_3 E_3 + p_4 E_4 = 0 , \tag{10}$$

and

$$F_1 + p_2 F_2 + p_3 F_3 + p_4 F_4 = 0 . \tag{11}$$

If $E_1 + p_2 F_2$ is negative the home country is lending and if positive, it is borrowing.

---

[6] This is expressed in terms of the domestic rate. The positive denominator is assured from positive prices and interest.

The home country can influence p_i by changing the E_i's $(i \neq 1)$. From the market clearing equations,

$$E_j + F_j(p_2, p_3, p_4) = 0, \qquad j \neq 1, \tag{12}$$

we have

$$\Sigma_k(\partial F_j/\partial p_k)(\mathrm{d}p_k/\mathrm{d}E_i) + \delta_{ij} = 0, \qquad \delta_{ij} = 1 \text{ for } i = j, \tag{13}$$

E_1 should be adjusted to the changes of E_i, $i \neq 1$, so as to clear its own market, i.e.,

$$(\mathrm{d}E_1/\mathrm{d}E_i) + \Sigma_j(\partial F_1/\partial p_j)(\mathrm{d}p_j/\mathrm{d}E_i) = 0, \qquad i \neq 1, \tag{14}$$

from

$$E_1 + F_1(p_2, p_3, p_4) = 0. \tag{15}$$

Finally, from (11), (13) and (14)

$$(\mathrm{d}F_1/\mathrm{d}E_i) + \Sigma_{j \neq 1} F_j(\mathrm{d}p_j/\mathrm{d}E_i) + \Sigma_{j \neq 1} p_j(\mathrm{d}F_j/\mathrm{d}E_i)$$
$$= -(\mathrm{d}E_1/\mathrm{d}E_i) + \Sigma_{j \neq 1} F_j(\mathrm{d}p_j/\mathrm{d}E_i) - p_i = 0. \tag{16}$$

Now taking the point of view of the home country, we notice that the optimal condition for the home country is the equality of the marginal rate of substitution in trade and that in domestic consumption and production, i.e.,

$$q_i = p_i - \Sigma_{j \neq 1} F_j(\mathrm{d}p_j/\mathrm{d}E_i), \qquad i \neq 1. \tag{17}$$

Hence, depending on whether q_i is larger or smaller than p_i, an import tariff (export subsidy) or an import subsidy (export tariff) is required.[7]) It must be emphasized that there is no need to impose a tax on (or give subsidy to) interest payments, provided that an import tariff (or subsidy) and an export tariff (or subsidy) are both possible in both periods. Of course, one could replace one of the tariffs (or subsidies) by an interest tax (subsidy). Suppose, for example, that an export tariff (subsidy) in the future is not permitted. Then, the domestic rate of interest should be higher or lower depending on whether q_3 is lower or higher than p_3, i.e., on whether a tariff or a subsidy is to be replaced. In this case, of course, the fourth commodity should be tariffed or subsidized according to $q_4/q_3 \gtrless p_4/p_3$.

Unfortunately, one cannot be certain whether a tariff or subsidy (tax or subsidy) is required, unless very stringent assumptions are made. For

[7]) The case of subsidy corresponds to the case of a loss leader in the theory of multi-product monopoly. See for example, Singer [10], pp. 180–2.

example, if there is no cross effect among markets, i.e., $(dp_j/dE_i) = 0$ for all $i \neq j$ in (17),[8]) then a tariff must be imposed in all markets (except numeraire) for optimality in the home country. Alternatively, one could have a subsidy on lending or a tax on borrowing, plus import tariffs in the present and in the future, since the domestic interest should be higher than the foreign rate and q_4/q_3 is larger than p_4/p_3.

4. Since the assumption of the existence of markets for future commodities or of perfect expectation in the previous section is very stringent, it may be worth while working through a less perfect model than the one just presented.

Suppose that future commodities are somehow aggregated into a single commodity, the third commodity. This aggregation would not be damaging if individual decision makers are assumed to disregard future price changes.[9]) This new model is formally identical with the one in the previous section except that p_4, q_4, E_4 and F_4 are deleted. A positive value for E_3 now signifies that the home country is lending and conversely.

As in the previous section, we have

$$q_i - p_i = -\Sigma_{j \neq 1} F_j(dp_j/dE_i), \qquad i \neq 1. \tag{17}$$

Again for optimality in the home country an import tariff (subsidy) is required if q_2 is larger (smaller) than p_2 and subsidy to (tax on) lending or tax on (subsidy to) borrowing is required when q_3 is smaller (larger) than p_3.

Firstly, one can show that

Theorem 1. Either an import tariff or a tax on interest should be imposed, i.e., a combination of subsidy to import and subsidy to interest will never be required for optimality. In other words, free trade and/or free capital movements should be restricted from the home country's point of view.

Proof. To see this, we solve (13) for dp_2/dE_i and dp_3/dE_i ($i = 2, 3$) and substituting into (17), we obtain

$$q_2 - p_2 = (F_2 F_{33} - F_3 F_{32})/|A|, \tag{18}$$

$$q_3 - p_3 = (F_3 F_{22} - F_2 F_{23})/|A|, \tag{19}$$

---

[8]) Graaf [3]. Since the choice of numeraire is arbitrary, the assumption is very stringent.
[9]) This may be related to Walrasian concept of net perpetual revenue. Walras [11], pp. 267–77.

where F_{ij} signifies $(\partial F_i/\partial p_j)$ and

$$A = \begin{bmatrix} F_{22} & F_{23} \\ F_{32} & F_{33} \end{bmatrix}. \tag{20}$$

If we assume that E_2 and E_3 are arbitrarily fixed by the home country, then from the local stability condition of

$$\begin{aligned} dp_2/dt &= F_2(p_2, p_3) + E_2 \\ dp_3/dt &= F_3(p_2, p_3) + E_3 \end{aligned} \qquad (t = \text{time}), \tag{21}$$

$|A|$ must be positive.[10] However, one may argue that the home country would fix the ratio of p_i and q_i and E_i's are not constants but functions of p_2 and p_3. Even so, we may alternatively be able to show the positive $|A|$ as follows. Suppose $|A|$ is negative. From (13), (14) and the optimal conditions $q_i = -dE_1/dE_i > 0$, $i = 2, 3$, we have

$$-F_{33}F_{12} + F_{32}F_{13} < 0, \tag{22}$$

$$F_{23}F_{12} - F_{22}F_{13} < 0. \tag{23}$$

On the other hand, by differentiating (11) with respect to p_2 and p_3 and solving for p_2 and p_3, we have

$$(-F_{33}F_{12} + F_{32}F_{13}) + (-F_2F_{33} + F_3F_{32}) < 0, \tag{24}$$

$$(F_{23}F_{12} - F_{22}F_{13}) + (F_2F_{23} - F_3F_{22}) < 0. \tag{25}$$

Assuming that the behavior of a country can be described by a trade indifference map, we have a Slutsky equation and can decompose F_{ij} into a Hicksian substitution term S_{ij} and an income term $-m_iF_j$,

$$F_{ij} = S_{ij} - m_iF_j, \tag{26}$$

where m_i is $\partial F_i/\partial Y$, Y being the national income in terms of the first commodity. Substituting (26) into (22)–(25), we have respectively

$$-m_1(F_3S_{32} - F_2S_{33}) + (S_{12}F_3 - S_{13}F_2)m_3 < 0, \tag{27}$$

$$-m_1(F_2S_{23} - F_3S_{22}) - (S_{12}F_3 - S_{13}F_2)m_2 < 0, \tag{28}$$

$$(1 - m_1)(F_3S_{32} - F_2S_{33}) + (S_{12}F_3 - S_{13}F_2)m_3 < 0, \tag{29}$$

$$(1 - m_1)(F_2S_{23} - F_3S_{22}) - (S_{12}F_3 - S_{13}F_2)m_2 < 0. \tag{30}$$

[10] See chapter 13. Since the real part of the characteristic roots of A must be negative, $|A|$ is positive.

by choosing the unit of commodities properly so that $p_2 = p_3 = 1$ and using the well known properties of substitution terms, $S_{ij} = S_{ji}$, $\Sigma_j S_{ij} = 0$ and $S_{22} S_{33} - S_{23} S_{32} > 0.$[11]) If we assume no inferiority, i.e., $m_i > 0$, $i = 1, 2, 3$, then $1 - m_1 > 0$, since $\Sigma_i m_i = 1$. There is a contradiction between (27) and (29) if $S_{12} F_3 - S_{13} F_2 \geqq 0$. On the other hand, if $S_{12} F_3 - S_{13} F_2 \leqq 0$, (28) and (30) are in contradiction. Therefore, assuming no inferiority, we see that $|A|$ must be positive at the optimal point. Now substituting (26) into (18) and (19), we have

$$q_2 - p_2 = (F_2 S_{33} - F_3 S_{32})/|A| , \tag{31}$$

$$q_3 - p_3 = (F_3 S_{22} - F_2 S_{23})/|A| . \tag{32}$$

As is well known,[12])

$$X_2 S_{22} X_2 + 2 S_{32} X_2 X_3 + S_{33} X_3 X_3 < 0 \tag{33}$$

is always true for any non zero X_2 and X_3. Substituting $-F_3$ for X_2 and F_2 for X_3, we have from (33)

$$F_3 (S_{22} F_3 - F_2 S_{23}) < F_2 (F_3 S_{32} - F_2 S_{33}) . \tag{34}$$

In the case of a home country which is lending, $E_3 > 0$ and $F_3 < 0$ and an import subsidy ($p_2 - q_2 > 0$) implies $F_2 S_{33} - F_3 S_{32} < 0$, since $|A|$ is positive. Because F_2 and F_3 are negative, this implies from (34) $F_3 S_{22} - F_2 S_{23} > 0$, or $p_3 - q_3 < 0$. Hence, for optimality in the home country, the domestic rate of interest must be lowered and there should be a tax on interest received from investment abroad. Similarly, in the case of a home country which is borrowing, $E_3 < 0$ and $F_3 > 0$, and the import subsidy implies $p_3 - q_3 > 0$ from (34). The domestic interest should be higher and a tax on interest earned by foreigners is required.

Similarly in the case of a single period three commodity model of pure international trade, we can show that trade of at least one commodity, except the numeraire, must be restricted by tariff from the view point of the home country. It never pays to subsidize import or export of two commodities. In other words, tariffs dominate subsidies in the optimal commercial policy of a nation. By analogy with the case of multi-product monopoly one would suspect that subsidies are required when there is complemen-

---

[11]) Hicks [4], p. 311.
[12]) See footnote 11.

tarity among commodities.[13]) For this reason it is interesting to consider the case of substitutability.

Theorem 2. If all commodities are substitutes, $S_{ij} > 0$ for all $i \neq j$, then both trade and capital movements must be restricted by tariff and tax if the home country is lending and trade must be restricted by tariff if it is borrowing. No definite conclusion is obtained for borrowing.

Proof. For the case of a lending country, this is easily seen from (31) and (32). Since F_2 and F_3 are negative and S_{32} is positive, both $q_2 - p_2$ and $q_3 - p_3$ are positive. It is a little more complicated in the case of a borrowing country. Firstly, by choosing the unit of commodities properly, we can make $p_2 = p_3 = 1$ at the optimal situations. Then, from (11), we have $|F_2| > F_3$ since both F_1 and F_3 are positive. Next consider the well-known property

$$A_{31} + p_2 S_{32} + p_3 S_{33} = 0 .^{14}) \tag{35}$$

From this we have $|S_{33}| > S_{32}$ and from (31) $q_2 - p_2 > 0$.

In a single period three commodity model of pure international trade, this theorem implies that imports must always be tariffed under substitutability when one of the exportables is numeraire, though whether other exportables must be tariffed or subsidized is not certain.

Finally, it might be interesting to add that the identical result is obtained in the case of the gross-substitutability, $F_{ij} > 0$, for all $i \neq j$.[15])

5. The guiding principle in the previous sections is that the problem of optimal trade and foreign investment in a two commodity world can be regarded as formally identical to the problem of optimal trade in a more than two commodity world, investment being considered as the excess of export over import. This is also true when investment is regarded as the movement of capital stock, as in the case of Kemp [6, 7] and Jones [5]. Even though we are critical of this view of foreign investment, it may be interesting to consider the Kemp–Jones problem of optimal trade and investment as the problem of optimal trade in a three commodity model so as to see the

---

[13]) See footnote 7.
[14]) See footnote 11.
[15]) It is also conceivable that the home country is either exporting or importing both of two commodities in the present. Generally, the lending in the former case (borrowing in the latter) must be restricted from (32).

formal relationship between our analysis of capital movement and those of Kemp and Jones.

Consider a two country three commodity model of an international economy. The formal structure of the model is identical to the one given in the preceeding section. Three commodities are, however, interpreted as two produced goods (the first and the second commodities) and the service of capital (the third commodity). The foreign investment in this model is, as in Kemp [6, 7] and Jones [5], the movement of capital stock or the export of the service of capital, i.e., $E_3 < 0$. Suppose each country is completely specialized, say, the home country specialized in the first commodity and the foreign country in the second.[16])

Then, we have the following theorem.

Theorem 3. All three commodities are substitutes (more exactly not complements) for each other in the foreign country and furthermore it always pays to restrict both trade and investment for the home country.

Proof. For the consumers, only two commodities (products of two countries) are relevant and therefore only the substitutability is possible, i.e., $S_{12}^c > 0$, $S_{13}^c = 0$, $S_{23}^c = 0$, c denoting consumers. Since only the second commodity is produced by the use of the service of capital and the given amount of labor force in the foreign country, a higher price of the service of capital p_3 implies smaller output and a higher output price p_2 implies larger demand for capital, i.e., $S_{23}^p > 0$, $S_{12}^p = 0$, $S_{13}^p = 0$, p denoting producers. Therefore, $S_{12} = S_{21} = S_{12}^c + S_{12}^p > 0$, $S_{13} = S_{31} = S_{13}^c + S_{13}^p = 0$, $S_{23} = S_{32} = S_{23}^c + S_{23}^p > 0$. In view of theorem 2 in the preceding section, we should have $q_2 - p_2 > 0$, $q_3 - p_3 > 0$ if $F_3 < 0$ and $q_2 - p_2 > 0$ if $F_3 > 0$. Since $F_3 < 0$ implies the borrowing of the home country and $F_3 > 0$ implies the lending of the home country, it always pays to restrict trade by tariff for the home country. As for lending, we must first notice that the home country investor wants to make $p_3 q_2/p_2 = q_3$ when the investment is not interfered with since their earnings in the foreign country must be paid in the form of the second commodity on which the home country imposes an import tariff.[17]) There-

[16]) As a matter of fact, the home country can be either completely or incompletely specialized. Our approach is inconvenient for the case of an incompletely specialized foreign country.
[17]) It is assumed that no duty is levied on repatriated dividends. In this case it is better for the home country investor to exchange his second commodity into the first in the home country than in the foreign country.

fore, $p_3/q_3 > (<)p_2/q_2$ implies the tax (subsidy) on the investment. From (31) and (32), $p_3/q_3 > (<)p_2/q_2$ implies

$$F_3 S_{22} - F_2 S_{23} < (>) F_2 S_{33} - F_3 S_{32} \qquad (36)$$

if units of commodities are properly taken so that $p_2 = p_3 = 1$. Since $S_{13} = 0$, $S_{32} = S_{23} = -S_{33}$ and $|S_{22}| > |S_{33}|$, we have

$$F_3 S_{22} - F_2 S_{23} < F_2 S_{33} - F_3 S_{32} \qquad (37)$$

when $F_3 > 0$. Therefore, lending must also be restricted by a tax. The case of borrowing can be similarly discussed since the foreign investor in the home country is paid in the form of the first commodity but it is better to exchange it into the second commodity in the home country. If $F_3 < 0$, we have $q_3 p_2/q_2 > p_3$ from

$$F_3 S_{22} - F_2 S_{23} > F_2 S_{33} - F_3 S_{32} \qquad (38)$$

and the borrowing must be taxed, too.

Let us make $p_2 = p_3 = 1$ below. Since $m_3 = 0$ and $|A| = F_{22} F_{33} - F_{23} F_{32}$ is reduced to $S_{33}(F_{11} + F_1)$, the tariff rate is calculated from (31) as one over one minus the foreign elasticity of the import, i.e., $(-1)/(1 + (F_{11}/F_1))$, where $F_{11}/F_1 < -1$. This expression happens to be identical to the optimal tariff formula in the case of a two commodity model of pure trade as is seen in (5) and (8). In view of (17) and (18), however, one must notice that this coincidence is limited only in the case of Kemp–Jones model. Denoting that $S_{31} = 0$, $m_3 = 0$, and using the well-known properties of substitution terms, the homogeneity of excess demand functions F_i's with respect to all prices p_1, p_2, p_3, and the budget constraint (11), the rate of tax on lending is obtained from the comparison of $p_3 q_2/p_2$ and q_3 and the use of (18) and (19) as $-(F_3/S_{33})[(q_2 m_1/p_2) + m_2]$, where $-(F_3/S_{33})$ signifies the elasticity of returns to capital invested overseas and q_2/p_2 equals to $(1 + (F_{11}/F_1))/(F_{11}/F_1)$. Similarly, in the case of borrowing the optimal tax rate is

$$(F_3/S_{33})(m_2 + m_1 q_2/p_2)/(1 + (F_3/S_{33})(m_2 + m_1 q_2/p_2)) .$$

References

[1] Atsumi, H. and H. Nikaido, 'Income distribution and growth in a monopolist economy,' *Zeitschrift für Nationalöconomie*, 28 (1968), 399–416.
[2] Caves, R.E., *Trade and economic structure*, Harvard, 1960.
[3] Graaf, J. de V., 'On optimal tariff structures,' *Review of Economic Studies*, 17 (1), no. 42 (1951–2), pp. 47–59.

[4] Hicks, J.R., *Value and capital*, 2nd ed., Oxford, 1946.

[5] Jones, R.W., 'International capital movements and the theory of tariffs and trade,' *Quarterly Journal of Economics*, 81 (1967), pp. 1–38.

[6] Kemp, M.C., *The pure theory of international trade*, Prentice-Hall, 1964, chapters 13 and 14.

[7] Kemp, M.C., 'Gains from international trade and investment,' *American Economic Review*, (1966), pp. 788–809.

[8] Ohlin, B., *Interregional and International Trade*, Harvard, 1933.

[9] Okita, S. and T. Miki, 'Treatment of foreign capital, a case study for Japan,' *Capital Movements and Economic Development*, Adler ed., Macmillan (1967), pp. 139–74.

[10] Singer, E.M., *Antitrust economics*, Prentice Hall, 1968.

[11] Walras, L., *Elements of pure economics*, Jaffé tr., Allen & Unwin, 1954.

PART 4

Second best

CHAPTER 10

The theory of second best
and separability

1. The problem of the second best is now well known. Imagine a problem of optimization whose degree of freedom is more than one, i.e., the number of variables exceeds that of constraints by at least two. You have as many optimum conditions as the degree of freedom. Suppose it is impossible to satisfy *all* of the optimum conditions. Then, does a change which brings about the satisfaction of *some* of the optimum conditions make things better? A naive man guided by common sense might answer in the affirmative. However, the correct answer is: it may make things better or worse, depending on situation. This is the problem of the second best and second best theories try to solve such questions as: in what situation the satisfaction of a certain optimum condition is still desirable and how a certain optimum condition should be modified in a certain situation, even if it does not lead to a maximum, when other optimum conditions are not satisfied.

For example, in the welfare maximization problem under given resources and technological constraints considered in chapter 1, marginal cost pricing is derived as the optimal condition for all industries. If there exist unavoidable discrepancies between price and marginal cost in some industries due to, say, the existence of monopolies, the question is whether we should still impose marginal cost pricing on other industries under our control. We have to consider in what circumstances marginal cost pricing is still desirable and generally what pricing policy is the best one, in the presence of monopolies in other industries.

Although the formal definition of the second best problem begins with Lipsey and Lancaster [9], we can go back to several earlier works in the field of applied welfare economics to look for interesting examples of second best problems. As will be seen in the next section, there is another second best problem, in addition to the one just mentioned, in the optimal pricing problem if the balanced budget condition is institutionally imposed in the case of decreasing cost. In the theory of public finance, we have encountered several second best problems, e.g., comparison of direct and indirect taxation. In view of the fact that free trade is optimal (chapter 2), most of the arguments on commercial policies in the theory of international trade are of a second best character. We have already pointed out in chapter 6 that the protective tariff for the infant industry is, though worthwhile, not the best solution. Chapter 11 will deal with other second best problems, i.e., restrictions on foreign trade and investments in the face of domestic distortions. The theory of customs unions, which made a considerable contribution to the general theory of the second best, will be briefly reviewed in the next section and studied further in chapter 12.

Summarizing experience in solving these various second best problems, the so called general theory of the second best is developed by Lipsey and Lancaster [9]. The general theory is of a negative character in the sense that the conditions for the second best are completely different from those of optimality in the ideal situations (Paretian conditions). Among several criticisms of Lipsey and Lancaster [9], the most controversial one was that of Davis and Whinston [3] which insists that even if one or more Paretian conditions are violated some of other Paretian conditions are still desirable when separability in terms of decision units properly exists. The outcome of the debate between Bohm [1], McManus [12] and Davis and Whinston [4] is by no means clear. The aim of this chapter is to consider the relationship between the second best conditions and separability and to clear the problem raised by Davis and Whinston [3].[1])

2.   Hicks's [6] classical arguments on optimal pricing when other industries are not competitive may be considered as one of the earliest examples of the second best theory. The optimality of perfect competition is demonstrated in terms of the surplus which accrued in the market of a particular commodity. The intersection of demand curve and marginal cost curve of the industry is optimal for the consumers and producers of this industry since the sum of the consumers' and producers' surplus is maximized. It is also optimal for an economy as a whole, if other industries are also competitive, since there would be no appreciable gain or loss to any third party if resources transferred from this industry were applied at (to this industry were taken from) the margin in another industry. However, it is not optimal when other industries are not competitive, since the extra unit produced in

---

[1]) This chapter is therefore to replace Negishi [17] which is quite unsatisfactory, as the essence of the problem was not seen.

other industries will be worth more than marginal cost and an additional surplus accruing to someone or other will be generated, if there is a contraction in output of the original industry and the excluded factors are transferred elsewhere. This means the social cost of the employment of factors in the original industry is greater than it appears at first and it is best taken care of by moving the cost curve upwards, its new intersection with the demand curve being optimal instead of the old one. In this way Hicks showed that perfect competition is not desirable if other industries are not competitive, which may seem to a casual reader as the second best theory.

However, the story is not so simple. In such a model of the economy as is conceived by Hicks, where every industry is integrated so that there exist no intermediate goods and owners of the factors of production do not reserve any part of their resources for their own use (i.e., factor supply is inelastic), the optimum condition is not necessarily perfect competition in every industry. Equal degree of monopoly in every industry will also do in such a model, i.e., the so-called Kahn–Meade model.[2]) If other industries are not competitive but the degree of monopoly is equal everywhere, then the optimum conditions are satisfied there and the new intersection of the demand curve and the shifted marginal cost curve (shifted proportionally to the common degree of monopoly) suggested above of the original industry is clearly not the point of the second best but the best point. On the other hand, if the degree of monopoly in other industries is not equal, i.e., the optimal conditions are not met, then the intersection of the demand curve and the shifted marginal cost curve is surely the point of the second best. However, it is not easy to tell how far the cost curve should be moved up, i.e., how large the degree of monopoly in the original industry should be. It is Green [5] who considered this problem in terms of general equilibrium analysis, as we shall see in the next section.

The optimal pricing problem of the public enterprise with diminishing costs and an institutionally imposed balanced budget condition is another example of the second best problem, since the best pricing, i.e., marginal cost pricing implies a deficit budget for the enterprise. It has been proposed that the degree of monopoly (the relative discrepancy between price and marginal cost) of each output must be inversely proportional to the price elasticity of its demand, by assuming that demands for joint outputs are independent each other and maximizing the sum of consumers' surplus.[3])

[2]) See chapter 3, section 7.
[3]) A modern version of this is given in Samuelson [19].

This proposition is certainly subject to the partial equilibrium character of the concept of consumers' surplus.[4]) On the other hand, Boiteux [2] analyzed the problem in general equilibrium analysis. It is important to note that he gave the rule of second best behavior in terms of artificial efficiency prices (prix fictifs) derived from the Lagrangean multipliers, clearly recognizing the difference between market prices (prix réels) and artificial efficiency prices, which is somewhat confused in the later debate on separability and the second best.

In addition to general pricing theory in welfare economics, we can find several pioneering works on the second best problem in the field of applied economics. For example, in the theory of public finance, Rolph and Break [18] argued that the excess burden of indirect taxes contention rests on an assumption that the resources allocation is ideal in the absence of e.g., excise taxes. In other words, otherwise we are in the second best situation and it cannot be said that direct taxes are superior to indirect taxes. Little [10] also argued as follows. Consider two commodities and leisure. A direct tax may reserve the equality of marginal rates of substitution in consumption and in production between two commodities but upsets the equality of marginal rates of substitution between commodities and leisure. On the other hand, an indirect tax on the consumption of a commodity makes the equality of marginal rates of substitution in consumption and in production between that commodity and leisure and between that commodity and the other commodity impossible, while it still keeps the equality of rates between the other commodity and leisure. Therefore, the superiority of two taxes cannot be easily decided since only some optimal conditions (equalities of marginal rates of substitution in consumption and production) are established in both cases.

In the sphere of international economics, the naive view on the optimality of free trade, tariff and customs unions was as follows. Free trade maximizes world welfare. A customs union reduces tariffs and is therefore a movement towards free trade. A customs union will, therefore, increase world welfare even if it does not lead to a world welfare maximum. It was Viner [21] who first showed that this argument is incorrect and that the trade creation effect of customs unions increases while the trade diversion effect diminishes world welfare. This is the second best theory, since a customs union implies partial free trade, a situation in which only some of the optimum conditions (free trade) are satisfied while other optimum conditions are not.

---

[4]) See chapter 3, section 1.

Following Viner, Meade [14] considered the problem of the customs union from a more generalized point of view. His method of analysis, which can be applied not only to the problem of the customs union but also to second best problems in general, such as the problem of direct and indirect taxation, etc., amounts to considering the infinitesimal change of social utility,

$$dU = u(dx(p_x - c_x) + dy(p_y - c_y) + \ldots),$$

where u is the marginal utility of income assumed identical for every one, dx is the change of amount sold and bought of the commodity x, p_x is the price of x payable by consumers, c_x is the supply price received by producers of x, and the like.[5]) The rest of his study of the second best problem is therefore devoted to the factors which will increase or decrease the volume of each commodity sold and bought, which is, however, by no means easy.[6])

3. The nature and significance of the second best problems are most generally demonstrated by Lipsey and Lancaster [9]. Consider the maximization of $F(x_1, \ldots, x_n)$, being subject to

$$G(x_1, \ldots, x_n) = 0. \tag{1}$$

Optimum conditions are $F_i - \alpha G_i = 0$, $i = 1, \ldots, n$, or $F_i/F_n - G_i/G_n = 0$, $i = 1, \ldots, n-1$, where α is the Lagrangean multiplier, F_i is the partial derivative of F with respect to x_i, and the like. Suppose the first condition is violated and

$$F_1/F_n - kG_1/G_n = 0, \tag{2}$$

where $k \neq 1$ is the given constant, is imposed. Then, conditions for the maximization of F subject to (1) and (2) are

$$F_i - \alpha G_i - \beta((F_n F_{1i} - F_1 F_{ni})/F_n^2) - k(G_n G_{1i} - G_1 G_{ni})/G_n^2) = 0$$

where β is the Lagrangean multiplier corresponding to (2). These are generally different from the original optimum conditions.[7])

The difficulty is that nothing can be said, in general, about the second best conditions without necessary knowledge on the second order partial derivatives of F and G.[8]) The formulation of the second best problem due

---

[5]) See Meade [14], 120–121, and also Meade [13], pp. 14–33.
[6]) For other comments on Meade, see Lipsey [9] and Vanek [20].
[7]) See also McManus [11].
[8]) Vanek [20], appendix.

to Lipsey and Lancaster is too general in one sense and too limited in another. It is too general since there is a possibility, in practice, of vanishing F_{1i}, F_{ni}, G_{1i} and G_{ni} for some i, with the result that some of the second best conditions coincide with the original optimum ones.[9]) It is too limited since k in (2) may be a function of x_i's, α's (i.e., efficiency prices) or market prices in general. For example, in the case where the violation of the original optimum conditions is due to the existence of taxation, k can be constant. However, when it is due to monopoly and imperfect competitions, the assumption of constant k is highly limitational. Actually, all the examples given in Lipsey and Lancaster [9] are cases of constant k, i.e., cases of taxation and tariff of constant rate and that of monopoly under a full cost pricing principle with a constant mark up ratio. One reason for this may be that at that time there was no general equilibrium model of imperfect competition at hand, which requires variable k, e.g., a model based on the marginal principle.[10])

Perhaps it was Kuroiwa [7] who first realized that the formulation of Lipsey and Lancaster is too general in the above-mentioned sense. In a non Robinson Crusoe economy, there are many independent decision units. Let the production function of the ith unit be

$$f_i(y_1^i, \ldots, y_n^i) = 0, \quad i = 1, \ldots, m, \tag{3}$$

where y_j^i signifies the amount of the jth commodity. For the Pareto optimal production of the total amounts of commodities, $\Sigma_i y_j^i, j = 1, \ldots, n$, equality of the marginal rate of substitution between every pair of commodities for every decision unit is required. Suppose this is violated for the first and second commodities and the first and second units and

$$f_1^1/f_2^1 - k f_1^2/f_2^2 = 0, \quad k \neq 1, \tag{4}$$

is imposed, where f_i^j signifies the derivative of f_i with respect to y_j^i. Kuroiwa demonstrated that the original optimum conditions, i.e., equality of the marginal rate of substitution for every pair of commodities, still hold for the units other than the first and second, as the condition for the Pareto optimum subject to (3) and (4).

---

[9]) Kuroiwa [7] and Davis and Whinston [3] realized the possibility of the separability of functions.

[10]) However see Negishi [16] and Davis and Whinston [3]. McManus [11] is the first to criticize Lipsey and Lancaster [9] in this respect.

Green [5] worked out a less abstract model of the economy. His problem is: if the ratio of price to marginal cost in certain industries is given what can be said about the optimal ratio of price to marginal cost in other industries? A single primary factor of production (labor), no joint output, and constant returns to scale are assumed so that the social transformation function is linear. Assuming perfect competition in the factor market (labor and intermediate products), the economy is on the transformation frontier. Define a unit of the commodity so that it requires a unit of labor to produce it and take the price of the latter as unity. Then, the marginal cost of each commodity is equal to unity and the market price of the ith commodity is $1 + t_i$, where t_i is the proportion by which the market price differs from the marginal cost. Suppose only t_i is free to vary (other t_j's, $j \neq i$, are constant).[11] At the point of the second best (optimal value of t_i under given t_j's), we have

$$\Sigma_j (1 + t_j) dx_j = 0 \tag{5}$$

from the differentiation of the social welfare function and

$$\Sigma_j dx_j = 0 \tag{6}$$

from that of the linear social transformation function, where x_j is the amount of the jth commodity produced. From (5) and (6) we have

$$t_i = \Sigma_{j \neq i} t_j dx_j / \Sigma_{j \neq i} dx_j .$$

Therefore, t_i lies between the largest and the smallest of the given t_j's, if the ith commodity is a Hicksian substitute for every other commodity (i.e., $dx_j > 0$, $j \neq i$, for $dt_i > 0$). This is an example of results obtained by Green. It may suggest that the general theory exaggerates the difficulty of the second best problem and that solving each concrete problem is much more fruitful than the abstract arguments of the general theory.

4. Davis–Whinston [3] starts, in a sense, from the place which Kuroiwa [7] had reached.[12] If Lipsey and Lancaster's [9] relevant functions are separable, i.e., $\partial^2 F / \partial x_i \partial x_j = \partial^2 G / \partial x_i \partial x_j = 0$, $i \neq j$, in the preceding section, the second best conditions coincide with Paretian conditions, with the exceptions of those concerned with the first and the nth variables. Such a

[11] The assumption of constant t_j corresponds to that of constant k in Lipsey and Lancaster [9].
[12] Of course, they are independent of each other.

separability is quite likely in actual economic problems since many decision making units are independent each other. Davis and Whinston criticized the formulation of the problem of Lipsey and Lancaster [9] to the effect that the decision making of consumers and firms is not explicitly considered.

Consider the maximization of the weighted sum of individual utilities,

$$\Sigma_i \alpha_i U_i(X_i) \, , \tag{7}$$

where $X_i = (X_{i1}, \dots, X_{im})$ is the consumption vector of individual consumer i ($i = 1, \dots, n$), U_i denotes his utility and α_i is a positive constant.[13]) Constraints are

$$\Sigma_i X_{ik} = \Sigma_r y_{rk}, \quad k = 1, \dots, m \, , \tag{8}$$

$$g_r(y_{r1}, \dots, y_{rm}, h_{r11}, \dots, h_{rms}) = 0, \quad r = 1, \dots, z \, , \tag{9}$$

$$\Sigma_k \Sigma_r h_{rkj} = H_j, \quad j = 1, \dots, s \, , \tag{10}$$

where g_r is the production function of the rth firm, y_{rk} is its output of the kth good, h_{rkj} is its use of the jth factor for the production of the kth good and H_j is the total amount of the jth factor. Paretian conditions, i.e., conditions for Pareto optimal resource allocation are

$$\alpha_i \partial U_i / \partial X_{ik} - \lambda_k = 0, \quad k = 1, \dots, m, \quad i = 1, \dots, n \, , \tag{11}$$

$$\lambda_k - \mu_r \partial g_r / \partial y_{rk} = 0, \quad k = 1, \dots, n, r = 1, \dots, z \, , \tag{12}$$

$$- \mu_r \partial g_r / \partial h_{rkj} - \rho_j = 0, \quad j = 1, \dots, s, \quad k = 1, \dots, m, \quad r = 1, \dots, z \, , \tag{13}$$

and (8), (9), (10), where λ_k, μ_r and ρ_j are Lagrangean multipliers respectively corresponding to (8), (9) and (10).

Paretian conditions are expressed as equalities of marginal rates of substitution by eliminating Lagrangean multipliers or as the perfectly competitive behavior of consumers and firms by interpreting Lagrangean multipliers as prices. If the behavior of some decision units is not competitive and can be expressed as a function of several variables ($X_{ik}, y_{rk}, h_{rkj}, \lambda_k, \rho_j$, etc.), e.g.,

$$X_{\tau k} = B_{\tau k}(\dots\dots\dots), \quad k = 1, \dots, m \, , \tag{14}$$

---

[13]) Davis and Whinston [3] explained α_i as the inverse of marginal utility of income, referring to Negishi [15]. However, as was demonstrated in chapter 1, it is so only in a competitive equilibrium situation. Generally, α_i should be regarded as a parameter in a social welfare function which specifies a certain Pareto optimum situation.

the second best problem is, according to Davis and Whinston [3], to maximize
(7) under (8), (9), (10) and (14). Condition (11) is replaced by

$$\alpha_i \partial U_i/\partial X_{ik} - \lambda_k - \Sigma_q \gamma_q \partial B_{\tau q}/\partial X_{ik} = 0, \quad i = 1, ..., \tau-1, \tau+1, ..., n,$$

$$k = 1, ..., m, \tag{15}$$

and (12) and (13) are replaced by

$$\lambda_k - \mu_r \partial g_r/\partial y_{rk} - \Sigma_q \gamma_q \partial B_{\tau q}/\partial y_{rk} = 0, \quad k = 1, ..., m,$$

$$r = 1, ..., z, \tag{16}$$

and

$$-\mu_r \partial g_r/\partial h_{rkj} - \rho_j - \Sigma_q \gamma_q \partial B_{\tau q}/\partial h_{rkj} = 0, \quad k = 1, ..., m,$$

$$r = 1, ..., z,$$

$$j = 1, ..., s, \tag{17}$$

where γ_q ($q = 1, ..., m$) are Lagrangean multipliers corresponding to (14).
Note that Lagrangean multipliers may enter into function $B_{\tau k}$ in (14). Davis
and Whinston [3] suggest first solving the maximizing problem by considering
λ_k, ρ_j, etc. in $B_{\tau k}$ as parameters and then equalizing such parameters with
corresponding Lagrangean multipliers obtained in the maximized problem
just solved. Then, it can be seen from (15), (16) and (17) that the second
best conditions and Pareto conditions are identical for those decision making
units whose behaviour has no direct influence on the behavior of those
deviating from the competitive (Pareto optimal) rule, i.e., if $\partial B_{\tau q}/\partial X_{ik}$,
$\partial B_{\tau q}/\partial y_{rk}$, etc. are zero.

Bohm [1] criticized Davis and Whinston [3] in that they ruled out every
possibility of letting prices to be faced by the deviant and those to be faced
by other decision units differ (i.e., the use of taxes and subsidies) or of
exerting indirect influences on the deviant through changes in prices. By a
simple example, he showed how Pareto optimality is achieved by the use
of such policies ruled out by Davis and Whinston even if a monopolist
exists. McManus [12] insisted that Lagrangean multipliers which express
social costs of goods and factors in terms of a welfare unit cannot be put
equal to prices measured in terms of a different unit, i.e., the monetary unit.
Suppose α_i's in (7) are doubled. The solution of the second best problem
should be unchanged in real terms, with Lagrangean multipliers doubled.
However, according to McManus, if prices (considered as parameters) in
functions $B_{\tau k}$ in (14) are equalized with Lagrangean multipliers, the real

solution of the problem must be changed by doubling α_i's, which indicates the invalidity of Davis and Whinston's [3] method. McManus suggests denoting prices in the deviant's behavior function $B_{\tau k}$ by $P_1, \ldots, P_{m+s}$ to be distinct from Lagrangean multipliers λ_k, ρ_j, and to maximize (7) under (8), (9), (10) and (14) with respect to X_{ik}, y_{rk}, h_{rkj} and P_t ($t = 1, \ldots, m+s$). In addition to (15), (16) and (17), the conditions for the maximization are

$$-\Sigma_q \gamma_q \alpha B_{\tau q}/\partial P_t = 0, \qquad t = 1, \ldots, m+s . \tag{18}$$

McManus also showed a simple case in which Pareto optimality, not the second best, is achieved by the suggested method in the presence of a deviant.

Davis–Whinston [4] is a rejoinder to Bohm [1] and McManus [12], particularly to the latter. They firstly emphasized the piecemeal character of the second best theory which permits the behavior of the deviant, thereby excluding from consideration the Pigouvian policy of taxes and subsidies suggested by Bohm and McManus since it aims to interfere with the behavior of the deviant and to lead to a Pareto optimal situation. As a reason for a second best theory which aims not at the best but at the second best solution, they enumerate the lack of information, the incompleteness of models, etc.[14]) Then, as for the relationship between prices and Lagrangean multipliers, they argued against McManus that the dimension of α_i's, being the inverse of the marginal utility of income, is money/utility and that of the marginal utility of goods is utility/goods. Therefore, from (11), the dimension of λ_k is money/goods, i.e., that of the price, being independent of utility units. If McManus's [12] doubling α_i's implies the doubling of monetary values, real variables remain unchanged with all prices doubled.[15]) On the other hand, if it implies changes in utility units, prices will remain unchanged.

It seems that the conclusion of Davis and Whinston [3] that separability makes some of the second best conditions identical to Paretian conditions is valid if the equality of marginal rates of substitution is implied by the latter conditions but not necessarily so if perfectly competitive behavior is implied by them. The crux of the problem is the nature of Lagrangean multipliers. Their ratios are identical to marginal rates of substitution.

---

[14]) Therefore, they seem to insist that the aim of the second best theory is to check the desirability of simple Paretian conditions in the second best situation rather than to derive delicate second best condition for the decision unit not separable from the deviant. However, the trouble is that the former is not assured unless the latter is established.

[15]) They seem to assume, quite rightly, that $B_{\tau k}$ functions in (14) are homogeneous of degree zero with respect to Lagrangean multipliers.

Therefore, they are identical to prices only in perfect competition. Davis and Whinston [3], by putting Lagrangean multipliers and prices equal, assume perfect competition from the beginning. McManus [12] is right saying that Lagrangean multipliers denote social costs, though his statement that they cannot be expressed by a common unit with prices is incomprehensible. However, Davis and Whinston's [4] argument against McManus in this respect has some difficulties, since α_i's are regarded as the inverses of marginal utility of income, which is true only in the equilibrium of perfect competition. Generally, α_i's are mere numbers and the dimension of λ_k's is utility/goods. Although the dimension of prices P_t is money/goods, P_t and λ_k are comparable since the absolute prices are indeterminate and proportional changes of P_t's mean no changes in real terms. If there is no money illusion, functions $B_{\tau k}$ in (14) must be homogeneous of degree zero with respect to P_t's. Therefore, McManus's [12] argument based on doubling α_i's makes no sense at all.

There is a difference in the definition of the deviant between Lipsey and Lancaster [9] and Davis and Whinston [3]. In the case of the latter definition in terms of behavior function like $B_{\tau k}$ in (14), the behavior of a single deviant can be cancelled by Pigouvian taxes and subsidies. The result is Pareto optimal and there is no room for the piecemeal second best theory, since the same result is also obtained by any proper pricing or quantity policies of other decision units which can exert influences on the deviant through price changes. Therefore, the difference between Bohm [1] and McManus [12] on one hand and Davis and Whinston [3] on the other does not lie in whether Pigouvian policies are taken into consideration. However, if there are multiple deviants, their behavior cannot be cancelled and the result is short of Pareto optimality, i.e., second best, unless prices are differentiated according to each different deviant. The second best problem arises when price differentiation for each different deviant is ruled out.

5. We are now ready, after the critical review of the debate on the second best and the separability, to state our positive view on the problem.

Consider an economy of a single consumer, three firms, three goods and three factors. Let the consumer's demands and supplies of goods and factors be denoted by D_i and S_i ($i = 1, 2, 3$) and prices of goods and factors by P_i and W_i ($i = 1, 2, 3$). Each good is produced by a single firm, with production function of the ith good (firm) being generally

$$X_i = f_i(Y_{i1}, Y_{i2}, Y_{i3}, Z_{i1}, Z_{i2}, Z_{i3}), \qquad (19)$$

where X_i, Y_{ij} and Z_{ij} denote the output of the ith good and the input of the jth good and of the jth factor for the production of the ith good. Suppose the first two firms are monopolistic in the market of output and each maximizes its profit $F_1(X_1; \overline{X}_1, P_1)X_1 - P_2 Y_{12} - \Sigma_j W_j Z_{1j}$ and $F_2(\overline{X}_2; \overline{X}_2, P_2) X_2 - P_1 Y_{21} - \Sigma_j W_j Z_{2j}$ respectively under

$$X_1 = f_1(Y_{12}, Z_{11}, Z_{12}) \text{ and } X_2 = f_2(Y_{21}, Z_{21}, Z_{22}), \tag{19'}$$

where F_i is the subjective inverse demand function perceived when current output $\overline{X}_i$ and price P_i are given, such that $P_i = F_i(\overline{X}_i; \overline{X}_i, P_i)$.[16]) Therefore, X_i, Y_{ij} and Z_{ij} are functions of $\overline{X}_i$, P_i and W_j, $i, j = 1, 2$.

Excluding the possibility of price differentiation for each different monopolist, we have a second best problem due to the existence of monopolies.[17]) We first maximize $U(D_1, D_2, D_3, S_1, S_2, S_3)$, i.e., the utility of the consumer, being subject to demand and supply equalities,

$$D_1 + Y_{21} = X_1, \tag{20}$$

$$D_2 + Y_{12} = X_2, \tag{21}$$

$$D_3 = X_3, \tag{22}$$

$$S_1 = Z_{11} + Z_{21}, \tag{23}$$

$$S_2 = Z_{12} + Z_{22}, \tag{24}$$

$$S_3 = Z_{33}, \tag{25}$$

behavior functions of monopolists,

$$X_i = X_i(\overline{X}_i, P_1, P_2, W_1, W_2), \quad i = 1, 2, \tag{26}$$

$$Y_{ij} = Y_{ij}(\overline{X}_i, P_1, P_2, W_1, W_2), \quad i, j = 1, 2, \tag{27}$$

$$Z_{ij} = Z_{ij}(\overline{X}_i, P_1, P_2, W_1, W_2), \quad i, j = 1, 2, \tag{28}$$

and the production function of the third firm which is under our control, i.e.,

$$X_3 = f_3(Z_{33}), \tag{19''}$$

---

[16]) See chapter 7.
[17]) We are permitting price differentiation between monopolists on one hand and the consumer and the third firm on the other which are under our control. It may be interesting to point out that in the problems considered by Hicks [6] and Green [5] the behavior of consumers is not under our control (i.e., they must be competitive) and any price differentiation is ruled out.

assuming that $\bar{X}_i$'s are parameters and then make $\bar{X}_i = X_i$, i, $i = 1, 2$, where X_i is the solution of the maximizing problem. The conditions obtained are

$$U_i - q_i = 0, \quad i = 1, 2, 3 , \tag{29}$$

$$U_j + V_j = 0, \quad j = 1, 2, 3 , \tag{30}$$

$$V_3 / q_3 = \mathrm{d}f_3 / \mathrm{d}Z_{33} , \tag{31}$$

$$\Sigma_i \beta_i X_{ik} + \Sigma_{i,j} \gamma_{ij} Y_{ijk} + \Sigma_{i,j} \delta_{ij} Z_{ijk} = 0, \quad k = 1, 2 , \tag{32}$$

$$\Sigma_i \beta_i X_{is} + \Sigma_{i,j} \gamma_{ij} Y_{ijs} + \Sigma_{i,j} \delta_{ij} Z_{ijs} = 0, \quad s = 1, 2 , \tag{33}$$

where U_i, U_j, q_i, V_j, β_i, γ_{ij}, δ_{ij}, X_{ik}, X_{is}, Y_{ijk}, Y_{ijs}, Z_{ijk} and Z_{ijs} are respectively marginal utility and disutility of goods and factors, Lagrangean multipliers corresponding to (20–22), (23–25), (26), (27), (28), the partial derivative of X_i, Y_{ij}, Z_{ij} with respect to P_k, W_s.

From (32) and (33), P_1, P_2, W_1 and W_2, i.e., market prices of the first two goods and two factors are determined up to scalar multiplication. Generally, q_1, q_2, V_1 and V_2, i.e., efficiency prices of two goods and factors are different from P_1, P_2, W_1 and W_2. Therefore, if the consumer behaves competitively, there must be taxes and subsidies designed to make consumer's prices q_1, q_2, V_1 and V_2 properly different from monopolists' prices P_1, P_2, W_1 and W_2. Or, alternatively, the consumer may behave non-competitively so that marginal rates of substitution (i.e., ratio of q_1, q_2, V_1 and V_2) are properly different from the ratio of market prices. As for the third good and third factor which are irrelevant for monopolists, Lagrangean multipliers q_3 and V_3 can be considered as prices. In other words, the consumer and the third firm must behave competitively in these markets.

We must note that the consumer and the third firm are (physically) separable from the deviant in the sence of Davis and Whinston [3], i.e., have no direct influences on the behavior of the monopolist.[18] Paretian conditions in the sense of an equal marginal rate of substitution are still applicable for the consumer and the third firm in the second best situation. Furthermore, the third firm is pecuniarily separable from monopolists, i.e., it cannot exert any indirect influence through price changes on monopolists. Paretian conditions in the sense of perfect competition without any corrective taxes and subsidies are still desirable for this firm. Since the behavior of the deviant must be based on some subjective functions like a perceived demand function

---

[18] I.e., (26–28) are independent of D_i, S_i, X_3 and Z_{33}.

where only a limited number of variables are strategically taken into consideration, the presence of physical and/or pecuniary separability may be more likely than is generally expected.[19]) We may recapitulate as

Theorem.   In a second best problem, the Paretian conditions in the sense of equal marginal rates of substitution are still desirable for decision units physically separable from the deviant and the Paretian conditions in the sense of perfect competition and laissez-faire remain untouched for decision units not only physically but also pecuniarily separable from the deviant.

References

[1] Bohm, P., 'On the theory of the second best,' *Review of Economic Studies*, 34 (1967), 301–14.

[2] Boiteux, M., 'Sur la gestion des monopoles publics astreints a l'équilibre budgetaire,' *Econometrica*, 24 (1956), 22–40.

[3] Davis, O. and A. B. Whinston, 'Welfare economics and the theory of the second best,' *Review of Economic Studies*, 32 (1965), 1–13.

[4] Davis, O. and A. B. Whinston, 'Piecemeal policy in the theory of second best,' *Review of Economic Studies*, 34 (1967), 323–331.

[5] Green, H. A. J., 'The social optimum in the presence of monopoly and taxation,' *Review of Economic Studies*, 29 (1961), 66–78.

[6] Hicks, J. R., 'The rehabilitation of consumers' surplus,' *Review of Economic Studies*, 8 (1940–1), 108–116.

[7] Kuroiwa, H., 'Jizenteki Saiteki no Riron,' *Journal of Kobe Commercial College*, 42 (1961), 1–25.

[8] Lipsey, R. G., 'The theory of customs unions; a general survey,' *Economic Journal*, 70 (1960), 496–513 (Caves and Johnson, ed., *Readings in international economics*, Irwin, 1968, 261–278).

[9] Lipsey, R. G. and K. J. Lancaster, 'The general theory of second best,' *Review of Economic Studies*, 24 (1956–7), 11–32.

[10] Little, I. M. D., 'Direct versus indirect taxes,' *Economic Journal*, 61 (1951), 577–84 (Musgrave and Shoup ed., *Readings in economics of taxation*, Irwin, 1959, 123–13).

[11] McManus, M., 'Comments on the general theory of the second best,' *Review of Economic Studies*, 24 (1959), 209–224.

[12] McManus, M., 'Private and social costs in the theory of second best,' *Review of Economic Studies*, 34 (1967), 317–323.

[13] Meade, J. E., *Trade and welfare*, Mathematical Supplement, Oxford University Press, 1955.

[14] Meade, J. E., *The theory of customs unions*, North-Holland Publishing Co., 1955.

[19]) See Davis and Whinston [4] and chapter 7.

[15] Negishi, T., 'Welfare economics and the existence of a competitive equilibrium,' *Metroeconomica*, 11 (1960), 92–97.

[16] Negishi, T., 'Monopolistic firm competition and general equilibrium,' *Review of Economic Studies*, 28 (1961–62), 196–201.

[17] Negishi, T., 'Perceived demand curve in the theory of second best,' *Review of Economic Studies*, 34 (1967), 316–7.

[18] Rolph, E. R. and G. F. Break, 'The welfare aspects of excise taxes,' *Journal of Political Economy*, 58 (1949), 46–54 (Musgrave and Shoup, ed., *Readings in economics of taxation*, Irwin, 1959, 110–120).

[19] Samuelson, P. A., 'Pure theory of public expenditure and taxation,' Margolis and Guitton, ed., *Public economics*, Macmillan, 1969, 98–123.

[20] Vanek, J., *General equilibrium of international discrimination*, Harvard University Press, 1965.

[21] Viner, J., *The customs union issue*, Carnegie Endowment for International Peace, 1950.

CHAPTER 11

Domestic distortions and second best foreign policies

1. As is discussed in the preceding chapter, the second best problem arises when the best solution is impossible or difficult while alternative solutions are easier, though less efficient. There are some situations in which domestic optimal policies (taxes and subsidies) for domestic distortions like market imperfections, externalities, etc. are very hard to carry out, though foreign policies, i.e., restrictions on foreign trade and investments etc., are possible, since foreign trade and investments are more likely to be under the government's control or supervision than domestic trade and investments. The aim of the present chapter is to discuss two cases of second best foreign policies designed to correct domestic distortions of recent interest. The first case is concerned with the corrective tariff when the marginal productivities of factors of production are different between different industries, owing to the wage differential between industries or the existence of non-capitalistic subsistence sector. Domestic distortion in the second case is non-optimal capital accumulation or saving due to market imperfection, i.e., the non-existence of futures markets and futures prices for all commodities.[1])

We have a long list of economic arguments for protection, which make it desirable for a country to trade less and to move to a position of greater autarky, the last of which is perhaps Hagen [6]. Hagen, in his attempt to justify the use of a tariff, appealed to the wage differential unfavorable to the import competing industry, and graphically demonstrated the case of a small country which is better off at autarky than with trade. Bhagwati and Ramaswami [2] first offered a counter example to Hagen, then generalized the arguments in terms of the second best theory and denied the general possibility of the second best tariff to correct domestic distortions. However, in our opinion (Kemp and Negishi [11]), not all of the conclusions obtained by Bhagwati and Ramaswami are correct and we can show the existence of

---

[1]) See Scitovsky [17].

the second best tariff which makes the country better off than at free trade.[2]) In other words, what Hagen wanted to demonstrate, but not the way he did it, was right. Below, we will explain the debate between Hagen and Bhagwati–Ramaswami (section 2) and show, in terms of general equilibrium analysis, the possibility of the second best tariff pointed out by Kemp and Negishi (section 3). A slightly different but highly related case of domestic distortion, i.e., the case of disguised unemployment in the subsistence sector, is also discussed (in section 4).[3])

The arguments that capital export tends to be excessive from the national point of view of the lending country and therefore foreign investment should be restricted can be based on several different points, among which the diminishing return to capital in the invested country is emphasized by MacDougal [13] and Kemp [9].[4]) However, our result from a simple dynamic model (Negishi [14]) that there are on the other hand situations in which capital export should be encouraged is different from that of Kemp which is based on an a-temporal model, i.e., it should always be restricted.[5]) Now these two contradicting results can be reconciled from the point of view of the second best theory (section 5), since the result obtained from the a-temporal model can remain valid in the dynamic analysis, if the amount of saving (capital accumulation) is optimal. The final section is devoted to putting in a dynamic form the theory of the optimal tariff[6]) and its relevance to the theory of the second best. It will be shown that the import of capital goods should be subsidized (tariffed) for a small country, for which free trade is optimal if statically considered, if saving is less (more) than optimal.

2. Let us begin with the review of Hagen [6]. In figure 11.1, the quantity of the manufactured goods is measured along the horizontal axis and that of the agricultural goods, along the vertical axis. The transformation curve is AQB when the resource allocation is optimal and there is no domestic distortion. If a wage differential exists, the transformation curve is ASB, since resources are wasted when both manufactured and agricultural goods

[2]) Bhagwati and Ramaswami have accepted this (Bhagawati and Ramaswami [2], 1969) and further generalized the argument in Bhagawati, Ramaswami and Srinivasan [3].
[3]) See Lewis [12].
[4]) Kemp [9], pp. 192–203.
[5]) Kemp himself has obtained different results by using a different model which permits incomplete specialization but is still static. See chapter 9.
[6]) For the optimal tariff, see chapter 9. A pioneering work making dynamic the theory of the optimal tariff is Atsumi [1].

are produced.[7]) Assuming the case of a small country, the constant international relative price of manufactured and agricultural goods is given by the slope of *PFT*. Since the relative wage is assumed to be higher in the manufacturing industry, the ratio of the marginal cost of manufacturing industry to that of the agriculture exceeds the marginal rate of transformation of the manufactured to agricultural goods.[8]) That is to say, a price line like *PFT* must be steeper than *ASB* at a production point like *P*. Under free trade, agricultural goods are exported and manufactured goods are imported.

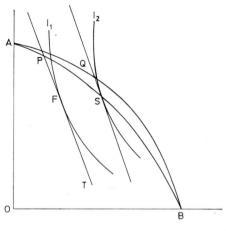

Fig. 11.1.

At the consumption point *F*, a social indifference curve I_1 is tangent to *PFT*. If the import competing manufacturing industry is protected by an import tariff, the domestic price of manufactured goods is relatively raised and the domestic relative price of manufactured and agricultural goods is expressed by the slope of *QS*, with the international one still being that of *PFT*. With a sufficiently high tariff, there is no trade at the autarky point *S*. A social indifference curve I_2, which is higher than I_1, is tangent to *QS* at *S*. Therefore, it pays to protect with a tariff the import competing industry which is paying a relatively higher wage. Such is the conslusion of Hagen [6].

---

[7]) We assume no price differentials for the service of other factors. As for the shape of the transformation curve, see Fishlow and David [4] and Johnson [8].
[8]) Hagen [6], pp. 507–8.

As far as the case of figure 11.1 is concerned, it pays to impose the prohibitive tariff on the import. However, we cannot jump, as Hagen did, from figure 11.1 to the conclusion that it always pays to prohibit trade when there is domestic distortion due to wage differentials. Bhagwati and Ramaswami [2] present figure 11.2 in which I_1 passes S and I_2 passes F,

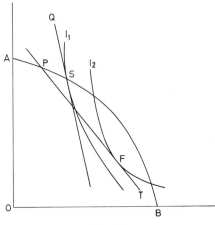

Fig. 11.2.

and insist that the above conclusion of Hagen must be rectified since prohibitive protection S is not necessarily superior to free trade F. They also point out that a subsidy on the production of manufactured goods or a tax on the production of agricultural goods which makes the international price line tangent to the transformation curve ASB yields a better solution than protection by tariff. But, Bhagwati and Ramaswami continue, a subsidy on the use of labor in the manufacturing industry or a tax on the use of labor in agriculture, which makes the international price line and the transformation curve AQB in figure 11.1 tangent with each other, produces the best result, attaining an optimum optimorum.[9]) In other words, the best policy for a domestic distortion is a domestic policy.

Bhagwati and Ramaswami generalize the above arguments as follows. The international relative price, i.e., the slope of *PFT*, can be called the foreign rate of transformation (FRT) since it is the rate at which a commodity can be transformed into another through trade. The slope of transformation

---

[9]) Hagen himself admitted this point.

curves like AQB, ASB is the domestic rate of transformation (DRT) while that of social indifference curves like I_1 and I_2 is the domestic rate of substitution (DRS). The achievement of an optimum solution for a country is characterized by the equality of FRT, DRT and DRS (assuming an interior maximum). Free trade implies FRT = DRS $\neq$ DRT as is seen at P and F in figures 11.1 and 11.2 and is not optimal. Domestic taxes and subsidies can change DRT so as to have FRT = DRS = DRT. On the other hand, a suitable tariff can equalize FRT and DRT but destroys the equality between DRS and FRT. Therefore, a tariff is inferior to the best policy of taxes and subsidies. Generally it is impossible to say which is better between situations of FRT = DRT $\neq$ DRS and of FRT $\neq$ DRS = DRT. From these arguments, Bhagwati and Ramaswami conclude that no tariff may exist that would yield a solution superior to that under free trade.

Of the two propositions on which Bhagwati and Ramaswami insist concerning the desirable form of intervention when the economy is subject to domestic distortion, there can be no objection to the first one to the effect that, in the case of domestic distortion, a suitable tax-cum-subsidy on domestic production is superior to a tariff. Kemp and Negishi [11] cannot, however, agree with the second proposition that no tariff (or trade subsidy) may exist that yields a solution superior to that under free trade,[10]) since given distortion there exists a level of tariff (or trade subsidy when it is negative) which is second best, i.e., superior to the free trade, though not to the suitable tax-cum-subsidy on production. The only reason which is given by Bhagwati and Ramaswami denying the possibility of the second best tariff is that a suitable tariff can equalize FRT and DRT but destroys the equality between DRS and FRT. If some of the Paretian conditions are violated, then the rest of the Paretian conditions are no longer desirable. Therefore, the tariff at a rate just sufficient to offset the distortion between FRT and DRT may not be superior to the free trade. It does not, however, follow from this argument that no tariff may exist that would yield a solution superior to that under free trade.[11])

---

[10]) On pages 45 and 46 Bhagwati and Ramaswami [2], 1963, may seem to mean that there may not exist a positive tariff superior to free trade, leaving open the possibility that there may exist a negative tariff superior to free trade. However, on pages 47 and 49 they make clear that they intend their statement to apply to both positive and negative tariff.

[11]) Similarly, for a country without domestic distortion but with appreciable monopoly power in trade, Bhagwati and Ramaswami state that it may be impossible to devise a tax-cum-subsidy that would yield an equilibrium superior to free trade. This is also incorrect.

3. Kemp and Negishi [11] argue as follows. Consider an initial free trade equilibrium in which something is consumed of each commodity. Suppose that this equilibrium is disturbed by the imposition of a tariff. At the initial equilibrium point the relevant community indifference curve is tangential to the world price line: hence the rate of change of the consumption gain or loss per unit increase in the tariff is zero. The rate of change of the production gain or loss, however, is not zero, for in the initial equilibrium the transformation curve cuts the price line. Thus the net rate of change of welfare must be non zero and we may be sure that there exists a tariff or trade subsidy which produces an equilibrium superior to that under free trade.

Let us demonstrate the above statement in terms of general equilibrium analysis. Consider a two commodity two factor model of a small country.[12]) The consumers' demands for two commodities and the utility indicator corresponding to the social indifference map are denoted respectively by D_1, D_2 and $U(D_1, D_2)$. Domestic output of two commodities and national income (in terms of the first commodity) are denoted by X_1, X_2 and Y. The international and domestic prices of the second commodity in terms of the first is denoted by p and q.

Since the country is small, p is given by the international market. Initially, free trade is assumed and q is equal to p. Then, D_1, D_2, X_1, X_2 and Y are determined by

$$(D_1 - X_1) + p(D_2 - X_2) = 0 , \tag{1}$$

$$X_1 = F(X_2) , \tag{2}$$

$$-F'(X_2) = t(X_2)q , \tag{3}$$

$$D_2 = D_2(q, Y) , \tag{4}$$

$$Y = X_1 + qX_2 + (q-p)(D_2 - X_2) . \tag{5}$$

The balance of trade condition is expressed by (1). Equation (2) signifies the transformation curve under domestic distortions, i.e., ASB in figures 11.1 and 11.2. Domestic distortion is given by $t(X_2)$ in (3), i.e., the relation between price lines and the transformation curve in figures 11.1 and 11.2. In view of (2) and (3), distortion is assumed to be generally a function of outputs of the two commodities. Let us assume that the second industry has

---

[12]) See Kemp [9], pp. 9–22, [10], pp. 5–30.

to pay a higher wage and therefore $t(X_2) < 1$. The tariff revenue is taken care of in the definition of Y, i.e., (5).[13])

Assuming the second commodity to be imported and starting from free trade, consider the effect of the imposition of an import tariff. If q is increased slightly from p by the imposition of a tariff, the change in social welfare is given by

$$dU/dq = \lambda(dD_1/dq + qdD_2/dq) , \tag{6}$$

where $\lambda > 0$ is the marginal social utility of income corresponding to U. Differentiating (1–5) by q, computing dD_1/dq and dD_2/dq, substituting them into (6) and noting that $p = q$, we have

$$dU/dq = \lambda t(X_2)(p + F'(X_2))/(-p)(F''(X_2) + qt'(X_2)) . \tag{7}$$

Differentiation of (3) gives

$$dX_2/dq = t(X_2)/(-F''(X_2) - qt'(X_2)) . \tag{8}$$

If there is no domestic distortion, a tariff implies the increase of X_1, since $F''(X_2) < 0$, i.e., the transformation curve AQB is concave to the origin in figure 11.1. Alternatively, if a tariff increases X_1 even under the domestic distortion, as in the case of figures 11.1 and 11.2, then $-F''(X_2) - qt'(X_2) > 0$, i.e., the denominator of the right-hand side of (7) is positive. As for the numerator, (3) gives us $p + F'(X_2) > 0$, since $t(X_2) < 1$ and $p = q$. Therefore, $dU/dq > 0$. Imposition of the import tariff, starting from free trade, increases the social welfare.

Now, we can state

Theorem 1. If the import competing industry has to pay a higher wage and the imposition of the import tariff increases the output of the import competing industry,[14]) then there exists a tariff superior to free trade.

Starting from free trade, initially an increase in the rate of tariff implies a welfare increase. If we continue to increase the tariff rate, however, eventually this may not be true and welfare may begin to decline. In the case of figure 11.1, the prohibitive tariff is superior to free trade, though whether

---

[13]) The last term in the right-hand side of (5) signifies the tariff revenue in terms of the first commodity.

[14]) If this condition is not satisfied, it may be a negative tariff, i.e., a trade subsidy which is superior to free trade.

a higher tariff rate implies a welfare increase at this stage is not certain. In the case of figure 11.2, the prohibitive tariff is inferior to free trade and a higher tariff rate must imply lower welfare at the rate of the prohibitive tariff. Of course, even in the case of figure 11.2, there must exist a tariff of a lower rate than the prohibitive one which is superior to free trade. To derive the rate of such a second best tariff explicitly, it is convenient to make some simplifying assumption on the distortion $t(X_2)$.

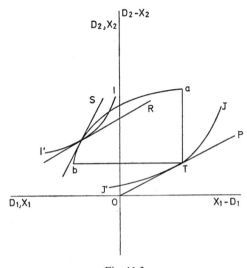

Fig. 11.3.

Consider figure 11.3.[15]) In the second quadrant are drawn a single social consumption indifference curve II' and the production block, i.e., ab which corresponds to ASB in figures 11.1 and 11.2. At point Q, the marginal rate of substitution in consumption R is minus the slope of the tangent to the indifference curve, and the marginal rate of transformation S is minus the slope of the tangent to the transformation curve ab. Because of the distortion, we have, from (2) and (3),

$$R = tS,\tag{9}$$

where $t < 1$ is now assumed to be constant.

---

[15]) See Kemp [10], pp. 310–13.

If we slide the production block around the indifference curve, maintaining the relation (9) between R and S we trace out the constrained trade indifference curve JJ'. To find the second best tariff we need the slope of JJ'.[16]) Consider the point T, which corresponds to point Q on the consumption indifference curve. If we change slightly the consumption D_1 of the first commodity by dD_1, the consumption of the second commodity must change by $dD_2 = -RdD_1$ so as to remain on II'. Since R on JJ' and S in (9) are respectively functions of D_1 and of X_1, we have from (9)

$$R'dD_1 = tS'dX_1 , \tag{10}$$

where the prime indicates differentiation with respect to the consumption D_1 or production X_1 of the first commodity. Then the change in X_1 corresponding to dD_1 is $dX_1 = (R'/tS')dD_1$ and the corresponding change in X_2 is $dX_2 = -SdX_1 = -(SR'/tS')dD_1$. Therefore, the slope of the trade indifference curve JJ' is

$$-(dD_2 - dX_2)/(dD_1 - dX_1) = (R - SR'/tS')/(1 - R'/tS') . \tag{11}$$

Since $R = 1/q$ and $S = 1/tq$ at equilibrium, the right-hand side of (11) is equal to $(1 - R'/ttS')/q(1 - R'/tS')$. Since the condition for the second best is the tangency of the trade indifference curve JJ' and the international price line p, we have

$$q/p = (1 - R'/ttS')/(1 - R'/tS') . \tag{12}$$

Now R' is negative, S' is positive; hence $-R'/S'$ is positive. Therefore, (12) implies $q > p$, since $t < 1$. It follows then that if the second commodity is imported, as in the figure 11.3, an import tariff is needed.[17])

From (12) and $t < 1$,

$$1/p = (1 - R'/ttS')/(1 - R'/tS')q < 1/q. \tag{13}$$

Therefore, $1/p < S$, since $S = 1/tq > 1/q$. If the tariff is just sufficient to offset the distortion, we have FRT = DRT, i.e., $1/p = S$. On the other hand, DRS = FRT $\neq$ DRT, i.e., $R = 1/p < S$ at free trade. In other words, the second best tariff is not at a rate just sufficient to offset the distortion but at

---

[16]) We have drawn JJ' with the usual curvature. It is easy to show that in the face of domestic distortions JJ' might contain stretches of abnormal curvature. In the neighborhood of any interior constrained optimum, however, the curvature must be normal.

[17]) If the second commodity is exported, i.e., the point T is in the third quadrant in figure 11.3, we must have an export subsidy.

a rate somewhat lower.[18]) It may be interesting to see that the second best tariff with FRT $\neq$ DRT $\neq$ DRS is superior to free trade with FRT = DRS $\neq$ DRT. Paretian conditions are relevant if all the conditions are simultaneously satisfied. Otherwise, the number of the conditions satisfied is irrelevant.

We may summarize as

Theorem 2. If the import competing industry has to pay a higher wage and the distortion t is constant, then the rate of the second best tariff is

$$1 - (1 - R'/ttS')/(1 - R'/tS') \, ,$$

which is lower than the rate to offset the distortion completely.

Theorems 1 and 2 are sufficient to conclude as follows. A wage differential against the import competing industry, if not corrected by tax-cum-subsidy on production, justifies the protection of the industry by tariff. Such a policy is, though by no means optimal, certainly the second best and superior to free trade in spite of the statement of Bhagwati and Ramaswami. Hagen's conclusion that protection will increase real income was right, if protection does not necessarily mean the prohibitive tariff. In essence Hagen was right; he simply claimed too much.[19])

4. Domestic distortion in the sense that the marginal productivity of labor differs in different industries is caused not only by wage differentials but by the existence of a subsistence sector. In such a sector production is not carried out by modern capitalistic enterprises but by traditional households. Output is equally divided among family laborers so that per head income is equal to the average product rather than the marginal product of labor. A modern capitalistic sector hires labor from the subsistence sector with a wage equal to the per head income in the latter sector. Since marginal productivity is short of the wage in the subsistence sector, a part of labor in that sector is actually a sort of surplus and we may call it disguised

---

[18]) Bhagwati and Ramaswami seem to consider mainly such a completely offsetting tariff.
[19]) Similarly, in the case of distortions due to external economies, the economy generating industry should be protected from foreign trade. Whether the tariff or the trade subsidy is needed depends on whether the economy generating industry is an import competing or an export industry rather than on whether the direction of the specialization is right or wrong. See Habeler [5] and Bhagwati and Ramaswami [2].

unemployment. Then a natural question is whether we should protect the modern sector so as to reduce disguised unemployment, if the subsistence sector is not modernized, i.e., if the best solution is impossible. Although labor moves between sectors, capital will concentrate on the modern sector, since there exists no surplus output to be imputed to capital in the subsistence sector. Therefore, we may consider land and labor in the subsistence sector, capital and labor in the modern sector.

The production function of the first, subsistence sector is

$$X_1 = f_1(L_1), \tag{14}$$

where X_1 and L_1 are respectively the output and the labor input of the first sector, the amount of land input being given constant. Similarly, in the second, modern sector production function is

$$X_2 = f_2(\bar{L} - L_1), \tag{15}$$

where X_2 and $\bar{L}$ are respectively the output of the second sector and the total amount of labor, the amount of capital input being constant. Since the wage is equal to the average product of labor in the first sector and to the marginal product in the second,

$$f_1/L_1 = qf_2', \tag{16}$$

q being the domestic price of the output of the second sector in terms of the output of the first. Therefore, from (14–16),

$$dX_1/dX_2 = -f_1'/f_2' = -qf_1'L_1/f_1. \tag{17}$$

On the other hand, from (16),

$$(f_1' - qf_2' + L_1 qf_2'') \, dL_1/dq = L_1 f_2'. \tag{18}$$

Since $f_2' > 0$, $f_2'' < 0$ and $f_1' < f_1/L_1$, (16) and (18) imply $dL_1/dq < 0$ and therefore $dX_1/dq < 0$ and $X_2/dq > 0$.

If we denote the international price corresponding to q by p and the amount of the import of the ith commodity, i.e., the ith sector's output by E_i, the condition of the trade balance is

$$E_1 + pE_2 = 0. \tag{19}$$

Assuming a small country (p is constant), we have

$$dE_1/dE_2 = -p \tag{20}$$

from (19). Denoting the consumers' demand for the ith commodity by D_i, the equality of demand and supply conditions are

$$D_1(q, Y) - X_1(q) - E_1 = 0 , \tag{21}$$

$$D_2(q, Y) - X_2(q) - E_2 = 0 , \tag{22}$$

where Y is the national income defined by

$$Y = X_1 + qX_2 + (q-p)(D_2 - X_2) , \tag{23}$$

which is alternatively expressed as

$$Y = X_1(q) + pX_2(q) + (q-p)D_2(q, Y) . \tag{24}$$

We can solve (22) and (24) for Y and E_2 when q is given. The differentiation with respect to q gives

$$dE_2/dq = \Delta/\{(q-p)D_{22} - 1\} , \tag{25}$$

where $D_{22} = \partial D_2/\partial Y$. If we exclude the inferior good, the denominator of the right-hand side of (25) is negative since $qD_{22} < 1$. On the other hand, the numerator is

$$\Delta = (D_{21} - X_2') \{(q-p)D_{22} - 1\} - D_{22} \{X_1' + pX_2' + D_2 + (q-p)D_{21}\}$$

$$= -X_2' qD_{22} + X_2' - D_{22}X_1' - D_2 D_{22} - D_{21} , \tag{26}$$

where $D_{21} = \partial D_2/\partial q$, $X_1' = dX_1\,dq$ and the like. Considering the fact that $D_2 D_{22} + D_{21}$ is the substitution effect on the demand for the second commodity of the change in the price of the second commodity and therefore is negative, we can easily see that Δ is positive since $X_2' > 0$, $X_1' < 0$ and $qD_{22} - 1 < 0$. Therefore, $dE_2/dq < 0$.

At the second best situation, i.e., the best situation under the distortion due to the subsistence sector, the marginal rate of substitution in consumption and that in supply must be equal. From (17), (20), (21) and (22),

$$dD_1/dD_2 = -q = (dX_1 + dE_1)/(dX_2 + dE_2)$$

$$= \{-(qf_1' L_1/f_1)\,dX_2 - pdE_2\}/(dX_2 + dE_2) . \tag{27}$$

This leads to

$$\{(qf_1' L_1/f_1) - q\}\,dX_2 = (q-p)\,dE_2 . \tag{28}$$

Since the sign of dX_2 and dE_2 for the same infinitesimal change of q (infinitesimal change of tariff rate) are opposite, and $f_1' < f_1/L_1$, we must have $q > p$. This implies that the modern sector must be protected by the second best tariff.

Let us recapitulate this section as follows.

Theorem 3. If the marginal productivity of labor in the modern sector is equal to the average productivity of labor in the subsistence sector, there exists a second best tariff superior to free trade.

5. The simplest model used in Kemp [9] to show that foreign investment tends to be excessive from the point of view of the investing country runs as follows.[20] Let the amount of capital in the investing country and the invested country be constant and respectively k and k^*. Assuming that each country which competes in the world market is producing one and the same commodity, let us denote the production functions of the investing and invested countries by f and f^*. Since labor is immobile between countries, the amount of labor is assumed to be constant and full employment is assumed, each country's output is given by $f(k-z)$ and $f^*(k^*+z)$, where z is the amount of capital movement. Under laissez faire, z is determined by the condition that the rate of return to capital is equal in two countries, i.e., $f'(k-z) = f^{*\prime}(k^*+z)$. On the other hand, the optimal amount of foreign investment z from the point of view of the investing country is determined by maximizing her national income, $f(k-z) + zf^{*\prime}(k^*+z)$, the sum of the domestic output and the return on the foreign investment. The condition for the maximization of the national income is $f'(k-z) = f^{*\prime}(k^* + z) + zf^{*\prime\prime}(k^*+z)$. This implies that $f'(k-z) < f^{*\prime}(k^*+z)$, since $f^{*\prime\prime} < 0$. The laissez faire z is larger than the optimal z, since in the former case $f' = f^{*\prime}$. It is necessary to restrict the amount of foreign investment by imposing a tax on the earnings of the capital invested in the foreign country. The rate of tax t is given by $f' = (1-t)f^{*\prime}$, i.e., $t = -zf^{*\prime\prime}/f^{*\prime}$.

In the above analysis, output and the factors of production are regarded as distinct items and the amount of factors of production are assumed to be constant. This implies either that the capital does not depreciate and only the consumers' goods are produced or that the analysis is that of the short-run or temporary equilibrium in the sense that the capital goods produced are not to be utilized in production within the period under consideration. As the result of these assumptions, in such a static or timeless model, new investment abroad, i.e., the changes in the amount of capital invested abroad

---

[20] Kemp [9], pp. 198–200.

is considered as the movement of capital stock. In other words, the capital stock already constructed and in use is assumed to be mobile between countries. However, being simply an export surplus, new investment abroad is more appropriately considered as the accumulation abroad of the flow of the newly produced capital goods or the acquisition of the capital stock already constructed and in use in the foreign country.[21]) We have to consider, therefore, the optimal foreign investment in the long-run analysis of the dynamic process of the production and accumulation of capital goods.

For the sake of simplicity, let us confine ourselves to optimal foreign investment in terms of long-run stationary equilibrium or balanced growth equilibrium.[22]) The point is that the change in the amount of foreign investment has an effect on the level of national income at the long-run stationary equilibrium or on the balanced growth path through changes in capital accumulation (investment and saving) caused by changes in national income and its distribution of the investing and invested countries. Suppose each country owns respectively k and k^* amount of capital stock and the amount of the foreign owned capital in the invested country is z. Under the assumption of full employment of the constant labor force, two countries produce respectively $f(k-z)$ and $f^*(k^*+z)$ amount of one and the same commodity which may be either consumed or invested as capital. There is, therefore, no movement of commodities between countries except for the new investment abroad and the interest payment on the capital stock invested in the foreign country. Let α denote the uniform rate of depreciation of the capital stock in two countries. Then the long-run level of the net income of the investing country, which is to be maximized, is

$$f(k-z)+zf^{*\prime}(k^*+z)-\alpha k , \tag{29}$$

i.e., domestic output plus interest earnings from abroad less depreciation. Proportions s and s^* of the capital earnings of the investing and invested countries are assumed to be saved, while all the wage income in both countries is assumed to be consumed.[23]) This assumption about saving, though special, has often been used in recent growth theory literature.[24]) Then the condition for the stationary state, i.e., of zero net investment, will be

$$s(k-z)f'+szf^{*\prime} = \alpha k \tag{30}$$

---

[21]) See chapter 9.
[22]) See for a more general model, e.g., Hamada [7].
[23]) We assume that $s<1$ and $s^*<1$.
[24]) See e.g., Takayama [18].

for the investing country and

$$s^* k^* f^{*\prime} = \alpha k^* \tag{31}$$

for the invested country. Our problem is to choose z which maximizes (29) under the restrictions of (30) and (31). We must note that k and k^* are not constant now, but variables to be determined by (30) and (31) when z is given. By changing the amount of the capital stock to be kept invested abroad, we are interested in maximizing, not the instantaneous net income (as in Kemp [9]), but the long-run maintained level of net income, just as in the theory of optimal saving we are interested in maximizing, not instantaneous consumption, but the long-run maintained level of consumption.[25])

From (31) above, the marginal productivity of capital in the invested country is constant, i.e.,

$$f^{*\prime} = \alpha/s^* , \tag{32}$$

if $k^* \neq 0$. Assuming $k^* \neq 0$, we substitute (32) into (29) and (30). If national income in the investing country is constant, the marginal rate of substitution between k and z in (29) is

$$(\mathrm{d}k/\mathrm{d}z)^1 = (f' - (\alpha/s^*)/(f' - \alpha) . \tag{33}$$

On the other hand, from (30), the marginal rate of k and z is given as

$$(\mathrm{d}k/\mathrm{d}z)^2 = (sf' + s(k-z)f'' - (s\alpha/s^*))/(sf' + s(k-z)f'' - \alpha) . \tag{34}$$

If there exists an optimal solution with positive k, k^* and z, these two marginal rates of substitution must be equal.[26]) Therefore, we have

$$(\mathrm{d}k/\mathrm{d}z)^1 = (\mathrm{d}k/\mathrm{d}z)^2 = s(k-z)f''/(s(k-z)f'' - \alpha + s\alpha) . \tag{35}$$

From the usual assumption that $f'' < 0$ and $s < 1$, it is clear that $0 < \mathrm{d}k/\mathrm{d}z < 1$. Applying this result to (33), we see that $f' > \alpha$ and $f' > f^{*\prime} = \alpha/s^*$ at the optimum. Since the private motive for foreign investment is satisfied when $f' = f^{*\prime}$, the amount of foreign investment tends to be too little under laissez faire.

Theorem 4. If two countries are competing in the international market with a single identical commodity which can be either consumed or invested

---

[25]) Phelps [15].
[26]) This implies that $s \neq s^*$.

and laborers do not save in each country, a subsidy rather than a tax on the foreign investment is needed from the long-run point of view of the investing country.

The optimum rate of subsidy is calculated from (33) and (35) as $t = s(k-z)(s^*-1)f''/(\alpha - s\alpha)$. The rationale of this result, which seems rather paradoxical from the short-run point of view, may be that, if capital accumulation is heavily dependent on capital earnings, it is wise for a country to encourage capital export so as to keep home capital earnings and, therefore, capital accumulation and the long-run level of consumption high. Another reason is that larger instead of diminishing returns are expected by increasing foreign investment since it will check the growth of domestic capital in the invested country.[27])

Different results from the static or short-run analysis and the dynamic or long-run analysis can be reconciled from the point of view of the second best theory. The implications of the assumption that saving is equal to $s \times 100\%$ of capital earnings is that there is no room for the policy which directly interferes with the amount of saving and therefore of capital accumulation. What we can do is to change the amount of saving indirectly through the changes in capital earnings by controlling the amount of foreign investment. Suppose now we can directly control the amount of saving in each country and therefore k and k^* are free from (30) and (31). k^* is determined by the policy of the invested country. With k^* given, the investing country maximizes her national income (29) with respect to k and z. Conditions for the maximization are

$$f' - \alpha = 0 \tag{36}$$

$$-f' + f^{*\prime} + zf^{*\prime\prime} = 0 . \tag{37}$$

Condition (37) is identical with the condition obtained in the static analysis, while condition (36) is that of the optimal saving.[28]) The conclusion from the static or short-run model remains unchanged in the dynamic or long-run situation, if the amount of foreign saving and that of capital are given and domestic saving is optimal in the sense that the national income is maximized.

[27]) See Negishi [14]. In the case of balanced growth, we have only to replace α by $\alpha + \beta$ in the above analysis, where β is the uniform rate of growth of the labor force in the two countries.

[28]) See Phelps [15], pp. 6–11.

Since $f' > \alpha$ in the case of theorem 4, the condition for optimal saving is not satisfied. Therefore, the policy suggested there (a subsidy on foreign investment) is a second best policy when the direct control of saving is impossible.

6. According to the theory of the optimal tariff developed in the static or short-run analysis of international trade, free trade (i.e., no tariff) is optimal for a small country for which international prices of commodities are given constants.[29]) In this section we are concerned with the question whether this is true in the dynamic or long-run analysis, in which the adjustment of capital to the changes in the rate of tariff is fully taken care of. Let us again confine ourselves to the case of the stationary or balanced growth state. Assuming that the first commodity is consumers' goods and the second, capital goods in a two commodity two factor model of a small country, conditions for an incomplete specialization equilibrium are as follows.

$$E_1 + pE_2 = 0 , \tag{38}$$

$$\mu k = X_2 + E_2 , \tag{39}$$

$$X_1 = F(X_2, k) , \tag{40}$$

$$-q = F_1(X_2, k) , \tag{41}$$

$$q\mu k = s(r(q)k + w(q) + (q-p)E_2) , \tag{42}$$

where unknowns to be determined are E_1, E_2, k, X_1, X_2, respectively signifying the import of the first and second commodities, the amount of capital stock, outputs of the first and second commodities, while the international and domestic prices of the second commodity in terms of the first (p and q) and the labor force (taken as unity) are given. Condition (38) is that of balanced trade. Condition (39) signifies the stationary state[30]) where μ is the rate of depreciation. The transformation curve between X_1 and X_2 and its tangency with the domestic price line are represented by (40) and (41). The equality of saving and investment is (42) under the assumption of a simple Keynesian saving function, where the rate of interest r and the

---

[29]) Kemp [9], pp. 169–73, [10], pp. 290–296.
[30]) In the case of the balanced growth, we have only to replace μ by $\mu + g$, where g is the growth rate of the labor force.

wage w (in terms of the first commodity) are assumed to be uniquely determined when q is given.[31])

Starting from the initial free trade situation $(p = q)$, and assuming that the second commodity is imported, we ask whether the imposition of a tariff increases the net national income $Y = rk + w + (q-p)E_2 - q\mu k$, i.e., whether $dY/dq > 0$.[32])

Let us first consider

$$dk/dq = (sr'k + sw' + sE_2 - \mu k)/(q\mu - sr),\qquad(43)$$

which is obtained from the differentiation of (38–42). It is easily seen from (42) that $q\mu - sr > 0$, under the assumption that $p = q$. Consider Walras' law $r(q)k + w(q) + (q-p)E_2 \equiv X_1 + qX_2 + (q-p)E_2$. The differentiation with respect to q yields $r'k + w' - X_2 = X_1' + qX_2'$, where the prime denotes the differentiation with respect to q under the assumption that k is constant, i.e., $X_1' = dX_1/dq$ and the like. Since $X_1' + qX_2' = 0$,[33]) and therefore $r'k + w' - X_2 = 0$, we see that $sr'k + sw' + sE_2 - \mu k < 0$, using (39) and $s < 1$. Therefore $dk/dq < 0$. Again using the fact that $r'k + w' - X_2 = 0$ and (39), the total differentiation of Y with respect to q is reduced to

$$dY/dq = (r - q\mu)dk/dq.\qquad(44)$$

Therefore $dY/dq \gtreqless 0$ as $r - q\mu \gtreqless 0$. On the other hand, if we differentiate Y with respect to k assuming q is constant (equal to p), we have

$$dY/dk = r - \mu q.\qquad(45)$$

Perhaps we may say that the saving and capital accumulation relative to labor force is more (less) than optimal when $r - q\mu < 0$ (> 0). We must restrict (encourage) the import of capital goods by a tariff (subsidy) when the saving is more (less) than optimal.

Since $r - \mu q$ is independent of k, however, the sign of dY/dq is unchanged when $p = q$, provided that the economy is incompletely specialized. If the optimization of saving is considered, and k is increased (decreased) when $r - \mu q > 0$ (< 0), therefore, the output of the industry which is more capital (labor) intensive is increased and that of the other industry is decreased, until the economy is completely specialized.[34])

[31]) Kemp [9], pp. 45–53, [10], pp. 77–82.
[32]) If the second commodity is exported, the question is whether an export subsidy increases the national income.
[33]) Kemp [9], p. 21, [10], p. 26.
[34]) Rybczynski [16].

When the economy is completely specialised in the first industry, we must replace (39–42) by

$$\mu k = E_2 , \tag{46}$$

$$X_1 = G_1(k) , \tag{47}$$

$$q\mu k = sX_1 + s(q-p)E_2 , \tag{48}$$

where (46) and (48) correspond to (39) and (42) and (47) is the production function of the second commodity since $X_2 = 0$. Instead of (43) we have from (46–48)

$$dk/dq = (1-s)\,\mu k/(sG_1' - q\mu), \tag{49}$$

where $sG_1' - \mu q < 0$, since

$$dk/dt = sX_1 + (q-p)E_2 - q\mu k , \quad (t = \text{time}) , \tag{50}$$

must be stable when $p = q$. Therefore, $dY/dq = (r - q\mu)dk/dq \gtreqless 0$, where $Y = X_1 + (q-p)E_2 - \mu qk$ and $r = G_1'$, as $(r - \mu q) \gtreqless 0$, i.e., the import of the second commodity must be tariffed or subsidized according to the level of saving relative to its optimal level. Since $r' = G_1'' < 0$, we can reach optimal saving by further increasing (decreasing) k when $r - \mu q > 0 \ (<0)$.

On the other hand, if the economy is specialized in the second commodity, we have to replace (40–42) by

$$X_2 = G_2(k) , \tag{51}$$

$$q\mu k = sqX_2 + s(q-p)E_2 , \tag{52}$$

where (52) corresponds to (42) and (51) is the production function of X_2, since $X_1 = 0$. Instead of (43) we have from (39), (51) and (52),

$$dk/dq = (1-s)\,\mu k/(sqG_2' - q\mu), \tag{53}$$

where the denominator of the left-hand side must be negative from the stability condition of

$$dk/dt = sqX_2 + s(q-p)E_2 - q\mu k, \quad (t = \text{time}, \, p = q) . \tag{54}$$

Therefore, $dY/dq = (r - q\mu)dk/dq \gtreqless 0$, where $Y = qX_2 - (q-p)E_2 - q\mu k$ and $r = qG_2'$, as $(r - \mu q) \gtreqless 0$, i.e., the export of the second commodity must be tariffed or subsidized as saving is less or more than optimal saving.

Summarizing the above arguments, we can now conclude as

Theorem 5. At a free trade equilibrium in a two-commodity (consumers' and capital goods) two-factor model of a small country, import of capital goods should be restricted (encouraged) by a tariff (subsidy) if saving in proportion to the national income is more (less) than optimal.[35])

References

[1] Atsumi, H., 'Long-run offer function and a dynamic theory of international trade,' *Journal of International Economics*, 1 (1971), 267–299.

[2] Bhagwati, J. and V.K. Ramaswami, 'Domestic distorsions, tariffs, and the theory of optimum subsidy,' *Journal of Political Economy*, 71 (1963), 44–50 (Caves and Johnson, ed., *Readings in international economics*, Irwin, 1968, 230–239, Bhagwati, *Trade, tariffs and growth*, Weidenfeld and Nicolson, 1969, 293–308).

[3] Bhagwati, J., V.K. Ramaswami and T.N. Srinivasan, 'Domestic distorsions, tariffs and the theory of optimum subsidy: further results,' *Journal of Political Economy*, 76 (1969).

[4] Fishlow, A. and P. David, 'Optimum resource allocation in an imperfect market setting,' *Journal of Political Economy*, 69 (1961), 529–46.

[5] Haberler, G., 'Some problems in the pure theory of international trade,' *Economic Journal*, 60 (1950), 223–40 (Caves and Johnson, ed., *Readings in international economics*, Irwin, 1968, 213–229).

[6] Hagen, E., 'An economic justification of protection,' *Quarterly Journal of Economics*, 72 (1958), 496–514.

[7] Hamada, K., 'Economic growth and long-term international capital movements,' *Yale Economic Essays*, VI-2 (1966), 49–96.

[8] Johnson, H., G., 'Factor market distortions and the shape of the transformation curve, '*Econometrica*, 34 (1966), 686–98.

[9] Kemp, M.C., *The pure theory of international trade*, Prentice-Hall, 1964.

[10] Kemp, M.C., *The pure theory of international trade and investment*, Prentice-Hall, 1969.

[11] Kemp, M.C. and T. Negishi, 'Domestic distortions, tariffs and the theory of optimum subsidy,' *Journal of Political Economy*, 76 (1969).

[12] Lewis, W.A., 'Economic development with unlimited supplies of labor,' *Manchester School of Economics and Social Studies*, 22 (1954), 139–91 (Agarwala and Singh ed., *The economics of underdevelopment*, Oxford University Press, 1958, 400–449.).

[13] MacDougal, G.D.A., 'The benefits and costs of private investment from abroad, a theoretical approach,' *Economic Record*, 26 (1960), 13–35 (*Bulletin of the Oxford University Institute of Statistics*, 22 (1960), 189–211, Caves and Johnson, ed., *Readings in international trade economics*, 1969, Urwin, 172–194).

[35]) If the capital goods are exported, we have to have a tariff (subsidy) on export as the saving is less (more) than optimal.

[14] Negishi, T., 'Foreign investment and the long-run national advantage,' *Economic Record*, 31 (1965), 628–32.

[15] Phelps, E. S., *Golden rules of economic growth*, Norton, 1966.

[16] Rybczynski, T. M., 'Factor endowment and relative commodity prices,' *Economica*, 22 (1955), 336–41 (Caves and Johnson, ed., *Readings in international economics*, Urwin, 1968, 72–77).

[17] Scitovsky, T., 'Two concepts of external economies,' *Journal of Political Economy*, 62 (1954), 143–51 (Agarwala and Singh, ed., *The economics of underdevelopment*, Oxford University Press, 1958, 295–308, Arrow and Scitovsky, ed., *Readings in welfare economics*, Irwin, 1969, 242–52.).

[18] Takayama, A., 'On a two-sector model of economic growth: a comparative statics analysis,' *Review of Economic Studies*, 30 (1963), 95–104.

CHAPTER 12

Customs union as a second best problem

1. The study of the customs union (or free trade area) is of great relevance, both from the practical point of view of international trade policies and from the theoretical point of view of second best theory.[1] From the world's point of view, world-wide free trade is optimal but the customs union, which is merely a partial liberation of trade within an area, can at most be the second best. Similarly, the formation of a customs union is also a second best problem from a single country's or the union's view point, unless the historically given rate of tariff on the import from the non-member countries is accidentally at the level corresponding to the optimal tariff structure. The basic model in the economics of the customs union is that of two commodities and three countries – the home country, the partner country and the foreign country (non-member country or the rest of the world).[2]

By assuming infinite elasticity of the foreign and partner supply and the non existence of tariffs imposed by the foreign and partner countries, it can easily be shown that the welfare of the home country is increased by the trade creation effect and may be diminished by the trade diversion effect, of the home country's granting a discriminatory elimination of its tariff on imports from the partner, while retaining its tariff on those from the foreign country.[3] An optimum rate of tariff for the home country on its imports from the partner country can be calculated from the comparison of these two effects, i.e., in terms of the changes of consumers' surplus, producers' surplus and tariff revenue of the home country. Such a rate is optimal simultaneously from the points of view of the home country, of the customs

---

[1] There are two possible approaches to the problem of customs unions. One is to apply the theory of trade gains due to economies of scale (as developed in chapters 5 and 8) to explain the gains from the union of homogeneous countries. The other is to apply the theory of the second best in considering the tariff discrimination of the union. This chapter, based on T. Negishi, 'The customs union and the theory of second best,' *International Economic Review*, 10 (1969), 391–8, is an attempt at the latter approach.

[2] See Johnson [1], [2], Kemp [4], Lipsey [5], Meade [6], Vanek [7] and Viner [8].

[3] See Johnson [2] and Viner [8].

union (the home and partner countries) and of the world (three countries), since welfare of the partner and foreign countries remain unchanged. If the optimum rate is zero, we can conclude that the formation of a customs union is preferable.

The assumption of infinite elasticity of foreign supply is, however, inappropriate for this problem, since under this assumption there is no incentive for the home country to impose any tariff on its imports from the foreign country. Free trade should be considered as the best solution and there must be, in fact, no place for arguing the optimal rate of tariff, i.e., a second best solution. Moreover, the assumption of the nonexistence of tariffs imposed by the foreign country cannot be expected as realistic, if the home country imposes a tariff on imports from the foreign country.

If one drops the assumption of an infinitely elastic foreign supply and/or that of no foreign tariff, one must solve the problem of the comparison of gains and losses of different countries. Optimality from the point of view of the customs union or of the world should, therefore, necessarily be that of Pareto, unless one makes a definite value judgement on the relative importance of the welfare of different countries.[4] In this chapter, we are interested in the Pareto optimality of a customs union, which completely or only partially liberalizes its internal trade, from the points of view of the union and of the world. Vanek [7] considered this problem by the use of geometry and conjectured some propositions. We can prove some of his conjecture rigorously in terms of analysis. It will be shown that analytical method is more useful for some problems of the customs union, despite Vanek's opinion to the contrary.[5]

2.   Consider a model of a world economy with three countries and two commodities. Suppose country 1 exports commodity 1 and imports commodity 2, countries 2 and 3 export commodity 2 and import commodity 1 (therefore, countries 2 and 3 do not trade with each other), and countries 1 and 2 form a customs union (the case of a customs union of two dissimilar countries). Since only one country of the union trades with the rest of the

---

[4] Johnson [1] and Meade [6] introduced such value judgements in their analyses.

[5] See Vanek [7], p. 11. Our analytical approach was followed by Kemp [4]. Another difference between Vanek [7] and this paper is that we introduced consumption taxes whose rate can be controlled. Therefore, we have a greater degree of freedom than Vanek, which makes the analysis extremely easy. However, the comparability with Vanek [7] is not lost, since it will be shown below that there should be no consumption taxes if the union with internal free trade is optimal.

world and therefore there is no problem of averaging the members' rate of tariff on imports from the rest of the world, the difference between a customs union and a pure free trade area disappears in our model. In this section, we discuss whether the formation of such a union is Pareto optimal from the point of view of the members of the union.

Let X_{ij} and Y_{ij} signify respectively the amount of consumption and production of commodity j by country i ($i = 1, 2, 3, j = 1, 2$). Next, let us denote by $U_i(X_{i1}, X_{i2})$ and $F_i(Y_{i1}, Y_{i2}) = 0$ respectively an ordinal utility index and production possibility in country i. Indifference (production) curves are strongly convex (concave) to the origin. Finally, let P_j signify the price of commodity j in country 1, $C_{ij} > 1$ (or < 1) signify $1 +$ the rate of consumption tax (or $-$ the rate of consumption subsidy) on commodity j in country i; t_{21} and t_{31} signify $1 +$ the rate of import tariff in countries 2 and 3 respectively; and t_{22} and t_{32} signify the inverse of $1 +$ the rate of tariff of country 1 on the exports of countries 2 and 3 respectively. We assume that there exists neither export tax nor export subsidy, while import subsidy can be conceived of as a negative tariff.

Assuming that perfect competition prevails within each country, we have

$$U_{11}/C_{11}P_1 = U_{12}/C_{12}P_2 \,, \tag{1}$$

$$U_{21}/C_{21}t_{21}P_1 = U_{22}/C_{22}t_{22}P_2 \,, \tag{2}$$

$$U_{31}/C_{31}t_{31}P_1 = U_{32}/C_{32}t_{32}P_2 \,, \tag{3}$$

$$F_{11}P_1 = F_{12}/P_2 \,, \tag{4}$$

$$F_{21}/t_{21}P_1 = F_{22}/t_{22}P_2 \,, \tag{5}$$

$$F_{31}/t_{31}P_1 = F_{32}/t_{32}P_2 \,, \tag{6}$$

where U_{ij} and F_{ij} are respectively the partial derivative of U_i and F_i with respect to X_{ij} and Y_{ij}. Unilateral income transfers are allowed within the union, but not between the union and the rest of the world, i.e., country 3. Therefore, the balance of payments of country 3,

$$P_1 Z_{31} + t_{32}P_2 Z_{32} = 0 \,, \tag{7}$$

where $Z_{3j} = X_{3j} - Y_{3j}$ (the net import of country 3), must be satisfied. From (3), (6) and (7), we can solve for Z_{31} and Z_{32} as functions of P_1 and P_2 when C_{31}, C_{32}, t_{31} and t_{32} are given.

We are interested in the Pareto optimal combination of U_1 and U_2 with respect to C_{11}, C_{12}, C_{21}, C_{22}, t_{21} and t_{22}, subject to the given values of C_{31}, C_{32}, t_{31} and t_{32}, conditions (1), (2), (3), (4), (5), (6) and (7), and conditions that supply equal demand for all commodities,

$$\Sigma_i X_{ij} = \Sigma_i Y_{ij} \quad \text{for all } j. \tag{8}$$

For the sake of the comparison, suppose t_{32} is not fixed, but is free to move. Then, five marginal rates of substitution (transformation), i.e., those of consumption and production in countries 1 and 2, and that of the offer curve of country 3, should be equal. A customs union within which internal and international free trade prevails is Pareto optimal if its tariff on imports from the rest of the world is optimal.

Let t_{32} be fixed at a certain value which is less than one. At a Pareto optimal state of the union under such a restriction on t_{32}, i.e., at a second best solution, the value of U_1 (or U_2) remains constant for any infinitesimal change of allocation of commodities which keeps the value of U_2 (or U_1) unchanged and does not violate the constraints of the problem.

Suppose P_1 and P_2 are held unchanged (therefore, conditions (3), (4), (6) and (7) remain satisfied), while C_{11}, C_{12}, C_{21}, C_{22}, t_{21} and t_{22} are adjusted so that conditions (1), (2), and (5) are not violated, when commodities are slightly reallocated among consumers of countries 1 and 2 and the producers of country 2. Then, we must have for stationarity of U_1 with constant X_{21}, X_{22}, i.e., constant U_2, and for stationarity of U_2 with constant X_{11}, X_{12}, i.e., constant U_1,

$$C_{11} P_1/C_{12} P_2 = C_{21} t_{21} P_1/C_{22} t_{22} P_2 = t_{21} P_1/t_{22} P_2 \tag{9}$$

from which we can conclude that

$$C_{21}/C_{22} = 1, \quad C_{11}/C_{12} = t_{21}/t_{22}. \tag{10}$$

If free trade prevails in the union, there should be no consumption taxes which distort competitive allocation.

Next, suppose $t_{21} P_1$ and $t_{22} P_2$ are held constant (therefore, conditions (2) and (5) remain satisfied) and C_{11}, C_{12}, t_{21} and t_{22} (consequently P_1 and P_2) are adjusted so as to keep conditions (1), (3), (4), (6) and (7) satisfied, when a small change occurs in the allocation of commodities among the consumers and producers of country 1 and the rest of the world. Then, for stationarity of U_1 with constant U_2, we must have

$$C_{11} P_1/C_{12} P_2 = -[dY_{12}+d(-Z_{32})]/[dY_{11}-dZ_{31}], \tag{11}$$

where dY_{12}, $d(-Z_{32})$, dY_{11} and dZ_{31} correspond to the same infinitesimal changes of P_1 and P_2. We have from (4) that

$$dY_{12}/dY_{11} = -P_1/P_2 . \tag{12}$$

We define the elasticity of the offer curve of country 3 as[6])

$$\alpha = -Z_{31}d(-Z_{32})/Z_{32}dZ_{31} . \tag{13}$$

Using (7), (12) and (13), (11) can be reduced to

$$C_{11}/C_{12} = [dY_{11} - (\alpha/t_{32})dZ_{31}]/[dY_{11} - dZ_{31}] . \tag{14}$$

Depending on the relation of α and t_{32}, we have following cases.

If $\alpha = t_{32}$, we see from (10), (11) and (14) that all rates of marginal substitution in countries 1 and 2 are equalized to that of the offer curve of country 3. Since $t_{21}/t_{22} = 1$, we must have free trade within the union or the import tariff of one country counterbalanced by the import subsidy of the other.

If $1 \geqq \alpha > t_{32}$, from (10) and (14), we have $t_{21}/t_{22} > 1$, i.e., the customs union which only partially liberalizes its internal trade can be Pareto optimal.[7]) This is, however, the case when the tariff rate of the union on its imports from the rest of the world exceeds its optimal rate, $1/\alpha - 1$. For such a union, therefore, it is preferable to reduce the external tariff rate (i.e., approach the best state) rather than to keep the internal rates of tariff at the second best rates.

If $\alpha < t_{32}$ (the external tariff rate is below the optimal rate), we have from (10) and (14) that $t_{21}/t_{22} < 1$. In this case, an import subsidy rather than a tariff is required for the internal trade of the union. If an import subsidy is not allowed in such a case, we must have a corner type maximum at $t_{21}/t_{22} = 1$, i.e., free trade within the union. To see this, suppose as before that $t_{21} P_1$ and $t_{22} P_2$ are kept constant and C_{11}, C_{12}, t_{21}, t_{22}, P_1 and P_2 are adjusted when more of commodity 1 and less of commodity 2 are produced, imported and consumed in country 1. U_1 is increased, provided that

$$C_{11} P_1/C_{12} P_2 > -[dY_{12} + d(-Z_{32})]/[dY_{11} - dZ_{31}] . \tag{15}$$

By such a reallocation of commodities, the relative price of commodity 1 in country 1, P_1/P_2 should increase, since more of commodity 1 and the less

---

[6]) See Kemp [3], p. 302.
[7]) If $\alpha \leqq 1$, dY_{11} is of the same sign with $-dZ_{31}$.

of commodity 2 are produced in country 1 and imported from country 3, whose offer curve elasticity is less than one and t_{32} is constant. Therefore, t_{21} must be diminished and/or t_{22} must be increased, since the relative price in country 2, $t_{21}P_1/t_{22}P_2$ is constant. If an import subsidy is not allowed, we have $t_{21} \geq 1$ and $t_{22} \leq 1$. If $t_{21} = t_{22} = 1$ and (15) still holds, we are at a corner maximum, since no further reallocation to increase U_1 is possible. If $t_{21}/t_{22} = 1$, using (7), (10), (12) and (13), (15) can be derived from $\alpha < t_{32}$.

If an import subsidy is not allowed, we can conclude that a customs union with internal free trade is Pareto optimal if and only if its rate of tariff on its imports from the rest of the world does not exceed the optimal rate. In other words, it is Pareto optimal if and only if the elasticity of the foreign offer curve is equal to or less than t_{32}. On the other hand, if such a condition is not satisfied, it is better to reduce the rate of tariff on imports from the rest of the world rather than to impose a tariff on the internal trade of the union. Therefore, *for the members of the union, internal free trade is, after all, favorable.*

Vanek [7] conjectured from his geometry that a union with internal free trade is Pareto optimal if the elasticity of the offer curve of the rest of the world is sufficiently diminished. He showed that it is not optimal when $\alpha = 1$ and suggested that it is optimal when $\alpha = 0$. Then he argued that between 1 and 0 there will be a limiting value of α below which the union must gain from its formation. We have, in the above, proved analytically that his conjecture is correct and have shown that such a limiting value of α is exactly t_{32}, i.e., the inverse of 1 + the rate of the external tariff.[8])

3.   Our next task is to consider whether a customs union is Pareto optimal from the point of view of the world as a whole. The model is virtually the same as in the preceding section. Assuming conditions (1), (2), (3), (4), (5), (6) and (8) (but not (7)), and the constancy of C_{31}, C_{32}, t_{31} and t_{32}, we seek conditions on C_{11}, C_{12}, C_{21}, C_{22}, t_{21} and t_{22} for Pareto optimality. If all C_{ij} and t_{ij} can be controlled freely, we are in the best situation when $C_{ij} = t_{ij} = 1$ for all i, j. Therefore, our problem is a second best problem under the restriction on C_{31}, C_{32}, t_{31} and t_{32}.

First, as before, we obtain

$$C_{11}/C_{12} = t_{21}/t_{22} \qquad\qquad (10)$$

---

[8]) See Vanek [7], pp. 107, 221.

from experimental redistribution among the consumers of country 1 and the consumers and the producers of country 2, keeping P_1 and P_2 constant.

Then, for the sake of simplicity, suppose $C_{31} = C_{32}$, and construct the trade indifference map of country 3, i.e., indifference curves of Z_{31} and Z_{32}. Consider the reallocation of commodities among the consumers and producers of country 1 and those of country 3, assuming that $t_{21}P_1$ and $t_{22}P_2$ are constant and moving alongside with a trade indifference curve of country 3. To be Pareto optimal, we must have

$$C_{11}P_1/C_{12}P_2 = -[\mathrm{d}Y_{12}+\mathrm{d}(-Z_{32})]/[\mathrm{d}Y_{11}-\mathrm{d}Z_{31}]. \tag{16}$$

Since from (4) and the construction of the trade indifference curve of country 3, we have

$$\mathrm{d}Y_{12}/\mathrm{d}Y_{11} = -P_1/P_2 \tag{17}$$

and

$$\mathrm{d}(-Z_{32})/\mathrm{d}Z_{31} = t_{31}P_1/t_{32}P_2. \tag{18}$$

From (10), (17) and (18), we obtain

$$t_{21}/t_{22} = [\mathrm{d}Y_{11}-(t_{31}/t_{32})\mathrm{d}Z_{31}]/[\mathrm{d}Y_{11}-\mathrm{d}Z_{31}]. \tag{19}$$

It is clear that $\mathrm{d}Y_{11}$ and $-\mathrm{d}Z_{31}$, which correspond to the same change in relative prices, are of the same sign. Therefore, we can conclude that t_{21}/t_{22} is greater than, equal to or less than one if and only if t_{31}/t_{32} is greater than, equal to or less than one. In other words, if country 1 and country 3 impose import tariffs on one another, and an import subsidy is not allowed within the union, countries 1 and 2 must also impose import tariffs on one another, and *a customs union with internal free trade is not Pareto optimal from the point of view of the world.*

From his geometry, Vanek conjectured that the desirability of a union from the point of view of the world as a whole depends on the size of the union.[9] In the case of a small union, he first showed that it can be either beneficial or detrimental to world welfare (i.e., it is not Pareto optimal) if the rest of the world adheres to free trade. He then argued that most likely the union will tend to reduce overall world welfare if the rest of the world is as restrictive in its trade as one of the members of the union, and that the higher the protection of the rest of the world the more probable is the reduction in world welfare.

---

[9] See Vanek [7], pp. 129, 224, 147–8 and 226.

By the smallness of the union, Vanek implied the infinite elasticity of the trade indifference curve of the rest of the world.[10]) In such a case, we have $dY_{11} = dY_{12} = 0$ in (19), and consequently $t_{21}/t_{22} = t_{31}/t_{32}$. It is clear that the higher value of t_{31} requires more restrictive trade within the union and Vanek's conjecture is correct for the case of a small union.

For the case of a large union, Vanek considered the limiting case of a union which includes the entire world, and concluded that the liberalization of trade leads to superior welfare for the world. He then conjectured that, as the union enlarges, the likelihood of increased world welfare will be increasing, and beyond some critical size, a union will always be desirable (i.e., Pareto optimal). However, the transition from the case of a small union (i.e., that of three countries) to the case of extremely large union comprising the entire world (i.e., that of two countries) is not a continuum, if one considers the Pareto optimality of world welfare and does not assume any comparable cardinal measure of welfare of different countries. Therefore, Vanek's conjecture for this case cannot be proved in the way he suggested. So long as the rest of the world does not disappear, our conclusion in the above – t_{21}/t_{22} is greater than one if t_{31}/t_{32} is greater than one – remains valid irrespective of the size of the union. Therefore, Vanek's conjecture for the optimality of the large union is incorrect.

Although he does imply a definition of the smallness of a union, Vanek does not define the index of the largeness of a union. However, if we define the largeness in terms of the infinite elasticity of supply in country 1 (dropping the assumption of strong convexity of the production possibility set), then our result in the above is modified somewhat.[11]) Under the assumption that supply in country 1 is infinitely elastic, we have $dZ_{31} = dZ_{32} = 0$ in (19), and consequently $t_{21}/t_{22} = 1$. Therefore, if an import subsidy is not allowed, we can conclude that in such a large union, trade should be liberalized for the welfare of the world as a whole, even if the union does not include the entire world.

---

[10]) This has been excluded so far by our assumption of strong convexity (concavity) of indifference (production) curves to the origin. Incidentally, this definition of the small union is not consistent with the definition given, e.g., on p. 98 of Vanek [7] i.e., α (the elasticity of the offer curve of country 3) = 1, unless country 3 does not impose tariffs.

[11]) It can be interpreted that Vanek [7] rather considered that the largeness of the union is implied by the constancy of the output of the rest of the world (p. 142). However, it is merely an effect of the large union which is to be explained by its largeness, not the largeness of the union itself.

Finally, let us add a remark on customs unions with external tariff compensation. In this case, the rate of tariff of the union on the exports of the rest of the world (i.e., t_{32}) can be changed so that the volume of trade of the rest of the world with the union remains unchanged. Since dZ_{31} and dZ_{32} are zero in (16), we have $C_{11}/C_{12} = C_{21}/C_{22} = t_{21}/t_{22} = 1$ from (10), (16) and (17). Then, the rate of compensating external tariff, t_{32}, should be determined from the balance of payments of country 3,

$$P_1 Z_{31} + t_{32} P_2 Z_{32} = 0, \tag{20}$$

where Z_{31} and Z_{32} are import and export of country 3, unchanged from the pre-union level. Except for the case of the Giffen paradox, the formation of the union (the change from $t_{21}/t_{22} > 1$ to $t_{21}/t_{22} = 1$) implies the increase in P_1 relative to P_2. Therefore, t_{32} should be increased, i.e., the external tariff of the union should be reduced. *Such a compensating union with free internal trade is Pareto optimal from the point of view of the world*, without allowing the transfer of income between the union and the rest of the world.[12]

However, if a subsidy on imports from the rest of the world is not allowed, i.e., $t_{32} \le 1$, then there is a possibility of a corner type maximum at $t_{32} = 1$ where

$$C_{11} P_1 / C_{12} P_2 > -dY_{12}/dY_{11} \tag{21}$$

holds instead of (16). So far as (21) holds, U_1 can be increased while U_2 and U_3 are kept constant, by increasing the consumption and production of commodity 1 in country 1, reducing P_2 relative to P_1. But, when $t_{32} = 1$, no further movement is possible without violating (20). From (10), (17) and (21), we have $t_{21}/t_{22} > t_{31}$. If the rest of the world imposes tariffs, and if the union's external tariff is zero, then no liberalization of internal trade is favorable for the world, since there is no way for the union to compensate the rest of the world.

References

[1] Johnson, H.G., 'A Marshallian analysis of customs union,' *Money, Trade and Economic Growth*, Harvard University Press, 1962, 63–74. ('Discriminatory tariff reduction: a Marshallian analysis,' *Indian Journal of Economics*, 38 (1957), 39–47,

[12] See Vanek [7], p. 163.

'Marshallian analysis of discriminatory tariff reduction: an extension,' *Indian Journal of Economics*, 39 (1958), 177–81).

[2] Johnson, H. G., 'The economic theory of customs union,' *Pakistan Economic Journal*, 10 (1960), 14–32 (*Money, trade and growth*, Harvard University Press, 1962, 46–62).

[3] Kemp, M. C., *The pure theory of international trade*, Prentice Hall, 1964.

[4] Kemp, M. C., *A contribution to the general equilibrium theory of preferential trading*, North-Holland Publishing Co., 1970.

[5] Lipsey, R., 'The theory of customs union: a general survey, '*Economic Journal*, 70 (1960), 496–513 (R. E. Caves and H. G. Johnson, ed., *Readings in international economics*, Irwin, 1968, 261–278, J. Bhagwati, ed., *International trade*, Penguin, 1969, 218–41).

[6] Meade, J. E., *The theory of customs unions*, North-Holland Publishing Co., 1956.

[7] Vanek, Jaroslav, *General equilibrium of international discrimination*, Harvard University Press, 1965.

[8] Viner, Jacob, *The customs union issue*, Carnegie Endowment for International Peace, 1950.

PART 5

Stability

CHAPTER 13

Stability and the gross substitutability

1. After he had demonstrated the 'theoretical or mathematical' solution of the equations of general economic equilibrium, Walras [28] studied the 'empirical or practical' solution of the market.[1]) This is nothing but the famous tâtonnement, a trial and error process representing the market mechanism under free competition. The intention of the original Walrasian tâtonnement was, therefore, to demonstrate simultaneously the existence and the stability of a general equilibrium by showing the eventual termination of the process in the equilibrium situation. However, Walras [28] could not solve the problem rigorously and it was left to modern analysis of stability to show the convergence of the process to an equilibrium, the existence of which is already proved.[2]) Hicks [12] formulated the problem in a very special way,[3]) which was generalized by Samuelson [26]. Recent contributions to this problem lie in the explicit use of economic laws, such as Walras' law and homogeneity, and the development of studies on non-tâtonnement processes. We shall discuss the former in this chapter under the general assumption of gross substitutability and the next chapter will be devoted to the latter problem.

The significance of the studies of the stability problem is twofold. Firstly, the study of comparative statics makes no sense at all unless stability is demonstrated under fairly plausible conditions. We have to compare two equilibria, the old and new ones prevailing before and after changes in data, e.g., the opening of foreign trade, the imposition of a new tax, technological improvements, etc. The comparison is meaningless if the economy, starting

---

[1]) See Walras–Jaffe [28], pp. 169–172, 243–54. For the theoretical or mathematical solution, see chapter 1.

[2]) Since we have surveyed modern development of the stability analysis of a competitive economy in Negishi [21], which is included in an easily available book of readings, this chapter and the next are designed to be an exposition of our results rather than a systematic survey of the general literature so that it is complementary rather than substitutable to [21].

[3]) See chapter 15.

from the old equilibrium which is now a disequilibrium situation, cannot converge to the new equilibrium. Secondly, the stability condition, i.e., the restriction on parameters of the system, can sometimes be used to derive some results in comparative statics, as seen, say, in chapters 9 and 17, which is the corresponding principle suggested by Hicks [12] and named by Samuelson [26]. The latter demonstrated how the results of comparative statics differ in the case of a single market according to its different dynamic adjustment processes, i.e., the so-called Walrasian and Marshallian ones.[4])

Since the existing literature is very confused, we must first clear up the relation between these processes, i.e., between what are often known as the Walrasian and Marshallian stability conditions, before studying 'Walrasian' stability of multiple markets.[5]) Then, the local stability of an equilibrium is proved under the assumption of gross substitutability by using Walras' law and the homogeneity of excess demand with respect to prices (section 3). Sections 4 and 5 are devoted to considering the relation between expectation and stability on the basis of the result obtained in section 3. Firstly, Hicksian argument on the relation between expectation and Hicksian static stability is reformulated from the point of view of Samuelsonian dynamic stability, which is related to the Keynesian impossibility problem, i.e., the instability of the full employment equilibrium with flexible money wages. Secondly, however, the economic system under gross substitutability is proved to be stable even if expectation is introduced, when expectation is extrapolative and in a sense rational. As for global stability, different proofs are possible according to different concepts of the distance from the equilibrium employed in the proof of stability, i.e., the convergence to the equilibrium. The Euclidian concept of distance is by no means the only one. In the final section, global stability is demonstrated under gross substitutability using Walras' law and the method suggested in Allais [2] based on the concept of the distance in terms of the sum of the absolute value of excess demands.

2.   It is commonly said that the Walrasian stability condition is the condition for the stability of the dynamic process in which the price of a commodity is changed according to its excess demand while the Marshallian stability condition is that in which the output of a commodity is changed as the demand price is different from the supply price. Let us demonstrate that

[4]) Samuelson [26], 263–4.
[5]) Section 2 owes very much to Newman [25], 106–8.

these two processes are special versions of the more general one, each appropriate in different circumstances.

Consider first a competitive market for a single commodity, with an industrial downward sloping demand curve and an industrial upward sloping supply curve, the latter being nothing but the marginal cost curve. Assuming the consumers' adjustment to a price change is instantaneous, the dynamic processes of price and output are generally given by

$$dP/dt = \alpha(D(P) - S), \tag{1}$$

$$dS/dt = \beta(P - C(S)), \tag{2}$$

where $D(P)$ and $C(S)$ are demand and inverse supply functions, indicating consumers' demand as a function of price and marginal cost (supply price) as a function of output, and P, S, t, α, β denote respectively the price and output of the commodity, time, and the coefficients indicating the speed of adjustment. Equilibrium is established when demand and supply are equalized with each other and the marginal cost is equalized with the price.

When there is no production involved as in the Walrasian equilibrium of exchange, (1) is the only relevant equation with S being constant. The stability condition, i.e., the condition for the convergence of $P(t)$ to $\bar{P}$ such that $D(\bar{P}) = S$ as t goes to infinity; $dD(P)/dP < 0$ is the so-called Walrasian condition.[6]) However, in the Marshallian argument of a temporary equilibrium, again (1) is the only relevant equation since no change of output takes place in such a very short run period.[7]) Therefore, there is no difference between Walras and Marshall in the case of pure exchange and very short run equilibrium.

In the equilibrium of production, Walras considered both (1) and (2) in each of multiple markets with $C(S)$ being assumed to be independent of S, i.e., constant returns to scale.[8]) On the other hand, in his theory of the short run normal price,[9]) Marshall is concerned with (2), with P replaced by the demand price $P(S)$, i.e., $D^{-1}(S)$. This is based on the assumption that for each given amount of output S, the temporary equilibrium $D(P) - S = 0$ is quickly established. Therefore, the Walrasian stability condition for the case of exchange, i.e., $dD(P)/dP < 0$, is implicitly assumed in the Marshallian process. In other words, we may say that the Marshallian process is a special

[6]) Walras–Jaffe [28], 107–114.
[7]) Marshall [16], 333.
[8]) See Morishima [18] and Walras–Jaffe [28], 243–54.
[9]) Marshall [16], 338–350.

case of (1) and (2) with the speed of adjustment in price α infinite. Thus, the so-called Marshallian process is appropriate for the short run competitive market adjustment where the adjustment of output is relatively slow compared with that of market clearance.[10]) The stability condition is $dP/dS - dC/dS < 0$.

Alternatively, the so-called Walrasian process can be obtained from (1) and (2) by assuming the speed of adjustment in output β infinite. It is (1) with S replaced by $S(P)$, i.e., the solution of the equilibrium of production $P - C(S) = 0$, $C^{-1}(P)$, which is assumed to be established quickly. Although it cannot be found originally in Walras [28], the modern analysis of stability has been mainly concerned with this process. It treats demand and supply of the consumers and producers symmetrically, both assumed to react to price changes instantaneously, with the stability condition that $dD/dP - dS/dP < 0$.

Though the demand curve must be downward sloping, the Marshallian process can be extended to the case of a forward falling industrial supply curve.[11]) Such a supply curve must be a long-run one explained by the economies external to firms but internal to the industry.[12]) The rising marginal cost curve of an individual firm is shifted downward by the increase of total industrial output. With the downward sloping demand curve given, the long-run equilibrium is established at an industrial output where the demand curve and the (horizontal) sum of individual marginal cost curves at the given industrial output intersect with each other. When the demand is increased, the equilibrium output is increased and the equilibrium price is diminished, since the individual marginal cost curves are shifted downward by the increased industrial output. The locus of such equilibrium pairs of output and price is called the industrial supply curve, which is the industrial average, not the marginal, cost curve, if entry to this industry is free. The adjustment of industrial output is certainly slow compared with that of price, which is a situation appropriate for the Marshallian process. It can be expressed by (2) with P replaced by $P(S) = D^{-1}(S)$ and $C(S)$ interpreted as the industrial average cost function. The stability condition is

---

[10]) Hicks [12] states that it is appropriate for the monopolistic adjustment which was followed by Negishi [21]. See [12], 62 and [21], 638. However, the marginal revenue rather than the demand price is relevant for monopoly. We would like to withdraw the statement on the Marshallian process in [21], which also wrongly denied the possibility of the short run application of the process.

[11]) Marshall [16], 806.

[12]) See chapter 5 and Adams and Wheeler [1].

that $|dP/dS| > |dC/dS|$, i.e., the demand curve must be steeper than the supply curve.[13])

On the other hand, the demand curve need not be downward sloping but the industrial supply curve must be rising in the so-called Walrasian process. The only conceivable case of the falling supply curve here is that of the supply of factors of production from households.

It may not be out of place to mention here one implicit assumption made in (1) and (2) concerning the possibility of trade at disequilibria. We must assume, strictly speaking, either that disequilibrium transaction is permissible but commodities are instantaneously perishable and taste and technology are unchanged or that no transaction is carried out until equilibrium is reached (i.e., the assumption of Walrasian tâtonnement), so that demand and supply curves are not shifted by the disequilibrium transactions.[14]) The second assumption might be appropriate for the case of short-run adjustment in a highly organized market while we must rely on the first assumption in the case of the longer run adjustments.

3. Consider the local stability of an isolated equilibrium of multiple markets by the 'Walrasian' process,

$$dP_i/dt = F_i(E_i(P)), \quad i = 1, ..., n, \tag{3}$$

where P_i is the price of the ith commodity, $P = (P_1, ..., P_n)$, t is time, E_i is the excess demand function for the ith commodity assumed to be differentiable and F_i is a strictly increasing differentiable function such that $F_i(0) = 0$. The nth commodity is chosen as numeraire so that $F_n \equiv 0$ and P_n is constant. The isolated equilibrium and local stability is defined as

Definition 1. An isolated equilibrium is a positive vector $\bar{P} = (\bar{P}_1, ..., \bar{P}_n)$ such that $E_i(P) = 0$ for $i = 1, ..., n$, which is unique within a certain open sub-set D of P in R^+ (the positive orthant in n-dimensional Euclidean space). It is locally stable if the solution of (3), $P(t; P(0))$ converges to it whenever the initial condition $P(0)$ belongs to a sufficiently small neighborhood of P, say, $C \subset D$. If we consider the linear approximation of (3) at $\bar{P}$,

$$dP_i/dt = F_i' \sum_j E_{ij}(P_j - \bar{P}_j), \quad i = 1, ..., n-1, \tag{4}$$

$$P_n \equiv \bar{P}_n,$$

[13]) For the stability analysis of the Marshallian process, see, e.g., Aoki [3] and Chipman [7].
[14]) For the case in which these assumptions are dropped, see chapter 14.

where F_i' and E_{ij}'s are the derivative of F_i and the partial derivative of E_i with respect to P_j at $\bar{P}$, then we have

Lemma 1. A sufficient condition for the local stability of (3) is the stability of (4). The necessary and sufficient condition for the latter is that the real part of all the characteristic roots of the $(n-1) \times (n-1)$ matrix $A = \{F_i' E_{ij}\}$, i.e., the solution $\lambda = (\lambda_1, \ldots, \lambda_n)$ of $|A - \lambda I| = 0$, are negative, where I is the identity matrix.[15]

Although we do not give the formal proof of lemma 1, the second half of the lemma is easily conjectured by substituting $P_j - \bar{P}_j = \Sigma_j k_{ij} \exp(\lambda_i t)$, where k_{ij}'s are constants, to (4) and checking the conditions for the non-trivial solutions. We can get rid of the coefficients of the speed of adjustment F_i' in A by choosing the unit of measurement for commodities properly. If we multiply the unit of measurement by the root F_i' (which implies the inversely proportional changes of quantities and proportional changes of prices), we can set F_i''s equal to one in (4) and the matrix A in the lemma is reduced to $\{E_{ij}\}$.[16]

Therefore, stability depends on the matrix A. We can make its off-diagonal elements positive by

Assumption 1. All the commodities are gross-substitutes, i.e., E_{ij}, i, $j = 1, \ldots, n$, the partial derivatives of E_i with respect to P_j, are all positive for any $P \in R^+$.

Then, by a proper scalar $t > 0$, we can construct a positive matrix $M = tI + A$, whose characteristic roots are t greater than those of A, to which we can apply Frobenius theorem.

Lemma 2. A positive matrix M (1) has a characteristic root $r > 0$ (Frobenius root) such that (2) to r can be associated an eigen-vector $x_r > 0$, i.e., $Mx_r = rx_r$; (3) if α is any characteristic root of M, $|\alpha| < r$; (4) r increases when any element of M increases; (5) r is a simple root; (6) if B is a principal submatrix of A and β a characteristic root of B, $|\beta| < r$.[17]

The following lemma is derived from lemma 2.

Lemma 3. If for a vector $x > 0$, $Mx < tx$, then $r < t$.

[15] See Liapounoff [15], 255–267 and Bellman [6], 75–79, 80–82, 14–17, 21–25.
[16] Fukuoka–Kamiya [10].
[17] Debreu–Herstein [8].

Proof. Let $y > 0$ be an eigen-vector of M' associated with r, i.e., $M'y = ry$. From $Mx < tx$, $x > 0$, we have $y'Mx < ty'x$, i.e., $ry'x < ty'x$. Since $y'x > 0$, $r < t$.[18])

Now we can prove

Theorem 1. Under assumption 1, an isolated equilibrium $\bar{P}$ is shown to be locally stable by the use of either (1) the zero degree homogeneity of excess demands with respect to P^{19}) or (2) Walras' law $\Sigma_j P_j E_j \equiv 0$.[20])

Proof. (1) From Euler's theorem on the homogeneous function, we have

$$-\sum_{j=1}^{j=n-1} E_{ij} \bar{P}_j = E_{in} \bar{P}_n, \quad i = 1, \ldots, n, \tag{5}$$

at $\bar{P}$. This can be rewritten as

$$Ax = (tI - M)x = y, \quad \text{i.e., } tx > Mx, \tag{6}$$

where $x = (P_1, \ldots, P_{n-1}) > 0$, $\quad y = (E_{1n}\bar{P}_n, \ldots, E_{n-1,n}\bar{P}_n) > 0$, $\quad t > 0$, $A = \{-E_{ij}\}_{i,j=1,\ldots,n-1}$. From assumption 1, M is positive for a proper t. From lemma 3, $r < t$, where r is the Frobenius root of M. For a characteristic root λ of A corresponds that of M, $t + \lambda$. From lemma 2, $|\lambda + t| < r$. Being not larger than $|\lambda + t|$, the real part of $\lambda + t$ is not larger than r. Then, the real part of λ is not larger than $r - t$. Since $r - t < 0$, the real part of λ is all negative and $\bar{P}$ is locally stable from lemma 1. (2) By differentiating Walras' identity by P_j at $\bar{P}$, we have

$$-\sum_{i=1}^{i=n-1} E_{ij} \bar{P}_i = E_{nj} \bar{P}_n, \quad j = 1, \ldots, n, \tag{7}$$

which can be written as

$$A'x = (tI - M')x = z, \tag{8}$$

where $z = (E_{n1}\bar{P}_n, \ldots, E_{n,n-1}\bar{P}_n) > 0$. The rest of the proof is similar to the case of (1).

4. In this section, we are concerned with the reformulation from the view point of dynamic stability analysis of the Hicks–Keynes proposition that elasticities of expectations is the cause of instability of the economic system

---

[18]) Debreu–Herstein [8].
[19]) Negishi [20].
[20]) Hahn [11] and Arrow and Hurwicz [5].

and that price rigidity is its possible stabilizer. Hicks [12] states that a static economy is inherently stable but the stability of the system is seriously weakened by the introduction of the elasticity of expectations and that price rigidity exercises a stabilizing influence. Hicks developed these arguments verbally and in terms of Hicksian stability. This is an extension of Keynes' famous proposition [13] that the reduction of money-wages expected to be a reduction relatively to money-wages in the future will be favorable to investment and consumption while the reduction which leads to the expectation of a further wage reduction in prospect will have precisely the opposite effect and that the maintenance of a stable general level of money-wages is the most advisable policy.[21])

Consider Walrasian tâtonnement (i.e., the process with no actual transaction carried out until it reaches an equilibrium) of a temporary equilibrium within a Hicksian week.[22]) Let there be n commodities (including bond, money, etc.), the nth one being money and numeraire and the $n-1$, labor service. An n-dimensional vector $P = (P_1, ..., P_n)$ is defined as the current price vector, where P_i denotes the price of the ith commodity. Similarly, an n-dimensional vector $q = (q_1, ..., q_n)$, $q_n \equiv P_n$, is the expected future price vector. We assume there is a Hicksian functional relation between expected and current prices (with homogeneity of degree one), $q_i = f_i(P)$, $i = 1, ..., n-1$.[23]) The excess demand for the ith commodity is $E_i(P, q)$, which is homogeneous of degree zero with respect to P and q.[24])

An equilibrium $(\bar{P}, \bar{q})$ is defined by the following conditions:

$$E_i(P, q) = 0, \ i = 1, ..., n, \ q_i = f_i(P), \ i = 1, ..., n-1, \ P_n \equiv q_n = 1 . \quad (9)$$

We assume there is an isolated equilibrium and are concerned with the local stability of it in the following dynamic price adjustment process,

$$\mathrm{d}P_i/\mathrm{d}t = E_i(P, q), \ i = 1, ..., n-1, \ q_i = f_i(P), \ i = 1, ..., n-1, \quad (10)$$

$$P_n \equiv q_n = 1 ,$$

[21]) Hicks [12], 256, 265, Keynes [13], 263, 270, and Negishi [24].
[22]) Hicksian temporary equilibrium is different from the Marshallian one. Hicks [12], 121–123. The problem of the stability of equilibrium over time (through Hicksian weeks) will be considered in the following section. See Hicks [12], 132.
[23]) It can be considered that the expected future price is a function of current price and past prices. But past prices are data in our analysis of current temporary equilibrium. Therefore an expectation function is reduced to a functional relationship between current and future prices only. See Hicks, [12], 204.
[24]) For the two period model of an economy, see chapter 16.

or its linear approximation;

$$dP_i/dt = \Sigma_j E_{ij}(P_j - \bar{P}_j) + \Sigma_j \Sigma_k E'_{ij} F_{jk}(P_k - \bar{P}_k),$$

$$i, j, k = 1, ..., n-1, \tag{11}$$

where $E_{ij} = \partial E_i/\partial P_j$, $E'_{ij} = \partial E_i/\partial q_j$, and $F_{jk} = \partial f_j/\partial P_k$. Let us denote the $(n-1) \times (n-1)$ matrices in the set of differential equations (11) as follows,

$$A = \{E_{ij}\}, \quad B = \{E'_{ij}\}, \quad C = \{F_{jk}\}, \quad i, j, k = 1, ..., n-1,$$

where differential coefficients are evaluated at $(\bar{P}, \bar{q})$, and assume

Assumption 2. All present and future commodities are gross substitutes, i.e., E_{ij}, $i, j = 1, ..., n$, $i \neq j$ and E'_{ij}, $i, j = 1, ..., n-1$, are all positive.[25])

Therefore, A is a positive off-diagonal matrix and B is a positive matrix. If we further assume

Assumption 3. Elasticity of expectations,[26]) $P_j F_{jk}/q_k$, are all non-negative, i.e., C is a non-negative matrix, then the stability of an equilibrium depends on $A + BC$, which is a positive off-diagonal matrix.

Now we can prove the following theorem.

Theorem 2. (1) If expectations are static, i.e., $q_i = P_i$, $i = 1, ..., n-1$, then (11) is stable. (2) If elasticities of expectation are large enough, (11) is unstable. (3) A necessary condition for the instability is that $E_{jj} + E'_{jj} F_{jj} > 0$ for some j while a sufficient condition is that $\Sigma_j (E_{jj} + E'_{jj} F_{jj}) > 0$.

Proof. (1) $A + BC$ is reduced to $A + B$, which corresponds to A in lemmata 1 to 3. Since we have Euler's identity like (5) from the homogeneity, the proof is similar to the case of theorem 1. (2) From lemma 2 there is a real characteristic root r' of $A + BC$ which is t smaller than r, r being the Frobenius root of $M = tI + A + BC$ where t is chosen so that M is a positive matrix. From (1), we have stability when $C = I$, i.e., $r' = r - t < 0$. Keeping t constant and increasing elements of C from I, r' is increased from a negative value to a positive one. (3) By extending $|\lambda I - (A + BC)| = 0$, we find

---

[25]) E'_{in} is not defined since $q_n \equiv P_n$. Assumption 2 implies that $E'_{uj} < 0$, $j = 1, ..., n-1$, from Walras' law, $\Sigma_i P_i E_i \equiv 0$. This can be interpreted as the rise in future prices decreasing the current demand for money reserve.

[26]) Lange [14], 20.

that the trace of $A + BC$ is equal to the sum of characteristic roots. From the homogeneity of E_i and f_i at least one diagonal element must be positive for instability.[27])

Next, let us introduce some price rigidity as a possible stabilizer. Consider a new equilibrium with some rigid price, say, the wage. The conditions of the equilibrium $(\hat{P}, \hat{q})$ with the fixed $\hat{P}_{n-1} > 0$ are,

$$E_i(P, q) = 0, \quad i = 1, \ldots, n-2, \quad q_i = f_i(P), \quad i = 1, \ldots, n-1, \tag{12}$$

$$P_{n-1} = \hat{P}_{n-1}, \quad P_n \equiv q_n = 1 .$$

We assume the unique existence of this equilibrium. In this case the adjustment process (11) is reduced to first $n-2$ equations with A, B and C respectively replaced by $(n-2) \times (n-2)$ matrices $\hat{A}$, $\hat{B}$ and $\hat{C}$, $i, j, k = 1$, ..., $n-2$, evaluated at $(\hat{P}, \hat{q})$. If $(\hat{P}, \hat{q})$ is very close to $(\bar{P}, \bar{q})$, then we can safely consider the matrix $\hat{A} + \hat{B}\hat{C}$ as a principal submatrix of $A + BC$. Then, we have,

Theorem 3. If some (not all) of the diagonal elements of $A + BC$ are positive and the adjustment process (11) is unstable, the introduction of rigid prices has a stabilizing effect on (11), unless all the diagonal elements of $A + BC$ corresponding to flexible prices are positive.

Proof. From lemma 2, the real part of all the characteristic roots of $\hat{A} + \hat{B}\hat{C}$ are smaller than the real characteristic root $r' = r - t$ of $A + BC$, where t is so chosen that $tI + A + BC$ is a positive matrix. Therefore, there is a possibility that r' is positive but the real part of all the characteristic roots of $\hat{A} + \hat{B}\hat{C}$ is negative. This is true even if there remain some positive diagonal elements in $\hat{A} + \hat{B}\hat{C}$. If there are still some characteristic roots of $\hat{A} + \hat{B}\hat{C}$ with positive real part, we can introduce another rigid price, and by repeating this procedure, we can finally get to the principal submatrix with all the diagonal elements non-positive, where the real part of all the characteristic roots are negative. This is seen from assumptions 2 and 3 and the homogeneity of E_i's and f_i's as in the case of theorem 1.[28])

5. The relation between stability and expectations can also be considered in the dynamic process over Hicksian weeks. Stability then implies the

---

[27]) The critical condition of stability and instability is that $|A + BC| = 0$, since r' is real.
[28]) If only the last column of C is positive as in the case of Keynes, the rigidity of wages is enough for stability.

convergence of the series of temporary disequilibria established in each Hicksian week to some stationary state, i.e., a temporary equilibrium which remains unchanged through Hicksian weeks. The expected future prices may now depend not only on current prices but also on past prices or the rates of change in prices. The relation between extrapolative expectations and stability was studied by Enthoven and Arrow [9] with the result that stability depends, when gross substitutability is assumed, on the magnitude of the coefficients of expectation, i.e., elastic expectations may be a cause of the instability, which is similar to the result in the preceding section.[29]) Negishi [23] is an attempt to argue the possible value of the coefficient of expectation by giving some rational basis to extrapolative expectation. The rational expectation hypothesis advanced by Muth [19] is that expectations are essentially the same as the predictions of the relevant economic theory; that the economy generally does not waste information; and that expectations depend specifically on the structure of the entire system. However, since there is a cost of gathering information and computation, expectations may also be called rational when they are formed as a prediction based on a simplified and approximated version of the economic theory, using only limited amounts of information on a part of the system. Extrapolative expectations are derived as the prediction of the equilibrium by the use of estimated excess demand functions, and it is shown that the coefficients of expectations thus derived are such that the system of multiple markets is stable when gross substitutability is assumed.

Consider the model developed in the previous section with Hicksian expectations replaced by an extrapolative version, $q_i = P_i + \eta_i dP_i/dt$, $i = 1, ..., n-1$, where η_i is the coefficient of expectation. Then, (11) is replaced by

$$dP_i/dt = \Sigma_j E_{ij}(P_j - \bar{P}_j) + \Sigma_j E'_{ij}(q_j - \bar{P}_j), \quad i, j = 1, ..., n-1, \qquad (13)$$

since $\bar{q}_i = \bar{P}_i$. Instead of assumption 3, we have, following Enthoven and Arrow [9],

Assumption 4. E'_{ij}'s, $i \neq j$, $i, j = 1, ..., n$, are all zero, which may be partly justified by supposing that specialist speculators in the ith market are interested mainly in the difference between P_i and q_i.

---

[29]) The model of Enthoven and Arrow [9] is formally equivalent to that of Walrasian tâtonnement, since the shifts of demand and supply functions caused by transactions at disequilibria are disregarded.

The expectation of future prices is assumed to be arrived at rationally, i.e., by the use of economic theory. Future prices q should be calculated as equilibrium prices of the system of excess demand functions estimated from past data on the entire economy. Since expectation q is not realized in the quantitative data, the estimation of excess demand functions may be the regression of E on P and dP/dt. However, we assume that, in the market of the ith commodity, only the excess demand E_i is estimated as a function of P and dP_i/dt, and the future price of the ith commodity q_i is predicted as the equilibrium price in that market, under the assumption that other future prices are not to change, i.e., $q_j = P_j, j \neq i$. The reason for the use of limited amounts of information is the cost of gathering information and computation.

We have the estimated excess demand function

$$E_i = \Sigma_j a_{ij} P_j + b_i (dP_i/dt) + c_i , \tag{14}$$

where a_{ij}, b_i and c_i are constants. As the equilibrium price, q_i is calculated by

$$0 = a_{ii} q_i + \Sigma_{j \neq i} a_{ij} P_i + c_i, \quad \text{i.e.,} \quad E_i = 0, \quad dP_i/dt = 0 . \tag{15}$$

If the estimation is good, we may suppose that the expressions on the right hand side of (13) and that of (14) will coincide with each other, both being expressions for the same E_i. Substituting $dP_i/dt = E_i$ into (14) and then (14) into (15) gives

$$q_i = P_i + \{(b_i - 1)/a_{ii}\}(dP_i/dt) . \tag{16}$$

The assumption of rational extrapolative expectations explained above amounts to,

Assumption 5. $\eta_i = (b_i - 1)/a_{ii}$.

Now we can prove,

Theorem 4.   Under assumptions 2, 4 and 5, (13) is stable.

Proof.   Substituting (16) into the right-hand side of (13) and comparing with (14), we have

$$a_{ii} = E_{ii} + E'_{ii}, \tag{17}$$

$$a_{ij} = E_{ij}, \tag{18}$$

$$b_i = E'_{ii}(b_i - 1)/a_{ii} . \tag{19}$$

From (17) and (19), therefore,

$$b_i = -E'_{ii}/E_{ii}.\qquad (20)$$

Considering (16) and (19), (13) is rewritten as

$$(1-b_i)(dP_i/dt) = \Sigma_j E_{ij}(P_j - \bar{P}_j) + E'_{ii}(P_i - \bar{P}_i).\qquad (21)$$

From the zero degree homogeneity of E_i with respect to P and q (i.e., q_i) and assumption 2, i.e., Euler's identity, we have $|E_{ii}| > E'_{ii}$ and therefore $0 < b_i < 1$. Then, again using Euler's identity, the stability of (21) is proved as in the case of theorem 1.

6. Finally, let us consider the global stability of the adjustment process

$$dP_i/dt = E_i(P), \quad i = 1, \dots, n,\qquad (22)$$

where price vector $P = (P_1, \dots, P_n)$ is not normalized, i.e., the role of numeraire is not assigned to any commodity. Excess demands E_i's are subject to zero degree homogeneity with respect to P and to Walras' law. We must first assume

Assumption 6. The differential system of equations has a solution $P(t; P(0))$ for any initial condition $P(0) \in N(P(0): P_j(0) \geq \gamma_j > 0)$, such that it satisfies $P_j(t) \geq \delta_j > 0$ for all j and is continuous with respect to time t and the initial condition $P(0),$[30])

and define the global stability as

Definition 2. The adjustment process (22) is globally stable when its solution $P(t; P(0))$ converges to an equilibrium vector $\bar{P}$ (such that $E_i(\bar{P}) = 0$ for all i) for any initial condition $P(0) \in N$.

Generally $\bar{P}$ is not unique, which is the reason why we speak of the stability of the process rather than the stability of an equilibrium in the case of global stability. However, under gross substitutability (assumption 1), we have

Lemma 4. The equilibrium price vector $\bar{P}$ is determined uniquely up to the scalar multiplication under gross substitutability. Therefore, the equilibrium

---

[30]) This can be assured by assuming that there are positive numbers $\gamma_s, \delta_s, \varepsilon_s, (\gamma_s > \delta_s)$, $s = 1, \dots, n$, such that $P_j \leq \delta_j, P_k \geq \delta_k, k \neq j, \Sigma_s P_s^2 \geq \Sigma_s \gamma_s^2$ implies $E_j \geq \varepsilon_j > 0$.

price vector which can be reached from the given initial condition $P(0)$ by the process (22) is unique.

Proof. Suppose both $\bar{P}$ and $\bar{\bar{P}}$ such that $\bar{P} \neq \lambda \bar{\bar{P}}$ for any scalar $\lambda > 0$ are equilibrium price vectors, and let $P_J/P_J = \min_j(\bar{P}_j/\bar{\bar{P}}_j)$. By the homogeneity of E_i's with respect to P, we may replace $\bar{P}$ by $\hat{P}$ such that $\hat{P} = \mu\bar{P}$, $\mu > 0$ and $\bar{P}_J = \hat{P}_J$. Then, $\hat{P} \leq \bar{\bar{P}}$, and hence by the gross substitutability and the definition of equilibrium, $E_J(\hat{P}) < E_J(\bar{\bar{P}}) = 0$, which contradicts with the supposition that $\bar{\bar{P}}$ is an equilibrium.[31]) Then, since $\Sigma_j P_j(t)^2 = \Sigma_j P(0)^2$, as is seen from the fact that $d\Sigma_j P_j(t)^2/dt = 2\Sigma_j P_j(t)(dP_j(t)/dt) = 2\Sigma_j P_j(t) E_j(P(t)) = 0$ by the process (22) and Walras' law, the equilibrium which can be reached from a given initial condition is unique.

Now we are ready to state a theorem on global stability under gross substitutability. The idea of the proof of stability, which is originally due to Liapounoff [15], is to consider a sort of generalized concept of the distance from an equilibrium and to show that it is decreasing through time, i.e., the solution of the dynamic system is approaching to an equilibrium. The most natural concept of the distance is of course that of Euclid, i.e., $\Sigma_i(P_i(t) - \bar{P}_i)^2$, which was used by Arrow, Block and Hurwicz [4] to prove stability under gross substitutability. Another concept of the distance, i.e., the distance in terms of the maximum norm, which is also considered in Arrow, Block and Hurwicz [4] is $\max_i\{|P_i(t) - \bar{P}_i|/\bar{P}_i\}$. The concept of the distance, on the other hand, which we are going to consider in the following theorem, is the sum of the absolute value of the excess demand for each commodity multiplied by its price. It is certainly positive out of equilibrium and zero at an equilibrium. The essense of the proof is to show that it is decreasing through time by the use of Walras' law.

Theorem 5. Under assumptions 1 and 6, the process (22) is globally stable.

Proof. Let us construct a characteristic function as follows;
$V(t) = \Sigma_{j \in J}^{+}{}_{(t)} P_j(t) E_j(P(t))$, where $J^{+}(t) = \{j; E_j(P(t)) > 0$, or $E_j(P(t)) = 0$, $dE_j(P(t))/dt > 0\}$. By Walras' law, we also have $V(t) = \Sigma_{j \in J}^{-}{}_{(t)} P_j(t) E_j(P(t))$, where $J^{-}(t) = \{j; E_j(P(t)) < 0$, or $E_j(P(t)) = 0$, $dE_j(P(t))/dt < 0\}$.[32]) For

---

[31]) Arrow, Block and Hurwicz [4].
[32]) The use of this function was first suggested by Allais [2], vol. 2, 486–9, and later studied by McKenzie [17] and Negishi [22].

sufficiently small $h > 0$, we have $V(t+h) = \Sigma_{j \in J}{}^+{}_{(t)} P_j(t+h) E_j(P(t+h))$ $+ \Sigma_{j \in J} P_j(t+h) E_j(P(t+h))$, where J is a suitable subset of $J^0(t) = \{j;$ $E_j(P(t)) = 0,\ dE_j(P(t))/dt = 0\}$. We wish to show that $W(t) = \overline{\lim}_{h \to 0}(1/h)$ $\{V(t+h) - V(t)\} = \lim_{v \to \infty}(1/h_v)\{V(t+h) - V(t)\} \leq 0$, where $\{h_v\}$ is a sequence such that $h_v \to 0$ as $v \to \infty$, and equality holds only at equilibrium. Because of the number of commodities, n, is finite, we can take a suitable subsequence of h_v and find $\lim_{v \to \infty}(1/h_v)\{V(t+h) - V(t)\} = \Sigma_{j \in J}{}^+{}_{(t)} d(P_j E_j)/$ $dt + \Sigma_{j \in J} d(P_j E_j)/dt$ for a certain $J \in J^0(t)$. From the definition of $J^0(t)$, $\Sigma_{j \in J} d(P_j E_j)/dt = 0$, and we have $W(t) = \Sigma_{j \in J}{}^+{}_{(t)} d(P_j E_j)/dt$. By the use of Walras' identity, then, we have

$$W(t) = -\Sigma_{k \in J^+(t)}\{\Sigma_{j \notin J^+(t)} \partial(P_j E_j)/\partial P_k\}(dP_k/dt)$$

$$+ \Sigma_{k \in J^-(t)}\{\Sigma_{j \in J^+(t)} \partial(P_j E_j)/\partial P_k\}(dP_k/dt),$$

which is negative from assumption 1, since $j \neq k$ in each term. At equilibrium, J^+ and J^- become null sets and we have $V = 0$, $W = 0$. The domain of $P(t; P(0))$ is bounded because we have $d(\Sigma_j P_j^2)/dt = 0$. Since $V(t)$ is bounded from below by 0, the fact that $V(t)$ decreasss through time implies the existence of $\lim_{t \to \infty} V(t) = V^*$. Let P_j^* be a limit of $P_j(t; P(0))$ as $t \to \infty$, i.e., $P_j^* = \lim_{k \to \infty} P_j(t_k; P(0))$, where $t_k \to \infty$ as $k \to \infty$. Then we have $V^*(t) = V^*(t; P^*) = \lim_{k \to \infty} V(t; P(t_k)) = \lim_{k \to \infty} V(t + t_k; P(0)) = V^*$, from the continuity of P_j and V. Hence, $W(t) = 0$ at P^*, i.e., P^* is an equilibrium. From lemma 4, therefore, (22) is globally stable.[33]

References

[1] Adams, R.W. and J.T. Wheeler, 'External economies and the falling supply curve,' *Review of Economic Studies*, 20 (1951), 24–39.

[2] Allais, M., *Traité d'économie pure*, Paris: Imprimerie Nationale, 1943.

[3] Aoki, M., 'A note on Marshallian process under increasing returns,' *Quarterly Journal of Economics*, 84 (1970), 100–112.

[4] Arrow, K.J., H.D. Block and L. Hurwicz, 'On the stability of the competitive equilibrium,' II, *Econometrica*, 26 (1959), 89–109.

[5] Arrow, K.J. and L. Hurwicz, 'On the stability of the competitive equilibrium,' *Econometrica*, 26 (1958), 522–552.

[6] Bellman, R., *Stability theory of differential equations*, McGraw-Hill, 1953.

[7] Chipman, J.S., 'External economies of scale and competitive equilibrium,' *Quarterly Journal of Economics*, 84 (1970), 347–85.

[33] See Uzawa [27].

[8] Debreu, G. and I. N. Herstein, 'Nonnegative square matrices,' *Econometrica*, 21 (1953), 597–607 (P. Newman, ed., *Readings in mathematical economics*, *I*, Johns Hopkins University Press, 1968, 57–67).

[9] Enthoven A. C. and K. J., Arrow, 'A theorem on expectations and the stability of equilibrium,' *Econometrica*, 24 (1956), 288–93.

[10] Fukuoka, M. and D. Kamiya, 'The stability conditions and the speeds of adjustment: a critical note,' *Economic Studies Quarterly*, 14-2 (1964), 76–8.

[11] Hahn, F. H., 'Gross substitutes and the dynamic stability of general equilibrium,' *Econometrica*, 26 (1958), 169–170.

[12] Hicks, J. R., *Value and capital* (2nd ed.), Oxford University Press, 1946.

[13] Keynes, J. M., '*The general theory of employment, interest and money*, Macmillan, 1936.

[14] Lange, O., *Price flexibility and employment*, The Principia Press, 1944.

[15] Liapounoff, M. A., 'Problème général de la stabilité du mouvement,' *Annales de la Faculté des Sciences du Toulouse*, 2nd series, 9 (1907), 27–496 (*Annals of Mathematical Studies*, 17, Princeton University Press, 1949).

[16] Marshall, A., *Principles of economics*, (8th ed.) Macmillan, 1920.

[17] McKenzie, L. W., 'Stability of equilibrium and the value of positive excess demand,' *Econometrica*, 28 (1960), 606–17.

[18] Morishima, M., 'A reconsideration of Walras–Cassel–Leontief model of general equilibrium,' *Mathematical methods in the social sciences*, Stanford University Press, 1960, 63–76 (Morishima, M., *Equilibrium, stability and growth*, Oxford University Press, 1964, 23–43).

[19] Muth, J. F., 'Rational expectations and the theory of price movements,' *Econometrica*, 29 (1961), 315–35.

[20] Negishi, T., 'A note on the stability of an economy where all goods are gross substitutes,' *Econometrica*, 26 (1958), 445–7.

[21] Negishi, T., 'Stability of a competitive economy, a survey article,' *Econometrica*, 30 (1962), 635–69. (P. Newman ed., *Readings in mathematical economics*, *I*, Johns Hopkins University Press, 1968, 213–47).

[22] Negishi, T., 'On the formation of prices, '*International Economic Review*, 2 (1961), 122–126.

[23] Negishi, T., 'Stability and rationality of the extrapolative expectations,' *Econometrica*, 32 (1964), 649–51.

[24] Negishi, T., 'Market clearing processes in a monetary economy,' Hahn and Brechling ed., *The theory of interest rates*, Macmillan, 1965, 152–163.

[25] Newman, P., *The theory of exchange*, Prentice Hall, 1965.

[26] Samuelson, P. A., *Foundations of economic analysis*, Harvard University Press, 1947.

[27] Uzawa, H., 'The stability of dynamic Sta process,' *Econometrica*, 29 (1961), 617–31.

[28] Walras, L., *Élements d'économie politique pure*, Corbaz (Lausanne), 1874–77 (1st ed.), 1926 (definitive ed.,) (W. Jaffe tr., *Elements of pure economics*, Irwin, 1954).

CHAPTER 14

The stability of non-tâtonnement processes

1. In Walrasian tâtonnement, which was studied in the preceding chapter, it is assumed that excess demands for commodities are functions of commodity prices only. This implies that no exchange transaction will be undertaken until a system of prices is reached which secures equilibrium in all parts of the market. The use of tickets or the possibility of recontract is suggested for this purpose.[1] Because of this assumption, the equilibrium becomes determinate in the sense that the process of adjustment does not alter the conditions of equilibrium.[2] In the absence of this assumption, the equilibrium is generally indeterminate and depends on the route followed by prices before the equilibrium is reached. The indeterminateness of the equilibrium arises through redistribution of incomes among individuals due to changes of prices in the midst of trading.[3] Excess demands, as functions of prices, will be shifted by the changed income distribution due to disequilibrium transactions. Although recontracting which ensures that no transactions take place out of equilibrium is an ingenious simplification, it is also a heroic assumption. Certainly it may provide a rough approximation of the process by which market equilibrium is attained, but it does not seem to be a very promising approach to the understanding of the behavior of markets while in disequilibrium. The aim of this chapter is, therefore, to investigate the implication of relaxing the recontracting assumption and of introducing the distribution effect of disequilibrium transactions on excess demands.

[1] Walras–Jaffe [25], p. 37, Edgeworth [7], pp. 311–14.
[2] Kaldor [9].
[3] See Hicks [13], pp. 127–9. Japanese literature like Morishima [14] and Yasui [26] had also expressed this possibility.

There is another problem which also arises when the tâtonnement assumption is relaxed, i.e., the so-called spillover effects.[4] An individual's actual attempt to buy in one market depends upon the transactions which are actually executed in other markets. The unsatisfied excess demands or supplies in some markets spill over to other markets. To take Clower's example, a worker's demand for commodities will generally depend upon his sale of labor services. If he sells less labor than he would like to sell at existing prices because of an aggregate excess supply of labor, he will not be able to buy the notional quantities of the various commodities which he would otherwise have liked to buy at the existing prices. Consequently, the excess demand function for any commodity should contain as arguments the excess demands realized in other markets. Certainly this spillover effect is most important in the realistic imperfect process of exchange in which one has to use a specified commodity, i.e., money, as the medium of exchange. However, in a Walrasian abstract but perfect model of exchange, with which our study on non-tâtonnement is concerned, the full flexibility and quick market clearing ability of prices are believed by competitive participants and therefore such a spillover effect is irrelevant. In perfect competition, the given market prices are the only information assumed to be necessary and relevant for individual decisions, i.e., an individual participant behaves believing that he can buy or sell as much as he wishes with the given market prices. In other words, the notional and actual demands (and supplies) are not different even in disequilibrium, since every commodity is believed to be a medium of exchange. Spillover effect becomes relevant only when the adjustment speed of some markets is very slow, almost nil as in the case of the Keynesian labor market, so that people give up their belief in the price mechanism and demand non-price information such as market excess demand or supply to make their decisions. This is the reason why we confine ourselves to the distribution effect of disequilibrium transactions in our study of a non-tâtonnement process.[5]

We shall start with the original Walrasian model of tâtonnement, in which markets are not simultaneously but successively adjusted. Transactions

[4] See Patinkin [20], 235–6. Clower [6] and Grossman [10].
[5] Arrow–Hahn [2] (chapter 13) and Fisher [8] skillfuly combined the spillover effect (i.e., the difference between notional and actual demands) and distribution effect by introducing money as the sole medium of exchange. Unfortunately, however, the role of money is considered in their model still in a very unsatisfactory way, since not the real value of money but the nominal value is considered in the utility function.

among individuals are now permitted even though the economy as a whole is in disequilibrium, provided that the relevant single market is in equilibrium. It turns out that such a process of successive price adjustment and transaction in each market is strongly stable in the sense that no restrictions on the form of excess demand functions are necessary for stability (section 2). Then, the system of simultaneous adjustments in all markets will be studied with disequilibrium transactions permitted according to certain transaction rules. This is the case of what has been called the non-tâtonnement process in the literature.[6]) We shall demonstrate that the non-tâtonnement process is stable in certain cases in which the tâtonnement process, a special case of the non-tâtonnement process, is known to be stable (section 3). It can be said that the combination of some restrictions placed on the forms of the excess demand functions, e.g., gross substitutability, and the very special transaction rule, i.e., that of no transaction, ensure the stability of tâtonnement. Therefore, we may expect that restrictions on excess demand functions and transaction rules can be traded for stability. In other words, no restrictions on excess demand functions are needed for the stability of the non-tâtonnement process, if some suitable rules are imposed on transactions. In section 4, the stability of the non-tâtonnement process will be demonstrated under the assumption of the so-called Hahn transaction rules. The final section is devoted to the study of dynamic systems under the assumption of the Hahn transaction rule and adaptive expectations.[7])

2. Let us begin with a sketch of the original form of Walrasian tâtonnement, i.e., not the process of simultaneous adjustment of all markets as formulated by Samuelson, but the process of successive adjustment in each market.[8])

Consider a competitive economy of m commodities. The price of and the excess demand for the jth commodity are denoted respectively by P_j and E_j. A competitive general equilibrium $(\bar{P}_1, ..., \bar{P}_{m-1})$ is achieved when

$$E_j(P_1, ..., P_{m-1}) = 0, \quad j = 1, ..., m-1, \tag{1}$$

is satisfied, with the mth commodity being numeraire. Suppose the initial set of prices $(P_1, ..., P_{m-1})$ does not satisfy the condition of general equi-

---

[6]) See Negishi [16].

[7]) Arrow–Hurwicz [4] and Arrow–Nerlove [5] assumed the instantaneous perishability of commodities in their study on stability and adaptive expectation. We on the other hand assume that commodities are permanently durable.

[8]) This section is based on Negishi [17]. See Walras–Jaffe [25], pp. 170–2, Samuelson [21], pp. 269–75.

librium (1), i.e., we are in a situation like

$$E_1(P_1, ..., P_{m-1}) > 0,$$

$$E_2(P_1, ..., P_{m-1}) < 0,$$

$$............................ \tag{2}$$

$$E_{m-1}(P_1, ..., P_{m-1}) < 0.$$

The price of the first commodity P_1 is adjusted by the excess demand for the same commodity E_1 and increased in situation (2) until an equilibrium in the first market

$$E_1(P'_1, P_2, ..., P_{m-1}) = 0 \tag{3}$$

is established. Under the new price system $(P'_1, P_2, ..., P_{m-1})$ the remaining $m-1$ markets may or may not be in equilibrium. If the second market is out of equilibrium, the price of the second commodity is changed from P_2 to P'_2 so as to satisfy

$$E_2(P'_1, P'_2, P_3, ..., P_{m-1}) = 0. \tag{4}$$

Generally this will upset the equilibrium of the first market (3). Under the price system $(P'_1, P'_2, P_3, ..., P_{m-1})$, then, the price of the third commodity P_3 is adjusted if the third market is out of equilibrium, upsetting the equilibrium of the second market (4) just established. In this way the last, $m-1$th market is eventually cleared by changing the price system from $(P'_1, ..., P'_{m-2}, P_{m-1})$ into $(P'_1, ..., P'_{m-2}, P'_{m-1})$ so as to satisfy

$$E_{m-1}(P'_1, ..., P'_{m-2}, P'_{m-1}) = 0. \tag{5}$$

By this time all the markets except the last, which were once cleared successively, have been generally thrown out of their respective equilibria again. The price system we have just arrived at $(P'_1, ..., P'_{m-1})$, and the initial system $(P_1, ..., P_{m-1})$ are not in equilibrium. The question is, then, which system is closer to general equilibrium (1). Walras argued that the former is closer to general equilibrium than the latter since, e.g., $E_1(P'_1, ..., P'_{m-1}) \neq 0$ is closer to 0 than $E_1(P_1, ..., P_{m-1}) \neq 0$. The reason is, according to Walras, that the change from P_1 to P'_1 which established (3) exerted a direct influence that was invariably in the direction of zero excess demand so far as the first commodity is concerned, while the consequent changes from P_2 to P'_2, ..., P_{m-1} to P'_{m-1}, which jointly moved the foregoing excess demand again away from zero, exerted indirect influences, some in the direction of equilibrium and some in the opposite direction, at least so far as the excess demand for the first commodity is concerned, so that up to a certain point they cancelled each other out. Hence, Walras concluded, by repeating the successive adjustment of $m-1$ markets along the same lines, we can move closer and closer to general equilibrium (1).

Although the above Walrasian argument seems highly probable, it is by no means necessary, as was emphatically discussed by Yasui [26]. We have to impose certain restrictions on the form of excess demand functions to enable Walrasian tâtonnement to move the price system closer and closer to general equilibrium.[9]) Why did Walras fail to demonstrate the stability of tâtonnement? It is clear that even if (3) is established no actual trade is carried out in the first market until all the markets are cleared. Otherwise excess demands must be functions not only of prices but also of individual stocks of commodities which are changed by trade carried out. Because of this no trade assumption, the equilibrium of the first market (3) can make no contribution towards moving the economy closer to general equilibrium (1), before the first market is thrown out of equilibrium by the subsequent changes in the prices of other commodities. Then our guess is that the equilibrium of the first market (3) can move the economy towards general equilibrium (1), which cannot be cancelled by the subsequent disequilibrium in the first market, if trade is actually carried out in the first market. In other words, trade may push the economy closer to general equilibrium even if price changes cannot. However, for trade in the first market to take place fully, equilibrium (3) is not sufficient, since the composition of different commodities which the demanders of the first commodity offer and that which the suppliers demand may not be identical, unless one commodity is specified as the sole medium of exchange with which the first commodity can be traded. We have to divide the first market into $m-1$ sub-markets in which the first commodity is exchanged with each different commodity. In an m commodity economy, we have to consider $m(m-1)/2$ markets in all.

Let there be n individuals in the economy. A positive constant, $\overline{X}_j$ is the amount of the jth commodity existing in the economy. A non-negative column vector $X_i = (X_{i1}, ..., X_{im})$ is a commodity vector of the ith individual and its component X_{ij} is the amount of the jth commodity. Finally, a non-negative matrix $X = (X_1, ..., X_i, ..., X_n)$ is a distribution matrix of commodities among individuals, such that $\Sigma_i X_{ij} = \overline{X}_j$ for all j. The utility

---

[9]) Uzawa [22].

functions of the individuals $U_i(X_i)$ are strictly quasi-concave such that for $U(x) = U(y)$, $1 > \alpha > 0$, we have $U\{\alpha x + (1-\alpha)y\} > U(x)$, and strictly increasing such that for $x \geq y$, we have $U(x) > U(y)$. A Pareto optimal distribution matrix of commodities among individuals is defined as follows: A distribution of commodities among individuals X is Pareto optimal if and only if there is no other distribution of commodities among individuals X' such that $U_i(X_i') \geq U_i(X_i)$ for all i and $U_i(X_i') > U_i(X_i)$ for some i. The set of Pareto optimal distribution matrices is denoted by $\{X^*\}$.

There are $m(m-1)/2$ markets in the economy in each of which the exchange of two commodities takes place. Adjustments in these markets are made successively, one by one. The order of $m(m-1)/2$ successive adjustments of markets may be different in each round. The initial distribution matrix at $t = 0$, $X(0)$ is given. As a result of exchange of commodities among individuals, distribution matrix $X(t)$ will be changed as $t = 1, 2, ...$, ad. inf.

Suppose we are now at $t = T$ and in the market for the exchange between the jth commodity and kth commodity. As a result of previous exchanges in other markets, distribution matrix $X(T)$ is given. In this market, the ith individual maximizes his utility $U_i(X_i)$, being subject to $X_{il} = X_{il}(T)$, for $l \neq j$, $l \neq k$, and $P_{jk}\{X_{ij} - X_{ij}(T)\} + \{X_{ik} - X_{ik}(T)\} = 0$ if either $X_{ij}(T) > 0$ or $X_{ik}(T) > 0$. Otherwise we have $X_{ij} = 0$, $X_{ik} = 0$. As a function of price or exchange ratio $P_{jk} > 0$, demand for the jth commodity X_{ij} and the kth commodity X_{ik} are determined. The single valuedness and continuity of these functions are assumed. The equilibrium price $P_{jk}^* > 0$ which satisfies $\Sigma_i X_{ij}(P_{jk}) = \bar{X}_j$ and $\Sigma_i X_{ik}(P_{jk}) = \bar{X}_k$ exists. We also assume its uniqueness. The convergence of the solution $P_{jk}(u)$ to equilibrium P_{jk}^* as $u \to \infty$ in the dynamic process $dP_{jk}/du = \Sigma_i X_{ij}(P_{jk}) - \bar{X}_j$ is already known.[10] Now new distribution matrix $X(T+1)$ is given by $X_{ij}(T+1) = X_{ij}(P_{jk}^*)$, $X_{ik}(T+1) = X_{ik}(P_{jk}^*)$, $X_{il}(T+1) = X_{il}(T)$, $l \neq j$, $l \neq k$, for all i. The matrix $X(T+1)$ is continuous and single valued function of matrix $X(T)$. It must be noted if $X(T+1) \neq X(T)$, then we have $\Sigma_i U_i\{X_i(T+1)\} > \Sigma_i U_i\{X_i(T)\}$ since the exchange takes place if and only if there is some utility gains.

In this way distribution matrix becomes a function of time with the given initial distribution matrix and is denoted as $X\{t; X(0)\}$. Then, we have

Theorem 1. The successive exchange process is stable in the sense that every limit of $X\{t; X(0)\}$ as $t \to \infty$ is Pareto optimal.

---

[10] Arrow–Hurwicz [3].

Proof. First, consider a function of time, $V(t) = V\{X(t), \ldots, X(t-a)\} = \sum_{d=t-a}^{d=t} \sum_i U_i\{X_i(d)\}$, where $a = m(m-1)/2 + 1$ and $t \geq a$. It is clear that if $X(t-a) \notin \{X^*\}$, then $V(t+a) - V(t) > 0$, since for some $t-a \leq d < t$, we have $X(d) \neq X(d+1)$. Because $X(t)$ is bounded, there is a limit such that $\lim_{v \to \infty} X(t_v) = \hat{X}$, where $t_v \to \infty$ as $v \to \infty$. Now consider a matrix starting from $\hat{X}$, $\hat{X}(t) = X\{t; \hat{X}\}$. From the continuity and the uniqueness of $X(t+1)$ with respect to $X(t)$, and therefore with respect to $X(0)$, we have $\hat{X}(t) = X\{t; \hat{X}\} = \lim_{v \to \infty} X\{t; X(t_v)\} = \lim_{v \to \infty} X\{t+t_v; X(0)\}$. Since the function $V(t)$ is bounded and non-decreasing, $V(t+1) - V(t) \geq 0$, we have $\lim_{t \to \infty} V(t) = \hat{V}$. For $\hat{X}(t)$, we have $\hat{V}(t) = V\{\hat{X}(t), \ldots, \hat{X}(t-a)\} = \lim_{v \to \infty} V\{X(t+t_v), \ldots, X(t-a+t_v)\} = \lim_{v \to \infty} V(t+t_v) = \lim_{t \to \infty} V(t) = \hat{V}, t \geq a$. Now $\hat{V}(t+a) = \hat{V}(t)$ implies $\hat{X} \in \{X^*\}$.[11] It is easy to see that the condition of general equilibrium (1) is satisfied at $\hat{X} \in \{X^*\}$, since the necessary and sufficient condition for Pareto optimality is $U_{ij}/U_{ik} = P_{jk}$ for all i, j, k such that $X_{ij} > 0$, $X_{ik} > 0$ and $U_{ij}/U_{ik} \leq P_{jk}$ if $X_{ij} = 0$, where $U_{ij} = \partial U_i/\partial X_{ij}$.[12]

So far we have devided the economy into markets for two commodity trade and assumed that adjustment takes place in one market after another successively. There is also another way to subdivide the economy, i.e., into bargains between two individuals. Bargains are assumed to be made successively, one bargain at a time. Suppose we are now at $t = T$ and in the bargain between the ith individual and the hth individual. As a result of previous bargains between other participants, a distribution matrix $X(T)$ is given. The status quo of this bargaining problem is $X_i(T)$, $X_h(T)$. A solution to this problem is (X_i, X_h). Then a distribution matrix $X(T+1)$ is given by $X_i(T+1) = X_i$, $X_h(T+1) = X_h$, $X_g(T+1) = X_g(T)$ $(g \neq i, g \neq h)$. It is generally agreed in the theory of the bargaining problem that a solution is in the Pareto optimal negotiation set and satisfies the following conditions;

(1) $X_i + X_h = X_i(T) + X_h(T)$.

(2) $U_i(X_i) \geq U_i\{X_i(T)\}$, $U_h(X_h) \geq U_h\{X_h(T)\}$.

(3) There is no other (U_i, U_h) possible such that $U_i \geq U_i(X_i)$ and $U_h \geq U_h(X_h)$.[13]

---

[11] See Uzawa [23].

[12] See Samuelson [21], p. 237.

[13] The negotiation set is, in terms of the Edgeworth box diagram, the part of the contract curve between two indifference curves which pass through the initial point of distribution of two commodities.

Then we have $\Sigma_i U_i\{X_i(T+1)\} > \Sigma_i U_i\{X_i(T)\}$ if $X(T) \neq X(T+1)$. The stability of the process i.e., convergence to $\{X^*\}$ is shown by using a function of time $V(t)$ given in the proof of theorem 1, but this time $a = n(n-1)/2+1$.

3.   Having studied the stability of the successive exchange process in which trade is carried out only when the relevant single market is in equilibrium, we now turn to the study of the more general process of simultaneous adjustment and consider the effect of trade carried out at disequilibrium.[14] Consider an exchange economy of n individuals and m commodities under perfect competition. Suppose, as in the preceding chapter, all the markets are adjusted simultaneously, i.e.,

$$\mathrm{d}P_j/\mathrm{d}t = E_j(P, X), \quad j = 1, ..., m, \tag{6}$$

where P_j, E_j, P, X and t denote respectively the price and excess demand of the jth commodity, the price vector $(P_1, ..., P_m)$, the distribution matrix of individual commodity stocks composed of X_{ij} (the amount of the jth commodity held by the ith individual) and the time.

The reason why excess demand is a function not only of P but also of X is easily understood since each individual is assumed to maximize his utility being subject to the budget constraint, i.e.,

Definition 1.   Excess demand E_j is defined as

$$E_j = \Sigma_i Z_{ij} - \Sigma_i X_{ij}, \quad i = 1, ..., n, \quad j = 1, ..., m,$$

where the ith individual's demand for the jth commodity Z_{ij} is derived from the maximization of his utility $U_i(Z_{i1}, ..., Z_{im})$ being subject to

$$\Sigma_j P_j Z_{ij} = \Sigma_j P_j X_{ij} \equiv M_i.$$

If recontract is always possible and no actual trade of commodities among individuals is carried out until general equilibrium is reached, the distribution matrix remains constant over time. This is the case of tâtonnement studied in the preceding chapter. If, on the other hand, some trade out of equilibrium is carried out, X is no longer constant and changed as the result of such disequilibrium transactions. We may describe the process of exchange transactions as

$$\mathrm{d}X_{ij}/\mathrm{d}t = F_{ij}(P, X), \quad i = 1, ..., n, \quad j = 1, ..., m, \tag{7}$$

---

[14] This section is based on Negishi [15].

where functions F_{ij} denote that the opportunity for individuals to change their stock of commodities X_{ij} by exchange with other individuals are assumed to depend on prices and on the distribution of commodities in the economy.

Disequilibrium transactions, of course, must be carried out according to certain transaction rules which are incorporated in the form of, or expressed in terms of, functions F_{ij}. Because we are considering the case of pure trade, in which total amounts of commodities $(\Sigma_i X_{ij})$ are constant, we must first impose on the functions F_{ij} the conditions

$$\Sigma_i dX_{ij}/dt = \Sigma_i F_{ij}(P, X) = 0, \quad j = 1, ..., m. \tag{8}$$

Since exchange will not take place if every individual is satisfied with the current distribution of commodities, it is natural to impose that

$$Z_{ij} = X_{ij} \text{ if and only if } F_{ij}(P, X) = 0, \text{ for all } i, j. \tag{9}$$

As a transaction rule, we may also assume that no transaction on credit is permitted, i.e., all transactions should be of the barter type. Since in a barter exchange, to get something one must offer something else of the same value in return, such an exchange does not alter the value of the commodity stocks held by an indivdual. It is therefore appropriate to impose the following restrictions on the functions F_{ij},

$$\Sigma_j P_j dX_{ij}/dt = \Sigma_j P_j F_{ij}(P, X) = 0, \quad i = 1, ..., n. \tag{10}$$

We are interested in the behavior of a solution of the process (6) and (7), which is often called non-tâtonnement process, through the initial price vector P^0 and the initial distribution of commodities X^0. It is an $m(n+1)$ dimensional function $[P(t; P^0, X^0), X(t; P^0, X^0)]$ of time such that

$$P(0; P^0, X^0) = P^0,$$

$$X(0; P^0, X^0) = X^0,$$

and

$$dP_j/dt = E_j[P(t; P^0, X^0), X(t; P^0, X^0)]$$

$$dX_{ij}/dt = F_{ij}[P(t; P^0, X^0), X(t; P^0, X^0)]$$

for $t \geq 0$ and all $i, j.$[15]

---

[15] We assume that this solution exists and is continuous with respect to time and initial conditions. Furthermore it is assumed that prices remain positive through time. See assumption 6 in chapter 13.

In a non-tâtonnement process, not only prices but also the distribution of commodities are adjusted so as to satisfy the condition of general equilibrium. On account of the redistribution of income among individual participants due to changes of prices in the midst of trading, the competitive equilibrium reached by a non-tâtonnement process is generally different from the one reached by a tâtonnement process. In this case, a vector P and a matrix X are called an equilibrium price vector and an equilibrium distribution matrix if

$$E_j(P, X) = 0, \text{ for all } j. \text{[16])} \tag{11}$$

The question is, then, whether the introduction of trade at disequilibria upsets the stability of the tâtonnement adjustment process, say, under the assumption of gross substitutability, i.e.,

Assumption 1. $\partial E_j(P, X)/\partial P_k > 0, \quad j \neq k$.

We shall show that the non-tâtonnement process (6) and (7) is also stable under the assumption of gross substitutability (assumption 1) and the transaction rules (8), (9) and (10). However, the concept of stability is slightly different from that of the global stability which was established in the case of tâtonnement, since the uniqueness of the equilibrium (11) can not be obtained even when gross substitutability is assumed. We have to satisfy with a weaker concept of the stability, as in the case of theorem 1, i.e.,

Definition 2. The adjustment process (6) and (7) is said to be quasi-stable when every limit point of its solution $[P(t; P^0, X^0), X(t; P^0, X^0)]$ is an equilibrium defined by (11). In other words, it is quasi-stable if the excess demands of all commodities $E_j, j = 1, ..., m$, converge to zero.

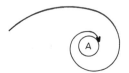

Fig. 14.1.

[16]) If (11) is established, excess demands remain zero inspite of the changes in X, since we have (10).

The concept of quasi-stability defined in definition 2 can be visualized in figures 14.1 and 14.2. If equilibria form a set A and the solution converges to this set, we have quasi-stability (figure 14.1). On the other hand, if equilibria, E's, are distinct (or if equilibrium is unique), quasi-stability is identical to global stability (figure 14.2). To demonstrate the quasi-stability, the Liapounoff's method can be used.[17]

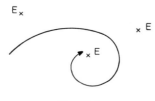

Fig. 14.2.

Now we can state,

Theorem 2. The non-tâtonnement process (6) and (7), with (8), (9) and (10) satisfied, is quasi-stable when assumption 1 (gross substitutability) is assumed.

A sketch of proof. The proof is identical with that of the case of tâtonnement given in chapter 13 as theorem 5, except that the effect of changing X is now to be taken care of. Construct a characteristic function $V(t) = \Sigma_{j \in J^+(t)} P_j(t) E_j(t)$, where $J^+(t) = \{j \mid E_j(t) > 0, \text{ or } E_j(t) = 0, \mathrm{d}E_j(t)/\mathrm{d}t > 0\}$. By Walras law, we have $V(t) = \Sigma_{j \in J^-(t)} (-P_j(t)) E_j(t)$, where $J^-(t) = \{j \mid E_j(t) < 0, \text{ or } E_j(t) = 0, \mathrm{d}E_j(t)/\mathrm{d}t < 0\}$. For a sufficiently small $h > 0$, we have $V(t+h) = \Sigma_{j \in J^+(t)} P_j(t+h) E_j(t+h) + \Sigma_{j \in J} P_j(t+h) E_j(t+h)$, where J is a suitable subset of $J^0(t) = \{j \mid E_j(t) = 0, \mathrm{d}E_j(t)/\mathrm{d}t = 0\}$. We wish to show that $W(t) = \overline{\lim}_{h \to 0} [\{V(t+h) - V(t)\}/h] = \lim_{v \to \infty} [\{V(t+h_v) - V(t)\}/h_v] \leq 0$, where $\{h_v\}$ is a sequence such that $h_v \to 0$ as $v \to \infty$, and equality holds only at equilibrium. Because the number of commodities, m, is finite, we can take a suitable subsequence of h_v and find that $\lim_{v \to \infty} [\{V(t+h_v) - V(t)\}/h_v] = \Sigma_{j \in J^+(t)} \mathrm{d}(P_j E_j)/\mathrm{d}t + \Sigma_{j \in J} \mathrm{d}(P_j E_j)/\mathrm{d}t$ for a certain $J \subset J^0(t)$. From the definition of $J^0(t)$, $\Sigma_{j \in J} \mathrm{d}(P_j E_j)/\mathrm{d}t = 0$. Therefore, we have $W(t) = \Sigma_{j \in J^+(t)} \mathrm{d}(P_j E_j)/\mathrm{d}t$. From the definition of E_j (definition 1), we have $\Sigma_{j \in J^+(t)} \mathrm{d}(P_j E_j)/\mathrm{d}t = \Sigma_k \Sigma_{j \in J^+(t)} (\partial(P_j E_j)/\partial P_k)(\mathrm{d}P_k/\mathrm{d}t) + \Sigma_i \Sigma_k \Sigma_{j \in J^+(t)} (\partial(P_j E_j)/\partial M_i)$

[17] See chapter 13, Hahn [11], Negishi [16] and Uzawa [23].

$(\partial M_i/\partial X_{ik})(\mathrm{d}X_{ik}/\mathrm{d}t)$, since the dependence of E_j on X_{ik} is through the income or asset of the ith individual $M_i = \Sigma_j P_j X_{ij}$.[18]) The last term of the right hand side of the above equation can be written as $\Sigma_i \Sigma_{j \in J}^+{}_{(t)}(\partial(P_j E_j)/\partial M_j)$ $\Sigma_k P_k(\mathrm{d}X_{ik}/\mathrm{d}t)$, which vanishes from (10), while the first term on the right-hand side is negative, as was shown in the proof of theorem 5, chapter 13. The domain of $X(t)$ as well as of $P(t)$ are bounded. Since $V(t)$ is bounded below by 0, the fact that $V(t)$ decreases implies the existence of $\lim_{t \to \infty} V(t)$ $= V^*$. Let P^* and X^* be a limit of $P(t)$ and $X(t)$ as $t \to \infty$, i.e., $P^* = \lim_{h \to \infty}$ $P(t_h; P(0), X(0))$ and $X^* = \lim_{h \to \infty} X(t_h; P(0), X(0))$, where $t_h \to \infty$ as $h \to \infty$. Then we have $V^*(t) = V^*(t; P^*, X^*) = \lim_{h \to \infty} V(t; P(t_h), X(t_h)$ $= \lim_{h \to \infty} V(t + t_h; P(0), X(0)) = V^*$, from the continuity of P, X and V. Hence, $W(t) = 0$ at P^* and X^*. We can, therefore, conclude that $E_j \to 0$ as $t \to \infty$.

Alternatively, to obtain the stability of the non-tâtonnement process, we can assume

Assumption 2.   The utility function $U_i(Z_{i1}, \ldots, Z_{im})$ is strictly quasi- concave and homogeneous with respect to all variables,

and

Assumption 3.   Utility functions of all individuals are the same, i.e., $U_i = U$, $i = 1, 1, \ldots, n$.

Then we find that the total demand for the jth commodity, $Z_j = \Sigma_i Z_{ij}$, is the solution of the maximization of $U(Z_1, \ldots, Z_m)$, subject to $\Sigma_j P_j Z_j$ $= \Sigma_j P_j \Sigma_i X_{ij}$, since from definition 1 and assumption 2, we have $Z_{ij} = A_{ij}(P_1, \ldots, P_m)\Sigma_j P_j X_{ij}$ and from assumption 3, we have $Z_j = A_j$ $(P_1, \ldots, P_m)\Sigma_j P_j \Sigma_i X_{ij}$. Total demands $Z_j(P)$ and the equilibrium P which satisfies (11) are independent of the distribution of commodity stocks X among individuals. As a result of the strong quasi-concavity of the utility function, the equilibrium is unique.

Since excess demands are independent of X, there is no difference between tâtonnement and non-tâtonnement so far as the price adjustment is concerned. We state now,

---

[18]) The fact that effects of transactions at disequilibria are income effects is clearly stated in Hicks [13], p. 128.

Theorem 3. Under assumptions 2 and 3, the price adjustment process (6), with E_j's independent of X, is globally stable.

Proof. By differentiating Walras identity $(\Sigma_j E_j \, \mathrm{d}P_j/\mathrm{d}t + \Sigma_j P_j \, \mathrm{d}Z_j/\mathrm{d}t = 0)$ and considering (6), we have $\Sigma_j P_j \, \mathrm{d}Z_j/\mathrm{d}t \leqq 0$, with equality holding only at equilibrium. If we set $U(t) = U(Z_1(t), \ldots, Z_m(t))$ and differentiate U with respect to time, we have $\mathrm{d}U/\mathrm{d}t = \Sigma_j (\partial U/\partial Z_j)(\mathrm{d}Z_j/\mathrm{d}t) = \lambda \Sigma_j P_j \, \mathrm{d}Z_j/\mathrm{d}t \leqq 0$, where λ is a positive function of t.[19]) Because $U(t)$ is decreasing and bounded below, and $P(t)$ is bounded, we can show that prices converge to the unique equilibrium.

4. In the preceding section, we have shown that in some important cases in which special assumptions are placed on the form of the excess demand functions tâtonnement stability is not violated by the introduction of disequilibrium transactions among individuals. Roughly speaking, this may imply that generally the non-tâtonnement process is as stable as the tâtonnement process. Little has been assumed, however, for the non-tâtonnement process about how individuals exchange their stocks of commodities. It is therefore expected that by adding some plausible assumptions on the exchange behavior of individuals, stronger results on stability may be established. In this section, we shall show that provided certain not unreasonable trading rules are postulated, the non-tâtonnement process is always stable, quite irrespective of the forms of the excess demand functions.[20]) In other words, the non-tâtonnement process is more stable than the tâtonnement process.

In the non-tâtonnement process (7), it is assumed that the opportunity for an individual to change his stock of commodities through exchange depends generally on prices and the distribution of commodities among individuals. In other words, the individual's opportunity to change his stock depends on the plans of other individuals to change theirs. If there is a surplus of a commodity i.e., if the total amount individuals want to increase their stock of this commodity is less than the amount they want to part with, any individual who seeks to increase his stock can easily and quickly achieve his plan. If there exists, on the other hand, a shortage of a commodity, any individual who wants to dispose of his stock can easily and quickly do so. Let us therefore impose the so-called Hahn condition on functions F_{ij} in (7),

---

[19]) See Allais [1], vol. 1, p. 26.
[20]) This section is based on Hahn–Negishi [12].

Assumption 4.   For all i, j, $\text{sign}(Z_{ij} - X_{ij}) = \text{sign } E_j$ if $Z_{ij} - X_{ij} \neq 0$, and if $E_j = 0$, then $Z_{ij} - X_{ij} = 0$ for all i.

The implication of assumption 4 is as follows. With prices given, all possible exchanges are instantaneously effected on a 'first come, first served' basis. Thus, if $E_j < 0$, all individuals demanding the jth commodity will be able to satisfy their demand, while some supplying individuals will be left with unsold commodities. Therefore, after exchange, there remain only negative individual excess demands (positive excess supplies) and sign $Z_{ij} - X_{ij}$ $= \text{sign } E_j < 0$. If $E_j > 0$, all supplying individuals will find they can supply all they had planned, while some demanding individuals will have their demands unsatisfied, with the result that sign $Z_{ij} - X_{ij} = \text{sign } E_j > 0$. Of course, this may require that some plans of individual demand and supply are overfilled. Since every commodity acts at least partly as a medium of exchange, there is a possibility that a commodity which was originally demanded must temporarily be sold and more than was originally demanded of another commodity must be bought so as to carry out exchange transactions of other commodities.[21])

Suppose in the time interval $(0, h)$, prices remain unchanged. In that interval trade takes place in such a way that the sign of the individual excess demand for any commodity and any participant is not the opposite of the sign of the corresponding total excess demand, i.e., assumption 4 is satisfied at $t = h$. At h, prices start changing as in (6) and trade takes place in such a way so as never to permit opposite signs between any individual and the corresponding total excess demands, i.e., assumption 4 is continuously satisfied. The possibility of such a process of trade, i.e., the existence of a solution of the non-tâtonnement process under assumption 4 is conjectured from the following example. Construct a process where the excess or the shortage of commodities is always shared by individuals in constant ratio.

$$j = 1, \ldots, m-1, \quad \mathrm{d}X_{ij}/\mathrm{d}t = \Sigma_k(\partial Z_{ij}/\partial P_k)\, E_k - \alpha_i\, \Sigma_k\, \Sigma_s(\partial Z_{sj}/\partial P_k)\, E_k,$$
$$i = 1, \ldots, n,$$

$$\mathrm{d}X_{im}/\mathrm{d}t = (-\Sigma_{j=1}^{j=m-1}\, P_j\, \mathrm{d}Z_{ij}/\mathrm{d}t)/P_m, \quad i = 1, \ldots, n,$$

(12)

where the α's are positive constants such that $\Sigma_i \alpha_i = 1$, i.e., the ratio by which an excess or shortage of commodities is allocated to individuals. It

---

[21]) See Negishi [19].

is easy to see that conditions (8), (9) and (10) are satisfied by (12). Then, from (10), we know that

$$dZ_{ij}/dt = \Sigma_k(\partial Z_{ij}/\partial P_k)(dP_k/dt) + \Sigma_k(\partial Z_{ij}/\partial X_{ik})(dX_{ik}/dt)$$
$$= \Sigma_k(\partial Z_{ij}/\partial P_k)E_k$$

since $\Sigma_k(\partial Z_{ij}/\partial X_{ik})(dX_{ik}/dt) = \Sigma_k(\partial Z_{ij}/\partial M_i)(\partial M_i/\partial X_{ik})(dX_{ik}/dt) = (\partial Z_{ij}/\partial M_i)$ $\Sigma_k P_k dX_{ik}/dt = 0$. From (12) we have $dX_{ij}/dt = dZ_{ij}/dt - \alpha_i\Sigma_i dZ_{ij}/dt, j \neq m$. Since at $t = h$, $Z_{ij}(h) - X_{ij}(h) = \alpha_i(\Sigma_i Z_{ij}(h) - \Sigma_i X_{ij}(t))$, for all j, we have $Z_{ij}(t) - X_{ij}(t) = \alpha_i(\Sigma_i Z_{ij}(t) - \Sigma_i X_{ij}(t))$, for all $i, j \neq m$, $t \geq h$, and from Walras' law and individual budget constraints, we have $Z_{im}(t) - X_{im}(t)$ $= \alpha_i(\Sigma_i Z_{im}(t) - \Sigma_i X_{im}(t))$, for all i and for $t \geq h$. Thus assumption 4 is satisfied by (12) and therefore non-vacuous.

The stability of the non-tâtonnement process (6) and (7), with (8), (9), (10) and assumption 4 satisfied, is stated as follows.

Theorem 4. Under (8), (9), (10) and assumption 4, the non-tâtonnement process (6) and (7) is quasi-stable.

Proof. Differentiating the budget constraint of the ith individual, we have $\Sigma_j P_j((dZ_{ij}/dt) - (dX_{ij}/dt)) + \Sigma_j(Z_{ij} - X_{ij})dP_j/dt = 0$. From condition (10), $\Sigma_j P_j dX_{ij}/dt = 0$, and from (6) and assumption 4, $\Sigma_j(Z_{ij} - X_{ij})dP_j/dt > 0$, we have $\Sigma_j P_j dZ_{ij}/dt < 0$ in disequilibrium. On the other hand, consider $V = \Sigma_i U_i(Z_{i1}, ..., Z_{im})$. By differentiation with respect to time, we have in disequilibrium, $dV/dt = \Sigma_i \Sigma_j (\partial U_i/\partial Z_{ij})(dZ_{ij}/dt) = \Sigma_i \lambda_i \Sigma_j P_j dZ_{ij}/dt < 0$, where λ_i is the marginal utility of income, a positive function of t. The domain of P and X are bounded. Since $V(t)$ is bounded from below, it will approach a limit, say, $V^* = V(P^*, X^*)$ such that $dV(P^*, X^*)/dt = 0$, i.e., an equilibrium.[22]

In view of some recent comments on Hahn and Negishi [12], it may not be out of place to add some remarks on the so-called Hahn condition.[23] It may be true, of course, that the utility of the individual commodity stock may not be increasing uniformly through time under assumption 4.[24]

---

[22] For the generalization of this theorem, see Arrow–Hahn [2] (chapter 13) and Fisher [8].

[23] See Veendorp [24].

[24] The non-tâtonnement process in which increasing utility by transaction is imposed is called the Edgeworth process. See Negishi [16].

Although the increasing utility of the individual commodity stock is a nice and plausible condition for the exchange process, the process is consistent with competitive behavior of the participants in the market even if such a condition is not satisfied. The rule of the game of competition is to assume that any one can exchange as much as he wishes at given market prices. Provided that market prices are considered to be given and unchanged, the utility of the commodity stock in the midst of the exchange process does not matter. Of course, such behavior is, though statically rational, dynamically irrational since prices are actually changing. However, we often have in economics examples of such ignorant but not extremely unrealistic behavior, e.g., the behavior of producers in the cobweb theory. On the other hand, it may be too stringent to require that we do not exchange unless the utility of our commodity stocks is always increasing through time. As a matter of fact, some buying a camera strictly speaking suffers a decrease in utility until he also buys some films.

5. Finally, let us introduce expectations into the non-tâtonnement process.[25] Imagine an exchange economy of n individuals and m commodities under perfect competition. At each moment of time, the individual with a given stock of commodities is faced with current prices announced in the market. He has expectations about future prices on the basis of the past history of prices and determines his excess demand both for the current and future periods by maximizing his utility under current and future budget constraints. No chance of borrowing or lending is assumed to be available to him. Exchange transactions take place among individuals; current prices change according to current total excess demands, and individuals' expectations of prices change adaptively. The future in this system is supposed to be a period only infinitesimally far from the current period. As time goes on, and when the future arrives, the individual is in a new situation with new prices and new commodity stocks, but exactly the same taste as he began with, and the process continues.

Let P_j and q_{ij} denote the current price of the jth commodity and its future value expected by the ith individual. The current and future demand for the jth commodity by the ith individual, Z_{ij} and Y_{ij}, are defined as

Definition 3. Z_{ij} and Y_{ij} are determined so as to maximize utility $F_i(U_i(Z_i), V_i(Y_i))$, where $Z_i = (Z_{i1}, ..., Z_{im})$, $Y_i = (Y_{i1}, ..., Y_{im})$, being

[25] This section is based on Negishi [18].

subject to the current budget constraint

$$\Sigma_j P_j Z_{ij} = \Sigma_j P_j X_{ij} \tag{13}$$

and the expected future budget constraint

$$\Sigma_j q_{ij} Y_{ij} = \Sigma_j q_{ij} Z_{ij}, \tag{14}$$

where X_{ij}'s signify the ith individual's current stock of the jth commodity. All commodities are assumed to be durable and depreciation by consumption is neglected. It is assumed that functions U_i and V_i are of the same mathematical form, F_i is increasing with respect to U_i and V_i, and it is strictly quasi-concave with respect to Z_i and Y_i.

We postulate that the rate of change in current prices are determined by current excess demands, $E_j = \Sigma_i Z_{ij} - \Sigma_i X_{ij}$, i.e.,

$$dP_j/dt = E_j(P, Q, X), \quad j = 1, ..., m, \tag{15}$$

where $P = (P_1, ..., P_m)$, $Q = \{q_{ij}\}$ and $X = \{X_{ij}\}$. The expectation of future price is adapted to the past history of that price, and we have,

$$dq_{ij}/dt = a_i(P_j - q_{ij}) \quad i = 1, ..., n; \quad j = 1, ..., m, \tag{16}$$

where a_i is the constant positive elasticity of expectation.[26] This equation may alternatively be interpreted in the following two ways: First, suppose the future price is formed as *the weighted average of past prices*, with the weights declining as one goes back in time. If the future price currently expected differs from the current price, the change of the former is likely to be in the direction of the latter, since the latter newly joins the formation of the new future price with the greatest weight. Secondly, if we assume that the future price is *the weighted average of current and past prices*, with the weights declining as one goes back in time, future prices higher (lower) than current imply the tendency of declining (rising) prices (i.e., current price is lower (higher) than the average of past prices) and downward (upward) change of future prices may be expected. Finally, as a result of exchange transactions, X will vary as time goes on. The desire of the ith individual

---

[26] We assume that an individual has the same elasticity of expectation for all commodities, which is more stringent than what Arrow–Hurwicz [4] and Arrow–Nerlove [5] assumed. However, we assume different expectations for different individuals, i.e., the existence of bulls (those who expect price rises, $q_{ij} > P_j$) and bears (those who expect price falls, $q_{ij} < P_j$), which is not done by Arrow–Hurwicz [4] and Arrow–Nerlove [5].

to exchange commodities will depend on what he wants to have, Z_{ij}, which is a function of P, q_{ij} and X_{ij}, $j = 1, ..., m$, and what he actually has, X_{ij}. The opportunity for him to exchange, on the other hand, depends on how other individuals want to exchange. Therefore, we may assume that changes in commodity distribution X are determined generally by all variables P, Q and X.

$$dX_{ij}/dt = F_{ij}(P, Q, X), \quad i = 1, ..., n, \quad j = 1, ..., m. \tag{17}$$

Let us now define the stationary equilibrium of the system (15), (16) and (17) as (P, Q, X) which satisfy $E_j(P, Q, X) = 0$, $q_{ij} = P_j$ and $F_{ij}(P, Q, X) = 0$, $i = 1, ..., n$, $j = 1, ..., m$. For the sake of convenience in analysis, let us also define a quasi-equilibrium (P^*, Q^*, X^*) as a point at which $E_j(P, Q, X) = 0$, $Z_{ij}(P, Q, X) = Y_{ij}(P, Q, X)$ and $F_{ij}(P, Q, X) = 0$, $i = 1$, ..., n, $j = 1, ..., m$. It must be noted that the equality of future expected price and current price, $q_{ij} = P_j$, is not established in quasi-equilibrium and, therefore, expected prices q_{ij} may change. On the other hand, the stationary equilibrium is always a quasi-equilibrium, since the equality of future and current prices implies $Z_{ij} = Y_{ij}$, which is easily seen from the first order condition of the maximization of F_i subject to (13) and (14) and the assumption that U_i and V_i are of the same form.

We first show the convergence of the solution of (15), (16) and (17) to a quasi-equilibrium.

Theorem 5. Under assumption 4 and (8), (9), (10), the dynamic system (15), (16), (17) is quasi-stable in the sense that any limit point of its solution, as t tends to infinity, is a quasi-equilibrium.[27]

Proof. From (13) we have Walras' law, $\Sigma_j P_j E_j \equiv 0$. We have $d\Sigma_j P_j^2/dt = 2\Sigma_j P_j E_j = 0$, which implies the boundedness of P. Since $q_{ij}^2 > \Sigma_j P_j^2$ implies $dq_{ij}/dt < 0$, the domain of $Q = (q_{11}, ..., q_{nm})$ is also bounded. By construction, X is clearly bounded.

By differentiating (13) with respect to t we have[28]

$$\sum_j \dot{P}_j(Z_{ij} - X_{ij}) - \sum_j P_j \dot{X}_{ij} + \sum_j P_j \dot{Z}_{ij} = 0.$$

---

[27] We assume that there exists a solution which is continuous with respect to time and initial conditions and that prices remain positive. See footnote 15 above.
[28] A dot signifies differentiation with respect to t.

From assumption 4 and (15) we have $\Sigma_j \dot{P}_j(Z_{ij} - X_{ij}) \geq 0$ for all i and $\Sigma_j \dot{P}_j(Z_{ij} - X_{ij}) > 0$ for some i if $E_j \neq 0$ for some j, and from (10) we have $\Sigma_j P_j \dot{X}_{ij} = 0$ for all i. Therefore,

$$\sum_j P_j \dot{Z}_{ij} \leq 0, \quad \text{for all } i,$$

$$\sum_j P_j \dot{Z}_{ij} < 0, \quad \text{for some } i \text{ if } E_j \neq 0 \text{ for some } j.$$

$$(18)$$

Differentiation of (14) with respect to t yields

$$\sum_j \dot{q}_{ij}(Y_{ij} - Z_{ij}) + \sum_j q_{ij}(\dot{Y}_{ij} - \dot{Z}_{ij}) = 0.$$

From (16) and (14), we have

$$\sum_j \dot{q}_{ij}(Y_{ij} - Z_{ij}) = a_i \sum_j (P_j - q_{ij})(Y_{ij} - Z_{ij})$$

$$= a_i \sum_j P_j(Y_{ij} - Z_{ij}).$$

By maximizing utility subject to (14),

$$F_i(U_i(Z_i), V_i(Y_i)) > F_i(U_i(Z_i), V_i(Z_i)) \text{ and } V_i(Y_i) > V_i(Z_i)$$

if $Y_i \neq Z_i$. Now suppose $\Sigma_j P_j(Y_{ij} - Z_{ij}) \leq 0$. Then, from the maximization of utility subject to (13),

$$F_i(U_i(Z_i), V_i(Y_i)) > F_i(U_i(Y_i), V_i(Y_i)) \text{ and } U_i(Y_i) < U_i(Z_i)$$

if $Y_i \neq Z_i$. However, since V_i and U_i are of the same mathematical form, this leads to a contradiction. We must, therefore, have $\Sigma_j P_j(Y_{ij} - Z_{ij}) > 0$, so that

$$\sum_j q_{ij}(\dot{Y}_{ij} - \dot{Z}_{ij}) < 0 \quad \text{if } Z_i \neq Y_i$$

$$\sum_j q_{ij}(\dot{Y}_{ij} - \dot{Z}_{ij}) = 0 \quad \text{if } Z_i = Y_i.$$

$$(19)$$

Finally, differentiation of F_i with respect to t gives

$$\mathrm{d}F_i/\mathrm{d}t = \sum_i \{(\partial F_i/\partial U_i)(\partial U_i/\partial Z_{ij}) \dot{Z}_{ij} + (\partial F_i/\partial V_i)(\partial V_i/\partial Y_{ij}) \dot{Y}_{ij},$$

$$= \lambda_i \sum_j P_j \dot{Z}_{ij} + \mu_i \sum_j q_{ij}(\dot{Y}_{ij} - \dot{Z}_{ij}).$$

The last equality follows from the familiar conditions for utility maximization subject to (13) and (14),

$$(\partial F_i/\partial U_i)(\partial U_i/\partial Z_{ij}) - \lambda_i P_j + \mu_i q_{ij} = 0,$$

$$\tag{20}$$

$$(\partial F_i/\partial V_i)(\partial V_i/\partial Y_{ij}) - \mu_i q_{ij} = 0,$$

where λ_i and μ_i are positive multipliers. From assumption 4 we find that $E_j = 0$ $(j = 1, ..., m)$ implies $F_{ij} = 0$ $(i = 1, ..., n; j = 1, ..., m)$. Hence it follows from (18) and (19) that $d\Sigma_i F_i/dt < 0$ unless quasi-equilibrium is established. Therefore, we can prove the quasi-stability.

Now our remaining task is to examine the relation of quasi-equilibrium to stationary equilibrium.

Theorem 6. Suppose the transaction functions $F_{ij}(P, Q, X)$ are homogeneous of degree zero with respect to Q. Then any quasi-equilibrium will eventually tend to stationary equilibrium, i.e., q_{ij}^* converges to P_j^*, $i = 1, ..., n, j = 1, ..., m$.

Proof. Since $Z_{ij} = Y_{ij}$ at (P^*, Q^*, X^*), we have from (20)

$$(\partial U_i/\partial Z_{ij})/(\partial U_i/\partial Z_{ik}) = (\lambda_i P_j^* - \mu_i q_{ij}^*)/\lambda_i P_k^* - \mu_i q_{ik}^*)$$

$$= (\partial V_i/\partial Y_{ij})/(\partial V_i/\partial Y_{ik}) = q_{ij}^*/q_{ik}^*, \text{ i.e., } P_j^* = b_i q_{ij}^*,$$

where b_i is a positive constant. Therefore, it follows from (16) that at quasi-equilibrium q_{ij} are changing proportionally. On the other hand, P and X remain unchanged since Z_{ij} and F_{ij} are unaffected by proportional changes of Q. Therefore, it is clear from (16) that q_{ij}^* converges to P_j^*.

References

[1] Allais, M., *Traite d'économie pure*, Paris: Imprimerie Nationale, 1952.
[2] Arrow, K.J. and F.H. Hahn, *Competitive equilibrium analysis*, Holdenday, forthcoming.
[3] Arrow, K.J., and L. Hurwicz, 'On the stability of the competitive equilibrium, I,' *Econometrica*, 26 (1958), 522–552.
[4] Arrow, K.J. and L. Hurwicz, 'Competitive stability under weak gross substitutability: non-linear price adjustment and adaptive expectations,' *International Economic Review*, 3 (1962), 233–55.
[5] Arrow, K.J. and M. Nerlove,' A note on expectations and stability,' *Econometrica*, 26 (1958), 297–305.

[6] Clower, R., 'The Keynesian counterrevolution: a theoretical appraisal,' F.H. Hahn and F.P.R. Brechling, ed., *The theory of interest rates*, Macmillan, 1965.

[7] Edgeworth, F.Y., *Papers relating to political economy*, vol. 2, Macmillan, 1925.

[8] Fisher, F.M., 'On price adjustment without an auctioneer,' mimeographed, 1970.

[9] Kaldor, N., 'A classificatory note on the determinateness of equilibrium,' *Review of Economic Studies*, 1 (1933–4), 122–36.

[10] Grossman, H.I., 'Theories of markets without recontracting,' *Journal of Economic Theory*, 1 (1969), 467–9.

[11] Hahn, W., *Theorie und Anwendung der direkten Methode von Lyapunov*, Springer-Verlag, 1959.

[12] Hahn, F.H. and T. Negishi, 'A theorem on non-tâtonnement stability,' *Econometrica*, 30 (1962), 463–9.

[13] Hicks, J.R., *Value and capital*, 2nd ed., Oxford University Press, 1946.

[14] Morishima, M., *Dogakuteki keizai riron (Dynamic economic theory)*, Kobundo, 1950.

[15] Negishi, T., 'On the formation of prices,' *International Economic Review*, 2 (1961), 122–6.

[16] Negishi, T., 'The stability of a competitive economy; a survey article,' *Econometrica*, 30 (1962), 635–669 (P. Newman ed., *Readings in Mathematical Economics*, I, Johns Hopkins University Press, 1968, 213–47).

[17] Negishi, T., 'On the successive barter process,' *Economic Studies Quarterly*, 12–2 (1962), 61–4.

[81] Negishi, T., 'The stability of exchange and adaptive expectations,' *International Economic Review*, 5 (1964), 104–111.

[19] Negishi, T., 'Market clearing processes in a money economy,' F.H. Hahn and F.P.R. Brechling ed., *The theory of interest*, Macmillan, 1965.

[20] Patinkin, D., *Money, interest and prices*, 2nd ed., Harper and Row, 1965.

[21] Samuelson, P.A., *Foundations of economic analysis*, Harvard University Press, 1947.

[22] Uzawa, H., 'Walras' tâtonnement in the theory of exchange,' *Review of Economic Studies*, 27 (1960), 182–94.

[23] Uzawa, H., 'The stability of dynamic processes,' *Econometrica*, 29 (1961), 617–31.

[24] Veendorp, R.E.C.H., 'A theorem on non-tâtonnement stability: a comment,' *Econometrica*, 37 (1969), 142–3.

[25] Walras, L., *Éléments d'économie politique pure*, Corbaz (Lausanne), 1874–77 (1st ed.), 1926 (definitive ed.) (W. Jaffe tr., *Elements of pure economics*, Irwin, 1954).

[26] Yasui, T., 'Kinko bunseki to katei bunseki (Equilibrium analysis and process analysis),' *Keizaigaku Ronshu (University of Tokyo Journal of Economics)*, 10 (1940) (*Walras omegutte (On Walras)*, Sobunsha, 1970, 353–472).

CHAPTER 15

The stability of foreign exchange[1]

1. There have been three types of approach to the problem of the 'stability' of the foreign exchanges or the effect of devaluation on the balance of payments in fully employed economies.

The first approach is represented by the famous articles of Robinson and Metzler,[2] which give the *necessary and sufficient* condition for 'stability' in terms of total elasticities of import demand and export supply in the home and foreign countries under certain simplifying assumptions of a seemingly partial equilibrium flavor. Another approach is illustrated by the general equilibrium analyses of Hahn [3] and Kemp [7, 8], which state that devaluation has a favorable effect on the balance of payments when commodities and currencies are gross substitutes and thus provide a *sufficient* condition for stability. The last approach is typified by two books by Meade [12, 13], which give a *necessary and sufficient* condition for 'stability' in terms of the elasticity of import demand and the marginal propensity to import in the home and foreign countries.[3]

The relationship between the results of these three approaches, however, does not seem to be well recognized so far; in particular, there seem to be some misunderstandings and confusions in the literature concerning the appropriateness of the first type of approach. Kemp [7, 8] and Meade [13] regard the Robinson–Metzler condition as acceptable only if there is no effect of income change on internationally traded goods. To exclude such an effect, the former requires the existence of domestic goods which dominate the consumers' budget, so that the income elasticity of demand for international goods is zero and the latter assumed that a constant income was entirely spent on goods, with no hoarding or dishoarding of money. Both

---

[1] This chapter is largely based on Negishi [17].

[2] See Robinson [21], 1949, p. 91 and Metzler [14], p. 226.

[3] See Meade [2], pp. 80–96, and Meade [13], pp. 69, 150. See also Pearce [19], p. 14, and Jones [6], pp. 205–6.

stress the partial equilibrium flavor of the first approach.[4]) However, the Robinson–Metzler condition can be derived from the general equilibrium model without making such assumptions. Nor has the close relationship of the devaluation problem to that of Hicksian 'stability' of multiple markets been sufficiently recognized.[5]) The Hicksian analysis is based on asymmetric assumptions concerning the speeds of adjustment in different markets (some markets are assumed to be instantaneously adjusted, others are assumed to be not adjusted at all); it has therefore been superceded by Samuelson's explicitly dynamic analysis. In the analysis of devaluation, however, the Hicksian analysis finds an appropriate application, for here it is a question of the effect on a single (currency) market of a parametric change in a price (the rate of exchange) when all other (commodity) markets adjust instantaneously.[6])

The aim of this chapter is to tie up these loose ends and to show that the Robinson–Metzler condition can be obtained under assumptions which are far less stringent than those imposed by Kemp and Meade.

First, we will show that a necessary and sufficient condition for the 'stability' of the foreign exchanges is that the currency market is imperfectly stable in the sense of Hicks, when commodity prices are assumed to be flexible and the stocks of currency at home and abroad are assumed to be constant. From this, the results of the first two types of approach mentioned above can easily be direved as corollaries, one as the necessary and sufficient condition for a simplified case and the other as a sufficient condition for the general case. It emerges, therefore, that the first two approaches are essentially of the same type and that the Robinson–Metzler condition can be interpreted in terms of general equilibrium analysis. Kemp's partial equilibrium interpretation is well taken but by no means the only one which is permissible.

Secondly, we will show that the monetary assumption implicit in the last approach is different from that of the first two. Under the first two types of approach to the devaluation problem, stocks of currencies are assumed to be kept constant in the short run though naturally increased (diminished) by

---

[4]) See Kemp [7], [8], pp. 235–6 and Meade [13], pp. 131–6. See also Jones [6], p. 209. However, Kemp [9], p. 339, followed Negishi [17] to give a general equilibrium interpretation of the first approach.

[5]) However, see Hahn [3], p. 121. For the discussion of Jones [6], pp. 202–4, see section 5 below and Chipman [1], p. 721.

[6]) See Hahn [3], p. 121, though the relevance of the Hicksian condition is not explicitly stated.

the trade surplus (deficit) in the long run.[7]) Under the third approach, however, it is assumed that even in the short run, i.e., before the effect of the trade surplus or deficit is felt, the supply of currencies is changed deliberately so that the wage in the general case or the price of the exportable in the simplified case remains constant in the face of the changed rate of exchange. Therefore, Meade's interpretation and criticism of the Robinson–Metzler condition is not relevant.

This conclusion will suggest, then, some criticisms of Harberger [4], Jones [6] and Tsiang [22] who interpret the Marshall–Lerner condition, originally the stability condition for a barter economy, as the 'stability' condition for the balance of payments, when a certain monetary policy is assumed to be pursued in each country.[8]) It will be shown that the effect of monetary wealth on consumption is not duly considered by these authors. The money which is a concrete commodity to be hoarded and dishoarded is not successfully integrated into the model of the barter economy in Harberger [4] and Jones [6], i.e., money is merely an abstract unit of account which has no function of the store of value and medium of exchange, as is clearly admitted by Chipman [1].[9]) Generally speaking, the Marshall–Lerner condition is neither the stability condition of commodity markets nor the condition for a favorable devaluation in a genuine monetary economy.[10])

2. In this section, the Hicksian stability condition is derived for a four commodity economy, since we have to consider at least four commodities in the discussion of the 'stability' of foreign exchanges, i.e., domestic and foreign currencies, exportables and importables of the home country. The Hicksian stability condition is a sort of extension of the Walrasian stability condition which is, as was explained in chapter 13, a stability condition for a two-commodity economy. The second commodity being numeraire, the

---

[7]) See Kemp [7], [8], p. 224.
[8]) For the so-called 'Marshall–Lerner' condition, i.e., the necessary and sufficient condition for the stability of a barter economy, see Kemp [8], pp. 61–2, 70. In spite of Harberger, it is not the Robinson condition, which is the 'stability' condition in a genuine monetary economy. The Robinson condition is generally different from the Marshall–Lerner condition but looks like the latter when supply elasticities are infinite (see Robinson [21], 1949, p. 92, Metzler [14], p. 227 and Lerner [10], p. 378) or when its sufficient condition version is considered (see Metzler [14], p. 227 and Vanek [23], pp. 71–2). The former case is ruled out by our full employment assumption. See also section 3 below.
[9]) See Chipman [1], p. 721.
[10]) As for the special cases in which the Marshall–Lerner condition truly coincides with the stability condition of the foreign exchanges, see chapter 17.

Walrasian stability condition is satisfied if and only if the price of the first commodity higher (lower) than the equilibrium one implies the existence of excess supply (demand) in the market of the first commodity so that the price is pulled back to equilibrium. Let us extend this condition to the case of four commodities with the fourth one being numeraire. The market of the first commodity is stable if, starting from an equilibrium, an increase (a decrease) in price induces an excess supply (demand). Since the excess demand (supply) of the first commodity is a function not only of its own price but also of prices of the second and third commodities, however, whether the stability condition of the first market is satisfied depends on the situation in the second and third markets which are also thrown out of equilibrium when the price of the first commodity departs from equilibrium. The Hicksian imperfect stability condition of the first market is obtained under the assumption that the second and third markets are instantaneously cleared by the adjustment of the second and third prices.[11]

Let us denote excess demand and the price of the ith commodity by E_i and p_i, respectively. From the equilibrium conditions,

$$E_1(p_1, p_2, p_3) = 0,$$
$$E_2(p_1, p_2, p_3) = 0, \tag{1}$$
$$E_3(p_1, p_2, p_3) = 0,$$

and the Hicksian assumption on the adjustments in the second and third markets, we have

$$dE_1/dp_1 = \partial E_1/\partial p_1 + \partial E_1/\partial p_2 \cdot dp_2/dp_1 + \partial E_1/\partial p_3 \cdot dp_3/dp_1$$
$$dE_2/dp_1 = \partial E_2/\partial p_1 + \partial E_2/\partial p_2 \cdot dp_2/dp_1 + \partial E_2/\partial p_3 \cdot dp_3/dp_1 = 0 \tag{2}$$
$$dE_3/dp_1 = \partial E_3/\partial p_1 + \partial E_3/\partial p_2 \cdot dp_2/dp_1 + \partial E_3/\partial p_3 \cdot dp_3/dp_1 = 0$$

where $\partial E_i/\partial p_j$'s are evaluated at an equilibrium. Since this can be solved for dE_1/dp_1, dp_2/dp_1 and dp_3/dp_1, the Hicksian imperfect stability condition of the first market is

$$dE_1/dp_1 = \begin{vmatrix} E_{11} & E_{12} & E_{13} \\ E_{21} & E_{22} & E_{23} \\ E_{31} & E_{32} & E_{33} \end{vmatrix} \bigg/ \begin{vmatrix} 1 & E_{12} & E_{13} \\ 0 & E_{22} & E_{23} \\ 0 & E_{32} & E_{33} \end{vmatrix} = |E_{ij}|_{123}/|E_{ij}|_{23} < 0 \tag{3}$$

where $\partial E_i/\partial p_j$ is denoted by E_{ij}.

[11] See Hicks [5], pp. 62–77, 315–317.

This condition can also be obtained as a special case of the dynamic stability condition which was, as discussed in chapter 13, the condition for the convergence of the solution of

$$dp_1/dt = a_1 E_1 (p_1, p_2, p_3)$$

$$dp_2/dt = a_2 E_2 (p_1, p_2, p_3) \qquad (4)$$

$$dp_3/dt = a_3 E_3 (p_1, p_2, p_3)$$

to an equilibrium, where t is time and a_i is positive constant. If the speed of adjustment of the second and third markets, a_2 and a_3, are infinite, (4) can be replaced by

$$dp_1/dt = a_1 E_1 (p_1, p_2, p_3)$$

$$E_2 (p_1, p_2, p_3) = 0 \qquad (5)$$

$$E_3 (p_1, p_2, p_3) = 0 .$$

By taking a linear approximation of (5), the local stability condition is $\lambda = |E_{ij}|_{123}/|E_{ij}|_{12} < 0$, where λ is the solution of

$$\begin{vmatrix} E_{11}-\lambda & E_{12} & E_{13} \\ E_{21} & E_{22} & E_{23} \\ E_{31} & E_{32} & E_{33} \end{vmatrix} = 0.$$

Since $E_i(p_1, p_2, p_3, p_4)$ is homogeneous of degree zero, we can see from Euler's theorem $\Sigma_j E_{ij} P_j = 0$ that $|E_{ii}| > E_{ij}$, $i \neq j$, if $E_{ij} > 0$, $i \neq j$, i.e., gross substitutability is assumed and, without loss of generality, equilibrium prices p_1, p_2, p_3 and p_4 are taken as unity. The co-factors of the matrix

$$[E_{ij}]_{123} = \begin{bmatrix} - & + & + \\ + & - & + \\ + & + & - \end{bmatrix}$$

are all positive, including $[E_{ij}]_{23}$. The inverse of $[E_{ij}]_{123}$ must be, therefore, either a positive or negative matrix. Again from Euler's theorem we have

$$E_{11}p_1 + E_{12}p_2 + E_{13}p_3 = -E_{14}p_4$$

$$E_{21}p_1 + E_{12}p_2 + E_{13}p_3 = -E_{24}p_4$$

$$E_{31}p_1 + E_{32}p_2 + E_{33}p_3 = -E_{34}p_4 .$$

Since $p_i > 0$, $E_{ij} > 0$, $i \neq j$, we see that the inverse of $[E_{ij}]_{123}$ must be a negative matrix. Gross substitutability implies Hicksian imperfect stability of all markets.[12])

A matrix is called Hicksian if all the principal minors have the sign of $(-1)^n$, where n is the rank of the minor. The matrix $[E_{ij}]_{123}$ is Hicksian if gross substitutability is assumed. A sufficient condition for Hicksian imperfect stability is that $[E_{ij}]_{123}$ is Hicksian. As a matter of fact, Hicksian $[E_{ij}]_{123}$ is the condition for Hicksian perfect stability, i.e., the imperfect stability of all the markets with rigid prices in any number of markets and instantaneous adjustments in other markets.

3. Consider a two-country (and therefore two-currency) and two-commodity world. Let p, q, r and s be respectively the prices of commodities x and y and of the currencies of the home and foreign countries. Assume that the stocks of foreign currency and of government bonds in each country are kept unchanged (neutral monetary policy) and that households and firms in each country are not interested in holding foreign currency. Then we can designate the excess demands (net imports) for commodities x and y by the home country as $X(p, q, r)$ and $Y(p, q, r)$ and those by the foreign country as $X^*(p, q, s)$ and $Y^*(p, q, s)$. These functions are homogeneous of degree zero since excess demand is a function of relative prices, real income and real assets. For example, $X(p, q, r) = X(p/d, q/d, (p\overline{X} + q\overline{Y} + rW)/d)$, where d is the price index (i.e., a certain weighted average of p and q), W is the public's net wealth (i.e., outside money and government bonds in money terms), $\overline{X}$ and $\overline{Y}$ are the outputs of the two goods and are functions of p/q.[13]) Actually, X may also be a function of the rate of interest, since $W = M + V/i$, where M is the amount of foreign currency, V is the number of government bonds issued and $1/i$ is the price of government bonds.[14]) However, the amount of foreign currency and the number of government bonds are fixed and the possibility of international lending and borrowing is assumed away; hence the interest rate is eliminated by the assumed equality of the demand for and supply of bonds within a country, just as, e.g., the wage is eliminated by the equality of the demand for and

[12]) See Negishi [15].
[13]) See Patinkin [18], p. 427, Kemp [6], [7], p. 223 and also Patinkin [18], pp. 515–23.
[14]) See Patinkin [18], pp. 289–90 and 295–302.

supply of labor.[15]) At the equilibrium of commodity markets, we have $X + Y^* = 0$, $Y + Y^* = 0$. The balance of payments of the home country in terms of its own currency B is then the excess demand for its currency z which is designated as $Z(p, q, r)$.[16]) Let the foreign currency be the numeraire $(s = 1)$ and the initial value of p, q, r and B be $\bar{p}$, $\bar{q}$, $\bar{r}$ and $\bar{B}$. Then we have, at $(\bar{p}, \bar{q}, \bar{r})$,

$$X(p, q, r) + X^*(p, q, s) = 0 \tag{6}$$

$$Y(p, q, r) + Y^*(p, q, s) = 0 \tag{7}$$

$$Z(p, q, r) = \bar{B} . \tag{8}$$

The 'stability' condition of the foreign exchanges, or the condition for a favorable impact effect (i.e., the short run effect under the assumption that stocks of currencies are not affected by the trade deficit or surplus)[17]) of devaluation on the balance of payments is $dZ/dr < 0$. A necessary and sufficient condition for this is that z in the system (6), (7) and (8) is imperfectly stable in the sense of Hicks, i.e., that the determinants of the matrix

$$\begin{bmatrix} X_p + X_p^* & X_q + X_q^* & X_r \\ X_p + Y_p^* & Y_q + Y_q^* & Y_r \\ Z_p & Z_q & Z_r \end{bmatrix} \tag{9}$$

[15]) Kemp [7], [8], p. 223, assumes, e.g., that $E_i^*(p_2/p_1, \bar{A}_1^*(p_2/p_1) - RA^*/P_1) = E_i^*(p_1, p_2, R)$, where E_i^* is the foreign demand for the ith good, p_i is the price of the ith good, R is the price of foreign currency in terms of home currency, A^* and $\bar{A}_1^*$ are the supply (assumed to be constant) and demand (in terms of the first good) of the foreign currency. That is, (excess) demand is a function of relative price and real expenditure, although, e.g., $\partial E_i^*/\partial p_1$ is obtained not under the assumption of constant expenditure, but under that of constant money supply. There is a hidden assumption in the left hand side that the desired amount of money is independent of the level of wealth (i.e., the stock of money) and that the marginal rates of substitution between goods are independent of the desired amount of money (i.e., separability). Generally, $E_i^*(p_1, p_2, R)$ should be $E_i^*(p_2/p_1, \bar{A}_1^*(p_2/p_1, RA^*/P_1) - RA^*/p_1, RA^*/p_1)$.
[16]) See Harberger [4].
[17]) Or, alternatively, that there is an autonomous capital movement from the surplus to the deficit country which offsets the change in the amount of currency induced by the surplus or deficit, as in Meade [12], pp. 80–96 and Jones [6], pp. 205–6.

and of the matrix

$$\begin{bmatrix} X_p + X_p^* & X_q + X_q^* \\ Y_p + Y_p^* & Y_q + Y_q^* \end{bmatrix} \tag{10}$$

are opposite in sign where X_p is the derivative of X with respect to p at $(\bar{p}, \bar{q}, \bar{r})$, and the like.

Therefore, a sufficient condition for exchange 'stability', the improvement of the balance of payments by devaluation of the home currency, is that the matrix (9) is Hicksian. Hahn [3] and Kemp [7, 8], pp. 221–39, assume gross substitutability, i.e., that X_q, X_q^*, X_r, X_s^*, Y_p, Y_p^*, Y_r, Y_s^*, Z_p and Z_q are all positive.[18] Then it is easily seen that the matrix of (9) has positive off-diagonal elements and is Hicksian by use of the fact that X, Y and Z are homogeneous of degree zero with respect to p, q, and r and X^* and Y^* are homogeneous of degree zero with respect to p, q and s (i.e., $pX_p + qX_q + rX_r = 0$, $pY_p + qY_q + rY_r = 0$, $pZ_p + qZ_q + rZ_r = 0$, $pX_p^* + qX_q^* + sX_s^* = 0$ and $pY_p^* + qY_q^* + sY_s^* = 0$). From Walras' law, $pX + qY + rZ = 0$; hence $pX_p + qY_p + rZ_p + X = 0$, $pX_q + qY_q + rZ_q + Y = 0$ and $pX_r + qY_r + rZ_r + Z = 0$. It follows that, if x is imported (i.e., $X > 0$), positive Z_p (i.e., gross substitutability) implies that the home elasticity of import demand with respect to its own price is greater than one, since $Z_p = (X/r)(-pX_p/X - qY_p/X - 1) > 0$.

By choosing the units of commodities and currencies properly, we can make $\bar{p} = \bar{q} = \bar{r} = 1$. In view of the homogeneity of X, Y and Z and Walras' law, (9) can be written as

$$\begin{bmatrix} X_p + X_p^* & X_q + X_q^* & X_p^* + X_q^* \\ Y_p + Y_p^* & Y_q + Y_q^* & Y_p^* + Y_q^* \\ -(X + X_p + Y_p) & -(Y + Y_q + X_q) & 0 \end{bmatrix}$$

and the Hicksian condition for the imperfect stability of z is that the ratio of

$$(Y + Y_q + X_q)((X_p + X_p^*)(Y_p^* + Y_q^*) - (Y_p + Y_p^*)(X_p^* + X_q^*)) -$$

$$-(X + X_p + Y_p)((X_q + X_q^*)(Y_p^* + Y_q^*) - (Y_q + Y_q^*)(X_p^* + X_q^*))$$

and $(X_p + X_p^*)(Y_q + Y_q^*) - (Y_p + Y_p^*)(X_q + X_q^*)$ is negative. If cross effects between commodities are zero, i.e., if $X_q = Y_p = X_q^* = Y_p^* = 0$, then the

---

[18] Since $rX_r = M\partial X/\partial M$, $sX_s^* = N\partial X^*/\partial N$, where M and N are respectively the home and foreign stocks of currency, positive X_r and X_s^* implies that x is not an inferior good.

Hicksian condition is equivalent to the Robinson–Metzler elasticity condition,

$$E(1+S)D^*/(S+D^*) - (1-D)S^*I/(D+S^*) > 0 \qquad (11)$$

where E, I, D, S, D^* and S^* are respectively the values of home exports and of home imports, the home elasticities of import demand and export supply and the foreign elasticities of import demand and export supply. This is easily seen by substituting zero for the cross effects in the Hicksian condition and dividing both the denominator and the numerator by XY. We have, assuming that $X > 0$ (home country imports x) and $Y < 0$ (home country exports y) and noting that $X = -X^*$ and $Y = -Y^*$,

$$((1+S)(-D-S^*)\,Y_q^* + (1-D)(S+D^*)\,X_p^*)/(-D-S^*)(S+D^*) < 0, \quad (12)$$

or

$$-Y(1+S)D^*/(S+D^*) - X(1-D)S^*/(S^*+D) > 0 \qquad (13)$$

where $D = -X_p/X$, $S = Y_q/Y$, $D^* = Y_q^*/Y$ and $S^* = -X_p^*/X$.

It is well known that if inferior goods are ruled out and $\bar{B} = 0$, i.e., $X + Y = 0$, a sufficient condition for (13) is that the sum of the home and foreign elasticities of import demand is greater than one, i.e., $-X_p/X - Y_q^*/Y^* - 1 > 0$.[19] In other words, a set of conditions sufficient for exchange 'stability' is

$$X_q = Y_p = X_q^* = Y_p^* = 0, \quad -X_p/X - Y_q^*/Y^* - 1 > 0.$$

Neither this set of conditions nor gross substitutability is stronger than the other, for while the latter seems to impose less stringent conditions on the cross effect between the exportable and the importable the former imposes the weaker restriction on the import elasticities. Furthermore, the assumption of no cross effects cannot be considered stricter than that of gross substitutability, i.e., positive cross effects, since the former can be justified by the principle of insufficient reason based on a positive substitution effect (the case of complementary goods), a negative substitution effect (the case of substitutes), a positive income effect (the case of export price change), a negative income effect (the case of import price change), a negative real cash balance effect and so on.

Such is the general equilibrium interpretation of the Robinson–Metzler condition. To assume no cross effects is not to engage in partial equilibrium

[19] See Metzler [14], p. 227 and Vanek [23], pp. 71–2.

analysis. It is merely to assume, on balance, a zero total effect, with some of its components positive and others negative. In the above analysis all prices, and therefore the purchasing power of money, were treated as flexible, while in the Marshallian partial equilibrium analysis (as in the partial equilibrium interpretation of the Robinson–Metzler condition by Kemp)[20] the constancy of the purchasing power of money, i.e., the constancy of prices of many important commodities, is among the 'other things' which are assumed as ,equal'.[21] Therefore, the partial equilibrium interpretation given by Kemp, though sufficient, is by no means necessary for the acceptability of the Robinson–Metzler condition.

4. Suppose (as in Meade [13] and Pearce [19]) that the excess demand for each good is a function of commodity prices and of total money expenditure on commodities, and is homogeneous of degree zero. This clearly presupposes the separability of commodities and monetary assets as is clearly recognized by Pearce.[22] Suppose further that countries are completely specialized in the production of their exportables and that by monetary policy the prices of exportables are held constant in terms of the currency of the exporting country (i.e., $q = r$ in the home country, $p = s = 1$ in the foreign country).[23] The conditions of equilibrium in the commodity markets are

$$X(p, q, rC) + X^*(p, q, sC^*) = 0 ,$$

$$(14)$$

$$Y(p, q, rC) + Y^*(p, q, sC^*) = 0 ,$$

where C and C^* are expenditures in excess of incomes from production, expressed in terms of the appropriate local currency.[24] Devaluation of the home currency leads to an exchange surplus for the home country if and only if $B = -qY - pX$ increases when r is decreased and C and C^* are adjusted so as to have (14) satisfied, under the assumption that $q = r$ and $p = s = 1$. Such is the model used to discuss the devaluation problem in Meade [12]; it is also the essential part of the simplified two goods model of Meade [13].[25]

---

[20] See Kemp [7], [8], pp. 235–6.

[21] Marshall [11], p. 62 and Friedman [2], pp. 66–67.

[22] Pearce [19], p. 6.

[23] Meade [13], p. 103.

[24] Income from production is generally a function of relative prices under the assumption of full employment. It is constant if each country specializes in the production of its exportable. Meade [13], p. 46.

[25] Meade [12], pp. 80–96, [13], pp. 131–6.

Suppose that initially $p = r = q = s = 1$. The necessary and sufficient condition for successful devaluation, i.e., $dB/dr < 0$, $q = r$, $p = s = 1$, is that the determinants

$$\begin{vmatrix} X_c & X_{c^*}^* & X_q + X_r + X_q^* \\ Y_c & Y_{c^*}^* & Y_q + Y_r + Y_q^* \\ Y_c + X_c & 0 & Y + Y_q + Y_r + X_q + X_r \end{vmatrix}$$

and

$$\begin{vmatrix} X_c & X_{c^*}^* \\ Y_c & Y_{c^*}^* \end{vmatrix}$$

are of the same sign. The second determinant reduces to $-(1 - X_c - Y_{c^*}^*)$, since $X_c + Y_c = 1$ and $X_{c^*}^* + Y_{c^*}^* = 1$. When $B = -C = C^* = 0$,[26]) the first determinant reduces to $X(1 + X_p/X + Y_q^*/Y^*)$, by the use of $X + Y = C$ and $X^* + Y^* = C^*$ (i.e., $X_q + X_r + Y_q + Y_r + Y = C$, $X_p + Y_p + Y = 0$ and $X_q^* + Y_q^* + Y^* = 0$), $X + X^* = 0$, $Y + Y^* = 0$, $X_c + Y_c = 1$, $X_{c^*}^* + Y_{c^*}^* = 1$ and the homogeneity of Y (i.e., $Y_p + Y_q + Y_r = 0$). Therefore, the 'stability' condition is

$$X(-X_p/X - Y_q^*/Y^* - 1)/(1 - X_c - Y_{c^*}^*) > 0.[27])$$ (15)

It is clear that the monetary policies to be pursued in each country cannot be the neutral one assumed in the first two approaches, since generally it is impossible in the model of the previous section to change q and r proportionately while p and s are kept unchanged without violating the equilibrium conditions (6) and (7). Therefore, generally speaking, some non-neutral policy (involving changes in the amounts of outside money and government bonds) is required in the Meade-type approach to the devaluation problem.

[26]) From Walras' law, or the basic absorption condition (Pearce [19], pp. 5, 10–11), we have $B = -qY - pX = -C$ and $B^* = -pX^* - qY^* = -C^*$. If $X + X^* = 0$, $Y + Y^* = 0$, then $B = -B^*$ and therefore $B = -C = C^*$.

[27]) By making use of $B = -C = C^*$, we can, alternatively, obtain the same 'stability' condition by substituting B for $-C$ and C^* in the expression for B and then differentiating B, i.e., without differentiating (14). Such is the procedure used by Pearce [19] and Jones [6], pp. 205–6; it is more appropriate to the model of Meade [12], pp. 80–96, while our procedure is nearer to the method of Meade [13], pp. 10–14, though the two procedures are essentially the same.

Meade, after working out his own model, criticized the Robinson–Metzler condition on the grounds that the effect of total expenditure and of the price of the exportable on imports are neglected.[28]) The latter point has already been discussed in the previous section. Now the neglect of cross price effects in the model of Meade [13] himself, where each country is assumed to be specialized in the production of its exportable and where, e.g., $\partial X/\partial p$ is calculated under the assumption of constant expenditure, would indeed be open to Meade's criticism. In the model of the previous section, however, the situation is somewhat different and the assumption of zero cross effects can be defended, for there $\partial X/\partial p$ signifies a total effect, i.e., the sum of the pure effect of a change in p and the effect of, e.g., the change in the interest rate induced by the change in p, under the assumption that the net wealth of the public, not its expenditure, is constant. Therefore, the former point is also not well founded, since total expenditure was clearly not assumed to be constant in the previous section. What was assumed there is a neutral monetary policy, i.e., a constant amount of outside money and of government bonds. The reason why Meade's comments on the Robinson–Metzler condition are irrelevant is that he assumed that the excess demand functions involved in the statement of the condition are of the kind incorporated in his own model. In fact they should be interpreted quite differently, as was seen in the previous section.

Following Meade [13], Pearce [19] discussed a model of the same type and criticized the Robinson–Metzler condition. He raised two points.[29]) Interpreting the four elasticities which appear in the formula as total elasticities in his sense (i.e., as the ratio of the relative change in the amount of a good traded to the relative change in the price ratio),[30]) Pearce implies that the Robinson–Metzler condition is trivially correct but useless. This criticism may be valid if applied to the simple necessary and sufficient condition obtained by differentiating the balance of payments definition with respect to the terms of trade – that the sum of two elasticities be greater than one.[31]) The Robinson–Metzler necessary and sufficient condition, however, is derived quite differently and involves four elasticities. Its two elasticities version is merely a *sufficient* condition for successful devalua-

---

[28]) Meade [13], p. 132.
[29]) Pearce [19], pp. 13–4.
[30]) Pearce [19], pp. 9–10.
[31]) Pearce [19], p. 9, equation (5). See also section 1, footnote 8.

tion;[32]) it is, therefore, entirely different from the condition just mentioned. Elasticities which appear in the Robinson–Metzler condition are sometimes called total elasticities. For example, $(\partial X/\partial p)(p/X)$ signifies the total elasticity of X with respect to p in the sense that adjustments in (e.g.) the labor and bond markets, involving the wage and interest rates, are carried out. Therefore, even if social indifference curves exist, the sign of $\partial X/\partial p$ cannot be easily inferred from theory, though it can be easily estimated by econometric studies.[33]) But it is by no means a total elasticity in Pearce's sense that import and export markets, including the market for x itself, are adjusted. The first comment of Pearce is therefore irrelevant. The second one is entirely wrong. Pearce supposed that demand is implicitly assumed to be independent of income in the Robinson–Metzler model. Then, by substituting the relative for the absolute price, an absurd result, that the absolute values of the demand and supply elasticities are equal, was derived. However, such a substitution is not possible since the demand function is not homogeneous if it is independent of income, i.e., income to be spent on it is constant. The essential point of the Robinson–Metzler model is that demand is assumed to be a function of absolute price.[34])

5. As has been shown in the previous section, the monetary policy which stabilizes the price of the exportable in each country necessarily has a wealth effect on demand when the exchange rate is changed. For this reason, Harberger's [4] interpretation of the Marshall–Lerner condition, that the sum of elasticities of import must be greater than one, cannot be accepted.[35]) In his 'modern full employment model', each country specializes in the production of its exportable and the domestic price of exports is stabilized, with the result that national income is held constant in each country and import demand is considered as a function of the exchange rate alone. This implies that the net wealth effect on demand is neglected. Of course, at the time of Harberger [4], the role of net wealth had not been well recognized, for which we are greatly in Patinkin's debt. The influence on demand of monetary policy designed to stabilize price must operate either through the Pigou effect or through the Keynes effect, i.e., either through the direct wealth effect or through its effect on the rate of interest. Since the rate of

---

[32]) Metzler [14], p. 227, Vanek [23], pp. 71–2.
[33]) Pearce [20], p. 153.
[34]) Kemp [7], [8], p. 236.
[35]) See section 1.

interest is eliminated from the model by the use of the bond equation, which necessarily contains the amount of net wealth, demand should be a function of the net wealth of the public in any case. Otherwise, the 'modern full employment model' degenerates into a moneyless model, i.e., 'the classical model' in which the Marshall–Lerner condition is the condition for the 'stability' of the commodity market, not that for the 'stability' of the currency market.

Jones [6] constructed a model of a fully-employed international economy with *flexible prices* in which each country plans to spend exactly the value of its current production and in which the excess demand (supply) of goods is cleared by the decumulation (accumulation) of inventories. This model is essentially the same and therefore has the same difficulty as the 'modern full employment model' of Harberger, i.e., the wealth effect is neglected. Without the wealth effect, a flexible price cannot be arbitrary fixed in terms of domestic currency by monetary policy. Prices should be rigid, i.e., they should be controlled or administered directly. Jones seems to suggest that there is no wealth effect on demand since international trade at disequilibrium, as such, does not change the value of each country's wealth, though its composition between I.O.U.'s and inventories is changed.[36] However, when the rate of exchange (i.e., relative price) is changed, it surely has the wealth effect on demand since the value of wealth is changed.

In a monetary economy, therefore, it is difficult to use the Marshall–Lerner condition as the 'stability' condition for the foreign exchange in the way suggested by Harberger and Jones. Nor is it true in a monetary economy that the Marshall–Lerner condition is the stability condition for the commodity markets, unless Say's identity is assumed for each country, i.e. $pX + qY = 0$ and $pX^* + qY^* = 0$, the absence of which is the sine qua non of the ordinary model of a monetary economy. In other words, the Marshall–Lerner condition is the stability condition for the commodity markets in a monetary economy, if and only if currency markets are always cleared and there exists no balance of payments problem. Jones [6] tried to get rid of this difficulty by considering the perfectly passive adjustment of inventories so that Say's identity does not necessarily imply balance of payments equilibrium. In Jones' model, there exists no rational behavior of inventory holding (i.e., no concept of optimal or desired level of inventory) and, therefore, no ex ante relation between inventory and the rational decisions on

---

[36] This is essentially the same assumption as assumption 1 in Negishi [16].

current demand and current production. There seems to be, however, no particular reason to construct such a model.[37])

Tsiang [22] also seem to neglect the existence of the effect of money balance on demand when he says that the denominator of the above stability condition due to Meade, i.e., (15), disappears, i.e., $1 - X_c - Y_{c*}^*$ becomes 1, if the propensities to import are defined with respect to money incomes rather than to expenditures. This denominator, expressing the effect of the changing amount of money, never disappears unless the Pigou effect does. Tsiang's neglect of the Pigou effect is due to his confusion of the Keynesian effect (through interest rate) and the Pigou effect of money on demand.[38])

References

[1] Chipman, John S., 'A survey of the theory of international trade: Part 2, The neo-classical theory,' *Econometrica*, 33 (1965), 685–670.

[2] Friedman, M., *Essays in positive economics*, University of Chicago Press (1953).

[3] Hahn, F.H., 'The balance of payments in a monetary economy,' *Review of Economic Studies*, 26 (1959), 110–25.

[4] Harberger, A.C., 'Currency depreciation, income and the balance of trade,' *Journal of Political Economy*, 58 (1950), 47–60 (Caves and Johnson, ed., *Readings in international economics*, 1968, Irwin, pp. 341–358).

[5] Hicks, J.R., *Value and capital*, 2nd ed., Oxford University Press, 1946.

[6] Jones, R.W., 'Stability conditions in international trade: a general equilibrium analysis,' *International Economic Review*, 2 (1961), 199–209.

[7] Kemp, M.C., 'The rate of exchange, the term of trade and the balance of payments in fully employed economies,' *International Economic Review*, 3 (1962), 314–27.

[8] Kemp, M.C., *The pure theory of international trade*, Prentice Hall (1964).

[9] Kemp, M.C., *The pure theory of international trade and investment*, Prentice Hall, 1969.

[10] Lerner, A.P., *The economics of control*, Macmillan (1946).

[37]) In the text the possibility of fiscal policy i.e., government expenditure, is ruled out. Indeed, the price of the exportable can also be stabilized by fiscal policy in the discussion of section 4 (see, Pearce [19], p. 6), while there is no room for fiscal policy in the model of section 3. However, the difficulty of Harberger [4] and Jones [6] discussed in section 5 cannot be resolved, even if fiscal policy is introduced. Government expenditure must be paid either by collecting taxes or by issuing government bonds and/or money. In the former case the demand for imports is a function of disposable income, which is not considered by Harberger and Jones. The latter case is essentially the same as that of the monetary policy.

[38]) Tsiang [22], 1968, pp. 395, 400.

[11] Marshall, A., *Principles of economics*, 8th ed., Macmillan (1920).

[12] Meade, J.E., *A geometry of international trade*, George Allen & Unwin (1952).

[13] Meade, J.E., *The balance of payments*, Mathematical Supplement, Oxford University Press (1951).

[14] Metzler, L.A., 'The theory of international trade,' *A Survey of Contemporary Economics*, Blakiston (1948), 210–254.

[15] Negishi, T., 'A note on the stability of an economy where all goods are gross substitutes,' *Econometrica*, 26 (1958), 445–7.

[16] Negishi, T., 'On the formation of prices,' *International Economic Review*, 2 (1961), 122–6.

[17] Negishi, T., 'Approaches to the analysis of devaluation,' *International Economic Review*, 9 (1968), 218–227.

[18] Patinkin, D., *Money, interest and prices*, 2nd ed., Row Peterson (1965).

[19] Pearce, I.F., 'The problem of the balance of payments,' *International Economic Review*, 2 (1961), 1–28.

[20] Pearce, I.F., *A contribution to demand analysis*, Oxford University Press (1964).

[21] Robinson, J., 'The foreign exchanges,' *Essays in the Theory of Employment*, Macmillan, 1937 (Ellis and Metzler, ed., *Readings in the theory of international trade*, Blakiston, 1949, 83–103).

[22] Tsiang, S.C., 'The role of money in trade-balance stability: synthesis of the elasticity and absorption approaches,' *American Economic Review*, 51 (1961), 912–36 (Caves and Johnson, ed., *Readings in international economics*, Irwin, 1968, 389–412).

[23] Vanek, J., *International trade, theory and economic policy*, Irwin, 1962.

PART 6

Dichotomy

CHAPTER 16

Dichotomy of value and monetary theories

1. In the real models of general economic equilibrium, as developed in the preceding chapters, the existence of money is assumed away. Because of the homogeneity, only the relative prices of non-monetary commodities are determined in such models. However, we are living in a monetary economy in which we have to have money to buy goods. Why and how, then, can the results obtained in the real models be used to describe the working of a monetary economy? The traditional way of dealing with this question is to consider that real models of the value theory describe only a limited aspect of a monetary economy, i.e., the real part or the real sector of the economy. While real phenomena in a monetary economy such as relative prices are explained by the value theory, monetary phenomena such as the absolute prices of commodities (prices in terms of money) are left to be explained by a complementary monetary theory. This is the so-called classical or neo-classical dichotomy of the pricing process. Value and monetary theories, which aim to explain different aspects of the same monetary economy, must be consistent with each other.

As is well known, Patinkin's [22] critical view is that there is a logical contradiction between neo-classical value theory, in which excess demand of commodities depend only on relative prices and not on the real cash balances, and monetary theory, in which the quantity of money determines the absolute price level by the effect of real cash balances on excess demands of commodities. This contradiction can be removed, Patinkin insists, not by resort to Say's law but by making the excess demand functions depend on real cash balances as well as relative prices, which, while it eliminates the dichotomy of value theory and monetary theory (to be precise, the third invalid dichotomy of Patinkin),[1]) it preserves the classical neutrality of money, the invariance of the real equilibrium of the economy, and relative

---

[1]) Patinkin [22], 1956, p. 455, 1965, p. 624.

prices, with respect to changes in the quantity of money (the first valid dichotomy of Patinkin).[2])

On the other hand, Archibald and Lipsey [2] argue that the real balance effect is a transient phenomenon and that in the long run equilibrium where individual real balances are at the desired levels, real balances can be dropped from the equations determining equilibrium, which can be then written as functions of relative prices only. Following the suggestion of Hickman [9], they could construct a consistent system, using excess demand functions homogeneous of degree zero in prices, supplemented by the quantity equation.[3]) Valavanis [28] also disputed with Patinkin in the dichotomy debate and showed that if Say's identity is imposed and the Cambridge equation is interpreted as an independent technical restraint which fixes the rate at which exchanges can occur with the help of a monetary medium rather than as a behavior relationship conflicting with Walras' law, there is no inconsistency.

While consistently dichotomized systems are constructed by these favorable interpretations of neo-classical dichotomy, they cannot cover the whole classical and neo-classical argument, since situations in which Say's identity is not established and individual cash balances are initially not at the desired levels are clearly discussed by some neo-classical authors.[4]) The aim of this chapter is, after reviewing Patinkin and anti-Patinkin interpretations of dichotomy, to offer the third interpretation of classical or neo-classical dichotomy, referring to some neo-classical arguments to which neither Patinkin nor anti-Patinkin interpretations of dichotomy can be successfully applied. It will be shown that a consistent dichotomy is obtained between the determination of relative prices in a monetary economy which is done by the value theory of a real or non-monetary economy[5]) and the determination of an absolute price level which is obtained from the excess demand function of money in the monetary economy, under certain

---

[2]) Patinkin [22], 1956, p. 454, 1965, p. 622. Samuelson [25] supports Patinkin in this respect. He even insists that this is the classical dichotomy, judging not from what Wicksell, Cassel, Marshall and Pigou wrote, but from what young Samuelson once had in mind.
[3]) See also Symposium [32] and Clower [4].
[4]) See, for example, Pigou [23], in which the Cambridge equation as the demand and supply relation of money is derived from individual choices between money and other resources.
[5]) Since this economy is a highly special barter economy which presupposes the existence of a trading post or central clearing institution and is not that of primitive isolated barter, it may be wise to avoid the use of the word barter economy. See chapter 14.

assumptions, say, the separability of the utility of money from that of other commodities and no distribution effect of income on spending.[6]) This, of course, does not deny the possibility of the false dichotomy in some of the classical or neo-classical literature between the real sector and the monetary sector both in the same monetary economy, the case to which Patinkin's criticism should be applied.

2. Suppose an economy consisting of commodities (including bonds) and money is divided into two sectors, a real sector described by the excess demand functions of commodities which depend only on relative prices (including the rate of interest), and a monetary sector described by the excess demand function of money which depends on the absolute price level as well as relative prices. Then Patinkin's third invalid dichotomy is obtained between value theory constituted by the determination of relative prices in the real sector and monetary theory constituted by the determination of absolute price level in the monetary sector.

Let there be n commodities (denoted by $i = 1, ..., n$), a bond which is the claim to a unit of money in the future (denoted by b) and money (denoted by m). Excess demands for commodities and bonds are respectively denoted by $E_i(p_1, ..., p_n, r)$, $i = 1, ..., n$, and $E_b(p_1, ..., p_n, r)$, where p_i is the price of the ith commodity in terms of money and r is the rate of interest, i.e., $1/(1+r)$ is equal to the price of bonds in terms of money, i.e., p_b. According to Patinkin, the neo-classical assumption of homogeneity is that E_i's are homogeneous of degree zero with respect to $p_1, ..., p_n$ and E_b is homogeneous of degree one with respect to $p_1, ..., p_n$. This assumption is certainly an extension of, but quite different from, the homogeneity of excess demand functions in a non-monetary economy where money is merely an abstract unit of account. In view of homogeneity, we may solve the real sector of the economy

$$E_i(p_1, ..., p_n, r) = 0, \quad i = 1, ..., n \tag{1}$$

$$E_b(p_1, ..., p_n, r) = 0, \tag{2}$$

for relative prices, i.e., $p_1/p_n, ..., p_{n-1}/p_n$ and the rate of interest r.[7])

[6]) Negishi [18].
[7]) From Walras' law, only $n+1$ equations are independent among $n+2$ equations (1), (2) and (3) below.

To determine absolute prices, Patinkin considers, an equation requiring the equality of demand and supply of money, e.g., the Cambridge equation

$$KdT - M = 0 \tag{3}$$

is added by neo-classical economists, where K, d, T and M are respectively a positive constant, the index of price level (homogeneous function of degree one with respect to $p_1, ..., p_n$), the volume of trade (function of demands and supplies of n commodities) and the amount of money. If $KdT > M$, then there exists a shortage of real cash balance, money is substituted for commodities and d is reduced by the reduction of commodity prices due to excess supply of commodities while, if $KdT < M$, the real cash balance is in excess, commodities are substituted for money and d is increased by excess demands for commodities. In other words, (3) is established through the real cash balance effect on commodity demands, which does not exist in (1) and (2).

With M and K given, d and therefore absolute prices $p_1, ..., p_n$ are solved when relative prices (and the interest rate) and therefore demands and supplies of n commodities are obtained from (1) and (2). This dichotomy of value theory (1) and (2) and monetary theory (3), which Patinkin calls the third dichotomy, is invalid. From Walras' law and (1) and (2), the excess demand for money is

$$-\Sigma_i p_i E_i - p_b E_b , \tag{4}$$

which is homogeneous of degree one with respect to $p_1, ..., p_n$ from the homogeneity of (1) and (2). However, the excess demand for money as expressed in (3) is not homogeneous. In other words, the excess demand for money (4) derived from the homogeneous system (1) and (2) which is independent of the real cash balance effect is in contradiction with the Cambridge equation (3). If we replace the right-hand side of (3) by (4), we cannot determine d by (3) since (3) is independent of absolute prices and always satisfied if (1) and (2) are satisfied. Patinkin concluded that the neo-classical dichotomy, which is regarded as a dichotomy of two sectors, is inconsistent (when the Cambridge equation holds) or absolute prices are indeterminate (when Cambridge equation does not hold).[8]

While there are some dichotomized models constructed by contemporary economists to which Patinkin's criticism can be successfully applied,[9] the

---

[8] Patinkin [22], 1956, pp. 108, 334–5, 1965, pp. 176, 475–77.
[9] Modigliani [16], Hicks [10], pp. 254–5, 333–5, Keynes [11], pp. 257–71.

explicit presence of such a dichotomy in the writings of Cassel, Fisher and Pigou is, as Patinkin himself admitted, not certain.[10]) The key to the false dichotomy is the absence or the existence of a real cash balance effect in excess demand for commodities. As a matter of fact, in the debate with Keynes, it is Pigou who defended neo-classical economics and emphasized the cash balance effect on consumption.

On the other hand, the dichotomy is clearly recognized in Divisia [5] in which relative prices are determined by real equations independent of cash balance and a monetary equation is added to determine absolute price level. However, the crucial point in this case is whether his monetary equation is the one expressing the equality of demand and supply of money. He begins with the statement that one necessary equation is missing in Pareto's system of equations since the excess demand for money is identically zero if money has no direct utility.[11]). Since demand and supply of money are already in Pareto's system and considered by Divisia as identical with each other, the monetary equation to be added by him cannot be that of excess demand for money. Divisia clearly stated that in the long run the demand and supply of money are identical and that the monetary equation is an empirical relation between the amount of money and the absolute price level.[12]) If so, Patinkin's criticism cannot be applied, since the monetary equation has no connection with excess demands for commodities through Walras' law and is not inconsistent with the homogeneous assumption.[13])

3. Perhaps Archibald and Lipsey [2] had in mind a dichotomized system like the one of Divisia [5], when they followed Hickman [9] and attacked Patinkin [22], emphasizing the difference between temporary or weekly equilibrium and full equilibrium in the sense of Hicks [10].[14]) Suppose for the sake of simplicity that there are no bonds and that all the non-monetary commodities are non-durable but individual initial holdings of them in each period are identical through periods. The condition for full equilibrium in

---

[10]) Patinkin [22], 1956, pp. 108, 455, 1965, pp. 176, 624. In the case of Walras [29], existence of this dichotomy, due to a careless application of the principle of approximation, is rather obvious. Patinkin [22], 1956, p. 403, 1965, p. 561. Of course, Walras did not insist on the absence of a cash balance effect, he merely neglected it by regarding it as small.

[11]) Pareto [19], p. 593. However, this is not true unless the amount of money is zero. Patinkin [21].

[12]) Divisia [5], pp. 413–5.

[13]) Patinkin [22], 1956, p. 456, 1965, pp. 624–5.

[14]) Hicks [10], pp. 115–40.

which classical economists are interested, i.e., a series of unchanged weekly equilibria, is that the individual excess demands for money are all zero in weekly equilibria, since otherwise there are weekly changes in equilibrium prices due to changes in weekly individual money stocks. If we are interested only in the full equilibrium situation, excess demands for commodities are considered as functions of relative prices only, since proportional changes in all prices, with proportional changes in individual money balances implicitly assumed so that we remain in full equilibrium, keep the commodity excess demands unchanged (homogeneity). Since demand and supply of money are identical in full equilibria, Say's identity is derived from Walras' law and one equation among equations of the equality of demand and supply for commodities is not independent. Therefore, we may obtain equilibrium relative prices from the real system of equations expressing the equality of demand and supply for commodities. Substituting these into what they call the Cambridge equation, which is completely independent of the system of equations in relative prices, Archibald and Lipsey obtained absolute prices.[15]) Real cash balance effect, though important in disequilibrium, is absent in full equilibrium.

Also following Hickman, Valavanis [28] constructed a similar dichotomized system. But his justification of the dichotomy is different from that of Archibald and Lipsey [2]. Money has no utility in classical economics, according to Valavanis, and is merely a veil just like Walrasian tickets in tâtonnement.[16]) It serves as a medium of exchange in one period but by no means as a store of value to be held over periods. It has no value until endorsed by the supply of commodities in each period. Say's identity is established, since no one really wishes to hold money. However, if the amount of such tickets in use is limited, each ticket must represent a larger value when the volume of transactions is increased. What Valavanis called the Cambridge equation is merely expressing this technical relationship. It has nothing to do with the behavior of consumers and firms and is independent of the demand and supply of commodities.

While dichotomized systems constructed by Hickman, Archibald and Lipsey, Clower and Valavanis are logically consistent, the question is whether such systems are really classical or neo-classical, e.g., whether their so-called Cambridge equation is really the one used by the Cambridge school. Unfortunately, they seldom make references to classical or neo-classical

[15]) Clower [4].
[16]) Schneider [26], p. 306, Patinkin [22], 1956, p. 457, 1965, p. 626.

literature in this respect. Nor is it easy to find classical or neo-classical arguments to support their interpretation of the monetary equation. While Hickman's reference to Cassel[17] may seem to justify his interpretation that the monetary equation has nothing to do with demand for money, Cassel's arguments in other places clearly indicate that the monetary equation is a behavior equation concerning the demand for money.[18] The Cambridge equation used by Marshall and Pigou is generally concerned with short-run changes in the absolute price level and describes the relationship between the demand for money and the price level. It is a behavior equation derived from marginal utility theory applied to individual decision making on how much of assets should be held in the form of money.[19] Although we have an example in Divisia [5], it therefore cannot be said that the dichotomized systems of the anti-Patinkin group respresent neo-classical models of value and monetary theories. Nor do such systems interest us very much since the role of money is extremely limited there.

4. Both Patinkin and the anti-Patinkin group concerned with the dichotomy of value and monetary theories in the sense of the dichotomy of real and monetary sectors in a monetary economy. Our review in the preceding sections concluded that such a dichotomy, consistent or not, is not the proper interpretation of the classical or neo-classical dichotomy. Consider, on the other hand, two economies, a real economy without money and a monetary economy which is constituted by introducing money into the real economy. Value theory determines relative prices in the real economy. In the monetary economy, relative prices and the absolute price level must be determined.[20] If relative prices obtained by value theory in the real economy can be substituted into relative prices in the monetary economy, then the absolute price level is determined by a zero excess demand equation for money in the monetary economy, which may be called monetary theory. A valid dichotomy of two economies rather than two sectors is obtained if relative prices in the real economy are successfully substituted into those in the monetary economy. This substitution, though not generally true, is possible, e.g., if the introduction of money does not cause any substitution among com-

---

[17] Cassel [3], 1923, p. 424, 1932, pp. 454–9.
[18] Cassel [3], 1923, pp. 430–2, 453–4.
[19] Marshall [14], pp. 38–46, 282–4, Pigou [23].
[20] Excess demands for commodities in the monetary economy depend on real cash balances which, by definition, do not exist in the real economy.

modities, i.e., utility of money is separable from that of commodities so that there is no substitution effect and there is no distribution effect of income on demand so that no income effect takes place.[21])

In the case of Cassel [3], value theory is clearly concerned with a real economy rather than a real sector in a monetary economy, since in his Book I it is stated that money is introduced only as a scale of reckoning and the existence of a material commodity used as money is ignored.[22]) Therefore, the dichotomy between his Book I and Book III where concrete money is introduced is a dichotomy of economies rather than that of sectors in the same economy and Patinkin's criticism on the third invalid dichotomy cannot be applied.

Wicksell [30] also starts with an economy where money is merely an abstract unit of account, leaving on one side the function that money fulfills as a store of value[23]) and later drops this assumption,[24]) describing the tâtonnement by which the absolute price level is determined. As Patinkin himself observed, demand for a commodity is at first independent of real cash balances, and then a fundamental role is attributed to the effect of real cash balances on demand when the quantity theory of money influences the absolute price level. This is not inconsistent, as Patinkin admitted, since different economies are discussed in the two cases.[25]) If these two economies are successfully dichotomized, Wicksell can safely assume unchanged relative prices in the cumulative process in which the absolute price level is changing.[26])

In an essay arguing that demand and supply analysis can be applied to the problem of money, Pigou [23] adopts the assumption that the value of all commodities other than money in terms of one another is determined *independently of the value of money*, a plan, according to Pigou, similar to that employed in Marshall [15]. Patinkin interprets the meaning of the

---

[21]) Negishi [18].

[22]) Cassel [3], 1923, p. 50. Incidentally, Patinkin states that Cassel as well as Fisher [6] confuse the dichotomy between money and accounting prices (second valid dichotomy) with the one between relative and monetary prices (the third invalid dichotomy). It must be noted, however, that in the real economy with abstract money monetary prices are equal to accounting prices, since money is merely a unit of account. See Patinkin [22], 1956, pp. 39, 436, 450, 1965, pp. 43, 600, 617.

[23]) Wicksell [30], p. 23.

[24]) Wicksell [30], pp. 39–40.

[25]) Patinkin [20], [22], 1956, 424, 1965, 586.

[26]) Wicksell [30], 106.

italicized phrase as determined by the value theory, i.e., in the real sector of a monetary economy, and classifies this as the third invalid dichotomy. However, the reference made by Pigou to Marshall [15] suggests interpreting it as 'determined by the real value theory *before money is introduced*' into the economy just as relative prices of exported goods are assumed to be 'determined by the pure theory of domestic value *before foreign trade is introduced*' in Marshall [15]. Then, this again is a typical example of the dichotomy of two economies.[27])

Patinkin, while admitting that the neutrality of money obtains, strictly speaking, if the mere conversion of a real economy to a monetary economy does not affect equilibrium relative prices, states that the comparison of two economies is generally not meaningful.[28]) Negishi [18] insists, on the contrary, that such a comparison is meaningful under assumptions very often made in the neo-classical literature. If Patinkin's statement that the real economy is a limit of the monetary economy when a nominal amount of money and prices of goods go to zero is right,[29]) it is true that our dichotomy of two economies coincides with his first valid dichotomy of a monetary economy. However, as Wonnacott [31] showed, the real balance is unchanged and we do not get closer to a real economy by changing the amount of money and prices proportionally, which is necessary for the first dichotomy. A real economy is a limit of monetary one when the real balance approaches zero. Then, the neutrality of money in the sense of the comparison of two economies and the first valid dichotomy of Patinkin do not coincide and the former can be valid only when certain assumptions are met.

5. Consider a two period (present and future) model of a real economy without money. Suppose there exist n consumers (denoted by $i = 1, ..., n$), r firms (denoted by $k = 1, ..., r$) and m goods (denoted by $j = 1, ..., m$). As in the preceding chapters, X_{ij}, $\overline{X}_{ij}$, y_{kj} and P_j respectively denote the consumption of the jth good by the ith consumer, the initial holding of the jth good (the service of primary factors) by the ith consumer, output (input, if negative) by the kth firm of the jth good and the price of the jth good. Asterisk (*) signifies the future while notations without asterisk refer to the present. Suppose, for the sake of simplicity, that expectations of future

---

[27]) Pigou [23], Marshall [15], p. 1, Patinkin [22], 1956, p. 444, 1965, p. 610.
[28]) Patinkin [22], 1956, p. 59, 1965, p. 75, Hayek [8], p. 130, Koopmans [12], p. 228.
[29]) Patinkin withdrew this in Patinkin [22], 1965, p. 75.

prices P_j^*'s are static, i.e., future prices are identical to the present ones, P_j's. The rate of discount D is defined as $1/(1+r)$, where r is the rate of interest. A bond is defined as a claim to the value equivalent to one unit of the abstract unit of account in the future. Its present price is D. The net demand for bonds by consumers and firms are denoted by B_i and B_k.

When prices and the rate of interest are given, the kth firm is assumed to maximize the discounted profit $\Sigma_j DP_j^* y_{kj}^* + \Sigma_j P_j y_{kj}$ being subject to the production function $f_k(y_k, y_k^*) = 0$, where $y_k = (y_{k1}, ..., y_{km})$, $y_k^* = (y_{k1}^*, ..., y_{km}^*)$. This is equivalent to maximizing

$$\pi_k = \Sigma_j P_j y_{kj} - DB_k \tag{5}$$

with $B_k = -\Sigma_j P_j^* y_{kj}^*$. The conditions for this are

$$f_{kj}/f_{k1} = P_j/P_1, \quad f_{kj}^*/f_{k1} = DP_j^*/P_1, \quad j = 1, ..., m, \tag{6}$$

where $f_{kj} = \partial f_k/\partial y_{kj}, f_{kj}^* = \partial f_k/\partial y_{kj}^*$, i.e., y_{kj}'s are determined by relative prices and the rate of interest. It must be noted that the accumulation and decumulation of physical capital is implicitly included in this two period plan of production.

Similarly, with prices and the rate of interest given, the ith consumer maximizes his utility $U_i(X_i, X_i^*)$, where $X_i = (X_{i1}, ..., X_{im})$ and $X_i^* = (X_{i1}^*, ..., X_{im}^*)$, being subject to the budget constraint

$$\Sigma_j DP_j^* X_{ij}^* + \Sigma_j P_j X_{ij} = \Sigma_j DP_j^* \overline{X}_{ij}^* + \Sigma_j P_j \overline{X}_{ij} + \Sigma_k \alpha_{ki} \pi_k, \tag{7}$$

where α_{ki} is the ratio of the profit of the kth firm distributed to the ith consumer. This is equivalent to maximizing utility under two constraints,

$$\Sigma_j^{?} P_j^* X_{ij}^* = \Sigma_j^{?} P_j^* \overline{X}_{ij}^* + B_i, \tag{8}$$

$$\Sigma_j P_j X_{ij} + DB_i = \Sigma_j P_j \overline{X}_{ij} + \Sigma_k \alpha_{ki} \pi_k .^{30)} \tag{9}$$

The conditions for the maximization are, in addition to the budget constraint,

$$U_{ij}/U_{i1} = P_j/P_1, \quad U_{ij}^*/U_{i1} = DP_j^*/P_1, \quad j = 1, ..., m, \tag{10}$$

where $U_{ij} = \partial U_i/\partial X_{ij}$, $U_{ij}^* = \partial U_i/\partial X_{ij}^*$. If the right-hand side of (7), i.e., the discounted income is denoted by Y_i, then X_{ij}'s may be said to depend on relative prices, the rate of interest and Y_i.

---

[30]) We assumed away difficulties due to the existence of past debts. See Hahn [7].

The equilibrium conditions for the markets are

$$\Sigma_i X_i = \Sigma_k y_k + \Sigma_i \overline{X}_i \,, \tag{11}$$

where $\overline{X}_i = (\overline{X}_{i1}, \ldots, \overline{X}_{im})$ and

$$\Sigma_i B_i + \Sigma_k B_k = 0 \,, \tag{12}$$

which are assumed in order to solve $P_1, \ldots, P_m$ and r.[31] It can easily be checked that the proportional changes of $P_1, \ldots, P_m$ keep the equilibrium undisturbed while one among (11) and (12) is not independent from (5) and (9). Therefore, we can determine only relative prices, say, $P_2/P_1, \ldots, P_m/P_1$ and r.

Let us now introduce money, which is used simultaneously as a unit of account, a medium of exchange and a store of value. The initial stocks of money held by the ith consumer and the kth firm are denoted by $\overline{M}_i$ and $\overline{M}_k$.

The kth firm is now assumed to maximize its utility, a function of discounted profit and stock of money, M_k, i.e., $U_k(\pi_k, M_k, P_1, \ldots, P_m, r)$, where $\pi_k = \Sigma_j DP_j^* y_{kj}^* + DM_k + \Sigma_j P_j y_{kj} + (\overline{M}_k - M_k)$ or equivalently $\pi_k = \Sigma_j P_j y_{kj} + (\overline{M}_k - M_k) - DB_k$, $B_k = -\Sigma_j P_j^* y_{kj} - M_k$. Conditions for the maximization are (6) and

$$\partial U_k / \partial M_k = (1 - D) \partial U_k / \partial \pi_k \,, \tag{13}$$

i.e., y_{kj}'s are determined by relative prices and the rate of interest in (6) and M_k is determined by (13), which implies the equilibrium of the liquidity of money and opportunity cost of carrying money, i.e., the portfolio selection of the firm.

The ith consumer is similarly to maximize his utility $V_i(X_i, X_i^*, M_i, P_1, \ldots, P_m, r)$, where M_i is his stock of money, being subject to

$$\Sigma_j DP_j^* X_{ij}^* + \Sigma_j P_j X_{ij} + (1 - D) M_i$$
$$= \Sigma_j DP_j^* \overline{X}_{ij}^* + \Sigma_j P_j \overline{X}_{ij} + \overline{M}_i + \Sigma_k \alpha_{ki} \pi_k \tag{14}$$

or to $\Sigma_j P_j^* X_{ij}^* = \Sigma_j P_j^* \overline{X}_{ij}^* + B_i + M_i$ and $\Sigma_j P_j X_{ij} + DB_i + M_i = \Sigma_j P_j \overline{X}_{ij} + \Sigma_k \alpha_{ki} \pi_k + \overline{M}_i$. The conditions for the maximization are, in addition to (14),

$$V_{ij} / V_{i1} = P_j / P_1, \quad V_{ij}^* / V_{i1} = P_j^* / P_1, \quad j = 1, \ldots, m, \tag{15}$$

$$V_{iM} / V_{i1} = (1 - D) / P_1 \,, \tag{16}$$

where $V_{ij} = \partial V_i / \partial X_{ij}$, $V_{ij}^* = \partial V_i / \partial X_{ij}^*$ and $V_{iM} = \partial V_i / \partial M_i$.

[31] For the existence proof of such a temporary equilibrium, see Arrow and Hahn [1], chapter 6.

It must be noted that (10) and (15) are corresponding but generally different conditions since the latter is not independent of M_i. (16) is the equilibrium condition for the consumer's portfolio selection.

The conditions for the market equilibrium are

$$\Sigma_i X_i = \Sigma_k y_k + \Sigma_i \overline{X}_i, \text{ where } \overline{X}_i = (\overline{X}_{i1}, ..., \overline{X}_{im}), \tag{17}$$

$$\Sigma_i B_i + \Sigma_k B_k = 0, \tag{18}$$

$$\Sigma_i M_i + \Sigma_k M_k = \Sigma_i \overline{M}_i + \Sigma_k \overline{M}_k. \tag{19}$$

We can generally determine absolute prices $P_1, ..., P_m$ and the rate of interest r.

Now we are ready to state

Theorem 1. If (1) consumers' tastes are identical (i.e., $V_i(X_i, X_i^*, M_i, P_1, ..., P_m, r) = V(X_i, X_i^*, M_i, P_1, ..., P_m, r)$ for all i), (2) the utility of money is separable from that of other goods (i.e., $V(X_i, X_i^*, M_i, P_1, ..., P_m, r) = V(U(X_i, X_i^*), M_i, P_1, ..., P_m, r))^{32})$ and (3) Engel curve is a straight line through the origin (i.e., V is a homogeneous function with respect to X_i, X_i^* and M_i), then real and monetary economies are dichotomized and relative prices and the rate of interest obtained in (11) and (12) are identical to those obtained in (17), (18) and (19).

Proof. From the assumptions, X_{ij}'s and X_{ij}^*'s in the real economy are expressed as $X_{ij} = A_j(P_2/P_1, ..., P_m/P_1, r) Y_i$ and $X_{ij}^* = A_j^*(P_2/P_1, ..., P_m/P_1, r) Y_i$. The left hand side of the equations in (10) are homogeneous of degree zero in all X_{ij}'s and X_{ij}^*'s and remain unchanged by the proportional change of X_{ij} and X_{ij}^* from $A_j Y_i$ and $A_j^* Y_i$ to $A_j \Sigma_i Y_i$ and $A_j^* \Sigma_i Y_i$ where X_{ij} is equal to $\Sigma_i \overline{X}_{ij} + \Sigma_k y_{kj}$ from (11) and $\Sigma_j P_j^* X_{ij}^* = \Sigma_k \Sigma_j P_j^* y_{kj}^* + \Sigma_i \Sigma_j P_j^* \overline{X}_{ij}^*$ from (12). On the other hand, X_{ij}'s and X_{ij}^*'s in the monetary economy are expressed as $X_{ij} = B_j(P_1, ..., P_m, r) Y_i$ and $X_{ij}^* = B_j^*(P_1, ..., P_m, r) Y_i$ where Y_i denotes the left hand side of (14). Because of the separability, (15) becomes identical to (10). The left-hand side of equations in (15) are homogeneous of degree zero in all X_{ij}'s and X_{ij}^*'s and remain unchanged by the proportional change of X_{ij}'s and X_{ij}^*'s

---

[32]) See Sono [27] and Morishima [17]. Many neo-classical economists, Marshall, Pigou and even Walras, assumed independent utilities which are also separable. Marshall [14], p. 838, Pigou [23], Walras–Jaffe [29], p. 320.

from $B_j Y_i$ and $B_j^* Y_i$ to $B_j \Sigma_i Y_i$ and $B_j^* \Sigma_i Y_i$ where X_{ij} is equal to $\Sigma_i \overline{X}_{ij}$ $+ \Sigma_k y_{kj}$ from (17) and $\Sigma_j P_j^* X_{ij}^* = \Sigma_k \Sigma_j P_j^* y_{kj}^* + \Sigma_i \Sigma_j p_j^* \overline{X}_{ij}^*$ from (18). Then, relative prices and the rate of interest are identical and determined both in real and monetary economies by

$$f_{kj}(y_k, y_k^*)/f_{k1}(y_k, y_k^*) = P_j/P_1, \quad f_{kj}^*(y_k, y_k^*)/f_{k1}(y_k, y_k^*) = DP_j^*/P_1,$$

$$U_j(\Sigma_i \overline{X}_i + \Sigma_k y_k, X_i^*)/U_1(\Sigma_i \overline{X}_i + \Sigma_k y_k, X_i^*) = P_j/P_1,$$

$$U_j^*(\Sigma_i \overline{X}_i + \Sigma_k y_k, X_i^*)/U_1(\Sigma_i \overline{X}_i + \Sigma_k y_k, X_i^*) = DP_j^*/P_1$$

$$\Sigma_j P_j^* X_{ij}^* - \Sigma_k \Sigma_j P_j^* y_{kj}^* - \Sigma_i \Sigma_j P_j^* \overline{X}_{ij}^* = 0, \quad j = 1, ..., m, \quad k = 1, ..., r,$$

where U_j and U_j^* are $\partial U/\partial X_{ij}$ and $\partial U/\partial X_{ij}^*$.

Therefore, to obtain absolute prices, we can first solve the real economy for relative prices and the rate of interest and then substitute them into (19) to obtain the absolute price level. The study of the seemingly unrealistic real model is thus worthwhile for the later study of the more realistic monetary model. Theorem 1 is an extension of the result given in Negishi [18] which deals only with a single period exchange economy. The introduction of money into the utility function is not a necessary condition for the dichotomy. For example, if the consumer's demand for money is related to the amount of his income through the so-called small Cambridge equation,[33] we can prove a theorem similar to theorem 1. What is necessary for the dichotomy is the independence of marginal rates of substitution among goods from the amount of money and from the distribution of income among consumers.

6. Rosenstein-Rodan [24], though accused by Patinkin [22] as an example of the third invalid dichotomy, actually discusses the neutrality of money, comparing the real and monetary economies.[34] However, unlike Patinkin and others he considers the case of metallic money rather than paper money. Neutrality is clearly defined there as the constancy of relative prices when a real economy is converted into a monetary economy, i.e., a commodity acquires a monetary function in addition to its commodity function. It is interesting to note that the neutrality is due, according to Rosenstein-Rodan, to the assumption of constant costs, a classical rather than neo-classical

---

[33] Clower [4].
[34] Patinkin [22], 1956, pp. 108, 456, 1965, pp. 175, 625.

assumption. This suggests an alternative set of conditions for our dichotomy of two economies, i.e., constant returns to scale, no joint output, single primary factor (a world of the substitution theorem)[35]) and the separability of money in the decision of firms.

   Consider a two-period model of a real economy with $m+1$ goods, where the $m+1$th good is the service of only one primary factor, say, labor. The assumption of no joint output makes the definition of an industry possible. Assuming that firms belonging to the same industry are identical, we can talk of the behavior of m industries rather than that of firms. Each industry has two processes of production, one for current inputs and current output, the other, a more complicated one, for current inputs and future output. Constant returns to scale are assumed for each process. Let $a_{kj}(P_1, ..., P_m)$ be the input coefficient of the current production in the kth industry, i.e., the amount of the jth good to be consumed for a unit of the current output of the kth good, where P_{m+1} is taken as numeraire ($j = 1, ..., m+1, k = 1, ..., m$). This is derived from the minimization of the unit cost. Similarly, $a_{kj}^*(P_1, ..., P_m)$'s are defined as the input coefficients for the future output of the kth good. Consumers' current demands for the jth good currently available X_j and that available in the future X_j^* are respectively denoted by $D_j(P_1, ..., P_m, DP_1^*, ..., DP_m^*)$ and $Dj (P_1, ..., P_m, DP_j^*, ..., DP_m^*)$. Assuming that the supply of the primary factor is a given constant, L, and there is no reserved demand for it by consumers, the equilibrium conditions are

$$D_k + \Sigma_k(a_{kj} X_k + a_{kj}^* X_k^*) = X_k,$$

$$D_k^* = X_k^*, \qquad k = 1, ..., m, \tag{20}$$

$$\Sigma_k(a_{k,m+1} X_k + a_{k,m+1}^* X_j^*) = L,$$

and

$$P_k = \Sigma_j a_{kj} P_j,$$

$$DP_k^* = \Sigma_j a_{kj}^* P_j. \tag{21}$$

Since the use of L is efficient from the optimality of perfect competition we can apply the substitution theorem so that relative prices P_j and DP_j^*, (prices in terms of P_{m+1}) are determined in (21) independently of quantities,

[35]) Koopmans [13], pp. 142–164.

which are subsequently determined in (20).[36]) Commodity rates of interest are obtained by $(P_j - DP_j^*)/DP_j^*$, some weighted average of which is the real rate of interest.

When money and bond, i.e., portfolio selection of consumers is introduced into the real system (20) and (21), (21) remains unchanged while (20) is replaced by

$$F_j(P_1, \ldots, P_{m+1}, DP_1^*, \ldots, DP_m^*, D, \overline{M}) + \Sigma_k(a_{kj} X_k + a_{kj}^* X_k^*) = X_j,$$

$$F_j^*(P_1, \ldots, P_{m+1}, DP_1^*, \ldots, DP_m^*, D, \overline{M}) = X_j^*, \quad j = 1, \ldots, m, \qquad (22)$$

$$\Sigma_k(a_{k, m+1} X_k + a_{k, m+1}^* X_k^*) = L,$$

$$M(P_1, \ldots, P_{m+1}, DP_1^*, \ldots, DP_m^*, D, \overline{M}) = \overline{M}, \qquad (23)$$

$$B(P_1, \ldots, P_{m+1}, DP_1^*, \ldots, DP_m^*, D, \overline{M}) = 0,$$

where F_j, F_j^*, M, $\overline{M}$ and B are respectively the consumers' demands for current output and future output (corresponding to D_j and D_j^*), consumers demand for money and their initial stock of money, and consumers' net demand for bonds.[37]) (22) is a natural extension of (20) while (23) is derived from the portfolio selection of consumers.

Relative prices (and the real rate of interest) obtained in (21) are identical either in the real system (20) and (21) or in the monetary system (21), (22) and (23). In addition to relative prices, absolute prices and monetary rate of interest are determined in the latter, i.e., P_{m+1} and D in (23). We may summarize

Theorem 2. If there exists only one primary factor of production and no joint output, returns to scale are constant, and there is no portfolio selection problem for industries, then relative prices (and the real rate of interest) are unchanged between real and monetary systems.[38])

---

[36]) It must be noted that current markets for future outputs (produced from current inputs) are assumed to be open. From budget constraints of consumers (Walras' law). one among (20) and (21) is not independent.

[37]) A bond is, as before, defined as a claim to a unit of money in the future. The current price of a bond is therefore D. The distribution effect among consumers is assumed away. From Walras' law, one among (21), (22) and (23) is not independent.

[38]) The assumption of no portfolio selection in industries has often been made in neo-classical literature. Samuelson [25], Walras [29], etc.

References

[1] Arrow, K.J. and F.H. Hahn, *Competitive equilibrium analysis*, Holden-Day, forthcoming.
[2] Archibald, C.C. and R.G. Lipsey, 'Monetary and value theory: a critique of Lange and Patinkin,' *Review of Economic Studies*, 26 (1958), 1–22 (R.W. Clower, ed., *Monetary theory*, Penguin, 1969, 149–161).
[3] Cassel, G., *The theory of social economy*, J. McCabe tr., T.F. Unwin, 1923, S.L. Baron, tr., Harcourt, Brace and Co., 1932.
[4] Clower, R., 'Classical monetary theory revisited,' *Economica*, 30, 1963, 165–70.
[5] Divisia, F., *Economique rationnelle*, Gaston Doin et Cie, 1928.
[6] Fisher, I. *The purchasing power of money.*
[7] Hahn, F.H., 'On some problems of proving the existence of an equilibrium in a monetary economy,' *The theory of interest rates*, Brechling and Hahn ed., Macmillan, 1965, 126–35 (R.W. Clower, ed., *Monetary theory*, Penguin, 1969, 191–201).
[8] Hayek, F.A., *Prices and production*, 2nd ed., G. Rontledge and Sons, 1935.
[9] Hickman, W.B., 'The determinancy of absolute prices in classical economic theory,' *Econometrica*, 18, 1950, 9–20.
[10] Hicks, J.R., *Value and capital*, 2nd ed., Oxford University Press, 1946.
[11] Keynes, J.M., *The general theory of employment, interest and money*, Macmillan, 1936.
[12] Koopmans, J.G., 'Zum Problem des 'Neutralen' Geldes,' Hayek ed., *Beitraege zur Geldtheorie*, Springer, 1933, 211–359.
[13] Koopmans, T.C., ed., *Activity analysis of production and allocation*, John Wiley, 1951.
[14] Marshall, A., *Principles of economics*, 8th ed., Macmillan, 1923.
[15] Marshall, A., *The pure theory of foreign trade*, London School of Economics, 1930.
[16] Modigliani, F., 'Liquidity preference and the theory of interest and money,' *Econometrica*, 12 (1944), 44–48 (Lutz and Mints ed., *Readings in monetary theory*, Irwin, 1951, 186–239).
[17] Morishima, M., 'Consumer's behavior and liquidity preference,' *Econometrica*, 20 (1952), 232–46.
[18] Negishi, T., 'Conditions for neutral money,' *Review of Economic Studies*, 31 (1964), 147–8.
[19] Pareto, V., *Manuel d'économie politique*, 2nd ed., M. Giard, 1927.
[20] Patinkin, D., 'The indeterminacy of absolute prices in classical economic theory,' *Econometrica*, 17 (1949), 1–27.
[21] Patinkin, D., 'The invalidity of classical monetary theory,' *Econometrica*, 19 (1951), 134–51.
[22] Patinkin, D., *Money, interest and prices*, Row, Peterson and Co., 1956 and 1965.
[23] Pigou, A.C., 'The value of money,' *Quarterly Journal of Economics*, 32 (1917–8), 38–65 (Lutz and Mints ed., *Readings in monetary theory*, Irwin, 1951, 162–83).
[24] Rosenstein-Rodan, P.N., 'The coordination of the general theories of money and prices,' *Economica*, 3 (1936), 257–80.
[25] Samuelson, P.A., 'What classical and neo-classical monetary theory really was,' *Canadian Journal of Economics*, 1 (1968), 1–15 (Clower ed., *Monetary theory*, Penguin, 1969, 170–190).
[26] Schneider, E., *Pricing and equilibrium*, T.W. Hutchison tr., W. Hodge and Co., 1952.

[27] Sono, M., 'The effect of price changes on the demand and supply of separable goods,' with a historical note by Morishima, *International Economic Review*, 2 (1961), 239–75.

[28] Valavanis, S. 'A denial of Patinkin's contradiction,' *Kyklos*, 8 (1955), 351–68.

[29] Walras, L., *Elements of pure economics*, Jaffe tr., Unwin, 1954.

[30] Wicksell, K., *Interest and prices*, Kahn tr., Macmillan, 1936.

[31] Wonnacott, P., 'Neutral money in Patinkin's money, interest and prices',' *Review of Economic Studies*, 26 (1958), 70–71.

[32] A Symposium on Monetary Theory, *Review of Economic Studies*, 28 (1960), 29–56.

CHAPTER 17

Terms of trade and the balance of payments

1. The theory of international trade is characterized by a dichotomy of real value theory and monetary analysis. The classical doctrine of comparative advantage and reciprocal demands, the Heckscher–Ohlin theory of trade based on differences in factor endowments, the welfare economics of gains from trade, the theory of the optimal rate of tariff, and Keynesian analysis of international income propagation in terms of open multiplier analysis, all run in terms of international barter trade with money appearing at most as an abstract unit of account. On the other hand, problems of the rate of exchange and the balance of payments should be, and actually are, discussed in terms of national currencies which have also the functions of medium of exchange and store of value.

Since the world we live in is a monetary, not a barter economy, one may naturally wonder whether the results obtained by the real analysis of a barter trade economy can remain valid in a monetary economy. This is essentially asking whether the dichotomy of real value theory and monetary analysis is possible in international trade theory.[1]

When Archibald and Lipsey [2] discussed the dichotomy of real and monetary analyses, one of their original aims was to answer this question in the affirmative. However, as was seen in the preceding chapter, the so-called dichotomy debate or Patinkin controversy is concerned mainly with the classical dichotomy in general with not much attention given to the possibility of the dichotomy in the particular field of international trade theory. Since the conditions under which the dichtotomy in general is possible are severe, the outcome of the controversy is rather negative and

---

[1] For the dichotomy, see Patinkin [16], Archibald and Lipsey [2], Negishi [14] and chapter 16. This chapter is a revision of Negishi, T., 'The dichotomy of real and monetary analyses in international trade theory,' mimeographed, University of New South Wales, 1967.

disappointing. However, in the field of international trade, as will be shown below, the possibility of the dichotomy is much greater. This is because of the existence of a multi-currency system and of the equilibrium condition for the balance of trade in international trade theory. The conditions for a successful dichotomy are conditions which were supposed to be so innocuous that they were often assumed in the monetary theory of international trade as simplifying assumptions without their full significance being recognized.

The first aim of this chapter is, therefore, to discuss under what circumstances a dichotomy in international trade theory is possible. Then use will be made of the dichotomy to consider the relation between economic growth and the balance of payments. Standard Keynesian analysis concludes that economic growth has no favorable effects on the balance of payments while Mundell [13] insists that high growth rates induce balance of payments surpluses, duly emphasizing the roll of the demand for money.[2]) We must note, however, that the effects of the changed terms of trade are disregarded in such macro analyses. The relation between economic growth and the terms of trade is, on the other hand, studied in detail by Hicks [5] and Johnson [6], though the original intention of the former seems to be the study of the relation between the balance of payments and economic growth. We will, therefore, study the relation between the terms of trade and the balance of payments and show that elastic demands for exports and imports are sufficient for the coexistence of growth and a balance of payments surplus.

2. Consider a monetary model of a two-country two-commodity international economy. Taking the currency of country 1 as numeraire, let us indicate prices of commodities and the rate of exchange by P_1, P_2 and R, respectively. The excess demand of country 1 for the ith commodity X_i can be conceived as a function of the relative price P_2/P_1, the real expenditure on the two commodities E/P_1, and the real amount of the desired monetary stock A/P_1. The expenditure E can be expressed as $E = I - (A(I, P_1, P_2, \bar{A}) - \bar{A})$, where I, A and $\bar{A}$ signify money income and the desired and existing monetary stock, respectively. Since the output of each commodity, and hence real income $I_1 = I/P_1$, depend on the relative price P_2/P_1 alone, and since the desired amount of monetary stock A is homogeneous of degree one in its arguments, we can write $X_i = X_i(P_2/P_1, A_1(P_2/P_1, \bar{A}/P_1) - \bar{A}/P_1, A_1(P_2/P_1, \bar{A}/P_1))$, where $A_1 = A/P_1$. Similarly, we have the excess demand of country 2 for the ith commodity $X_1^* = X_1^* (P_2/P_1, A_1^* (P_2/P_1, R\bar{A}^*/P_1)$ $- R\bar{A}^*/P_1, A_1^*(P_2/P_1, R\bar{A}^*/P_1))$, where $A_1^* = A^*/P_1$ and $A^*, R\bar{A}^*$ signify respectively the desired and existing amounts of monetary stock of country 2, in terms of the currency of country 1.

Then, the condition of equilibrium in the commodity markets is

$$X_i(P_2/P_1, A_1(P_2/P_1, \bar{A}/P_1) - \bar{A}/P_1, A_1(P_2/P_1, \bar{A}/P_1))$$

$$+ X_i^*(P_2/P_1, A_1^*(P_2/P_1, R\bar{A}^*/P_1) - R\bar{A}^*/P_1, A_1^*(P_2/P_1, R\bar{A}^*/P_1)) = 0,$$

$$i = 1, 2 \tag{1}$$

and that of equilibrium in the currency markets is

$$A_1 - \bar{A}/P_1 = 0, A_1^* - R\bar{A}^*/P_1 = 0.^3) \tag{2}$$

In the case of floating exchange rates, the system (1) and (2) determines P_1, P_2 and R when $\bar{A}$ and $\bar{A}^*$ are given. On the other hand, in the case of the gold standard $(R = 1)$ or of a monetary policy following the rules of the gold standard game $(R = \text{constant})$, (1) and (2), in addition to

$$\bar{A} + R\bar{A}^* = \text{constant}, \tag{3}$$

determine P_1, P_2, $\bar{A}$ and $\bar{A}^*.^4)$

The balance of trade of country 1 is, assuming she is importing the first commodity,

$$B = (P_2 X_2^* - P_1 X_1)/R. \tag{4}$$

It must be noted that we have $RB = - P_2 X_2 - P_1 X_1 = PX_2^* + P_1 X_1^*$ from (1). Since $\Sigma_i P_i X_i + A - \bar{A} = 0$ and $\Sigma_i P_i X_i^* + A^* - R\bar{A}^* = 0$, we have also

$$RB = A - \bar{A} = -(A^* - R\bar{A}^*). \tag{5}$$

Consider next the case of Keynesian underemployed economies with price rigidities.$^5)$ Let us denote the level of output, the demand for home goods, the demand for imports and the desired and existing amounts of monetary stock for country 1 by X, D, M, A and $\bar{A}$, respectively, and those of country 2 by the same notation with *. The equilibrium condition for the

---

$^3)$ Of course, one of the equations in (1) and (2) is redundant because of Walras' law.
$^4)$ See Meade [10], Mathematical Supplement, p. 13 and Kemp [7], pp. 222–225.
$^5)$ See Kemp [7], pp. 273–276.

commodity markets is

$$X = D(X, R, A(X, R) - \bar{A}, A(X, R)) + M^*(X^*, R, A^*(X^*, R)$$

$$- \bar{A}^*, A(X, R)),$$ (6)

$$X^* = D^*(X^*, R, A^*(X^*, R) - \bar{A}^*, A^*(X, R)) + M(X, R, A(X, r)$$

$$- \bar{A}, A(X, R)) .^6)$$

and that for the money markets is

$$A - \bar{A} = 0, \quad A^* - \bar{A}^* = 0 .^7)$$ (7)

Since prices are rigid in each country in terms of its currency, the rate of exchange R stands also for the relative price of home and foreign goods. In the case of floating exchange rates, (6) and (7) determines X, X^* and R, given $\bar{A}$ and $\bar{A}^*$. On the other hand, in the case of the gold standard, or a monetary policy following it, (6) and (7), together with (3), determine X, X^*, $\bar{A}$ and $\bar{A}^*$. The balance of trade is

$$B = M^*/R - M .$$ (8)

Since $X = D + RM + A - \bar{A}$ and $X^* = D^* + M^*/R + A^* - \bar{A}^*$, we have from (6)

$$RB = A - \bar{A} = - R(A^* - \bar{A}^*) .$$ (9)

3. Our problem is to consider under what circumstances the equilibrium relative price P_2/P_1 in the monetary system (1) and (2), or the equilibrium levels of output X, X^* in the monetary system (6) and (7), can be inferred from the real model of barter trade without being involved in monetary considerations.

First consider the case of (1) and (2). We can solve (2) for R and P_1 in terms of (P_2/P_1). Substituting these into (1), we have a system of equilibrium conditions for commodity markets exclusively in terms of (P_2/P_1). Alternatively, solving (2) and (3) for A, A^* and P_1 in terms of (P_2/P_1), R being assumed constant, and substituting them into (1), we have again a system of equilibrium conditions for commodity markets exclusively in terms of $(P_2/P_1) .^8)$ In any case, however, such a system is merely a quasi-

---

$^6)$ X, D, M^*, A and $\bar{A}$ are in terms of the currency of country 1 and X^*, D^*, M, A^* and $\bar{A}^*$ are in terms of the currency of the country 2.

$^7)$ Same as footnote 3.

$^8)$ This is Hahn's [4] interpretation of the dichotomy of Archibald and Lipsey [2]. However, see footnote 11 below.

real system, i.e., not a real system in the true sense of the word. For example, the elasticity of imports with respect to the relative price obtained in such a system is a total elasticity, taking account of the change in the real amount of the desired monetary stock, i.e., $\partial X_i/\partial(P_2/P_1)\cdot(P_2/P_1)/X_i+\partial X_i/\partial A_R\cdot$ $\partial A_R/\partial(P_2/P_1)\cdot(P_2/P_1)/X_i.$[9]) One can estimate, by use of an econometric method, such a quasi-real system from the data of a monetary economy. However, no theoretical inference derived from the consideration of a pure barter trade model can be applied to such a system.[10])

To obtain a truly real system, one has to introduce an assumption which has often been made in international trade theory without its significance for the dichotomy necessarily being recognized. This is the assumption of the separability of commodities and money, i.e., the marginal rate of substitution between commodities is independent of the amount of money.[11]) Under this assumption, excess demand for commodities can be expressed as a function of the relative price (P_2/P_1) and real expenditure E/P_1. Then, (1) is rewritten

$$X_i(P_2/P_1, A_1(P_2/P_1, \bar{A}/P_1)-\bar{A}/P_1)+$$

$$+X_i^*(P_2/P_1, A_i^*(P_2/P_1, R\bar{A}^*/P_1)-R\bar{A}^*/P_1) = 0, \quad i = 1, 2,\text{[12]}) \qquad (10)$$

and by (2) we have

$$X_i(P_2/P_1, 0)+X_i^*(P_2/P_1, 0) = 0, \quad i = 1, 2. \qquad (11)$$

Since $A_1 - \bar{A}/P_1 = E/P_1 - I/P_1$ and the like, and we have $E = I$ in the case of the barter trade model, (11) is exactly the real system of equilibrium conditions for such a model.[13])

Therefore, we have,

Theorem 1. Under the assumption of separability, the equilibrium relative price in the monetary economy can be inferred from the real model of barter

[9]) For example, the elasticity which appears in the exchange stability condition of Robinson [19] is also a total elasticity. See chapter 15 and Negishi [15].
[10]) See Pearce [18], p. 153.
[11]) For separability, see chapter 16, Sono [20], Pearce [17] and Negishi [14]. It is implicitly assumed, without its significance for the dichotomy being recognized by Kemp [7], p. 223, Meade [10], Mathematical Supplement, p. 10 and even Archibald and Lipsey [2], p. 17.
[12]) One of equations of (10), as well as of (11) below, is redundant. See footnote 3 above.
[13]) In each country, the individual utility functions are assumed to be identical and homogeneous so that there exists a consistent community indifference map. See Negishi [14] and Chipman [3].

trade. Specifically, the same equilibrium relative price is established both in the case of the floating exchange rate and in that of the gold standard.

Next consider the case of (6) and (7). In view of (7), (6) can be written in the form of

$$X = D(X, R) + M^*(X^*, R)$$

$$X^* = D^*(X^*, R) + M(X, R),$$ (12)

either by solving (7) and (3) for $\bar{A}$ and $\bar{A}^*$ in terms of X, X^* and R and substituting them into (6) (the quasi-real system) or by assuming the independence of demand for commodities from A and A^* (the real system). The latter case, with R constant, is that of the real multiplier analysis in post-Keynesian manner. The equilibrium X and X^* remain valid even in the monetary economy. It must be noted, however, that they cannot remain so in the case of a floating exchange rate.[14])

4. We have shown that the values of real variables such as relative prices, the level of output, etc., in a monetary economy can be inferred by the use of the real model of barter trade provided that the marginal rate of substitution between real variables is independent of monetary variables and that money markets are cleared. The latter condition, in view of (5) and (9), can be reduced to the condition that either one of two countries is adjusting the rate of exchange R instantaneously so that $B = 0$ is continuously satisfied (in the case of (1) and (2)) or that both countries are following the gold standard rule so that $B = 0$ is continuously satisfied (in the case of (1) and (2) and that of (6) and (7)).

However, if one is interested in the comparative statics of the shift of the equilibrium relative price or level of output due to a change in some hidden parameter in the system (11), one has sometimes to rely on the stability condition of such a barter trade system (the correspondence principle). If the results of comparative statics based on the use of the stability condition of the barter trade economy are to be valid in a monetary economy, such a stability condition should also be the condition for the stability of markets in a monetary economy.

---

[14]) Similarly, as is pointed out by Metzler [12], the condition of exchange stability or the stability of floating exchange rates, i.e., $\mathrm{d}B/\mathrm{d}R > 0$, with $\bar{A}$ and $\bar{A}^*$ being constant and the stability of the gold standard, i.e., $\mathrm{d}B/\mathrm{d}\bar{A} < 0$, $\mathrm{d}\bar{A} + R\mathrm{d}\bar{A}^* = 0$, with R being constant coincide for the system of (1) and (4). However, it is not so in the system of (6) and (8). See also Kemp [7], pp. 286, 289.

The stability condition of the barter trade model (11), i.e., the so-called Marshall–Lerner condition is obtained as the local stability condition of

$$d(P_2/P_1)/dt = f(X_2(P_2/P_1, 0) + X_2^*(P_2/P_1, 0)), f(0) = 0, f'(0) \geq 0, \quad (13)$$

i.e.,

$$\partial X_2(P_2/P_1, 0)/\partial(P_2/P_1) + \partial X_2^*(P_2/P_1, 0)/\partial(P_2/P_1) < 0 \quad (14)$$

at the equilibrium, where t is time. Since $X_1 + (P_2/P_1)X_2 = 0$ and

$$X_1^* + (P_2/P_1) X_2^* = 0 \text{(i.e., } \partial X_1/\partial(P_2/P_1) + (P_2/P_1) \partial X_2/\partial(P_2/P_1) +$$
$$+ X_2 = 0, \partial X_1^*/\partial(P_2/P_1) + (P_2/P_1) \partial X_2^*/\partial(P_2/P_1) + X_2^* = 0),$$

it is identical to

$$X_2^*/(P_2/P_1) \cdot (1 - (P_2/P_1)/X_1 \cdot \partial X_1/\partial(P_2/P_1) +$$
$$+ (P_2/P_1)/X_2^* \cdot \partial X_2^*/\partial(P_2/P_1)) < 0, \quad (15)$$

at the equilibrium where $X_1 + X_1^* = 0$ and $X_2 + X_2^* = 0$. If $X_2^* > 0$ and $X_1 > 0$ (country 1 imports the first commodity and country 2 imports the second commodity), it implies that the sum of the two import price elasticities must be greater than 1.[15]

As for the stability condition of the monetary model (1) and (2) in the case of floating exchange rates, i.e., say, that of

$$d(P_2/P_1)/dt = (X_2 + X_2^*)/P_1 - (X_1 + X_1^*) P_2/P_1^2,$$
$$dP_1/dt = X_1 + X_1^*, \quad (16)$$
$$dR/dt = A_1^* - R\bar{A}^*/P_1, [16]$$

we have

Theorem 2. A necessary condition of the local stability of (16) is (14), if separability is assumed.

Proof.[17] Consider the linear approximation of (16) at an equilibrium where, without loss of generality, we can make $P_2/P_1 = P_1 = R = 1$. The relevant

[15] See Kemp [7], 61–2.
[16] See chapter 15.
[17] This is suggested by, though slightly different from, Amano [1].

matrix,[18]) the characteristic roots of which must have negative real part, is

$$
A = \begin{bmatrix} X_{2k}+X_{2k}^*-X_{1k}-X_{1k}^* & X_{21}+X_{21}^*-X_{11}-X_{11}^* & X_{2R}^*-X_{1R}^* \\ X_{1k}+X_{1k}^* & X_{11}+X_{11}^* & X_{1R}^* \\ A_{1k}^* & A_{11}^*+\bar{A}^* & A_{1R}^* \end{bmatrix},
$$

where $X_{ik}=\partial X_i/\partial(P_2/P_1)$, $A_{1k}^*=\partial A_1^*/\partial(P_2/P_1)$, $X_{i1}=\partial X_i/\partial P_1$, $A_{11}^*=\partial A_1^*/\partial P_1$, $X_{iR}^*=\partial X_i^*/\partial R$, $A_{1R}^*=\partial A_1^*/\partial R-A^*/P_1$ and the like. The determinant of A must be negative. Since $X_{ik}=\bar{X}_{ik}-X_i'A_{1k}$, $X_{i1}=X_i'(A_1'-1)\bar{A}$, $A_{11}^*=-A_1^{*\prime}\bar{A}^*$, $X_{iR}^*=-X_i^{*\prime}(A_1^{*\prime}-1)\bar{A}^*/P_1$, $A_{1R}^*=(A_1^{*\prime}-1)\bar{A}^*/P_1$, where $\bar{X}_{ik}=\partial X_i(P_2/P_1,0)/\partial(P_2/P_1)$, $X_i'=-\partial X_i/\partial(A_1-\bar{A}/P_1)$, $A_1'=\partial A_1/\partial(\bar{A}/P_1)$ and the like, $|A|$ can be reduced to

$$
\begin{vmatrix} \bar{X}_{2k}+\bar{X}_{2k}^*-X_2'A_{1k} & X_2'\bar{A}(A_1'-1) & 0 \\ \bar{X}_{1k}+\bar{X}_{1k}^*-X_1'A_{1k} & X_1'\bar{A}(A_1'-1) & 0 \\ A_{1k}^* & -\bar{A}^*(A_1^{*\prime}-1) & (A_1^{*\prime}-1)\hat{A}^*/P_1 \end{vmatrix}.
$$

Assuming $A_1'-1<0$, $A_1^{*\prime}-1<0$ (two goods are jointly non-inferior), therefore, we must have $\bar{X}_{2k}+\bar{X}_{2k}^*<0$, since $\bar{X}_{2k}+\bar{X}_{1k}+\bar{X}_{2k}^*+\bar{X}_{1k}^*=0$ (from $X_1+(P_2/P_1)X_2+A_1-\bar{A}/P_1=0$, etc.,) and $X_1'+X_2'=1$. This is by definition identical to (14).[19])

The possible dichotomy of the real and monetary analyses is not limited to the case of neutral monetary policy ($\bar{A}$, $\bar{A}^*$ being constant) or of the gold standard and extends to the case of more active monetary policies. Consider the dichotomy in Meade's system of international trade theory, i.e., [10] and [11]. Meade seems to insist that the real analysis in [11] can be defended because of the assumption of the equilibrium balance of trade.[20]) Since the separability assumption is implicit in his monetary analysis,[21]) and the equilibrium balance of trade implies, in view of (5), the satisfaction of (2), the dichotomy of his 'The theory of international economic policy' into 'The balance of payments' and 'Trade and welfare' is all right if the use of the Marshall–Lerner condition in the comparative statics of the latter is justified.

---

[18]) See chapter 13.
[19]) The case of the gold standard can be similarly discussed.
[20]) Meade [11], pp. 3, 5.
[21]) See footnote 11 above.

The monetary policies assumed in the former are such that the prices of exports are held constant in terms of the currency of the exporting country,[22] assuming that each country is specialized in the production of its export commodity. The stability condition of the foreign exchange, i.e., the condition for a favorable effect of devaluation on the blance of payments under the assumption that commodity markets are instantly cleared is $(e_1 + e_2 - 1)/(1 - m_1 - m_2) > 0$, where e_i and m_i are the price elasticity of and the marginal propensity to import of the ith country.

This certainly presupposes the stability of the commodity markets under the given rate of exchange. Since the assumed monetary policy keeps the relative price P_2/P_1 constant, excess demands are functions of the expenditure only. Assuming that expenditures are adjusted by fiscal or monetary policies so that full employment is achieved, the dynamics of the commodity markets is

$$-dE^*/dt = X_1(E) + X_1^*(E^*) \tag{17}$$

$$-dE/dt = X_2(E) + X_2^*(E^*),$$

where $E(E^*)$ is the expenditure on commodities in terms of the local currency, $X_i(X_i^*)$ is the excess demand (import) of the ith commodity, the first country specializes in the production of the second commodity. A necessary condition for the stability of (17) is that

$$\begin{vmatrix} X_1' & X_1^{*\prime} \\ X_2' & X_2^{*\prime} \end{vmatrix} < 0, \tag{18}$$

where $X_i' = dX_i/dE$ and the like. Since $X_1' + X_2' = 1$, $X_1^{*\prime} + X_2^{*\prime} = 1$, (18) coincides with $1 - m_1 - m_2 > 0$, when $X_2^* > 0$ and $X_1 > 0$, i.e., the second country imports the second and exports the first commodity. Therefore, $e_1 + e_2 - 1 > 0$, i.e., (15) is the required stability condition in the foreign exchange market.

Theorem 3. The dichotomy of Meade's real and monetary system is possible and the use of (15) in the former is justified by the stability condition of the latter.

---

[22] See chapter 15, Meade [9], 80–96, [10], Mathematical Supplement, 150, Pearce [17] and Negishi [15].

5. Standard Keynesian argument on the balance of payments and economic growth is as follows. The balance of payments B (ignoring capital movements) is the difference between export X and import M, the latter being a function of national income Y, $a+mY$, where a and m (marginal propensity to import) are constant. Therefore,

$$B = X - mY - a . \tag{19}$$

The foreign demand for export X is determined exogenously. If Y is larger relative to X, i.e., a country's growth rate is higher relative to that of the rest of the world, then B is smaller, i.e., she is more likely to have a balance of payments deficit. Although this simple model can explain the experiences of some growing countries (e.g., the case of Japan before 1965), it is in conflict with the fact that surplus countries (e.g., Germany, Japan after 1965, etc.) have grown rapidly and deficit countries (e.g., U.S., U.K., etc.) have grown relatively slowly.

On the other hand, Mundell [13] insists that high growth rates induce a balance of payments surplus, not deficit. The difference between national income Y and expenditure E is absorbed into the increased demand for money which is proportional to the change in income dY, i.e.,

$$E = Y - kdY = (1 - k\lambda) Y , \tag{20}$$

where k (propensity to hoard) and λ ($= dY/Y$, growth rate) are constants. If λ is larger, E is smaller relative to Y. This affects both exports and imports. But Mundell assumes exports X as given, since, according to him, it is the most unfavorable case for his argument. On the other hand, imports M is assumed to be a function of E, rather than of Y, i.e., $a' + m' E$. Then we have

$$B = X - m'(1 - k\lambda) Y - a' \tag{21}$$

from which high λ implies larger B, i.e., the balance of payments surplus.[23]

The essence of the differences between the two theories lies in the fact that Mundell considers the effects of growth as an increased or constant supply of exports, diminished demand for imports and the increased demand for money while standard Keynesian analysis regards them as the constant supply of exports and the increased demand for imports, which must imply, by Walras' law, diminished demand for money. The assumption of a

---

[23] As a matter of fact, Mundell is assuming a balance of payments surplus from the beginning by assuming constant k with increased λ, since the difference between Y and E is nothing but the balance of payments surplus. The direction of change of k, however, cannot be inferred in the macro model.

constant supply of exports in the standard Keynesian analysis is due to the assumption of constant exogenous demand. If prices are rigid, it implies a constant amount of demand, which may not be unjustified. However, in the process of growth, prices cannot be rigid, unless the country is very small. The assumption of constant X implies the special case of the unitary elasticity of demand with respect to prices, if price is flexible. If the amount of the supply of exports is increased and the demand elasticity is large, X is increased and the demand for money can also be increased even if the demand for imports is increased. Therefore, growth may not necessarily imply a balance of payments deficit in such a case. Similarly, Mundell's assumption that X is not diminished implies that the demand elasticity for exports is greater than one, if growth increases the amount of the supply of exports. A constant X may not therefore be the most unfavorable assumption to him, since X is decreased and a balance of payments deficit may result if the demand elasticity is less than one.

To see the effects of growth on the balance of payments with flexible prices, it is not sufficient to consider the macro model of a single country as was done by Keynesians and Mundell. We have to analyse the two country two commodity model of an international economy. Consider, for example, (10) and the second equation of (2), with g, i.e., the index of economic growth (the amount of factors, the state of technology, etc.) being added.

$$X_2(P_2/P_1, A_1(P_2/P_1, \bar{A}/P_1, g) - \bar{A}/P_1, g)$$
$$+ X_2^*(P_2/P_1, A_1^*(P_2/P_1, R\bar{A}^*/P_1) - R\bar{A}^*/P_1) = 0,$$
$$X_1(P_2/P_1, A_1(P_2/P_1, \bar{A}/P_1, g) - \bar{A}/P_1, g) \tag{22}$$
$$+ X_1^*(P_2/P_1, A_1^*(P_2/P_1, R\bar{A}^*/P_1) - R\bar{A}^*/P_1) = 0,$$
$$A_1^*(P_2/P_1, R\bar{A}^*/P_1) - R\bar{A}^*/P_1 = 0.$$

By putting as $P_2/P_1 = P_1 = R = 1$ at an equilibrium defined by (22) and differentiating (22) with respect to g at the equilibrium, we have firstly

$$d(P_2/P_1)/dg = |B|/|A|, \tag{23}$$

where A is the matrix defined in the proof of theorem 2 whose determinant is negative from the stability condition and B is the matrix

$$\begin{bmatrix} -X_{2g} & X_{21} + X_{21}^* & X_{2R}^* \\ -X_{1g} & X_{11} + X_{11}^* & X_{1R}^* \\ 0 & A_{11}^* + \bar{A}^* & A_{1R}^* \end{bmatrix}$$

which can be reduced to $(A_1^{*\prime}-1)\bar{A}^*(X_{1g}X_2^{\prime}-X_{2g}X_1^{\prime})(A_1^{\prime}-1)\bar{A}$, where $X_{ig}=\partial X_i/\partial g$. Suppose the first country is exporting the second commodity. Following Hicks [5], Johnson [6] studied the effects of growth on the terms of trade, i.e., (P_2/P_1), by the use of a model without money. In most cases, growth results in the worsening of the terms of trade. Since the dichotomy is possible, we may assume $d(P_2/P_1)/dg<0$ in (23), i.e., $|B|>0$. Assuming $A_1^{*\prime}-1<0$, $A_1^{\prime}-1<0$, this implies that $X_{1g}X_2^{\prime}-X_{2g}X_1^{\prime}>0$.

Secondly, the differentiation of (22) with g gives

$$dR/dg = |C|/|A|, \tag{24}$$

where C is the matrix

$$\begin{bmatrix} X_{2k}+X_{2k}^* & X_{21}+X_{21}^* & -X_{2g} \\ X_{1k}+X_{1k}^* & X_{11}+X_{11}^* & -X_{1g} \\ A_{1k}^* & A_{11}^*+\bar{A}^* & 0 \end{bmatrix}$$

whose determinant is reduced to

$$\begin{vmatrix} \bar{X}_{2k}+\bar{X}_{2k}^*-X_2^{\prime}A_{1k} & X_2^{\prime}(A_1^{\prime}-1)\bar{A} & -X_{2g} \\ \bar{X}_{1k}+\bar{X}_{1k}^*-X_1^{\prime}A_{1k} & X_1^{\prime}(A_1^{\prime}-1)\bar{A} & -X_{1g} \\ A_{1k}^* & -\bar{A}^*(A_1^{*\prime}-1) & 0 \end{vmatrix}$$

Therefore, for the favorable effects on the balance of payments of the first country, i.e., $dR/dg<0$, $|C|$ must be positive, i.e.,

$$A_{1k}^*\bar{A}(A_1^{\prime}-1)(X_1^{\prime}X_{2g}-X_2^{\prime}X_{1g})-\bar{A}^*A_{1k}(A_1^{*\prime}-1)(X_1^{\prime}X_{2g}-X_2^{\prime}X_{1g})$$
$$+\bar{A}^*(A_1^{*\prime}-1)(\bar{X}_{2k}+\bar{X}_{2k}^*)A_{1g}>0, \tag{25}$$

where use is made of the fact that $X_{1g}+X_{2g}+A_{1g}=0$ and $\bar{X}_{1k}+\bar{X}_{2k}+\bar{X}_{1k}^*$ $+\bar{X}_{2k}^*=0$.[24]) Since $\bar{X}_{2k}+\bar{X}_{2k}<0$, $A_{1g}>0$, $A_1^{\prime}-1<0$, $A_1^{*\prime}-1<0$, $X_1^{\prime}X_{2g}$ $-X_2^{\prime}X_{1g}<0$, a sufficient condition for (25) is that $A_{1k}<0$ and $A_{1k}^*>0$. From Walras' law, $A_{1k}=-X_2(1+X_{2k}/X_2+X_{1k}/X_2)$ and $A_{1k}^*=-X_2^*$ $(1+X_{2k}^*/X_2^*+X_{1k}^*/X_2^*)$. Since $X_2<0$, $X_2^*>0$, $X_2=-X_1$, $X_2^*=-X_1^*$, we have

Theorem 4. A sufficient condition for the coexistence of growth and a balance of payments surplus is $1-D+S<0$ and $1-D^*+S^*<0$ while a

---

[24]) These are derived from Walras' law, $X_1+(P_2/P_1)X_2+A_1-A/P_1=0$, etc. A_{1g} is, of course, $\partial A_1/\partial g$.

necessary condition for the coexistence of growth and a balance of payments deficit is the violation of at least one of these inequalities, where $D = X_{1k}/X_1$ and $S = X_{2k}/X_2$ ($D^* = -X_{2k}^*/X_2^*$ and $S^* = -X_{1k}^*/X_1^*$) are respectively the elasticity of demand for imports and that of the supply of exports of the growing country (the rest of the world), provided growth deteriorates the terms of trade.[25])

References

[1] Amano, A., 'Stability conditions in the real and monetary models of international trade,' unpublished.

[2] Archibald, G. C. and R. G. Lipsey, 'Monetary and value theory: a critique of Lange and Patinkin,' *Review of Economic Studies*, 26 (1), 1958, 1–22.

[3] Chipman, J. S., 'A survey of the theory of international trade, part 2, The neo-classical theory,' *Econometrica*, 33, 1965, 685–760.

[4] Hahn, F. H., 'The Patinkin controversey,' *Review of Economic Studies*, 28 (1), 1960, 37–43.

[5] Hicks, J. R., 'An inaugural lecture,' *Oxford Economic Papers*, 5 (1953), 117–35 (Caves and Johnson, ed., *Readings in International Economics*, Urwin, 1968, 441–54).

[6] Johnson, H. G., 'Economic development and international trade,' *Nationaloekonomisk Tidsskrift*, 97 (1959), 273–253–72 (Caves and Johnson, ed., *Readings in international economics*, Urwin, 1968, 281–299).

[7] Kemp, M. C., *The pure theory of international trade*, Prentice Hall, 1964.

[8] Komiya, R., 'Economic growth and the balance of payments: a monetary approach,' *Journal of Political Economy*, 77 (1969), 35–48.

[9] Meade, J. E., *A geometry of international trade*, George Allen & Unwin, 1952.

[10] Meade, J. E., *The theory of international economic policy, 1, The balance of payments*, Oxford, 1951.

[11] Meade, J. E., *The theory of international economic policy, 2, Trade and welfare*, Oxford, 1955.

[12] Metzler, L. A., 'The theory of international trade,' *A survey of contemporary economics*, Blakiston, 1948, 210–254.

[13] Mundell, R. A., *International economics*, Macmillan, 1968.

[14] Negishi, T., 'Conditions for neutral money,' *Review of Economic Studies*, 31 (2), 1964, 147–148.

[15] Negishi, T., 'Approaches to the analysis of devaluation,' *International Economic Reveiw*, 9 (1968), 218–227.

[16] Patinkin, D., *Money, interest and prices*, 2nd ed., Row Peterson, 1965.

[17] Pearce, I. F., 'The problem of the balance of payments,' *International Economic Review*, 2, 1961, 1–28.

[25]) Komiya [8] studied the case of constant terms of trade where the first two terms in the left-hand side of (25) vanish and gave some conjectures on the case of the variable terms of trade.

[18] Pearce, I. F., *A contribution to demand analysis*, Oxford, 1964.

[19] Robinson, J., 'The foreign exchanges,' *Essays in the theory of employment*, Macmillan, 1937 (Ellis and Metzler, ed., *Readings in the theory of international trade*, Blakiston, 1949, 83–103).

[20] Sono, M., 'The effect of price changes on the demand and supply of separable goods,' with a historical note by Morishima, *International Economic Review*, 2, 1961, 239–75.

[21] Spraos, J., 'Devaluation under a policy of full employment,' *Economica*, 31 (1964), 270–278.

Subject index

Author index

(B 1175)   Imprimé en Belgique par Ceuterick s.a.
Brusselse straat 153   3000-Louvain
Adm.-dir. L. Pitsi   Bertemse baan 25   3008-Veltem-Beisem